Fiction and Imagination in Early Cinema

Fiction and Imagination in Early Cinema

A Philosophical Approach to Film History

Mario Slugan

BLOOMSBURY ACADEMIC
LONDON · NEW YORK · OXFORD · NEW DELHI · SYDNEY

BLOOMSBURY ACADEMIC
Bloomsbury Publishing Plc
50 Bedford Square, London, WC1B 3DP, UK
1385 Broadway, New York, NY 10018, USA
29 Earlsfort Terrace, Dublin 2, Ireland

BLOOMSBURY, BLOOMSBURY ACADEMIC and the Diana logo are trademarks
of Bloomsbury Publishing Plc

First published in Great Britain 2020
Paperback edition published 2021

Copyright © Mario Slugan, 2020

Mario Slugan has asserted his right under the Copyright, Designs and Patents Act,
1988, to be identified as Author of this work.

For legal purposes the Acknowledgements on p. xi constitute an extension
of this copyright page.

Cover design: Charlotte Daniels
Cover image: *The Merry Frolics of Satan*, 1906, directed by Georges Méliès
(© Photo 12 / Alamy Stock Photo)

All rights reserved. No part of this publication may be reproduced or transmitted
in any form or by any means, electronic or mechanical, including photocopying,
recording, or any information storage or retrieval system, without prior
permission in writing from the publishers.

Bloomsbury Publishing Plc does not have any control over, or responsibility for, any
third-party websites referred to or in this book. All internet addresses given in this
book were correct at the time of going to press. The author and publisher regret any
inconvenience caused if addresses have changed or sites have ceased to exist, but can
accept no responsibility for any such changes.

A catalogue record for this book is available from the British Library.

A catalog record for this book is available from the Library of Congress.

ISBN: HB: 978-1-7883-1412-1
PB: 978-1-3501-9481-6
ePDF: 978-1-3501-1568-2
eBook: 978-1-3501-1569-9

Typeset by Newgen KnowledgeWorks Pvt. Ltd., Chennai, India

To find out more about our authors and books visit www.bloomsbury.com
and sign up for our newsletters

For minusiplus

Contents

List of Illustrations	ix
Acknowledgements	xi
Introduction	1
1 The status of fiction in early cinema: Train and trick films	21
Are there textual criteria for fictionality?	21
Extratextual criteria of fictionality	29
Reception and exhibition context	32
Train films and *The Arrival of a Train*	33
The importance of exhibition context and magic theatre	38
A Trip to the Moon and trick films	41
Production and promotion context	48
2 Hale's Tours and adjacent cultural series: Illusion, immersion, imagination	59
Panoramas and terminological conflation	61
Travelogues as ersatz-tourism: Any place for imagination?	70
Phantom rides: From fiction of travel to non-fiction of place	75
Hale's Tours	83
The myth of a 'demented fellow'	83
The troubles with hybridity	88
Historicizing the imagined seeing thesis	93
3 Re-enactments in early cinema: Fake, fiction, fact	99
What is a fake?	100
Fakes, indexicality and fictionality	114
Fakes and imaginary participation	126
4 The lecturer and make-believe: The borders of the text and explicit mandates	135
The relation of the film lecturer to the text	139
Ideal, printed and delivered lectures	149
The lecturer and the performance of the film narrator through deixis	157

5	Implicit mandates and fictional narrators	165
	Narrative and narrator in early cinema	167
	Narrative	167
	Narrator	172
	Contemporary narratological discourse	178
	Genette's theory of voice	186
	The near-ubiquity thesis for literary fiction	191
	The near-absence thesis for fiction film	194
	The enunciator as the filmic narrator	194
	The return of the great image-maker	198
	Exceptions to near-absence thesis for fiction film	201
Conclusion		205
Notes		211
Bibliography		247
Index		261

Illustrations

Figures

0.1	Sandro Botticelli, *The Birth of Venus* (c. 1484–6)	6
0.2	Gian Lorenzo Bernini, *The Rape of Proserpine* (1621–2)	7
1.1	A photograph of a horse with an attached horn, or, a photographic representation of a unicorn. Still from *Blade Runner: Director's Cut* (Ridley Scott, 1992)	24
1.2	Still from *Lichtspiel: Opus II* (Walter Ruttmann, 1921)	28
1.3	Montparnasse derailment, 22 October 1895	35
1.4	*Recalcitrant Decapitated Man* at Théâtre Robert-Houdin	43
1.5	*A Trip to the Moon* at Pan-American Exposition, Buffalo (*Akron Daily Democrat*, 26 July 1900, p. 6)	45
1.6	Louis Abel-Truchet's poster for the Cinématographe Lumière	49
1.7	Age of Movement (American Mutoscope and Biograph Company, 1901)	50
2.1	Cross-section of Robert Barker's Panorama Rotunda at Leicester Square, London (Robert Mitchell, *Plans and Views in Perspective of Buildings Erected in England and Scotland,* London, 1801 p. 59)	65
2.2	Trans-Siberian Panorama (*Scientific American Supplement*, 18 August 1900, p. 20603)	77
2.3	Illustration of the 'Pleasure Railway' patented by George C. Hale and Fred W. Gilford (*Official Gazette of the U.S. Patent Office*, 19 September 1905, p. 788)	83
2.4	Inside Hale's Tours (*Kinematograph and Lantern Weekly*, 1 October 1908, p. 481)	84
2.5	(a–d) Stills from the first four shots of *The Hold-Up of the Rocky Mountain Express* (American Mutoscope and Biograph Company, 1906)	91
3.1	Still from *Bombardment of Matanzas* (Edward H. Amet, 1898)	103
3.2	Colorado National Guard soldiers threaten the local sheriff with lynching	109
3.3	The 1893 programme for Buffalo Bill's Wild West	129
3.4	An illustration of the Deadwood Coach	130

4.1	The Passion Play (*John L. Stoddard's Lectures*, Vol. 4, Boston, 1890, p. 326)	147
4.2	Still from *Enoch Arden* (D. W. Griffith, 1911)	157
4.3	Moving away from the Tower of Pisa. E. Burton Holmes (*The Burton Holmes Lectures*, Vol. 7, New York, 1901, pp. 20–1)	160
5.1	The first issue of *Photo Playwright*, April 1912	180

Table

5.1	A typology of narrators based on their narrative levels ('extra-' or 'intradiegetic') and relation to the story ('hetero-' or 'homodiegetic')	188

Acknowledgements

I would like to thank Daniel Morgan, Yuri Tsivian, D. N. Rodowick and Daniël Biltereyst for their comments at various stages of the manuscript. I would also like to thank the members of the Centre for Cinema and Media Studies at Ghent University for their discussion of specific chapters. I have also benefited greatly from the presentation and the ensuing dialogue on what would become various aspects of the monograph at the following conferences and annual meetings of learned societies and networks: Society for Cinema and Media Studies, Society for the Cognitive Study of the Moving Image, History of Moviegoing, Exhibition and Reception Network, The International Association for Media and History, Historical Fictions Research Network, Screen Studies Conference, British Association of Film, Television and Screen Studies, German Screen Studies Network, New Approaches to Silent Film Historiography, Researching Past Cinema Audiences, Philosophy without Theory, Docusophia, The Aesthetic Potential of the Virtual, Film-Philosophy and Rethinking the Attractions-Narrative Dialectics. Lastly, many thanks to Ivana Kardum, Dino Dobošić, Valentin Grégoire and Anna Stoeva for sharing their knowledge of unicorns in cinema with me and to Marija Krnić for finalising her PhD thesis at an opportune moment.

This work was supported by the European Union's Horizon 2020 research and innovation programme under the Marie Skłodowska-Curie grant agreement No 746619, the British Academy under Grant number SG162670 and the German Academic Exchange Network.

An earlier version of a part of Chapter 2 appeared as 'The Role of Imagination in Early Cinema: Fiction and Non-Fiction in Phantom Rides, Travelogues, and Hale's Tours.' In *A Treasure Trove. Friend of the Photoplay – Visionary – Spy? New Trans-Disciplinary Approaches to Hugo Münsterberg's Life and Ouevre*, edited by Rüdiger Steinmetz, 25–46. Leipzig: Leipzig University Press, 2018. A version of a section from Chapter 3 was published as 'The Turn-of-the-Century Understanding of "Fakes" in the US and Western Europe.' *Participations: Journal of Audience & Reception Studies* 16(1) 2019: 718–37, available online http://www.participations.org/Volume%2016/Issue%201/35.pdf. Chapter 5 is derived in part from an article published in 'The Film Narrator and Early American Screenwriting Manuals.' *Early Popular Visual Culture* 17(3)

2019: [print forthcoming] copyright Taylor & Francis, available online https://www.tandfonline.com/doi/full/10.1080/17460654.2019.1623058. A variant of another section of Chapter 5 originally appeared as 'Deixis in Literary and Film Fiction: Intra-Ontological Reference and the Case of Controlling Fictional Narrators'. In *How to Make Believe: The Fictional Truths of the Representational Arts* (= Narratologia 49), edited by J. Alexander Bareis and Lene Nordrum, 185–202. Berlin; Boston: De Gruyter Press, 2015.

Introduction

When watching Edwin S. Porter's 1903 *Uncle Tom's Cabin* we nowadays say that we are watching a fiction film. Among other things, we say that we see Eliza escaping across a frozen river, Uncle Tom saving Eva, and Legree beating Uncle Tom to death. We are far less inclined to say – as contemporaries regularly did – that we are watching an actuality film whose subject is the theatrical performance of various episodes from Harriet Beecher Stowe's 1852 novel of the same name. We certainly do not categorize the film as an actuality. But why? Why do we opt to call this film an actuality only when pressed to admit the fact that all non-manipulated analogue photographic films are in a sense documentary of whatever is recorded? A few months after the premiere of Porter's film, for instance, the writer of the 'Theatrical Chat' column for the *Grand Forks Daily Herald* speaks of *Uncle Tom's Cabin* as a film recording of William H. Brady's theatre production of the novel: 'Edison, the inventor of the moving picture machines, suggested to Mr. Brady the advisability of having films made of this mammoth production.'[1] For the film's contemporaries, it seems, it would take as much convincing to regard *Uncle Tom's Cabin* as a fiction film as it would for us to take it as non-fiction. Our default engagement with the film in question, in other words, has shifted from non-fiction to fiction over the years.

This is no isolated incident. Take Georges Méliès's *The Astronomer's Dream or the Man in the Moon/La Lune à un mètre* from 1898. To us this is even a better example of a fiction film representing an astronomer whose observation of the moon turns into a series of fantastical mishaps ranging from disappearing objects and seductive apparitions to being gobbled up by the moon and then reassembled by a benevolent maiden. Next to such a fantastical storyline there is an extensive use of a trick technique specific to film – substitution splicing – so from a present-day perspective it seems unclear how one would even go about denying the film's fictional status. It again turns out, however, that the turn-of-the-nineteenth-century audiences did precisely that: seen the film as 'a life motion picture reproduction of a celebrated French spectacular piece'.[2] For them, even the most fantastical trick films were primarily recordings of stage magic. At this point we might start to wonder what would need to happen for a representational work of art based on photographic reproductions of actual objects to be construed as a fictional work in its own right.

Both traditional film history and new film history have mostly taken the categories of fiction and non-fiction for granted.[3] For traditional film history the dichotomy was exemplified by Méliès's trick films and the Lumière brothers' actualities. Under this model, Siegfried Kracauer, for instance, writes: 'The films they [Lumière and Méliès] made embody, so to speak, thesis and antithesis in a Hegelian sense.'[4] Although new film history downplayed the fiction/non-fiction dichotomy by focusing on the attractions common to many early motion pictures and perceived some early cinema genres as characterized by ontological hybridity, it did not question the initial categorization. Méliès's trick films and Lumière brothers' train films continue to be categorized as fictions and non-fictions, respectively. Consider, for instance, the categorization from Richard Abel's *Encyclopedia of Early Cinema*: whereas genres like animation, chase films, comedy, crime films, fairy plays, mythologies, Shakespeare films and trick films are all cited as fictions, boxing films, ethnographic films, industrial films, phantom train rides and travelogues are among genres listed under non-fiction.[5] In other words, both brands of film history identify the categories of fiction and non-fiction primarily with recourse to content and films' other stylistic features without analysing in much detail the very nature of fiction.

The underlying idea of this monograph is that the inquiry into the nature of fiction which builds on theories from philosophical aesthetics can reveal a lot about early cinema which has been overlooked by existing models. It is undeniable that new film history has been instrumental in criticizing theories of film spectatorship which have often conflated the notions of fiction and illusion to argue that the condition of spectatorship is one of constant vacillation between being aware that one is only watching a film and confusing what the film represents for reality. By putting the veracity of the stories about the audience evacuating the seating in terror during the alleged first screening of the Lumière brothers' *The Arrival of a Train/L'Arrivée d'un train en gare de La Ciotat* at the Salon Indien du Grand Café into question and by interpreting those stories as founding myths of cinema concerned with hyping its power of illusion, new film history has jettisoned the idea that the earliest audiences, let alone later ones, were ever naïve enough to confuse representation for reality.[6] Yet by continuing to invoke the notions of 'willing suspension of disbelief' and 'diegetic illusion' when speaking of fiction, new film history continues to obscure the fact that it is not illusion that is constitutive of fiction.[7] This essential place should be, instead, yielded to imagination or make-believe. Following the argument Kendall L. Walton's makes in his seminal *Mimesis as Make-Believe* I intend to demonstrate just that.[8]

Since Walton's monograph there has been a virtual consensus among analytic philosophers that imagination is the defining trait of fiction.[9] Kathleen Stock, for instance, cites Walton as '[one of the two] cornerstones of this literature outlining positions that set the discursive agenda for years to follow'.[10] In their entry on imagination and make-believe for the third edition of *The Routledge Companion to Aesthetics* Gregory Currie and Anna Ichino acknowledge similarly:

> Imagination and make-believe, along with fantasy, pretense and play, are regular components of theories of art and aesthetics. Imagination is the central idea; the others generally appear as forms of imaginative activity or its manifestations. The special importance of make-believe in recent aesthetic thinking reflects the influence of Kendall Walton's ideas.[11]

Put most simply, fiction, according to Walton, is a subclass of imaginings or make-believes where make-believe is an attitude taken towards a certain state of affairs, that is, it is the imagining that a certain state of affairs obtains. Unlike beliefs, which are either true or false, questions of veracity are irrelevant for make-believes. The truth-value of sentences from, say, Bram Stoker's *Dracula* (1897) is completely beside the point. This is not to deny that there are sentences in *Dracula* which, when read literally, have a truth-value. 'In the population of Transylvania there are four distinct nationalities' clearly has a truth-value when taken to refer to the actual 1890s Transylvania. But it is to claim that when the content of these sentences is imagined that their truth is irrelevant. Moreover, whereas it is impossible to hold a belief that something both is and is not, there is no problem in holding a contradictory make-believe. Although we cannot believe that something is both dead and alive, we have no such problem in imaginatively engaging Count Dracula.

Prior to Walton's work, imagination/make-believe often played only a minor role in theories of fiction. In fact, a popular theory of fiction in the 1970s and 1980s was the one which built on David Lewis's and Saul Kripke's possible-world theory such as Thomas Pavel's and Lubomír Doležel's work.[12] According to the possible worlds account, the actual world is made up from the totality of the states of affairs. However, not all things need have happened as they had and it is possible that, for instance, it was Hillary Clinton and not Donald Trump who was elected as the 45th president of the United States. Such a world is one of possible worlds, and there are as many possible worlds as there are combinations of the totality of counterfactuals. Fictions, under this account, are a subclass of possible worlds. According to this model the world in which Jonathan Harker encounters Count Dracula is something that could have happened – even though it did not happen in the world we live in. Unlike Walton's proposal, these approaches do not give much importance to imagination. Instead, they are primarily concerned with semantics, that is, truth-values, and with whether terms like 'Count Dracula' denote anything (in Bertrand Russell's sense).[13] However, even here there are considerable difficulties, particularly in the case of how to deal with fictions that contain contradictions. According to Lewis's and Kripke's theories, there are statements which are true in all possible worlds such as 'A is A' or 'the value of pi is 3.14 …'. This means that their negations cannot appear in any possible world or that there is not a single possible world in which these claims are false. But that would mean there could not be a fictional story in which, for instance, a mathematician finds out that the value of pi is in fact 4.[14] Under Walton's account, by contrast, it is perfectly simple to imagine a different pi-value and to engage such a story.

An alternative to possible worlds approach to fiction which did attach importance to imagination drew heavily on speech act theory to construe fiction.[15] For instance, according to a previously influential account by John Searle, fiction was regarded as an illocutionary act in which the author *pretends* to be making an assertion but without any intention to deceive.[16] In that sense, Bram Stoker is only pretending non-deceptively to be making assertions about Count Dracula who feasts on the blood of the living. The key problem with this account is that there are acts of non-deceptive pretence which do not constitute fictions – namely, imitations. If a person mimics the voice and gestures of a well-known politician for the audience's amusement and insists, for instance, that over the years she has never financially profited from her public life and concludes by stating 'I am not a crook', she is pretending to be the politician in question (e.g. Richard Nixon) in a non-deceptive fashion but this act still does not amount to fiction.

In another variant of this model the proposal is that there is no pretence in fiction but rather that the fictional assertions are generated through genuine speech acts. In this case fictional assertions differ from non-fictional ones insofar speakers *intend* their audience to *make-believe* what is said rather than to believe it.[17] Walton counters with a thought experiment in which, by complete coincidence, naturally occurring cracks in the rocks form a pattern which reads

'Once upon a time there were three bears …' According to Walton, there is no reason to preclude make-believing the content of this pattern taken as a sentence. In other words, there need not be any *intentional* action behind an object which we engage in a make-believe fashion. If this example seems far-fetched, we can easily write a computer program which generates random letter strings of certain length. Because the program will go through every possible combination of letters, not only will at least one of these letter strings be identical to 'Once upon a time there were three bears …', but there will be other strings which will constitute fully intelligible stories as well. There is no reason we cannot make-believe the propositional content of stories generated in such a manner and yet we can hardly say that they were intentionally produced for the only intention behind the program was to generate random letter strings.

Due to the speech act model these theories employ they, not unlike possible world theories, are also heavily invested in claims to truth (here qualified as fictional).[18] It is understandable why this would be of importance in the case of literature – the usual model for fiction on this approach. Standard sentences from literary fiction appear to have a truth function not unlike that of 'serious' sentences. Harker's journal entry from *Dracula*, for example, is filled with assertions such as 'I was not able to light on any map or work giving the exact locality of the Castle Dracula.' There appears to be truth to these sentences at least *in* fiction. Somebody in the fiction asserts these claims as true. And, as Currie recognizes in his application of the speech act model to visual media, theatre and film regularly make similar assertions.[19] Unlike approaches building on Lewis and Kripke these theories have no problems with contradictory fictions because they do not subscribe to possible worlds – only to make-believing that something is asserted as true. Still, there are problems. What about fictions in which it is not readily clear that there are any assertions, that is, claims to truth? Walton asks us to consider representational artworks from painting, sculpture, photography and so on which employ no natural language, but which still amount to fictions. Take, for example, Sandro Botticelli's painting *The Birth of Venus* (Figure 0.1) or Gian Lorenzo Bernini's sculpture *The Rape of Proserpine* (Figure 0.2). Although they both depict mythological events – the goddess of love emerging from the sea and the abduction of Persephone by the god of the underworld, respectively – it is far from certain that depiction amounts to assertion. In fact, the general absence of linguistic structures such as the subject and the predicate from pictorial and plastic arts gives more reason to think that these media do not make any assertions. And even if this issue were somehow to be solved satisfactorily for the speech act theorist, there would still be no reason

Figure 0.1 Sandro Botticelli, *The Birth of Venus* (c. 1484–6).

to privilege one medium of fiction over another especially if a model can be found which is readily applicable to all media. Walton proposes precisely such a model.

The model for fiction, according to Walton, should not be literary fiction in particular and speech acts in general but an activity people undertake from an earliest age – children's games of make-believe. From very early on children have make-believe tea parties, dress up as pirates or play out imaginary scenarios with their toys. Crucially, these do not need to involve any assertions no more than making a move in a game of chess includes any claims to truth. Children's make-believe, moreover, is not even necessarily a form of communication as speech acts are. By make-believing a one-eyed parrot on her shoulder or by imagining Ken saving Barbie from the burning house the child is not only not making any assertions, but she is not even communicating anything to anybody. What she is doing is using different objects as props – a plastic parrot and Ken and Barbie dolls, respectively – in a game of make-believe. And it is props rather than assertions that are readily applicable to all forms of fiction. Sentences in the novel are props for imagining Harker doing so and so. The images and sounds in the latest film adaptation of *Dracula* are props for make-believing Harker's film version doing something else. Finally, Botticelli's painting and Bernini's sculpture are props for imagining Venus's birth and Persephone's abduction, respectively. Particular strength of Walton's theory is, therefore, not only that it

Figure 0.2 Gian Lorenzo Bernini, *The Rape of Proserpine* (1621–2).

rids us of the notion of fiction as 'parasitic' on language and that, by introducing props, it privileges no medium of fiction over another. Instead, it identifies a practice – children's game of make-believe – which precedes other fiction-making activities like storytelling both phylogenetically and ontogenetically.

What *is* important for make-believes, according to Walton, is not their truth-value or logical coherence but whether they are mandated or not. And this is also what distinguishes fiction from the more prevalent category of imaginings. For instance, I can imagine that a person in the street is Elsie Stoneman from D. W. Griffith's *The Birth of a Nation* (1915) but this is unlike using images and sounds of Lillian Gish from *The Birth of a Nation* to imagine the same. When watching D. W. Griffith's film *everybody* is *supposed to* make-believe that Lillian Gish is Elsie Stoneman by using the images of the actress as props. This is a normative category. I, by contrast, am perfectly free to imagine that the passer-by is Elsie Stoneman but there is nothing normative about this imagining. Nor is anybody who sees that person supposed to imagine Elsie Stoneman in her place. We could say that from the perspective of a potential prop in a game of make-believe the random person in the street, unlike images of Lillian Gish in *The Birth of a Nation*, simply does not constitute a prop for all. The distinction between the two types of props is what Walton understands as mandate. In other words, whereas all fictions are imaginings, only mandated imaginings are fictions.

To flesh out the idea of mandate further we need to introduce Walton's notion of the principles of generation and articulate their connection to props. A prop, according to Walton, 'is something which, by virtue of conditional *principles of generation*, mandates imaginings. Propositions whose imagining are mandated are *fictional*, and the fact that a given proposition is fictional is a *fictional truth*'.[20] In other words, fictional worlds are merely collections of mandated imaginings. To make this clearer, Walton gives an example of a game of make-believe in which participants agree that coming across a stump in a forest amounts to encountering a bear. Stumps are clearly props in such a game. Conditional on their presence the explicit rules of the game (principles of generation) mandate imagining that there is a bear. This makes it fictional that there is a bear. In the fiction that is this game of make-believe then there are as many bears as there are stumps, and they are to be found on the spots the stumps stand. Of course, participants can fail to recognize stumps and therefore fail to abide by the rules of the game (implement principles of generation) and make-believe bears in their place. But this does not negate the point that in this particular game of make-believe there is a bear where the stump is. This is the normative nature of the implementation of principles of generation.

Whereas in the case of stumps the principles of generation, that is, the rules of the game were explicitly made, in the case of most representational works they are implicit. With some exceptions, whatever is explicitly represented is mandated. To continue with the example above, while watching *The Birth of a Nation* we are mandated, among other things, to imagine that Elsie Stoneman marries Ben Cameron. This does not mean that we are not *free* to imagine a number of other things but that is not the same as being mandated to imagine such things. For instance, I am free to imagine that I am making love with Ben Cameron but it is certainly not the case that I am mandated to imagine this. It is not a part of the story-world that I – the author of this book – am making love with Ben Cameron. I am never shown on screen as making love with him, and nothing shown implies that I am making love or have made love with him.

Another way of clarifying mandates is to articulate them in terms of what Walton refers to as work-worlds and game-worlds. For Walton something is work-fictional so long as it holds for *any* game the work prompts. Otherwise it is game-fictional. My imaginings of seducing Ben Cameron are game-fictional because not everybody (in fact, nobody) watching the film is supposed to imagine my affair with him. Everybody, by contrast, is supposed to imagine that Ben Cameron is romantically involved with Elsie Stoneman. In other words, given that the principles of generation informing fiction film (and representational arts) generally mandate us to imagine whatever is explicitly (and implicitly) represented and given that explicit (and implicit) representations act as props in fiction film, there is nothing to mandate me imagining making love to Ben Cameron. Mandated make-believes, then, are work-fictional and non-mandated ones are game-fictional.

One of the key questions in this model has been to determine what imaginings are *implicitly* mandated. In the case of narrative fiction film, a crucial question has been whether we imagine seeing what is represented or whether we imagine propositions about what is represented. In other words, do we imagine *seeing* the curls of Elsie Stoneman's hair or do we just imagine *that* Elsie Stoneman has curly hair? And if we do imagine seeing what is represented then do we imagine seeing the events while being physically present at the event location or do we just imagine seeing them while not entertaining any imaginings about being present?

An even more hotly debated question regarding implicit mandates has been determining the status of what Currie has dubbed the controlling fictional narrator – an agency which we are mandated to *imagine* as responsible for all of the information we read, see or hear in a given representational artwork.[21] In the case of a novel like F. Scott Fitzgerald's *The Great Gatsby* (1925) it is explicit that there is a fictional character whose utterances coincide with the sentences of the novel – Nick Carraway. In a novel like Stoker's *Dracula*, however, the issue becomes far less clear. It is undeniable that various characters taken together – Harker, Minna, Dr Seward and the like – narrate all the events of the story. But is there an overarching agency – a controlling fictional narrator – who we are mandated to imagine as presenting all these letters (and other textual elements like transcripts of phonograph recordings or newspaper clippings) compiled in a single volume? Not the flesh and blood author Stoker but a fictional agency like the anonymous editor of letters in Pierre Choderlos de Laclos's *Dangerous*

Liaisons (1782). In the case of cinema, the question is no less difficult. Is there an agency distinct from the actual D. W. Griffiths who we are mandated to imagine to be presenting all the images and sounds that make up *The Birth of a Nation*? Some of the most influential accounts of the birth of narrative fiction cinema, for example, have invested heavily in the idea that such an agency is present in all narrative fiction films.[22] Some philosophers have even proposed that whether we imagine any such agency follows directly from whether we imagine seeing what is represented.[23] A significant portion of the monograph, therefore, devotes itself to answering these questions.

Another problem with Walton's theory is that it says very little about how principles of generation are activated in the first place. Walton recognizes that there are non-fictional works such as biographies or documentary films which clearly have representational content but chooses to focus only on fictional ones. (In fact, he reserves the term 'representational' for fiction alone.) He certainly does not explain why we are not mandated to imagine the events and characters represented in somebody's biography (on top of believing them). When the implicit rules of generation are applied to the case of *Uncle Tom's Cabin* and *The Astronomer's Dream or the Man in the Moon* it is also not clear why the mandate to take the *films* as props (as we do) rather than the *performances* recorded (as contemporaries did) would apply. And although on the example of myths Walton recognizes that what for some historical audiences would have been non-fiction is for present-day ones fiction, he does not give an account of how this shift took place.

This is where a study of early cinema can help. Clearly, early cinema is a challenge for philosophical aesthetics as much as it once presented a challenge for film history. At the same time, much like early cinema offered a unique way for rethinking cinema overall, early cinema can also allow us new insights into the nature of fiction.

From the philosophical aesthetics point of view the hypothesis of this monograph is that because of its relative youth and the availability of the material surrounding its advent, early cinema presents an exceptional opportunity for understanding how a representational medium becomes employed in the production of fictions. The case of early cinema is particularly interesting because it allows us to address the category of fiction from a historical perspective, to better understand the role of the representational medium in fiction-making, and to shed light on contemporary debates on what precisely we are implicitly mandated to imagine when watching fiction films. In the first case, unlike for literary fiction which has been regularly used as *the* model for understanding fiction, there exists sufficient information about the earliest formations of the category of fiction in cinema. We can see the earliest motion pictures, read contemporary reports by audiences, peruse trade press accounts, identify advertising strategies, analyse catalogue descriptions of moving pictures, investigate how they were programmed and try to reconstruct their exhibition contexts. This abundance of paratextual material is regularly neglected by analytic aestheticians and yet, as I will argue, it goes a long way in accounting for how Walton's mandates get off the ground in the first place.[24] In the second case, the primarily photographic medium of early cinema forces us to reconsider literature as a model for fiction yet again. Whereas words appear to be capable of representing fictional entities directly – saying 'Uncle Tom' will suffice for the job – in photographic cinema we need to show an actual person which we can only then take as representing the famous fictional character. Regarding imagined seeing, finally, contemporary reports from early film history suggest that only some moving pictures – primarily phantom rides – elicited audiences to imagine viewing objects on screen from *within* the represented world. Similarly, it is only on very specific occasions – namely, certain travelogue lecturing practices – that audiences *imagined* being *shown* the sights on the screen, that is, that they imagined film narrators in control of the image track.

From the film history point of view, once fiction is understood as mandated imaging, we can begin to understand numerous aspects of early film history from a new angle. For instance, we can start to appreciate the overlooked role imagination played in the earliest screenings of train films. In other words, it is not only that moving pictures like *The Astronomer's Dream or the Man in the Moon* and *Uncle Tom's Cabin* migrated from non-fiction to fiction over the years, transitions also went in the opposite direction. As I will argue at length in the first two chapters, the earliest train films were in fact both billed and perceived as fictional films insofar they mandated imaginings about trains bursting through the screen and into the auditorium. Méliès, for instance, describes how he was prompted to imagine the train 'as if about to leave the screen and land in the hall'.[25] To cite another example of the importance of imagination for early cinema, analysing contemporary discourse on film in terms of imagination can also shed light on the concept of immersion which has, like fiction, been discussed in terms of illusion all too often. In the case of Hale's Tours, for instance, I will show that the immersion these early examples of 'virtual reality' afforded did not lead to a confusion of what was represented on screen for reality any more than the first public film screening of *The Arrival of a Train* caused the spectators to flee in panic. Investigating whether audiences engaged early moving pictures imaginatively or not, moreover, can also help us determine whether genres such as fakes were primarily understood as illustrations or fictions. Finally, this grasp of the notion of fiction as mandated imagining also paves the way for reconceptualizing our understanding of the history of film narrators. Instead of looking for their earliest instances in the early story films, we should instead ask ourselves which genres hitherto categorized as non-fictions could have in fact been understood as fictions by their contemporaries. One of the key examples is none other than travelogues. Showmen who used motion pictures in their accounts of travel to distant lands could transform the images of actual places into props for make-believe by a simple turn of phrase. In our investigation of the origins of the fictional film narrator we can, therefore, learn much by turning to lecturing practices informing early travelogues.

The exploration of these ideas is organized into five chapters. I start off Chapter 1 with a discussion of the two standard criteria for determining whether something is fiction or not: the intentionalist (preferred by the majority of analytic philosophers) and the textual (espoused by the majority of film scholars). Whereas according to the former something is fiction if the author intends it as fiction (and non-fiction if the author intends it otherwise), according to the latter fiction and non-fiction are distinguishable based on the film's content and style. By pointing out that there are cultural texts which can migrate across fiction/non-fiction boundaries I put forward an alternative model: it is the institutional context – the interplay of production, distribution, exhibition and reception – that determines a text's fictional status. The same, I claim, holds true for two paradigmatic early cinema genres – train and trick films. Whereas nowadays *The Arrival of a Train* is regularly cited as an actuality and Méliès's trick films as fictions, around the year 1900 these genres were billed and engaged with in very much the opposite terms. At the time trick films like *The Four Troublesome Heads/Un homme de têtes* (Méliès, 1898) were advertised and construed as *recordings* of famous magic tricks performed in popular magic theatres. (We, by contrast, *imagine* the fiction of the magician taking his head off.) Similarly, when the turn-of-the-nineteenth-century audiences watched the earliest train films they *imagined* that the train is going to crash through the screen and into the auditorium, that is, they saw them as fictions. (We, by contrast, see these films simply as *actualities* of trains pulling into stations.)

Whereas in the first chapter I offer a reinterpretation of the myth of the panicking audience by arguing that the 'train effect' can be understood in terms of imaginary engagement as much as the looming effect, in Chapter 2, I further articulate the importance of imagination for construing early cinema. By looking at the scholarship on techniques of immersion, I argue that the concept has too often been conflated with that of illusion. Although an analysis of the contemporary commentaries of the prime nineteenth-century technique of immersion – the panorama – shows that on occasions the experience of actual illusion was afforded, that is, that the audiences sometimes actually confused representation for reality, this was an exception rather than the rule. Once advertising, patents and review patterns are examined, the same, I argue, holds for phantom rides and their later revival within the context of Hale's Tours. Regularly described in terms of illusion, Hale's Tours are, I claim, better understood as eliciting imaginings. Such motion pictures did not fool their contemporaries into *believing* that they were actually taking a ride as many argue. The oft-cited tale of a 'demented fellow' is no less of a myth than the story of the panicking audience at the Salon Indien. Instead, Hale's Tours make it *fictional* that there is a single agency that is the source of all the film's information: audiences are mandated to imagine themselves as agents watching the on-screen sights from *within* that world. As such, Hale's Tours are by no means fiction/non-fiction hybrids – they are fictions through and through.

Chapter 3 offers an opportunity to disentangle another set of terms that are often conflated: faking and fiction. After refining the historical understanding of the category of 'fake films', on the example of boxing and war re-enactments from the first decade of early cinema I demonstrate that both staging as an essential ingredient of fakes and deception as a fairly common practice in the promotion, distribution and exhibition of such moving pictures do not entail the introduction of any fictional elements into moving pictures. Rather, the main criterion for engagement with such motion pictures was their illustrative nature – either as a judgement about how alike to the represented event and its actors the moving images were or in their potential to give an impression of how the event looked like in the case there were no genuine recordings of it available. Although concluding that in general contemporaries treated fakes as non-fictions whose main function was illustrative, I do admit that on occasions fakes were *promoted* as inviting imaginary participation within the depicted locale similar to phantom rides and Hale's Tours. However, unlike with phantom rides and Hale's Tours these mandates were not picked up by the audiences, thereby leaving re-enactments in the non-fiction domain.

The reshuffling of the categories of fiction and non-fiction in early cinema continues in Chapter 4. There I examine the relationship between lecturing practices and the material shown on screen. First, I argue that during early cinema it was not the recorded film that constituted the text as it is the case today. Instead, the whole screening was a hybrid text made up of both the lecture *and* the images. Second, using the example of E. Burton Holmes, I demonstrate that lecturers had the power to transform travelogues into games of make-believe with a simple turn of phrase. In other words, what we think of as matter-of-fact accounts of travels to foreign lands were often presented as fictions to contemporary audiences. Finally, I argue that Holmes's performances constitute the earliest instances of controlling fictional narration in cinema known to date – the narrator responsible for all the images we see and for all the sounds we hear. He secures this through a combination of narrative present tense, the careful rhetorical deployment of 'we' and the use of images and motion pictures. In other words, Holmes's 'verbal track' secures the continuity and spatial overlapping of the elements in the 'image track' making the latter appear as the visual representation of the observers' point of view.

In Chapter 5 I take up the debate about the (in)existence of film narrators in narrative fiction film. I again mount my argument from both philosophical and historical perspective. In the latter case, I demonstrate that the discourse contemporary to formative years of storytelling cinema evinces no signs of imaginative engagement with fiction film as being *fictionally* shown. At most, the contemporary trade press and screenwriting manuals suggest that on occasions spectators are invited to imagine certain diegetic events and/or objects. From the philosophical aesthetics point of view, moreover, imagining seeing something does not entail any imaging that there is any showing of that thing taking place or imagining that anybody is showing that thing. In other words, the mandate for imagining an agency in control of all the audiovisuals on screen is absent in the greatest majority of narrative fiction films. And the key reason for its absence is that according to the set of institutional factors valid since at least the transitional era any mandate for imagining fictional narrators hinges on the presence of salient textual cues. These, however, appear only in a small number of films such as mockumentaries and the cycle of horror films shot from the position of a camera from within the fictional world.

Methodologically, then, throughout the monograph I combine conceptual analysis in the analytic vein with arguments based on historical evidence from contemporary materials. Doing two things at the same time clearly risks alienating both groups of readers. Whereas film historians might feel that too much space was afforded to the superfluous philosophical arguments, those interested in analytic philosophy could find historical evidence tangential. My hope, however, is that by the end of the book I will have demonstrated that to understand both the importance of imagination for historical spectatorship and its relevance for the category of fiction overall one cannot proceed without the other.

Having briefly outlined the analytic method by which one arrives at Walton's definition of fiction in terms of sufficient and necessary conditions above, a discussion is in order about what counts as proofs of historical mandates, especially when it comes to the reconstruction of historical spectatorship. Ever since the late 1970s when revisionist film historians became interested in the questions of film history which could not be answered by looking at films alone, there has been a healthy dose of scepticism about what we can really know about flesh and blood historical audiences.[26] For instance, do audience member writings penned down clearly with some time remove attest to whatever was going on in their minds at the time of viewing? In the case of newspaper and trade press pieces, how informative are these reports which oftentimes amounted to thinly veiled advertisements or almost verbatim copies from other sources? These are all important questions which are difficult to resolve. My focus on mandates, however, makes the problem tractable because they are a normative category. In other words, to reconstruct mandates it is not necessary to demonstrate that audience members actually imagined such and such, but only that they were supposed to do so. Newspaper and trade press reports, together with production and promotional materials and exhibition context, even in their present form, suffice to make this claim. While allowing me to argue about what normative response should have looked like and, by extension, about how categories of fiction and non-fiction were construed in the early period, this approach does not deny that historical individuals could have responded to films in a myriad of unique ways ranging from oppositional engagement to mandates, through failure to register them, to wholehearted acquiescence to them.

The second set of questions relates to issues of extrapolation and how much we can say about the audiences in general based on the cited historical data. Given that my sources are predominantly English- and German-language ones, I can hope to say little about mandates outside of the United States, the UK and Germany. And even here I provide no strong statistics, so I can only hope to outline some general trends. At the same time, the study has benefitted enormously from the recent boon of digitally available materials which allow for the identification of pertinent data at a hitherto unimaginable pace and scale as well as for the revisiting of some of the classic pieces of new film history. This by no means implies that I have even remotely approached the extensive archival knowledge amassed by new film history pioneers some of whose seminal contributions to the field I engage with on the following pages. But I do believe that the sources cited here present enough of a challenge for some entrenched generalizations about fiction and illusion in early cinema to consider alternatives when it comes to the specific problem of mandates.

Crucially, when I do criticize some of the classical works of new film history the criticism is not that their authors should have somehow been better at analytic philosophy, that they should have been using terms in the way Walton uses them, or that they should have made the investigation of fiction/non-fiction distinction a central feature of their work. Rather, when I criticize I do it on the scholars' own terms. For instance, if the point of these seminal works is to get a better appreciation of historical spectatorship as is regularly the case and the claim is that a certain class of films involves specific audience engagement such as false beliefs about what is represented, then reinterpreting the originally documented evidence and citing contemporary reports which point in the direction of imaginative engagement instead is a perfectly valid approach. And so is trying to disentangle terminological conflations when it comes to sufficiently distinguishable terms such as disbelief, belief and make-believe; imagination, immersion and illusion; or faking and fictionalizing. Similarly, if an author argues, for example, that every narrative has a narrator, then pointing to inconsistencies in the argument's formal structure or the issues that derive from conceptual imprecision of terms used in the premises is no less valid.

Lastly, it has to be admitted that this study has little to say about the potential differences between audiences according to distinct social categories such as gender, race, ethnicity, immigration status, urban/rural milieu, class, age and so on. Early cinema scholars' focus on these topics has undoubtedly been crucial for gaining a better understanding of historical audiences.[27] And if there is a single lesson to be learnt from this work is that the social experience of movie-going was distinct for different groups. While I am certainly not denying the wealth of the social dimension of spectatorship, the mandate for imaginative engagement is, to repeat, a normative matter which would have been dictated precisely through the sources I focus on (catalogues, promotional materials, trade press, newspapers, etc.) and which privileged white, male, middle-class, adult urbanites.

Moreover, on the continuum of phenomena ranging from cognition to social practices mandated engagement is closer to image comprehension than to, say, interpretative activity and the social use of cinema and as such tends to be more uniform. It is undeniable that in the case of *The Corbett-Fitzsimmons Fight* (1897), for instance, people of different socially constructed identities responded to the film differently. For some women, according to Miriam Hansen, the film afforded 'the forbidden sight of male bodies in seminudity, engaged in intimate and intense physical action'.²⁸ By contrast, those involved with the *Women's Christian Temperance Union*, Dan Streible demonstrates, campaigned against the film's distribution.²⁹ When it comes to ethnic affiliation, that despite the fact that Fitzsimmons was regularly described as English-born and Corbett as Irish and that the match took place on St Patrick's Day, Denis Condon found no evidence of ethnic partisanship during the film's showing in Dublin.³⁰ Irrespective of their social identities and the different responses to the film flowing from these identities, however, none of these scholars claims that able-bodied viewers could not easily comprehend the film's profilmic reference as a representation of the titular heavyweight championship boxing match. After all, the viewers could have hardly responded in these varied ways, if they did not have a baseline comprehension of the images. Given that the mandate for imagining is essentially either present or not and given that it concerns a mental faculty which, much like image comprehension, operates on the level of cognition, it is my contention that unlike the different responses outlined above it is less susceptible to variations owing to socially constructed identity. Over the years, mandates, undoubtedly, get activated or deactivated but this does not appear to be due to divergences along the lines of these identities.³¹

Before proceeding it remains to discuss one last aspect of Walton's work as it pertains to analogue photography and, by extension, early cinema. According to Walton, all analogue photographs allow us to see their subjects indirectly in the sense that mirrors and binoculars allow us to see objects indirectly through the manipulation of light.³² But next to this, Walton claims that photographs also mandate imagining seeing the subject represented *directly* as though we were in the subject's presence:

> Even when one looks at photographs which are not straightforward works of fiction, it can be fictional that one sees. On seeing a photograph of a long forgotten family reunion, ... [I] should add that it is fictional that I see Aunt Mabel *directly*, without photographic assistance. ... Fictionally, one is in the presence of what one sees.³³

According to this logic, all photographically based representations from family albums and actualities to documentaries and news reports are transformed into fictions for they mandate not only imagining seeing the objects of representation but also imagining being face to face with them. On this account, moving pictures like Louis Lumière's *Workers Leaving the Lumière Factory in Lyon/La Sortie de l'usine Lumière à Lyon* (1895) become fictions of presence and direct seeing – we are mandated to imagine seeing the workers from the position of the camera and being in that very position. This would mean, though, that using Walton's theory to determine the fictional status of early cinema would be an overkill, for practically all of early cinema would have to be treated as fictional (and so would all later cinema). *Uncle Tom's Cabin* and *The Astronomer's Dream or the Man in the Moon* would also revert to being fictions but not because they would now mandate imaginings about their storylines but because they would mandate imagining seeing the members of their cast directly from the position in the (magic) theatre auditorium where the camera is placed. This particular aspect of Walton's theory, however, fails from the perspective of both analytic philosophy and new film history.

Analytically speaking, there is nothing in Walton's general theory of fiction that entails that all visual representations mandate imagining seeing. Walton would be hard-pressed to claim that visual representations such as maps, encyclopaedic illustrations, anatomical atlases, cross-sectional views, instructions for use, graphs, diagrams, letters on a page and so on mandate any imagining seeing. The reason for the claim that practically all analogue photographs entail imagining seeing can be better understood if we tackle Walton's point that this imagining seeing is *direct*. As Walton puts it:

> A major source of the confusion which infects writings about photography and film [derives from the] failure to recognize and distinguish clearly between the special kind of seeing which actually occurs and the ordinary kind of seeing which only fictionally takes place, between a viewer's *really* seeing something *through a photograph* and his *fictionally* seeing something *directly*. A vague awareness of both, stirred together in a witches' cauldron, could conceivably tempt one toward the absurdity that the viewer is really in the presence of the object.[34]

In other words, imagining seeing something in a photograph directly is for Walton necessary to explain the specific experience of photography and cinema. But if it is the notion of presence that is really at stake here then there is no need for invoking imagining seeing something directly – for, as Walton himself puts it, seeing something through a photograph is like seeing something through a telescope, a microscope or a mirror. And all these visual aids are routinely seen as bringing the objects whose images they reflect closer to us, as bringing them into our presence. Crucially, Walton himself cites André Bazin's comparison of film to a mirror as a prime example of the articulation of the experience of presence in film scholarship:

> It is false to say that the screen is incapable of putting us 'in the presence of' the actor. It does so in the same way as a mirror – one must agree that the mirror relays the presence of the person reflected in it – but it is a mirror with a delayed reflection, the tin foil of which retains the image.[35]

For Bazin it is through the reflection of light which was in direct contact with the object that the presence is relayed in mirrors. And it is precisely their mirror-like quality that brings objects into our presence in the case of photographs.[36] In other words, any recourse to some form of default mandate for imagining seeing in photographs is superfluous. And given that Walton's theory of fiction does not necessitate any imagining seeing in the case of visual representations either it is best to avoid any unnecessary additions to the theory. Simply put, photographs do not necessarily entail any imaginings – we can and regularly do engage looking at photographs without imagining anything.

New film history take on the same matter gives further credence to my proposal. As I will demonstrate at length in Chapters 1 and 2 there were early motion picture genres which mandated imagining seeing the objects on screen such as train films and phantom rides. This, however, is precisely what *distinguished* them from other films. Train films and phantom rides were special because of such peculiar mandates. When imagining seeing was mandated, moreover, it did not necessarily entail *direct* seeing. Whereas early phantom rides did mandate such seeing numerous train films including *The Arrival of a Train* only mandated imagining seeing a train about to plunge from the screen into the auditorium without mandating imaginary relocation into the station where the train is pulling in. All of this can be gleaned from contemporary discourse on early cinema.

Of course, not even these resources can give us the complete understanding of historical spectatorship because they themselves are oftentimes inconclusive and filled with lacunae. Although catalogues list and describe far more moving pictures than have been preserved, catalogue collections themselves are far from complete. Albeit contemporary press sometimes describes moving pictures at length, such accounts are exceptions rather than the norm. While trade press gives us a lot of information about numerous aspects of promotion, distribution, exhibition and reception, it is not available from the earliest days of moving images. Though exhibition materials elucidate early cinema programming structures, we hardly have information on all venues in which moving pictures would have been shown. But all the materials that do exist – and I focus here mostly on English- and German-language sources – can give us a good general impression of the importance of imaginative engagement with moving pictures in this period. It is precisely this wealth of information that together with the help of philosophical aesthetics can offer new insights into both fiction and early cinema.

1

The status of fiction in early cinema: Train and trick films

Are there textual criteria for fictionality?

As Charlie Keil reminds us, film historians used to regularly cite the films of Lumière brothers and Georges Méliès as incontestable evidence of the existence of two competing tendencies since the earliest days of cinema – fiction and non-fiction.[1] More precisely, they distinguished between fiction and documentary (a category narrower than non-fiction film), but given that the key trait of documentaries for these historians was precisely their non-fictional nature, it was the non-fiction/fiction binary opposition that organized these histories. Since the advent of new film history, however, this founding dichotomy has been questioned on at least two fronts. On the one hand, scholars such as Tom Gunning have argued that the early cinema was perceived primarily in terms of attractions rather than the distinction between fiction and non-fiction.[2] On the other, Keil has claimed that although the categories of fiction and non-fiction were not unimportant during this period the line between the two was not as clear-cut as the earlier generations of film historians had us believe.[3]

    In this chapter my aim is to probe further into the question of relevance of the categories of fiction and non-fiction for early film history. More specifically, my guiding questions will be: what were the early cinema audiences mandated to make-believe? What were they expected to believe? What were they tricked into believing? What could they but disbelieve? Next to allowing us to articulate some of the key aspects of early cinema, these questions will also allow me to address wider concerns about the nature of fiction in general. Primarily, I will be interested in historicizing Kendall L. Walton's notion of make-believe by answering, on the example of early cinema, where the mandates to use representations as props for imaginings come from in the first place.[4] From the perspective of analytic philosophy, this will allow us to better explain how fictional status is attributed to representational works. In other words, it will reveal how in this process factors such as film reception and exhibition context play as important a role as intention and textual features do. From the perspective of new film history, this investigation will reveal the importance the notion of imagination played in the promotion and reviews accompanying early cinema. More specifically, it will force us to reconsider standard categorizations of exemplary early cinema genres – Méliès trick films and Lumière brothers' train films – in terms of fiction and non-fiction.

Regardless of whether the importance of categories of fiction and non-fiction is downplayed as in the case of cinema of attractions or their boundaries made more permeable, new film historians appear to assume that it is the textual features that determine whether something is fiction, non-fiction or something in between. In their introduction to *American Cinema, 1890–1909* Gaudreault and Gunning, for instance, distinguish between fiction films and actualities (understood as early non-fiction film):

> The switch from the predominance of actuality to the predominance of fiction films took place during the dawn of the nickelodeon era. The first film programs featured very brief scenes (often less than a minute) of staged performances or scenes of daily life. ... However, after the initial novelty period, a number of fictional genres became popular. ... Trick films, gag comedies, and chase films (both dramatic and comic) were easy to understand without dialogue, dependent as they were mainly on physical action.[5]

Both are described in reference to the content they depict; whereas actualities depict everyday events, acrobatic feats, views of various locales and the like, fiction films include trick films, gag comedies, chase films and so on. Such focus on textual features as the defining trait of the status of both fiction and non-fiction is typical not only of how other volume's contributors apply the terms in question but also of the more detailed taxonomy provided in the thematic entry list in Richard Abel's *Encyclopedia of Early Cinema*.[6] Next to actualities, non-fiction films, for instance, also include content-defined genres such as phantom train rides, travelogues, boxing films and so on.

Detailed discussions of what counts as fiction in early cinema are rare. One exception is Keil but even he is only sceptical about the applicability of the Lumière/Méliès dichotomy to the whole of early cinema and its definability in terms of content.[7] In the case of *The Arrival of a Train/L'Arrivée d'un train en gare de La Ciotat* (1897)[8] and *A Trip to the Moon/Le Voyage dans la Lune* (1902) he, however, does not dispute 'the obvious differences between the engine of steam and steel pulling into Ciotat station and the cardboard rocket hurtling toward a papier-mâché moon.'[9] Keil continues: 'we can distinguish fiction films from nonfiction by the means of presentation rather than by content.'[10] In other words, fiction/non-fiction distinction is not about what the film represents but how the film represents it (mise-en-scène, camera angle, distance, etc.). So, the distinction is less about the difference between an everyday event and a fantastical exploration of celestial bodies and more about the on-location shooting of a train as opposed to the use of theatrical props and film tricks.

Even under this modification, however, the criteria for whether something is fiction or not remain exclusively textual.[11] My point, by contrast, is that there is nothing *internal* to the two motion pictures that would allow us to classify *The Arrival of a Train* as non-fiction and *A Trip to the Moon* as fiction. If we are to approach Lumière brothers' film simply on the terms of its representational content and technique, what is to preclude us from taking it as a film depicting an arrival of, say, an undercover agent (hidden somewhere in the disembarking crowd) to a foreign town? Somebody sharing Keil's view might point out that in virtue of its presentation the whole scene comes across as unstaged or, to put it in Gunning's terms, that it exhibits the 'view' aesthetic – a standard trait of documentaries, a key category of non-fiction.[12] Given that the film elicits an impression of an everyday train arrival with people going about their daily business we must be dealing with non-fiction. But this would imply that no fiction film can make use of non-scripted performances and on-location shooting, and that is patently false. Another objection might be that there is clearly a moment when one of the disembarking passengers looks at the camera and then quickly leaves the shot, most probably because the cameraman has asked him to do so. But how does this preclude us from engaging the film as, say, a fiction about a cameraman who has had the bad luck of somebody ruining his shot? In other words, there is no reason a fiction film could not employ any and all stylistic features usually connected with documentaries – actual locations, use of non-actors as characters, minimal or no staging and so on. The same applies for the features and presentation techniques of the broader category of non-fiction which may include the elimination of narrative structures and representational form.[13]

In the case of the Méliès's film we are faced with an obverse predicament. There is undeniably a fictional story about a certain expedition to the moon that can be inferred from watching the film. There are, moreover, images of entities which clearly represent objects and agents non-existent at the time: flying rockets, humanoid Moon inhabitants and an anthropomorphic moon, just

Figure 1.1 A photograph of a horse with an attached horn, or, a photographic representation of a unicorn. Still from *Blade Runner: Director's Cut* (Ridley Scott, 1992).

to name a few. We need not, however, immediately take this as a sign that we are dealing with a fiction film. The fact remains that all the images cited are photographic reproductions of some actual objects. Much like it is possible to entertain a photographic image of a unicorn as essentially a photographic reproduction of a horse with a horn attached to its head (Figure 1.1), it is also reasonable to think of a Moon person on screen as an actor dressed up in a suit in front of a camera. The introduction of temporal dimension in film in contrast to photography and the articulation of a narrative does not necessarily mandate any imaginings either.[14] The above unicorn is still just a horse with an artificial horn attached, albeit it is now galloping around. In other words, no internal trait of the film stops us from engaging *A Trip to the Moon* simply as a recording of dressed-up actors playing certain characters across a number of stage-sets and scenes, a point that André Bazin has made.[15] And while at it why not also simply take the shots of the cardboard rocket and the papier-mâché moon as documents of how everyday material can be used to prompt imaginings of all sorts? The idea of cinema as 'canned theatre' used primarily to dismiss cinema as art in the early twentieth century certainly allows for this approach.

An answer to these semi-rhetorical questions might be that, following Keil's logic about the key role of presentation techniques in determining non/fictional status, Méliès's film is not really an instance of 'canned theatre', and not even an instance of 'canned magic theatre' because there are clearly film specific effects in it. After all, the notion of 'canned magic theatre' has been criticized for decades by scholars such as Jacques Malthête.[16] First, there are numerous occasions of antagonists simply disappearing from the shots clearly accomplished by means of substitution splicing. Moreover, multiple exposure plays a key role at least in the shot in which the rocket plunges from the moon back to the earth and the ocean. Finally, some prints of the film were hand-coloured so at least in some versions there are objects other than those reproduced by the camera that contribute to the representational content. Allow me to address these concerns in order. The use of substitution splicing does not change the fact that the shots across the splice are of actual objects – the first with the actor dressed up as a Moon inhabitant and the second without him. Nothing changes as far as the *option* to engage the film as a recording of actual people participating in a game of make-believe about a mission to the moon. Though the technique can certainly aid us in imagining that hitting a Moon person over the head with an umbrella will make him disappear, we are still perfectly free to regard the scene as a great example of how actors are able to stand perfectly still as one of them departs the shot and then continue performing once the cameraman has started shooting again. Multiple exposure presents no problem for similar reasons. Again it is from actual objects that the photographic images are derived – that they are composed into a single image only documents how film can make it look like a rocket is falling into an ocean, though from our perspective it is really a matter of juxtaposing a cardboard rocket against a stock footage of the sea and then having the former move towards the lower edge of the frame as the shot progresses. In other words, we can treat this as a combination of stop-motion animation and multiple exposure. The colour, admittedly, is not a result of shooting anything in front of the camera but a matter of adding pigments onto the filmstrip itself. Moreover, it is undeniable that, as Gunning and Joshua Yumibe have explained, colour in early cinema was used for fantastical effects and as an attraction in itself more often than for realistic reproduction.[17] But this changes nothing: we as viewers still have an *option* to treat colour as means for representing how the actual sets looked like. Given that the technology of the time did not allow for satisfactory colour reproduction, hand-painted additions are here to help us see, for instance, what the colours of dresses the actors wore actually were. In other words, we are still in the realm of Keil's presentation techniques. Returning to the point made about *The Arrival of a Train*, in the same sense that fiction films are free to use any stylistic features characteristic of non-fiction, non-fiction may capitalize on any stylistic traits typical of fiction films.

    To recapitulate, the argument is not that *A Trip to the Moon* is an instance of 'canned magic theatre' – the range of filmic methods employed in the production of the film makes such a claim patently false. Rather, the point is that the nature of the recorded image always allows us to focus on the profilmic and articulate the image as a recording of the profilmic while downplaying or fully dismissing any further fictional representations that the profilmic might instantiate. The discourse on 'canned magic theatre' was only one historical form of such emphasis on the profilmic. At the same time, our ability to engage any object as a prop in a game of make-believe makes it possible to, based on textual features alone, treat even recordings such as *The Arrival of a Train* as fictions.

The claim about the presentation techniques as defining features of fiction and non-fiction alike is only a part of a broader argument Keil is making. He wishes to produce an alternative to the strict fiction/non-fiction dichotomy by exploring what he calls the 'quality of being *part* of the fiction, while also existing *apart* from it' in three types of early films – 'motion films with interpolated fictional material, travel films, and fiction films'.[18] Keil is trying to articulate the idea that the boundaries between fiction and non-fiction in early cinema were particularly fuzzy because the actualities embedded in fictional contexts retained 'an indisputable ... separateness'.[19] In films like *Honeymoon at Niagara Falls* (Edwin S. Porter, 1906) location shots, despite being integrated into the fictional story of the honeymoon, still preserve the status of a documentary record. I am not denying this residual documentary quality in the films Keil is discussing but there are two key problems with his argument. First, not only some but all photographic films share the quality Keil wishes to address for they are all, as my discussion of *A Trip to the Moon* demonstrates, actualities in a perfectly legitimate sense. As we have seen, they are at the very least actualities of whatever was in front of camera during shooting, irrespective of the amount of post-production that in terms of substation splicing and/or colouring they might have undergone. Second, Keil fails to see that before a set of films is chosen to explore the intermediary qualities of fiction and non-fiction, we first need to address the question under what conditions the recording itself, rather than the performance recorded, is taken as a prop for certain imaginings. As I have mentioned in the Introduction and will articulate in more detail below, turn-of-the-nineteenth-century films like *Uncle Tom's Cabin* (Porter, 1903) which we nowadays identify as fictions were seen by their contemporaries as recordings of performances.

The lesson then to be learnt here is that textual information (content and/or presentational techniques) on its own cannot reveal the (non-)fictional status of photographic film. I speak of photographic film only because this does not appear to apply to at least some instances of digitally animated cinema. For instance, it seems that so long as we recognize their representational nature, there is no way of engaging films like *Toy Story* (John Lasseter, 1995) but imaginatively.[20] Because they have not been photographically derived from actual objects we cannot say that we are simply watching recordings of actual make-believe performances as we could in *A Trip to the Moon*.[21] The film's protagonists (living toys), moreover, have no place in the world as it actually is because living-breathing toys are figments of imagination. We are forced to take the images themselves as props for imagining all the toys' adventures. We might get a purchase on the representational difference crucial for determining fictionality by comparing *Toy Story* to *Mascot* (Vladislav Starevich, 1933) and *Steamboat Willie* (Ub Iwerks and Walt Disney, 1928). In a film like *Mascot* any invitation to make-believe live puppets, which have no more place in the actual world than walking-talking Buzz Lightyear and Woody, can still be dismissed with recourse to the stop-motion technique. We can simply say that the film documents the effectiveness of using stop-motion technique to produce an impression of movement in inanimate objects. Photographically derived films like *Steamboat Willie* similarly also allow for thinking about them as documentary recordings of a sequence of drawings, one replacing the other every 1/24th of a second. Though there is no Mickey Mouse in the actual world, the trick is to downplay whatever imaginings the drawings prop and focus on the fact that these drawings still needed to have been recorded for there to be a film.[22]

The matter, therefore, does not come down to whether a shot was made with an actual object in front of the camera for digitally animated cinema can also be used as non-fictional illustration. In digitally animated flight announcements, for instance, we are simply asked to behave somewhat like the animated characters behave on screen when lifting the window blinds, and not to imagine some characters behaving like that.[23] Therefore, we can only say that there are some digitally animated films which, unlike photographic ones, determine their fictional status on their own. In other words, the absence of actual objects in front of the camera is a necessary but not sufficient condition for a film to be able to fix its status as fictional with recourse to textual parameters alone. In digitally animated cinema, moreover, the sufficient condition for a film to be fictional is that whatever is represented cannot be identified among actually existing entities.[24]

This finding can be expounded into a principle applicable to all fiction regardless of the medium in which it is implemented. We can say that a representation necessarily mandates imaginings if its *direct* representational content is an entity which does not exist in the actual world. The notion of direct representation here is meant to draw attention to the fact that representations can be embedded within representations. The word 'unicorn', for instance, directly represents a unicorn, whereas a photograph can represent a unicorn only by representing something that represents a unicorn.[25] Therefore, any linguistic text speaking of unicorns will *necessarily* mandate imaginings about unicorns (this sentence and a large part of the monograph is, therefore, fictional). A painting of a unicorn will do the same. A theatre play in which an actor acts out a unicorn likewise. A photograph of a unicorn, as I mentioned earlier, will not because its direct representational content is in fact a dressed-up horse (or a horn and a horse in the case of composite photography).

The question remains, if there are some non-photographic films which internally determine their fictional status, might there be photographic films which are necessarily non-fictional? Or, more generally, if fictionality is tied up with representation perhaps non-representational works regardless of whether they are derived digitally, photographically or otherwise are automatically non-fictional? Consider, for instance, films like Walter Ruttmann's *Lichtspiel Opus* series from the early 1920s (Figure 1.2) or Peter Kubelka's *Arnulf Rainer* (1960). Given that they do not represent anything or that, at best, the former represents only various abstract shapes with or without colours and the latter only black and white does this not entail that there is simply nothing to imagine when watching them? The problem with this entailment is that we are always free to imagine something, and there is certainly nothing *internal* to these films that mandates me *not* to imagine anything. Focusing on the content and technique alone I am certainly free to imagine objects and/or colours changing shapes and doing so in case of Ruttmann. Similarly, I am free to imagine, say, a screen being turned off and on when watching Kubelka. We are left with the conclusion that even in the most 'non-representational' works there is always something in front of us

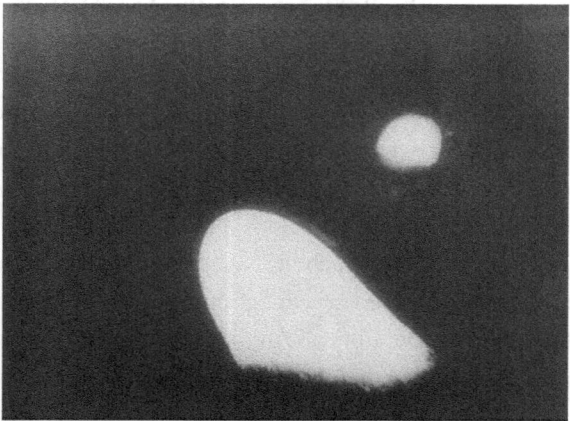

Figure 1.2 Still from *Lichtspiel: Opus II* (Walter Ruttmann, 1921).

to entertain and this something can always be used as a prop for imaginings. What we need to figure out, therefore, is where does the *mandate* to imagine something based on what is presented to us come from? In other words, how did it come about that we do virtually automatically take *A Trip to the Moon* to be fiction?

Extratextual criteria of fictionality

What, then, is this additional extratextual information that is necessary for attributing (non-)fictional status? Analytic philosophers have suggested that the key extratextual information in this context is the authorial one (where the author is usually understood as the director in the case of cinema). According to Noël Carroll, for instance, a film is a work of fiction if the author *intends* the audience to imagine whatever the film represents.[26] The obverse claim that the film is non-fiction if the author does not intend the audience to imagine anything about the film is also shared by other notable theorists such as Trevor Ponech and Carl Plantinga.[27] The proposal seems enticing because determining authorial intentions about whether the author categorizes her film as fiction or non-fiction is relatively easily accomplished by looking at the film's title, its generic specifications in TV guides and specialized internet portals, interviews, press releases, promotional campaigns and the like. The problems arise, however, when it becomes clear that the intentionalist model for film is merely a special case of these philosophers' views on fiction. In other words, a representation is fiction according to this model if its author intends the audience to imagine whatever is represented. Otherwise, it is non-fiction. For instance, *Oliver Twist* (1839) is a fictional work because Charles Dickens intended it to be fictional and not because there never existed such a boy like Oliver. Similarly, *A People's History of the United States* is not fictional because Howard Zinn did not intend the audience to take it as fictional.

This general model fails to accommodate the status of a large and foundational body of texts such as mythologies, however. Consider Hesiod's *Theogony*, that is, the genealogy of the birth of the gods, from circa 700 BCE. Nowadays, Greek mythology with *Theogony* as one of its most comprehensive accounts is categorized as fiction. It would be reasonable to assume, however, that for Hesiod the history of the gods (though not necessarily fact) was a matter of belief rather than make-believe. Over the years it became apparent that gods do not belong to the class of actually existing entities classifying them, as we have learnt in the previous section, fictions for present-day consumers. But according to the intentionalist model Hesiod's intentions fix *Theogony* as non-fiction once and for all. The intentionalists could resolve this counter-intuitive result by emphasizing that their definition of (non-)fiction is normative so later imaginative engagements with a text that was initially intended as non-fiction do not matter at all. They could claim that we are mistaken in categorizing mythologies as fictions and that we need to treat them instead as accounts of the universe which merely turned out to be wrong. It is certainly possible to treat *Theogony* and mythologies as incorrect descriptions of the world, but the fact remains that we regularly categorize them as fictions instead (in bookstores, libraries, education, etc.) precisely because they involve non-existing entities. The question is, given that it differs substantially from the way fiction is ordinarily construed, should the intentionalists' proposed redefinition of fiction trump the current ordinary categorization? The answer is no. Normative definitions of ordinary language phenomena cannot be supported by the mere fact that they make categorization relatively easy. If they diverge substantially from how the phenomenon is usually understood, then they need to provide better reasons for the proposed redefinition especially when the redefinition would involve such a large and important category as mythologies.

Though conceding on the matter of fiction in general the intentionalists might point out that demonstrating that texts can migrate across boundaries between fiction and non-fiction does not evince that films can do the same. Therefore, so long as there is no proof of the latter the intentionalist model is still applicable at least to cinema. Let us consider this objection by looking at number of early cinema productions based on the Bible and passion plays in particular.[28] Given the American and European early twentieth-century cultural and religious context it is safe to assume that for the greatest majority of filmmakers working at the turn of the century the Bible was a matter of belief rather than make-believe. Following this logic most, if not all, passion plays constitute non-fiction. Siegmund Lubin, for instance, the producer of one of the earliest passion plays – *Passion Play* (1898) – and a convert to Christianity from Judaism introduces his film and the accompanying lecture he himself penned by clearly articulating the intention to present the true story of Jesus Christ as recorded by 'the Holy Scripture':

> A brief, clear and vivid narrative of the birth, life, sufferings and death of our Lord Jesus Christ is here presented under the title of THE PASSION PLAY, which has not alone proven beneficial to the young in Bible classes, but has

served to impress on the minds of all who are interested a better knowledge and clearer knowledge of Holy Scripture.[29]

But with the waning of the power of Christian religion throughout the twentieth century (which is essentially no different from growing out of mythology be it Greek, Polynesian, Judeo-Christian or otherwise) we can say that at this point a great number of people, myself included, can perfectly legitimately call these works instances of fiction. At the very least, the intentionalists must admit that there is place for transformation of non-fiction to fiction even in cinema.[30]

If a text intended as non-fictional can migrate into the fictional domain then clearly (non-)fiction must be a category that hinges on something other than authorial intentions. The best way to approach fiction, therefore, is institutionally.[31] Rather than privileging authorial intentions we should look at the nexus of production, promotion, exhibition and reception to establish how each of these nodal points contributes to the formation of (non-)imaginative engagement with film. This is particularly important for early cinema where disclaimers like 'All persons fictitious' or labels such as 'documentary' and 'fiction' were not in circulation.[32] In other words, though nowadays we most often know well in advance to what category the film we are going to see belongs to, we cannot assume that the same institutional framework was in place during the earliest days of cinema.

It is important to note, moreover, that up to now I have mainly discussed *The Arrival of a Train* and *A Trip to the Moon* with the wisdom of hindsight, that is, with the knowledge of the history of film and film genre as well as of special effects. The point was to demonstrate that even such knowledge is neither necessary nor sufficient to determine whether something is fiction or not. There is little sense in using the standard traits of photographic non-fiction, however, to argue that something is a member of that class for at the time of the initial screening of Lumière's moving picture, the audience would have simply not been familiar with the class as we are. In the context of the myth of the panicking audiences and its subsequent debunking, moreover, what is to stop us from saying that even if they did not exactly vacate their seats in terror at the sight of its arrival, the early audiences were at least swept up in make-believe that the onrushing train is in their immediate proximity? Furthermore, with all the literature on early actualities as ersatz tourism in mind, is it unreasonable to think that on top of showing how these famous locales actually looked like, these films also invited the audiences to imagine that they are present at the locale?[33] In the case of *A Trip of the Moon* it would similarly be unfair and anachronistic to think that the audiences had the knowledge of how the film's special effects were achieved. In that sense, is it unrealistic to assume that the early cinema audiences, contrary to what our hypothetical critic might say, did see such films as instances of 'canned magic theatre' where it might have been a matter of disbelieving or not being able to believe what one sees rather than make-believing it? Let us, therefore, consider in order what information reception, exhibition, production and promotion contexts reveal as far as the intended and actual beliefs, disbeliefs and make-believes early cinema audiences entertained are concerned.

Reception and exhibition context

Stephen Bottomore's discussion of what Yuri Tsivian has termed the 'the train effect', that is, 'an anxious or panicky reaction to films of approaching vehicles', most notably its appendix 2, presents us with an unparalleled wealth of contemporary sources addressing the earliest screenings of numerous films depicting various vehicles rushing towards the camera.[34] Bottomore demonstrated that although some contemporary reports describing the audience as flinching or even screaming certainly exist it is only a decade or two later that these would be exaggerated into what would constitute the founding myth of cinema – the terrifying effect of cinema's hyper-realism. Focusing on contemporary reports, Bottomore has made use of the perceptual phenomenon known as the 'looming effect' and Tsivian's notion of 'a viewer with untrained cognitive habits' to explain audience's panicky reactions without resorting to the idea that the audiences actually believed that they were faced with an onrushing vehicle. The 'looming effect' is an optical illusion in which rapid expansion of two-dimensional images is automatically perceived as an approaching object giving rise to avoidant behaviour. In other words, like other optical illusions it is a *perceptual* illusion, that is, illusion which, unlike *cognitive* illusion, is perceived regardless of our knowledge about the nature of the illusion.[35] Even when we are told and we know that we are presented with just a rapidly expanding two-dimensional image, we still perceive it as three-dimensional object due to the way our brains process stimuli. Cognitive illusion, by contrast, takes place when we falsely believe that this two-dimensional image is a rapidly approaching three-dimensional object. It is, therefore, reasonable to see why the early audience, essentially unaccustomed to the speed of motion the novel representational form of cinema inaugurated, would have flinched at the sight of films like *The*

Arrival of a Train without having actually entertained the false belief that the train is going to run them over.

In this section I wish to build on Tsivian's and Bottomore's exemplary work by drawing attention to a recurrent theme in contemporary accounts they do not address systematically – the role of imagination – and propose an alternative account of 'the train effect'.[36] In other words, by expanding on Martin Loiperdinger's identification of hypothetical structures in contemporary accounts of train films, I will propose that for the very earliest audience moving pictures such as *The Arrival of a Train* presented instances of *fiction* insofar they were regularly seen as mandating imaginings about the onrushing vehicle and one's spatial placement in relation to it.[37] I will also address Gunning's explanation of 'the train effect' in terms of the tradition of the magic theatre and the experience of disbelief to get a better sense of what role a special brand of *illusion* distinct from looming understood as perceptual illusion played in the earliest engagement with these films.[38] This will serve to set up the discussion of the trick film in which I will argue that at least a large subclass of them was perceived as non-fiction. Films like *The Four Troublesome Heads/Un homme de têtes* (Georges Méliès, 1898), I will claim, and on occasions even *A Trip to the Moon* were plausibly perceived as *recordings* of theatrical performances, rather than fictions in themselves.

Train films and *The Arrival of a Train*

Let me begin with one of the most widely cited accounts of contemporary screening of *The Arrival of a Train* – Maxim Gorky's:

> It speeds right at you – watch out! It seems as though it will plunge into the darkness in which you sit, turning you into a ripped sack full of lacerated flesh and splintered bones...[39]

The assertion with which the paragraph opens and the subsequent imperative certainly present the train as a danger. The graphic description at the end of the paragraph undeniably brings the threat home. The menace is not only visceral but murderous. Notice, however, that these rhetorical strategies are essentially qualified with the phrase 'it seems as though'. This phrase serves less as a description of the looming effect than a sign of the imaginative mode underlying the whole passage. Nothing is actually going to plunge into the darkness. Nobody is actually going to be ripped into a thousand pieces. You need not actually watch out. Rather, you are supposed to entertain the prospect of a dreadful crash. You are invited to ruminate the contact with the implacable steel and your limbs as they are shred to pieces. You are asked to ponder the spectacle of your mangled body in the locomotive's awful wake. In other words, you are invited to *imagine* that that the train will break out of the screen destroying everything in its path with you in front. And this is why the description of the impossible consequences is so vivid. It is less an account of an actual threat than a prop for entertaining the most terrifying threat imaginable. In other words, Gorky is conveying in words the specific mandate for *imaginings* he finds to be present in the Lumière brothers' film.

In fact, Gorky is feeding into the sensationalist press Ben Singer demonstrated to be already in wide circulation at the turn of the century hyping all sorts of possible (though improbable) urban catastrophes, with traffic accidents and particularly train ones at the forefront.[40] The exhibition context of moving pictures that Bottomore is addressing could, therefore, easily prompt imaginings which take loss of life and limb as their subject matter. A particularly infamous train derailment did take place in Montparnasse in Paris in October shortly before the premiere of Lumière's train film when a train broke through the station wall and plummeted on the street bellow killing a pedestrian (Figure 1.3). One railway operator described another accident that almost took place like this: 'For a moment I pictured the awful horrors of such a calamity; listened to the wails and shrieks of the mangled and dying, and saw in imagination the crushed and bloody corpses intermingled with the debris of that terrible wreck.'[41] This is why the 'thinking' at the end of the following quotation describing the screening of *The Arrival of the Paris Express* (1896) in Britain easily stands for actually imagining those very things:

> In the distance there is some smoke, then the engine of the express is seen, and in a few seconds the train rushes in so quickly that, in common with the most of the people in the front row of the stalls, I shift uneasily in my seat and think of railway accidents.[42]

Much like Gorky, this anonymous reviewer cannot help but *imagine* all sorts of terrors the train on the screen could cause. Here we can also see more clearly how it is in fact imagining the accident rather than experiencing the looming effect that prompts one to fidget nervously. The reviewer does not simply automatically fidget in his seat but does so with time to conjure up an image of a train wreck in his mind.

Equivalents to Gorky's 'it seems as though' phrase – which evinces the role of imagination in the earliest audiences' engagement with the film – can be also found in reports about both Lumières' and other train films. In the first case,

Figure 1.3 Montparnasse derailment, 22 October 1895.

in the then leading Parisian magazine *L'Illustration* Félix Regnault writes: 'The locomotive appears small at first, then immense, as if it were going to crush the audience.'⁴³ President of the Vienna Photographic Society, Ottomar Volkmer, commented: 'At last the train arrives, the locomotive appears tremendous; it seems as if it were going to run into the spectators.'⁴⁴ Upon seeing the film, Méliès, similarly, writes to a friend: '... the train dashes towards us, as if about to leave the screen and land in the hall'.⁴⁵ A British reviewer of the cinématographe writes in the same vein: 'One of the most startling pictures is that of a railway station. You see the people hanging around the platform, and then all at once business is jerked into them. The train comes dashing along as if it were going to take a header right into the middle of the audience, and the people hurry and skurry for their seats in a most amusing manner...'[46] An account of an American Mutoscope and Biograph Company train films reads: '[the train] approaches at a fearful speed and appears as though it were going to burst from the picture into the audience'.[47]

In all these accounts 'as if' and 'as though it were' play the same role as Gorky's 'as though'. They all express a hypothetical stance in which the spectators are well aware that the train is *not* going to burst into the auditorium, yet they entertain it as a possibility. In entertaining a counterfactual possibility, they are essentially imagining an alternative state of affairs. In other words, they are playing a game of make-believe with the image of the train as a prop.[48]

An emphasis on imagining as the main (though not exclusive) cause of fright and even screaming is given in the following report of the screening of *The Empire State Express* (American Mutoscope and Biograph Company, 1896) in the United States as well:

> Suddenly the Empire State Express looms in sight way off in the distance and comes steaming towards you – right dead at you at full speed. It makes even unimaginative person kind of shiver and wish he could get off to one side, but women – it scares them to death. Two ladies who were in the box last night screamed and fainted.[49]

The suggestion is that although the experience is visceral even for the unimaginative viewers (which could be explained in terms of the looming effect), the most intensive effect is afforded to those who engage the recording imaginatively. The full force of the train becomes apparent only when it is imagined as the harbinger of doom which will leave nothing but mangled bodies and contorted steel in its wake. Much like in a horror film, it is in imagining the scenario on screen that the spectator can experience *genuine* fright.[50] If one's imagination is lacking, by contrast, the effect is not completely lost but it does not amount to more than fidgeting nervously in the chair.[51]

According to contemporary reception from across the world including the United States, Russia, France, Britain, Austro-Hungary and Algeria imaginings can be thought of as at least as legitimate an explanation of 'the train effect' as the combination of the looming effect and the unfamiliarity with the new medium. Moreover, because these films are taken as mandating consistent imaginings there is good reason to think of them as fictional, at least at the time of their earliest screenings. For Bottomore, cinema's founding myth misrepresents what was a perceptual illusion causing avoidant behaviour and stemming from the looming effect for a cognitive illusion cueing false belief about onrushing trains and deriving from the audiences' gullibility. What the myth of the panicking audience belies from the perspective of make-believe, by contrast, is the status of imagination in early cinema – what is initially articulated as a matter of active make-believe by contemporary audiences is in later mythical accounts misrepresented as false belief based on cognitive illusion. In other words, the articulation of the myth is a sign of how short it can take to transform what was initially perceived as genre of fiction into non-fiction.

As I have noted in the introduction to this section, Loiperdinger has also addressed the myth in question. He was, in fact, the first one to my knowledge to notice the 'as if' structure in numerous cited contemporary accounts. For him, however, the hypothetical is simply an 'attempt to give readers an understanding of the film image's projected spatial effect in *Arrival of the Train*' rather than a sign of mandated imaginings.[52] Though he connects the hypothetical to the notion of fantasy he does not define the latter in terms of fiction but rather as a 'fantastic experience' following Susan Sontag: 'For those first audiences, the very transcription of the most banal reality – the Lumière brothers filming *Arrival of the Train to La Ciotat Station* – was a fantastic experience. Cinema began in wonder, the wonder that reality can be transcribed with such immediacy.'[53] It is clear from the quotation that 'fantastic experience' describes an experience of amazement with perceptual illusions of image movement and depth rather than an act of make-believe in Walton's sense. That, unlike me, Loiperdinger never identifies *Arrival of the Train* as fiction for the earliest audiences is unequivocally evinced by the following claim: 'Paradoxical as it may appear today, the audience's interest in the projected *documentary* images of the Cinématographe Lumière was of a primarily *fantastic* nature.'[54] In fact, Loiperdinger only questions the film's genre *within* non-fiction, rearticulating *The Arrival of a Train* as an amateur film rather than an actuality. The impetus to do that, moreover, comes not from the analysis of the film's production, promotion, exhibition and reception discourse together but from its production aspect alone. In other words, it is solely a combination of authorial intentions and textual features that guide Loiperdinger's categorizations of genre – an approach I have criticized in the first section of this chapter.

The importance of exhibition context and magic theatre

In order to flesh out my point about imagination as opposed to the 'fantastic experience' associated with various types of illusions so prominent in the culture of the late nineteenth century that Loiperdinger discusses it is worth comparing my account to another seminal reinterpretation of the train effect – Gunning's discussion of it in relation to attraction.[55] From Gunning's perspective the myth of the panicking audience transforms the positive appeal of attractions into a disturbing experience while neglecting the early exhibition context. For Gunning it is crucial that the projections of *The Arrival of a Train* and similar films usually started with the initially static images which would only later be replaced with images conveying the illusion of movement. In that sense, the myth of the panicking audiences shifts the contemporary emphasis from the shock with the transformation of static into moving images to the illusion of threat of the oncoming train. In Gunning's own words: 'The audience's sense of shock comes less from a naive belief that they are threatened by an actual locomotive than from an unbelievable visual transformation occurring before their eyes, parallel to the greatest wonders of the magic theatre.'[56]

The claim feeds into Gunning's larger argument in which he aims to demonstrate that once the early spectator is historically contextualized, she can no longer be used to prop up theoretical models of the present-day spectator whose main premise is the force of cinematic illusion: 'Cinema's first audiences can no longer serve as a founding myth for the theoreticalisation of the ent[h]ralled spectator ... the first spectator's experience reveal not a childlike belief, but an undisguised awareness (and delight in) film's illusionistic capabilities ... screams of terror and delight were well prepared for in advance by both showmen and audience.'[57] Since the early spectator was aware of the film's illusion to begin with, there is little point in drawing on her to legitimize a view of the present-day spectator theorized to be engulfed by illusion.

Let us leave the discussion of whether the present-day spectator is generally under the sway of illusion for later chapters – a view which is far from eradicated from film studies[58] – but point out that if she is that this is at least partially based on the illusion of motion and depth a majority of photographic films convey. Instead, let us concentrate on the relation between Gunning's understanding of illusion and the structure of his argument. To make his argument formally valid, Gunning appears to conflate different types of illusions. My point here, to repeat, is not to criticize the conclusion of Gunning's argument and his larger point about theorizing present-day spectators but to emphasize the difference between his premise and mine by drawing attention to how he lumps together different things under the umbrella term of illusion without addressing the crucial role of imagination – hence, of fictions.

For Gunning, Lumière train film, trompe l'oeil and contemporary magic theatre are all illusions which 'exploited their unbelievable nature, keeping a conscious focus on the fact that they were only illusions'.[59] Though there is nothing wrong in principle with this general description, for in ordinary language all of these indeed are illusions, the quotation glosses over the different kinds of illusions we are dealing with. The impression of motion and depth in Lumière train film and the impression of three-dimensionality in trompe l'oeil are perceptual illusions, whereas magic theatre is not. Magic theatre uses sleights of hand, staging, lighting and other intricate devices to produce its effect, but the effect is not one of *perceptual* illusion. If the trick is explained, then the spectator will be able to pay attention and see the trick for what it really is. For instance, woman wiggling her toes after being sawn in half will generally cause amazement, wonder and disbelief if one is not aware of the design behind the trick. But after the design is revealed the spectator clearly does not see woman wiggling her toes any more, rather the spectator sees that another person hidden in the lower portion of the trunk is wiggling her feet or, in another version, notices that the feet are too mechanic in their movements to be real. The spectator certainly does not see the woman whose head is coming out of the other part of the truck *as* wiggling her feet. If, on the other hand, the spectator is informed of the technique behind both early motion pictures and trompe l'oeil, she will still see a two-dimensional object *as* three-dimensional and see the image of the train *as* moving. In magic there is always a diversion, whereas in projection of motion and trompe l'oeil there is no such thing.

Gunning's analogy with magic theatre from the perspective of illusion of motion (and depth), it would appear then, does not quite get at the aspect of illusion crucial to early film (and trompe l'oeil) – perceptual illusion. Gunning might object that I have been deliberately misreading his article, that is, that if we examine one of his key points and a passage of his I even quote above, it will become clear that it is the *transformation* from static to moving images that is the more important aspect of analogy with magic theatre, as compared to perceptual illusion of the moving image itself. This is a fair point. The first thing to notice, however, is that shifting emphasis from perception of movement (and depth) to transformation of static into moving images, makes a dent in the formal validity of Gunning's argument because whatever the claims about present-day enthralled spectator are they can hardly hinge on any similar transformations. More importantly, the transformation remains in the realm of perceptual illusions, a domain it does not share with the magic theatre.

At this point it might be conceded that there are issues with the formal validity of the argument but that, if we bracket off the validity of the conclusion, what is really at stake is how good an account of the train effect Gunning produces. In other words, though they might differ as far as the class of illusion they belong to, Lumière train film, trompe l'oleil and contemporary magic all have the same structure of incredulity for the contemporary spectator, that is, they 'make visual that which it was impossible to believe'.[60] Nobody believes the woman to be sawn in half and wiggling despite seeing her *as* sawn in half and wiggling her toes and nobody believes that images actually began to move despite seeing them *as* moving. This observation holds but it does not give us the full picture. What Gunning's account is missing is imagination.

Consider an excerpt from the letter by Gorky's compatriot – Vladimir Stasov – to his brother which has all the elements of Gunning's account:

> All of a sudden a whole railway train comes rushing out of the picture towards you; it gets bigger and bigger, and you think it's going to run you over, just like in Anna Karenina – it's incredible.[61]

The incredulity Gunning speaks of is certainly invoked ('it's incredible') and the unexpectedness of the moving image is implied ('all of a sudden'). However, there is more to it. There is a context to thinking the train is dangerous and it is an exemplary piece of Russian fiction – Tolstoy's *Anna Karenina* (1878). Stasov is not only jolted and amazed but actively imagining that the train is going to run him over, just like he imagines the train runs over Anna Karenina. Illusions, be they perceptual or of the magic theatre kind do not mandate any imaginings. One simply sees an object as three-dimensional, an image as moving or a woman as wiggling her toes.

Notice, moreover, that in Stasov's account as in all the others cited up to now, there is still a threat of the hurling train on top of the incredulity with perceptual illusions of both movement and transformation. Though shifting the emphasis away from the perceived threat Gunning still must grapple with it somehow. Bottomore needs no recourse to what the rapidly approaching image represents given that for the looming effect any two-dimensional image would do. In other words, his account invokes no beliefs about what is represented. Gunning approaches it differently: 'What is displayed before the audience is less the impending speed of the train than the force of the cinematic apparatus. Or to put it better, the one demonstrates the other.'[62] In other words, Gunning still falls onto the explanation of the train's perceived threat in terms of (false) beliefs about representations. When discussing the above quotation from Gorky, Gunning states the following: 'Describing *The Arrival of a Train* Gorky senses its impending threat. … Belief and terror are larded with an awareness of illusion.'[63] However much it might be pushed to the fringe, credulity, that is, formation of (false) beliefs about representational contents as causes of emotional states, still plays a role for Gunning. No such thing is necessary in the account focusing on imagination.

Gunning then conflates perceptual illusion of motion (and depth) in film, magic illusion, and illusion giving rise to false belief about an onrushing train. The last is essentially a cognitive illusion and this is what I wish to deny to the urbanite audiences Gunning speaks of. Gunning's dialectics of credulity and incredulity though shifting emphasis on the latter still allow for the former. My proposal, like Bottomore's, dispenses with credulity but, unlike Bottomore's, points to a neglected role of imagination and the ways in which it is distinct from all types of the above illusion. And it is precisely by virtue of imagination that is, the mandates that the contemporary audiences took to be operational with striking regularity that we should talk of *The Arrival of a Train* and similar films as fictional genre in a proper sense. This group of moving pictures also presents an example of how fiction can turn into non-fiction over (a very short amount of) time. By the time the myth of the panicking audience was articulated these films have already turned into non-fiction.

A Trip to the Moon and trick films

At least a subclass of trick films – a tradition *A Trip to the Moon* is clearly a part of – must have gone the other route if their relation to the magic theatre is considered. If, as I have argued, magic theatre tricks mandate no imaginings, but, as Gunning points out, it hinges on making visible that which one cannot believe, then there is good reason to think that numerous moving pictures such as *The Vanishing Lady/Escamotage d'une dame chez Robert-Houdin* (Méliès, 1896) provoked the same response. If disappearances and reappearances were a regular part of Méliès's repertoire at Théâtre Robert-Houdin which he owned and for which he was quite famous, then it is safe to assume that someone seeing a similar trick on screen would have the same response – incredulity accompanied by no imaginings whatsoever. What is more, the film would have been screened at the actual theatre.[64] Of course, considerably different devices were behind the disappearance of the lady and her later reappearance in the stage and screen version – intricate stagecraft in the former and substitution splicing in the latter. But neither is this something which would have been immediately obvious to the early spectator, especially given the exhibition context, nor, even if the distinction were apparent, would it have necessarily made a difference. How the trick is accomplished is irrelevant for the structure of incredulity and absence of mandated imaginings. In other words, what is important is that nobody believes that disappearance and reappearance actually take place and that nobody is mandated to imagine anything.

We could say the same even of a motion picture like *The Four Troublesome Heads*. In it Méliès takes off his head which continues to talk as he makes his head appear again and then proceeds to repeat the stunt two more times (eventually, the heads become too annoying so he hits the two of them with his guitar causing them to disappear and picks up the remaining one to replace his own head he had just taken off his shoulders and thrown off screen). Miriam Rosen notes that one of Méliès's most famous theatre tricks was *Recalcitrant Decapitated Man* wherein a professor's head is cut off mid-speech only to continue speaking until it is returned on his shoulders (Figure 1.4).[65] Within such context it would have been quite easy to see *The Four Troublesome Heads* and similar motion pictures as a further development of tricks Théâtre Robert-Houdin was already famous for – ingenious and incredible but by no means putting any mandated imaginings into play. To rephrase a derogatory term and put a positive spin on it, such moving pictures would have easily been perceived as instances of 'canned magic theatre'. Or, to use Gaudreault's and Phillippe Marion's formulation, such motion pictures were seen as 'attractional packages' – performances which were 'already predetermined, predefined, and preformatted in and by an extracinematic cultural series'.[66]

That this was an important context for contemporaries in construing cinema is supported by reports such as the following account of what was, as Richard Abel points out,[67] actually Méliès's *The Astronomer's Dream or the Man in the Moon/La Lune à un mètre* (1898):

> An important adjunct to the continuous vaudeville bill will be the Parisian novelty 'A Trip to the Moon,' shown at this house last week for the first time in America. 'A Trip to the Moon' is a life motion picture reproduction of a celebrated French spectacular piece. The entire spectacle has been reproduced, the film being the longest ever made.[68]

Notice how much emphasis is placed on reproduction by using the term on two separate occasions in two adjacent sentences. The matter is even more interesting

Figure 1.4 *Recalcitrant Decapitated Man* at Théâtre Robert-Houdin.

here because, unlike films like *The Vanishing Lady* or *The Four Troublesome Heads*, *The Astronomer's Dream or the Man in the Moon* from our perspective appears to have not only a storyline but a fictional storyline at that. The above citation still suggests that the film was seen as a photographic *reproduction* of a game of make-believe rather than as something mandating make-believe on its own. The deciding factor for this appears to be that, as Gunning himself points out, this has also originally been a trick by Méliès performed first in 1891 as *The Moon's Pranks and the Misadventures of Nostradamus* at Théâtre Robert-Houdin.[69] In Gaudreault's and Marion's vocabulary, the 'attractional package' was clearly the magic trick. We can therefore follow Turquety Benoit in saying that 'tricks were adapted or reinvented for film; but they nevertheless came straight from the stage, and were perceived by spectators as "versions" of the older, familiar magical numbers that some of them had seen performed on the city stages'.[70]

A Trip to the Moon is certainly far more than a trick film – not only is there a plethora of attractions which are, strictly speaking, not tricks but there is also an important narrative aspect to the film. Frank Kessler, moreover, reminds us of an important generic context of féerie – 'a form of theatrical entertainment combining visual splendor, fantastic plots, amazing tricks, colorful ballets, and captivating music'.[71] Ian Christie, furthermore, points to the context constituted by internationally famous novels *From the Earth to the Moon* (1865) by Jules Verne and *The First Men in the Moon* (1901) by H. G. Wells.[72] Richard Abel also draws attention to the popularity of the adaptations of Verne's novel – a melodrama by French writer Adolphe d'Ennery from 1874 and an operetta with music by Jacques Offenbach from 1875 – in both France and the United States.[73] In the case of the United States, finally, Abel documents in detail the hype surrounding the cyclorama by Frederic Thompson and Elmer 'Skip' Dundy which premiered at 1901 Pan-American Exposition in Buffalo (Figure 1.5) and then moved to Steeplechase Park in 1902 where it remained for a number of years.[74] The context then includes a number of adjacent and overlapping cultural series – theatrical forms (féerie, operetta, melodrama), illusions (féerie, cyclorama) and literary fictions (melodrama, novel).[75] From the perspective of literary fiction, on the one hand, the film could have been perceived as mandating imaginings about the travel to the moon. From the perspective of theatrical forms and illusions, on the other, the film could have been perceived as an instance of canned (magic) theatre mandating no imaginings. In this light the response could have been similar to that of a newspaperman describing the illusory nature of the attraction at Coney Island:

> Aside from the spectacle of 'Twenty Thousand Leagues Under the Sea' are numerous illusions of varied interest, as may suit the fancy of the spectator. [One of them is the] 'trip to the moon' illusion, wherein the visitor feels with unfailing certainty that he is being lifted into ethereal space, and finally sees the moon, larger and larger, approaching from the zenith...[76]

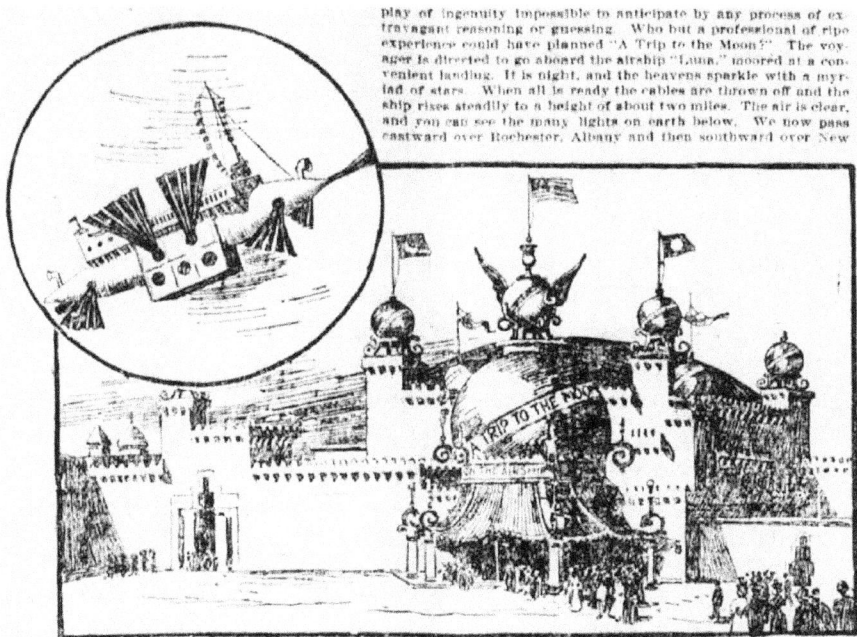

Figure 1.5 *A Trip to the Moon* at Pan-American Exposition, Buffalo (*Akron Daily Democrat*, 26 July 1900, p. 6).

That illusions of similar type could have been incorporated in stage craft is attested in a review of a play given at Krug Theater in Omaha, Nebraska:

> Report pronounces one of the scenic effects of 'Hearts Adrift', the season's big melodramatic success by Bangdon McCormick, an illusion of rare splendor and thrilling interest. In the third act of drama an airship is shown flying through the air at incredible speed, the effect of height and flight being realized by a cunning combination of moving panorama of sky, with the earth indicated far below on a perspective canvas.[77]

In fact, there are contemporary accounts that formulate the spectacular theatrical context as the prevailing one. In a list of amusements for the Christmas entertainment at St. Charles Orpheum vaudeville theatre in New Orleans the following is stated: '"A Trip to the Moon" is a delightful feature of the present bill, and as beautiful spectacular production as has ever been seen here.'[78] Given that the title is not identified as a film but simply as a 'feature' and a 'spectacular production' and that it is immediately followed by a list of stage acts including Cressy and Dayne's 'The Village Lawyer', Gargany's comedy acrobats and soprano Edith Helena it is safe to assume that within the vaudeville context it is simply deemed to be (a recording of) one of the theatrical/performance acts. An even better example of a contemporary account of Méliès film in which *A Trip to the Moon* is actually categorized as an instance of recorded pantomime (an English version of the féerie genre as Kessler reminds us) can be found in a digest of the upcoming shows at Maryland Theater in Baltimore:

> The New Year attraction ... will combine the finest features of the vaudeville stage, together with a real novelty in the form of English pantomime just as it is seen in leading London theaters, presented in a most life-like and realistic manner by the latest marvel of the moving picture line – the American Vitograph. A different pantomime will be given each day, and will consist of from five to eight scenes, showing hundreds of moving beings just as in the actual performance with the magnificent spectacular scenic effects and bright costumes in all colors. ... Among the selections will be the following: Monday, 'Gulliver's Travels' ... together with a 'Trip to Luna,' in 30 magnificent scenes, based on the famous story of 'A Trip to the Moon' by Jules Verne.[79]

This view, as we know from the cinema-debates in Germany during the transitional period, the contemporary discourse on *The Cabinet of Dr. Caligari/ Das Cabinet des Dr. Caligari* (Robert Wiene, 1920) and the debates about 'canned theatre' in the French cinema of the 1930s, is not an uncommon one.[80] The important difference is that the earliest accounts of cinema as essentially a recording of theatrical performances were presented in a positive light, rather than as a criterion for evaluative dismissal of a given film or cinema in general as in the later years: 'It is indeed not easy to discern the essence of cinematic representation.... Film producers and authors of film pieces fancy having theatre in front of them. ... They produce no filmic representations, but recordings of pantomimes.'[81]

The understanding of *A Trip to the Moon* as a *recording* of a game of make-believe, however, is not the one that prevails in the press reports of the time. It is the context of the Verne's novel, present even in the above citation, which pushes audiences' engagement with film toward imaginings. A reviewer from Nebraska, for instance, spoke of 'a most marvelous portrayal of the story of the same name by the famous French novelist, Jules Verne'.[82] It is a story that is portrayed rather than a performance of a story, as it is the case in the account from *Baltimore American*. Emphasis on film representing the make-believe story is present in a number of other reviews:

> Among [new Vitagraph views] is 'The Trip to the Moon,' in which are shown the adventures of a band of Frenchmen who visit the moon. They have an airship

built, embark in it, are fired from a huge cannon, sail to the moon, have all kinds of strange adventures there with the 'Moon Folk,' sail back to earth, land in the ocean, and are brought to land and rejoin their friends.[83]

The moving pictures will be 'A Trip to the Moon,' the film being 900 feet in length. This film is produced from extravaganca [sic] under the personal supervision of Edison. See the astronomer induce the professors to enter his large steel carriage to be loaded into a cannon and the ascent through space to the moon, and the imaginary beings that inhabit the moon, and the spilled milk, a funny combination of possibilities.[84]

[Méliès's] work is done in the little Houdin Theatre in Rue Chamberd, where the exhibition of moving pictures forms the entire evening's entertainment. But these motion pictures are by no means the conventional series of reproductions of everyday sights and scenes now so familiar to vaudeville patrons. On the contrary, the Melies' pictures are absolutely novel in their way. They run without interruption for nearly twenty minutes, all in one long film of nearly 1,200 feet, and they tell a complete story, usually of some weird or grotesque kind, that is simply wonderful in its different phases. 'The Trip to the Moon' and 'Robinson Crusoe' have already become familiar to the patrons of Proctor's theatres...[85]

As we can see from the reviews it is a matter of imagining the story in all its elements – from the astronomers' meeting and the shooting of the cannon to the return to earth – rather than one of being dumbfounded by stage illusion. Moreover, although, as the contemporary review from *Baltimore American* evinces, the film was at least on some occasions seen as a recording of a pantomime, the abundance of reports which speak of imaginary characters and effects directly without evoking any intermediary recordings strongly suggest that the prevalent way of engaging *A Trip to the Moon* was one of make-believe. This should, however, not lead us to think that early trick films in general were seen as fictions. Due to the exhibition and magic theatre illusion context films such as *The Vanishing Lady*, *The Four Troublesome Heads* and even *The Astronomer's Dream or the Man in the Moon* would have been perceived as mandating no imaginings.

Whereas early trick films were often initially perceived as non-fictions or reproductions of stage productions and are now regularly categorized as fantasy films or fictions, the engagement with early train films' 'actualities' has shifted in the exactly opposite direction. As Tsivian has shown, in Russia it took less than two decades since the earliest screenings for the myth of the panicking audience to be articulated.[86] During the earliest years, however, sources from around the world, from Gorky's famous newspaper account to Regnault's description in *L'Illustration* and press reports from around the globe, articulate the importance of make-believe in the train effect, a point consistently overlooked by scholars. With striking regularity these earliest viewers engaged the film as mandating imaginings about the train rushing out of the screen and running them over – a clear sign of fiction if there ever was one.

Production and promotion context

At the beginning of this chapter I argued that neither textual features nor authorial intentions are sufficient or necessary conditions for demarcation between fiction and non-fiction in photographic films. This is not to say that they have no role whatsoever, for there must be something to engage with – be it as make-believe or not. In the case of train films, for instance, there must be at the very least the representation of an approaching train. A similar point can be made regarding filmmaker's intentions. When the reception of *A Trip to the Moon* is examined, references to the filmmaker – be it Méliès or Edison (by mistake) – are not infrequently present. Based on these accounts, it is safe to state that the filmmakers in question were seen as authors whose intentions were the key causal force behind the film representing what it does and, by extension, allowing for imaginative engagement.

Perhaps the most effective way for filmmakers and film producers of the time to influence their audience to engage the film imaginatively or not would have been advertising campaigns including ads in the newspapers, posters and catalogues. In his discussion of an 1896 poster for Cinématographe Lumière by Louis Abel-Truchet, for instance, Loiperdinger correctly notes that although the railway is represented as protruding through the screen the two ladies in front of it are far from being represented as recoiling in terror (Figure 1.6).[87] For Loiperdinger the protrusion simply represents continuous motion of the rail on the train. I would add that such a representation also invites us to *imagine* that the train is going to exit the screen and enter the auditorium. This point appears to be supported by another publicity product for Cinématographe Lumière – an illustrated dinner plate.[88] The illustration depicts an amazed audience looking at the onrushing projected train with the caption 'one would think that it's true' ('on croirait que c'est vrai'). One would but one does not. Instead, one is *invited* to imagine that the train is going to jump out of the screen.

Similar invitations to imagine the train can be found in contemporary catalogues as well. The American Mutoscope and Biograph Company's catalogue

Figure 1.6 Louis Abel-Truchet's poster for the Cinématographe Lumière.

from 1901 repeats the words from the 1897 version, but the image which now accompanies it together with the words invoke a stunning effect (Figure 1.7):

> An express train traveling at the rate of a mile a minute is seen approaching, a mere speck in the distance. On it comes! 'Tis here!! Going by!!! Gone!!!! All with the vividness of reality, and so realistic that it does not require a great stretch of imagination to hear the roar and feel the breeze it makes.[89]

It is not only that this marvellous device allows for perceptual illusion of motion and depth, but it also beckons the viewer to imagine herself hear the thumping engine and feel the gust of accompanying wind on her skin. In other words, although the key to mandating imaginings is the device's capability to reproduce visual phenomena in time, the spectator is supposed to go beyond mere visual make-believes and imagine a multi-sensory experience which includes both auditory and tactile phenomena. The invited game of make-believe, according to the catalogue, will provide an immersive experience of presence which appeals to the eye, ear and body alike. A similar call to imagination when watching train films can be found at least as late as 1902 in the description of *The Rivals* (American Mutoscope and Biograph Company, 1902) – a film depicting a race between two fast trains: 'Our camera succeeded in taking a picture of one of these races and was placed directly between the two tracks, so that the effect is as if the two trains were rushing toward the spectator at high speed.'[90] Here again

Figure 1.7 Age of Movement (American Mutoscope and Biograph Company, 1901).

we see the hypothetical structure much like that of Gorky's which introduces mandates for imaginings.

We can track such articulations of mandates for make-believe in catalogues of other producers of the time. The F. M. Prescott catalogue, for instance, advertises *Third Avenue Elevated Train, New York* as follows: 'When looking at it you would really think you were in New York.'[91] The same film is also advertised word-for-word in Lubin Manufacturing Company's complete catalogue.[92] On the same page of the catalogue the following description of *Boston and New York Express* can be found: 'The train is down in a hollow and finally rushes up the hill with lightning rapidity, and shoots toward the audience who invariably rise in their seats as though they were in fear of being run down.'[93] Again, one is not actually afraid but asked to make-believe that the train is going to crash into the auditorium.

It is also, although not always with the fullest precision, possible to distinguish between two general trends among these examples – though both invoke the presence of the train one seems to articulate the train crashing into the audience and invading the auditorium more (e.g. Truchet's poster) whereas the other appears to emphasize the mandate that the spectator is transported on site (e.g. F. M. Prescott catalogue). This is in contrast with the accounts which dominantly took the train to be invasive rather than inviting (remember Gorky in particular). The following chapter will examine the distinction in more detail but for our present purposes it suffices to say that both trends constitute mandates for imaginings and as such serve as some of the earliest articulations of fiction-generating protocols in cinema.

What about trick films in general, and *A Trip to the Moon* more specifically? In the section on film reception and exhibition context it was argued that, contrary to present-day categorizations, a number of trick films were not seen as fictions but rather as film reproductions of stage acts mandating no imaginings. This also held for moving pictures with more pronounced storylines such as *The Astronomer's Dream or the Man in the Moon* and, on occasions, even for *A Trip to the Moon*. Catalogues appear to evince the same view for the most part.

For instance, the entry for the American Mutoscope and Biograph Company's *Vanishing Lady* (1897) insists on the film's magic theatre origin: 'This is the familiar trick of the magician...'[94] More importantly, it continues by stating that the trick is 'executed by Paul Gilmore in an artistic manner.'[95] As Gilmore was a well-known theatre actor of the time it is safe to say that the catalogue presents the film merely as a recording of Gilmore's performance.

The same emphasis on the reproduction of magic theatre performance can be found in 'Star' Films' catalogue entry on *The Four Troublesome Heads*:

> One of the most marvelous tricks ever cinematographed. The magician approaches and, after the usual bow, proceeds with the tricks of taking off his head, placing same on a table at his side. ... to show the audience that there is no illusion about the trick, he crawls upon the table, upon which is supported his first head. ... [Upon completing the trick] the magician then makes his bow and retreats from the scene. A most surprising and marvelous illusion.[96]

The trick is presented as cinematographed. Moreover, there is no mention of the possibility that the trick is made by filmic means, rather the suggestion is that it must be some stage craft if the magician is crawling under the table. Furthermore, the magician addresses the audience bowing twice, prior and following the trick, precisely how he would do in the theatre. Finally, catalogue entry emphasizes again that we are dealing with an illusion – something I have argued mandated no imaginings, but rather incredulity as Gunning's and Matthew Solomon's analyses show.[97]

With films such as *The Astronomer's Dream or the Man in the Moon*, however, catalogue entries stop speaking of magicians and actors performing illusions but of fictional characters who undertake mysterious actions or are victims of mystical events. The catalogue of the Edison Manufacturing Company from 1901, which is repeated almost verbatim in the Selig Polyscope Company's catalogue tells the following story:

> The old Astronomer is at work over his calculations. Through the aperture in the dome the full moon is visible. ... The moon comes down right from the sky, right in the observatory. He has eyes that move and a mouth that opens and shuts. ... Then the old Astronomer awakens – alas! it is all a dream.[98]

Compare this to the 1899 account from *Philadelphia Inquirer* in the previous section where emphasis is put on reproduction by photographic means rather than on performance effectively presenting the film as an instance of 'canned magic theatre'. In the Edison Manufacturing Company's and Selig Polyscope Company's catalogues, by contrast, it is the storyline that takes centre stage. Story does not necessarily amount to fiction (or vice versa) but given that the direct representational content of the story is an anthropomorphic moon – a non-existent entity – we have a mandate to imagine such and such a moon and, by extension, the whole story as fictional. This mandate comes across as even stronger in Lubin Manufacturing Company's catalogue entry which not only articulates the narrative in more detail but takes notice of numerous other non-existent entities including the Fairy Queen and the Satan.[99]

That the filmmaker and the film's copycats intended the audiences to engage *A Trip to the Moon* imaginatively as well, that is, as fiction, is also attested in a number of catalogue entries about the film. One catalogue, for instance, presents the film as an adaptation: 'A JOURNEY TO THE LUNA in thirty stupendous dissolving scenes. The most wonderful motion picture creation ever created. Based on the story by Jules Verne, "From the Earth to the Moon Direct"'.[100] Another similarly articulates the idea that one can engage the film as showing a fictional story directly rather than as reproducing a performance of the story: 'A wonderful piece of photography, showing the method adapted by six learned astronomers to explore the moon. The inhabitants of the moon are shown, together with other interesting scenes.'[101] Finally, Méliès's own catalogue as well as the catalogues of the Warwick Trading Company, which was at the time the authorized distributor of Méliès's films and Lubin Manufacturing Company's catalogue, all resort to the strategy employed in the entries describing *The Astronomer's Dream or the Man in the Moon* – direct representation of non-existent entities in detailed narratives – to articulate the mandates for imagining.[102] Among others Phoebus, Saturn, the selenites and selenite King make the list of fictional entities.

A few paragraphs are also in order about the classifications to be found in the catalogues. At the beginning of the chapter I have claimed that nowadays the crucial way in which we determine whether something is fiction or not is by taking a look to which existing category the film was assigned to. In fact, in the greatest majority of cases we already know in advance whether we are going to see fiction or non-fiction. If we go to see a horror or a comedy we know that we are watching fiction. If we are interested in the latest documentary we are watching non-fiction. In those minority instances when we are confused with what we have seen, as for instance with why every episode of the first season of the TV show *Fargo* (2014 –) opens with a superimposed text stating 'This is a true story', then we might take a look at the Internet Movie Database, Rotten Tomatoes, Wikipedia or some other source to resolve the matter.[103] Do catalogues in those early days provide comparable guidance?

The shortest answer would be: no. The earliest catalogues classify moving pictures more according to their length rather than in terms of some generic categories. For instance, Maguire and Baucus's catalogue of Edison Films dated 20 January 1897 primarily distinguishes between 50- and 150-foot motion pictures, and only within the 50-foot category does it separate the 'New Niagara Falls Series' from 'New Subjects'.[104] Among the latter *Black Diamond Express* is, for instance, side by side with thematically varied moving images such as *Burning Stable, Governor's Guard, Cock Fight* or *Surf Scene*. The Prestwich Manufacturing

Company catalogue from next year does something similar by distinguishing between 'P', 'S' and 'W' series according to film length.[105] This practice is already on its way out by then for as early as the fall of 1897 Maguire and Baucus's catalogue of Lumière, Edison, and International Films distinguishes between 'Miscellaneous Subjects', 'Comic Subjects', 'Military Views', 'Henley Regatta' and a number of views according to the country where they were made to list a few categories.[106] Whereas this catalogue still does not include a separate category for either train or trick films, the Warwick Trading Company's catalogue from 1897–8 does. There the train films can be found under the heading of 'Railway Pictures' and 'Panoramas' (which also include views from boats), while trick films appear under 'Robert Houdin Films'.[107] Even here both types of motion pictures are also listed under other categories, so a moving picture like the *Arrival of an Excursion Train* appears in a general category lacking a title and another like *The Conjuror* among 'Humorous Subjects'.[108] Nevertheless, the groundwork for the categorization of early film genre is set.

By 1900 the categories become more robust. In American Vitagraph Company's catalogue we find trick films, including *The Astronomer's Dream; or, The Man in the Moon*, under 'New Magical Subjects' as opposed to 'Comedy Subjects'.[109] Though train films such as *The Brockville Disaster* ('Realistic Reproduction of the Great English Railway Disaster')[110] still appear there under 'Miscellaneous Subjects', by at least July next year there is a separate 'Trains' category in the Edison Manufacturing Company's catalogue.[111] The 'Mystical' category also appears in the same catalogue.[112] The Warwick Trading Company has by then refined its categorization to distinguish numerous subjects including 'Railway Subjects' and 'Panorama from Moving Train, Steamer, and Tram', on the one hand, and 'Magical and Trick Series', on the other.[113] By 1902 the two categories would prove quite stable as they appeared in American Mutoscope and Biograph Company's catalogue with descriptions of the categories themselves.[114] The persistence of the same categories at the time can also be tracked in other catalogues, including Lubin Manufacturing Company's which identifies 'Magical Films and Illusions' and 'Railroad Films'[115] and Selig Polyscope Company's which lists 'Mythical and Mysterious Subjects' and 'Railway Scenes'.[116] R. W. Paul includes 'Novel Trick and Effect Films' and 'Original Trick and Effect Subjects' in his company's catalogue, while Hepworth Company lists 'Trick and Magical' and 'Railway Scenes' among its subjects.[117]

These categories on their own, however, do not specify whether a film belonging to the category is fiction or not. Consider American Mutoscope and Biograph Company's account of the train film, that is, 'Railroads':

> The Biograph has always been famous for its railroad views. The greatest sensation ever produced in moving pictures is our wonderful picture of the Empire State Express, the celebrated train of the New York Central & Hudson River Railroad. Our cameras, working at a speed of from 30 to 40 pictures a second, have a capacity for this class of work which has not to be found in smaller machines. We have covered the picturesque side of railroading all over the civilized world, and we point with pride to the completeness and comprehensiveness of our list. We have travelled in special cars from the Atlantic to the Pacific, all over Great Britain and the Continent; we have the armored train on the South African Veldt, and the daily express arriving at Shanghai, China. A large proportion of these views have a stereoscopic value which must be seen to be appreciated.[118]

On first inspection, it might seem that this is a description of an actuality genre which mandates no imaginings whatsoever. A variety of factual trains are listed as constituting the category as well as countries in which these views are taken. This, however, paints only half of the picture. Consider the reference to the *Empire State Express* as the 'greatest sensation ever produced in motion pictures'. It is the illustration of this very train that accompanies the company's 1901 Age of Movement publication which replicates the mandate-generating description from 1897: 'it does not require a great stretch of imagination to hear the roar and feel the breeze it makes'.[119] With this context in mind it can be as easily said that train films are about imagining the presence of the train in one way or another. In other words, the description of the category of train films as it appears is, on its own, underdetermined as far as decisions about the status of fiction in it are concerned.

The explanation of the trick film from the company's same 1902 catalogue provides no better guidance:

> To take a good trick picture requires long experience, the best of properties, and the greatest care in photographic manipulation. We have been so long in the business that we feel justified in claiming that our work along this line is unequalled.
>
> Our list of subjects is full of good things, and the comedy element will be found to be largely predominating. A trick picture that gets a laugh is doubly good, and we have worked on the theory that the public is more interested in mirthful magic than in mere mystery.[120]

It is true that it is suggested that tricks are filmic rather than a part of stagecraft – and many film descriptions go on to explain the nature of the trick.

But that does not guarantee any mandates for imaginings on their own if magical illusion remains the context. Films in this category like *Demolishing and Building up the Star Theatre* (F. S. Armitage, 1901) evince the point. There the trick is in making an exposure every four minutes, eight hours a day and then playing the film in reverse. That 'the effect is very extraordinary' can be simply understood as incredible rather than mandating imaginings.[121] It is true that the comedy element is emphasized as particularly important of this category but on its own this element again cannot determine either fiction or non-fiction. In other words, much like with the 'Railroads' category we need to move beyond the generic description, that is, into the accounts of specific films to gauge whether the film in question is fiction or not. Thus, for instance, although both are in the same trick category *Sherlock Holmes Baffled* (Arthur Marvin, 1900) is presented as an instance of fiction,[122] but *A Mermaid Dance* (American Mutoscope and Biograph Company, 1902) is not, that is, it is described as a clever use of composite photography of a dancer and an aquarium scene[123]. We could say then that although the labels of trick and train films clearly constitute some of the earliest film genres, unlike most of the modern genres their instances are not to be found exclusively on one or the other side of the line of demarcation between fiction and non-fiction.

The starting point for this chapter was Walton's notion of fiction as mandated imaginings. I argued that textual parameters and/or authorial intentions are neither sufficient nor necessary conditions for determining whether mandates for make-believe are in place in photographic film. Instead, these mandates are determined by broader parameters, including production, promotion, exhibition and contemporary commentaries. I turned to early cinema and its accompanying discourse as a unique source for construing the history of such mandates – something that analytic approaches in philosophy are in dire need of – to argue that present categorizations of fiction and non-fiction film were not operational in the first years of early cinema and to demonstrate that fiction can turn into non-fiction and vice versa. But this was not simply an exercise in articulating some theoretical concept by means of a yet unexplored example. It was also a full-fledged engagement with cinema history in its own right.

I sought to articulate the hitherto unexplored aspect of early cinema audience's engagement with a new representational form – make-believe. I have argued that although the attraction of perceptual illusion of motion and depth undeniably play a key role in the engagement with cinema, and that although looming and untrained spectatorship are valid accounts of the train effect, a wide range of contemporary sources attest to the idea that there was more to these films – specific games of make-believe articulated by reviewers, exhibitors, producers and promoters alike. In other words, train films like *The Arrival of a Train*, I argued, were effectively categorized as fiction in the earliest days of cinema. By the time the myth of the panicking audience appeared they were already transformed into non-fiction.

I also demonstrated that whereas a part of trick films were categorized as fictions as they are today, a number of them were billed and received as reproductions of stage performances mandating no imaginings in their own right. These were not only films like *Vanishing Lady* but also those which we nowadays see as having more pronounced fictional storyline including *The Astronomer's Dream or the Man in the Moon* and, most notably, *A Trip to the Moon*. The last two seem to have occasionally been categorized as non-fiction though the fictional categorization was the dominant one.

The discussion of *A Trip to the Moon* also sheds light on the period in early cinema, usually described as the cinema of attractions following Gunning's exemplary work.[124] This period lasting to about 1905 is seen as one of exhibitionist cinema (as opposed to the voyeuristic classical one) which solicits the attention of the spectator either by its own status as a technical novelty, or by aligning itself with the modes of representation of the performing arts rather than those of dramatic illusion. It is characterized by preference of display over the construction of diegesis, of temporal punctuality over chronological development, and of direct address to the spectator over effacement of its rhetoric potential. It is undeniable that a number of films fit the bill, but, as Charles Musser has pointed out, it is far from certain that attraction rather than narrative was the dominant for as long as Gunning claims it to have been.[125] This is particularly contentious in films with discernible storylines like *The Gay Shoe Clerk* (Porter, 1903), *The Great Train Robbery* (Porter, 1903) and, closer to examples from this chapter, films like passion plays and *A Trip to the Moon*. Although, as we have seen, the attraction of the reproduction was emphasized at least on one occasion,[126] the dominant mode of engagement was to address the story the film represented ('Melies' pictures … tell a complete story'[127]). In the case of catalogues, which arguably articulated how the producers and promoters wanted the audience to perceive the films, the film's storyline was presented at length and at the expense of emphasizing specific attractions. This speaks in favour of Musser's rather than Gunning's view which is even more relevant because Gunning has recently reiterated his position and stated that '*A Trip to the Moon* does tell a story, but it is secondary to the display of attractions..'[128] Of course, the story is not the same as fiction, but in these instances, due to the use of direct representations of non-existent entities the stories in question are fictional.

At the very least, therefore, articulating the role of imagination in early cinema contributes to our understanding of the period. Focusing on imagination may even help to resolve some important debates in film scholarship revolving not only around the same era but extending into full-fledged narrative cinema and up to present day. These include discussions on the relationship between immersion and illusion, faking and fiction, the hybridity of fiction and non-fiction, the nature of visual imagination film fiction invites, and the existence of film narrators. In the following chapters I take up precisely these issues. I start off with an analysis of nineteenth-century immersion techniques in order to further accentuate the importance of imagination for early cinema.

2

Hale's Tours and adjacent cultural series: Illusion, immersion, imagination

In the first chapter I historicized Kendall L. Walton's mandates for imagining through an analysis of the institutional discourses surrounding early cinema and provided a reinterpretation of the myth of the panicking audience from the perspective of make-believe. Here I wish to address the status of another highly popular early cinema phenomenon which, unlike the screening of *The Arrival of a Train/L'Arrivée d'un train en gare de La Ciotat*, remains regularly described in terms of illusion – Hale's Tours and Scenes of the World.[1] Popular between 1905 and 1910, Hale's Tours were the first of a number of amusement rides which simulated the experience of travel by visual, tactile, sonic and ambulatory means. In a sort of a hybrid between an amusement ride and a film show the patrons sat in a make-shift train car while phantom rides and other types of films were projected on screen in front of them. I will propose that we are dealing with another myth and that, although patents and advertisements regularly emphasize the illusory strengths of the product sold, Hale's Tours in fact fell short of fooling spectators into believing that they were taking a train ride while looking at the unfolding scenery from the point of view of the cowcatcher and instead mandated imaginings about those very same things. Hale's Tours, admittedly, were highly immersive, but even immersion, as I will demonstrate, is not to be confused with illusion. In other words, Hale's Tours provide an opportunity to articulate the distinction between the all too often conflated notions of illusion, immersion and imagination.

Because typical Hale's Tours programmes did not include phantom rides only but motion pictures representing action taking place inside the train car as well, the phenomenon also presents itself as a perfect subject to address the issue of hybridity. Whereas it is commonplace to cite Hale's Tours as mixing fiction and non-fiction, my point is that Hale's Tours were hybrids only stylistically.[2] There are certainly numerous textual traits that set phantom ride segments apart from the train car ones, but this does not change the fact that both mandated imaginings. Put differently, Hale's Tours were fictions through and through (although one part of the Hale's Tours programme mandated imaginings about the train ride and another about what was taking place on the train).

Hale's Tours also allow us to address the notion that the viewers imagine themselves watching events unfold from within the fictional world. The classic articulation of this idea in film theory can be found in Vsevolod I. Pudovkin's 1928 *Film Technique and Film Acting* under the name of the ideal observer and is current in present-day debates about the nature of imagined seeing in analytic philosophy circles.[3] The juxtaposition of the moving pictures from the point of view of the cowcatcher with the ones from depicting the inside of the train car typical of Hale's Tours brings into sharp relief the specific mandates about one's own position in relation to the represented. Whereas the former parts of the programme mandate the spectator to imagine her own presence on the cowcatcher the latter do not mandate any such presence in the train car. As such, Hale's Tours allow us to discard the version of the imagined seeing thesis according to which spectators imagine being physically present in the depicted world as a general model for engaging film fiction.

From the perspective of analytic philosophy, then, this chapter helps resolve one of the pressing questions raised by Walton's theory of fiction – the nature of imagined seeing in fiction film. The discussion of Hale's Tours also demonstrates that, contrary to a recent influential proposal, no form of imagined seeing entails any fictional showing.[4] In other words, this chapter establishes that the discussion of the controlling fictional narrators in film is separate from the analysis of imagined seeing. Finally, the discussion of phantom rides also demonstrates how mandates to imagine something may wane over time giving further credence to the proposal that fiction depends on a number of institutional factors rather than on authorial intentions alone.

From the perspective of new film history, this chapter allows us to dispel some of the lingering myths about the illusory power of cinema and the alleged naïveté of early film audiences. It further elucidates how radical stylistic diversity within a film programme such as Hale's Tours does not entail any hybridity as far as the programme's fictional status is concerned. This chapter, finally, gives us a more precise understanding of what it would have been to sit in one of the make-shift cars at the beginning of the twentieth century and how this experience would have differed from the experience of watching other related contemporary genres such as scenics or travelogues. Crucially, despite prominent views to the contrary, in general scenics and travelogues of the time mandated no imaginings.[5]

Art history, media archaeology and new film history teach us that Hale's Tours were far from the first visual mass medium to afford immersion through imaginary presence. Phantom rides, for instance, appeared as early as 1896, years before the first patent behind Hale's Tours.[6] Films such as *The Arrival of a Train* furthermore, prompted viewers to imagine that a train is going to run them over by crashing out of the screen and into the auditorium (as Chapter 1 has shown). Moreover, panoramas which, according to Stephan Oettermann, constitute the earliest visual mass medium and which were extremely popular in the nineteenth century are nowadays regularly acknowledged by film scholars such as Alison Griffiths and Erkki Huhtamo as a part of the cultural series capitalizing on immersion.[7] Finally, 360-degree representations which invite the spectator to imagine herself present at the site that is represented have been tracked to at least as early as antiquity and the Great Frieze in the Villa dei Misteri at Pompeii from around 60 BCE.[8] Given that a number of studies cited in this paragraph evince the same conflation of illusion and imagination as the discussions of Hale's Tours, I will open the chapter with an analysis of this indiscrimination in the scholarship on panoramas, travelogues and phantom rides.

Panoramas and terminological conflation

As I have argued at length in Chapter 1, illusion is a form of deception where what is represented is perceived as actually being the case. Cinema, of course, is most famous for its illusion of movement. If the frequency of the images of the successive stages of motion is sufficiently high the spectator will see the images as actually moving. Illusion, moreover, may entail false beliefs. Somebody unfamiliar with the projection apparatus may actually believe that the images are moving.[9] Similarly, later (unfounded) reports on the panicking audiences clearly articulate a form of illusion where spectators actually believe that the train is going to run them over and, in response, vacate the premises in terror. Imagination, by contrast, entails no false beliefs. Imagining something is completely independent from believing anything about the subject imagined. As I have argued, early train film audiences regularly imagined the train to be a threat without actually entertaining the belief that it was one. The fact that these imaginations were mandated with regularity through a negotiation of factors including production, distribution, exhibition and contemporary reviews constitutes these films as fictions during the early cinema period.

Illusion and imagination so construed, then, are clearly sufficiently distinct notions. In film scholarship, however, either the focus is unduly on illusion or the two are conflated. I have tackled the former in Chapter 1 when I argued that describing the early cinema film genres which have been traditionally understood as non-fictional in terms of illusion misses the importance imagination had for these genres. The latter is regularly the case in the discussions of works of fiction. 'Diegetic illusionism', for instance, is a standard trope in early cinema history and far beyond.[10] Theoretically, it is certainly not impossible to speak of illusion and effectively mean 'imagination' and/or 'immersion' rather than 'deception' and/or 'false belief'. In practice, however, the fact that these studies never define what fiction is and instead assume the widely used formula of 'willing suspension of disbelief' makes the above possibility extremely unlikely. It is crucial to recognize that the original formulation pertains to the design behind William Wordsworth's and Samuel Taylor Coleridge's *Lyrical Ballads* (1798):

> The thought suggested itself (to which of us I do not recollect) that a series of poems might be composed of two sorts. In the one, the incidents and agents were to be, in part at least, supernatural; and the excellence aimed at was to consist in the interesting of the affections by the dramatic truth of such emotions as would naturally accompany such situations, supposing them real. And real in this sense they have been to every human being who, from whatever source of delusion, has at any time believed himself under supernatural agency. For the second class, subjects were to be chosen from ordinary life; the characters and incidents were to be such, as will be found in every village and its vicinity, where there is a meditative and feeling mind to seek after them, or to notice them, when they present themselves. ... it was agreed, that my endeavours should be directed to persons and characters supernatural, or at least romantic; yet so as to transfer from our inward nature a human interest and a semblance of truth sufficient to procure for these shadows of imagination that willing suspension of disbelief for the moment, which constitutes poetic faith.[11]

The quotation makes it clear that the 'willing suspension of disbelief' is not synonymous with 'imagination' but revolves around the issue of belief versus disbelief. For Coleridge it is not sufficient to imagine 'these shadows'. It is also necessary to afford them 'a semblance of truth' which is done by temporarily falsely believing the matter at hand.

Apparatus theorists, moreover, present the most glaring example of how film studies have not distinguished between illusion and fiction, that is, mandated imaginings. As Noël Carroll demonstrated, such conflations lead to invalid theories of spectatorship.[12] At their worst, then, film studies have deliberately obfuscated the distinction between illusion and imagination to produce influential theories of spectatorship. At best, film studies fail to appreciate the importance of imagination which precludes them from consistently construing the notion of fiction. In the case of early cinema, for instance, Chapter 1 has argued how there is little or no traditional understanding for the contemporary accounts of story films as non-fictions and train films as fictions.

Although the talk of illusion in film studies is hardly free from the baggage that comes with the notion of (willing suspension of) disbelief, it is undeniable that such talk tries to highlight something like immersion. In its ordinary sense immersion denotes a heightened engagement with an experience. One is drawn into an experience, meaning that at the same time one is drawn away from something else. One is, so to speak, engulfed by an experience and, in virtue of that, lost to other things.

Focusing on visual objects of immersion, Oliver Grau in his widely cited book *Visual Art* states thus:

[I]n most cases immersion is mentally absorbing and a process, a change, a passage from one mental state to another. It is characterized by diminishing critical distance to what is shown and increasing emotional involvement in what is happening. ... [Virtual immersive spaces] offer the observers, particularly through their totality, the option of fusing with the image medium, which affects sensory impressions and awareness. ... The quality of apparently being present in the images is achieved through maximization of realism and is increased still further through illusionism in the service of an immersive effect.[13]

As we can see the key for immersion in visual experience is the impression of being present at whatever is represented. It is important to note that Grau, like many others, uses 'illusion' to denote both illusion proper and imagination:

In virtual space, both historically and in the present, the illusion works on two levels: first, there is the classic function of illusion which is the playful and conscious submission to appearance that is the aesthetic enjoyment of illusion. Second, by intensifying the suggestive image effects and through appearance, this can temporarily overwhelm perception of the difference between [sic] mage [sic] space and reality. This suggestive power may, for a certain time, suspend the relationship between subject and object, and the 'as if' may have effects on awareness.[14]

Grau's first level corresponds to accounts of fiction which make recourse of the willing suspension of disbelief and the 'as if' mode. In my account following Walton, this is the domain of mandated imaginings. Grau's second level is the one at which the spectator is deceived into thinking that the represented is in fact the reality. For Grau, therefore, the state of immersion takes place at the point where make-believe morphs, however temporarily, into false belief.[15]

Ordinarily speaking, however, immersion demands no such transformation. We can be immersed in both exclusively fictional and exclusively non-fictional experiences. I can immerse myself in the view from my hotel bedroom as much as I can immerse myself in an imaginary world. I can spend hours just looking through the window and losing track of time or I can play the latest video game to a point of forgetting to eat. In the example of the video game, moreover, there is no reason I should succumb even for a moment to thinking any of it was real to speak of immersion. If I play the latest instalment of *Fallout* there need not be any moment at which I should believe (falsely) that I am present on a street in the apocalyptic Wasteland where the game takes place to be able to describe the experience as immersive. Similarly, Chapter 1 argued that train films engendered no false beliefs in the audiences, yet we would be hard-pressed to claim that the experience of watching such films was not one of 'diminishing critical distance to what is shown and increasing emotional involvement in what is happening' accompanied by an imagination of 'being present'. (Though precisely what is imagined as 'being present' I will discuss in more detail in the section on phantom rides.) In that sense immersion is independent not only of both whether something is fiction or not and whether something is an illusion or not but also of whether the transformation from one to the other takes place.

Grau could object that I am making this argument in bad faith because the focus of his monograph are 360-degree visual objects rather than examples such as framed screens cited above. His key historical example of immersion is, instead, the panorama. Therefore, the above technical definition according to which immersion takes place at the point where make-believe transforms into false belief need not apply to visual objects in general as long as it pertains to 360-degree visual objects such as *The Battle of Sedan* (1883). Let us consider this objection.

The term 'panorama' originally appeared near the end of the eighteenth century to denote a fully cylindrical canvas of large size which depicted a

360-degree view in accurate perspective. The process of the production of such a view was patented by Robert Baker under the name 'la nature à coup d'oeil' ('nature at a glance') on 17 June 1787.[16] In good part, its inception was due to the needs of military for the accurately perspectival representations of landscape. After short experimentation with different presentational apparatuses, purpose-built rotundas quickly won out as the presentational vehicle for panoramas. The first purpose-built rotunda opened on Leicester Square on 17 May 1793 to house Baker's *The Grand Fleet at Spithead 1791* (Figure 2.1). In general, the visitors enter the rotunda via staircases which lead to the viewing platform. The eye is in line with the horizon line of the painting and the balustrade precludes the viewer from being able to see the upper and lower frames of the painting. Unbeknownst to the spectator the natural light comes from above to double as the source of the light for the painting. Later rotundas would also use *faux terrain* – three-dimensional objects at the foot of the painting – to further the illusionistic impression.

Anton von Werner's panorama *The Battle of Sedan* opened on 1 September 1883 in Berlin to celebrate the battle fought thirteen years prior which effectively

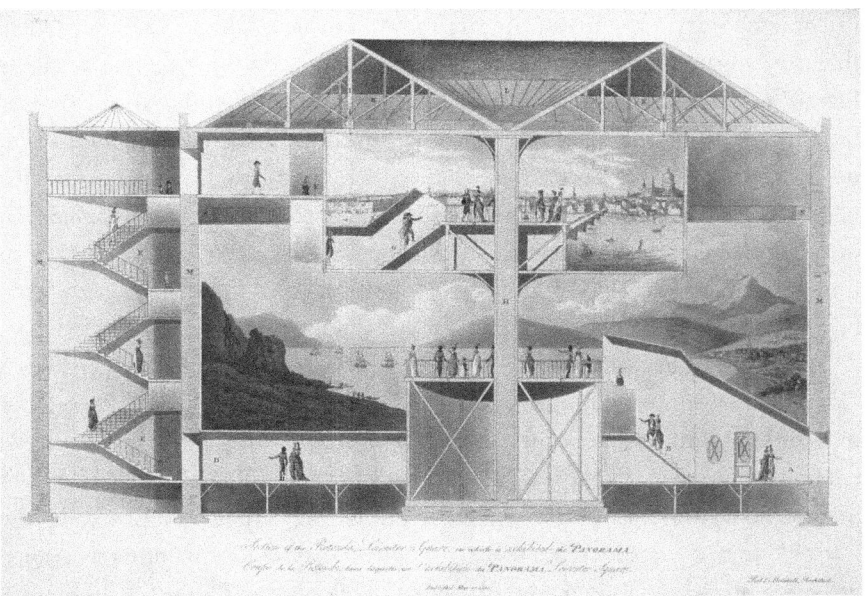

Figure 2.1 Cross-section of Robert Barker's Panorama Rotunda at Leicester Square, London (Robert Mitchell, *Plans and Views in Perspective of Buildings Erected in England and Scotland,* London, 1801, p. 59).

decided the Franco-Prussian War in favour of Prussia and ushered in the Second German Empire under Wilhelm I. It represents the disarray of the French cavalry whose desperate attempts at breaching the Prussian encirclement is met by a hail of infantry bullets. As a first-class political propaganda event, the effect of the panorama, as Grau and others have pointed out, rested in great part on its immersive traits. But is Grau right to claim that these hinged on the transformation from make-believe to false belief about one's presence at Sedan?

Grau marshals contemporary accounts to support his claims about immersion:

> The visitor is gripped immediately; he is taken completely by surprise and instinctively holds back. One is afraid of being trampled by the horses' hooves and feels the urge to concentrate on going backwards.[17]

> One believes that one is standing in the surging midst of the terrible battle.[18]

> One does not notice that one is still in the capital: one thinks one is on high ground, inexplicably surrounded by a railing, yet looking down on the battlefield of Sedan.[19]

> It is exactly as His Majesty the Kaiser is reported to have said: It does not look painted at all; it is reality.[20]

The reports undeniably articulate false beliefs – the very thing that was lacking in contemporary accounts of the train film audiences. Here people do report that they are afraid of being trampled by horses; they do think themselves to be literally in the midst of the battle, or at least on the high ground nearby. However briefly, it seems that a good number of visitors actually believed themselves to be witnessing the event depicted, that is, that they literally experienced the panorama as an illusion. In other words, they were immersed in the *illusion* of being present at the scene. It might appear then that Grau's point about immersion is vindicated – a number of viewers at least momentarily confused being present in the rotunda for being present at the real thing.

However, when read carefully the panorama reports, unlike the early train film accounts, reveal no *imaginative* engagement with the image. Remember that for Grau immersion occurs only once illusion *replaces* imagination. In the citations above people simply report believing to be standing on the battle field – there is no sign of make-believe preceding this. They are literally scared by the horses – they do not imagine being trampled. They talk of painting as reality, not of painting impelling them to imagine the famous past event. And there is certainly nothing problematic in this for we have already seen that there is no reason immersion could not be based exclusively on illusory effects. Contrary to

Walton, moreover, there is no reason seeing-in would entail any imaginary seeing as the discussion in the Introduction has demonstrated. Non-photographic images may act as illustrations no less than photographic ones can. Whereas illustrations will serve as means of recognition for the people who are already familiar with the object of representation, for those who have never seen the object in question they will provide sufficient visual information to recognize them when and if such an opportunity arises. As the promotional material for another panorama claims: 'those familiar with the scenes depicted will recognize their truthfulness of the representations, and enjoy the reminiscences, while others will form as accurate an idea of the appearance of the various places...'[21]

There is good reason to doubt, then, that the contemporaries reported any wavering between make-believe and belief of the type Grau speaks of taking place during the visit to the panorama of *The Battle of Sedan*. The immersion was simply the result of illusion. The question remains, however, whether in general there is a point when engagement with imaginary entities is such that one starts harbouring (false) beliefs about them and whether such a point should be privileged for the technical definition of immersion. Perhaps contemporary accounts from other panoramas paint a picture closer to Grau's.

Let us investigate the reports cited as proofs of Grau's notion of immersion in another study of the nineteenth-century panorama – Alison Griffiths's *Shivers Down Your Spine*.[22] Consider a contemporary account of Robert Baker's *The Battle of the Nile* (1799) she herself quotes:

> As soon as you enter a *shiver runs down your spine*. The darkness of night is all around, illuminated only by burning ships and cannon fire, and all is so deceptively real ... that you imagine you can see far out to sea in one direction and the distant coastline in the other.[23]

Undeniably, the invocation of shivers attests to a visceral experience. The illusionistic elements of the panorama are in full swing ('all is so deceptively real') and the darkness appears to engulf the viewer. It would again appear, then, that we are dealing with an illusion which guides the impression of immersion no different from in the aforementioned examples. There is something else going on, however. The effect of deception is not only immersion but imaginings ('you imagine you can see ...'). At this point it appears that Grau's definitional formula of immersion is inversed – instead of imagination causing brief illusion, illusion brings forth sustained imagination. This is true, but we need to be careful about the type of illusion that is at the basis of imagination here.

It would be mistaken to think that this is an illusion of the type articulated in the accounts of *The Battle of Sedan* above – namely an illusion of presence. There is no talk of believing of being in the midst of things here, nothing like a fear of an actually perceived threat. What is deceptively real, instead, is the perspectively accurate representation of the sea battle. And there is nothing strange about this because all perspectival paintings secure at least one perceptual illusion – precisely the illusion of depth. What the contemporary report about *The Battle of the Nile* articulates, then, is how impressive the perceptual illusion of depth is. But the immersion, that is, the notion of presence, is not one of false belief as it was in *The Battle of Sedan*, rather one of imagination. Again, this should not surprise us because it was precisely the illusion of depth and movement that played a crucial role in the mandates about the onrushing train for the early cinema audiences. Here, then, we have an example of a panorama in which, if the above quotation is representative, immersion hinged on imagination rather than illusion (beyond that of depth).

There is further proof that the immersive effect of panoramas was more often one of *imagining* one's own presence than one of falsely believing it. In fact, most of the panoramas Griffiths discusses in her monograph are better described in terms of imaginary immersion. A contemporary reviewer that Griffiths also quotes herself had the following to say about another battle panorama – *The Battle of Gettysburg* (1883):

> The battleground with its dead and wounded soldiers, the smoke of cannon, the bursting of shells, the blood stained ground are all drawn with a realism that is almost painful. The spectator can almost imagine that he hears the rattle of musketry and the brave regiments as they charge upon each other to sink amid the smoke and carnage. ... Standing on the little platform, the spectator seems to look out for miles upon a stretch of cornfields and farms.[24]

The painting's verisimilitude is extremely striking but still just stops short of producing the illusion of presence – the realism of the images is *almost* painful, the viewer *seems* to be looking at the battleground. Instead, imaginings are invoked to give the full account of the immersive experience – one can even almost imagine the sounds of the battle and the battle unfolding in front of one's eyes.

Something similar also happens in the case of moving panoramas. Unlike the 360-degree panoramas Grau focuses on, moving panoramas consisted of long rolls of canvas that were slowly unfurled between two rollers. Whereas the spectator had to walk around the viewing platform to see the whole static panorama the frames of which she could not discern, in the case of the moving panorama the spectator usually sat as the canvas unrolled on a sort of a stage. What moving panoramas had in common with the 360-degree ones according to both Griffiths and Huhtamo, however, is that they were as successful in effecting immersion. Griffiths, for instance, cites a contemporary account of a river journey panorama by John Banvard – *Panorama of the Mississippi River* (1846) – which was seen by as many as 400,000 people including the queen of the United Kingdom of Great Britain and Ireland,

> [D]rawn along on two cylinders, a small portion [of the panorama] was exhibited at a time, so that the audience may imagine they are performing the journey along the river, especially as the illusion is heightened by diorama effects representing changes of the day.[25]

Again, it is the imagination that is key for the immersion. Of course, the illusion of depth and, in this case, the lighting effects, play no small role but in the end the notion of presence is secured through imagining taking a journey rather than falsely believing it.[26]

Unfortunately, in Griffiths and other scholars interested in the matter these subtle yet important distinctions between imagination and illusion appear to be lost. This leads to problems in her account. Consider the following conflation of imagination and illusion:

> [W]hile one reviewer [of the Frankenstein's 1853 *Panorama of Niagara*] claimed that it required 'only the least degree of imagination to believe our bodies are keeping company with our thoughts, and that we are in person surveying this indescribable work of Almighty,' another was at pains to point out that despite the 'striking naturalness of the scene,' the panorama was still 'almost a reproduction' of the World's Wonder, not, we should note, the real thing.[27]

Griffiths thinks that the first report articulates the illusion of looking at Niagara and, therefore, contrasts it with another which makes it clear that we are dealing only with a representation. But there is nothing contradictory in the two accounts. The first one is also fully aware of the representational nature of Frankenstein's panorama, for the reviewer does not actually believe that she is 'in person surveying' the Niagara. Rather, she *imagines* the state of believing this position and does so with the painting as a prop.

Indeed, much like in train films, the dominant contemporary reports by panorama visitors convey the idea that however immersive mandated imaginings may be, they do not spill over into illusions of presence. We can, therefore, conclude that there is little need for technical definition of immersion along Grau's lines. Not only are there any contemporary accounts that can support such a definition, it is even unclear how an occasion when make-believe turns into false belief would look like. Even particularly visceral experiences which invited imagining loss of limb and life, as in the case of train films discussed in Chapter 1, never amounted to false beliefs about actual threats. It seems, instead, that the ordinary meaning of immersion as a particularly engaging experience better explains contemporary accounts of panoramas, early train films and a number of other phenomena as it allows for both imaginary and illusory experiences to be described as immersive.

Travelogues as ersatz-tourism: Any place for imagination?

We have seen how although some panoramas such as *The Battle of Sedan* could literally fool spectators into believing themselves there, most of the panoramas simply constituted fictions of presence and travel. Much like with early train films, their fictional status seems to be lost to the scholars due to the vague notions of illusion and traditional distinctions between actualities and fiction film. This view remains commonplace in early film scholarship with Jennifer Lynn Peterson's 2013 monograph on travelogue films – *Education in the School of Dreams* – presenting perhaps the most striking example.[28]

Peterson's work is an extremely informed study about the neglected genre of travelogue film in the early period with the focus on the transitional era, and, although it is insightful on numerous subjects, when it comes to the notion of fiction there are considerable issues. Peterson writes: 'I define travelogue films as nonfiction motion pictures that represent *place* as their primary subject.'[29] Yet only a few pages later she 'argue[s] that early travelogue films invite the spectator to imagine himself or herself in the role of traveler, or Author'.[30] For Peterson then travelogues remain non-fictions despite her claims that they uniformly mandate imaginings – the very definition of fiction. To further vex the issue she also makes continuous recourse to illusion when, in fact, as the chapter on lecturers will demonstrate at length, fiction is the case: '[E. Burton Holmes] strove to create for his audience the illusion of actually traveling.'[31] There is, finally, talk of 'fictionalizing strategies' in the discussions of the turn-of-the-century imperial nature of representational strategies in travelogues which further obfuscates matters. Orientalization and exoticization of foreign lands in the service of imperialism is for the most part misrepresentation rather than fiction-making. Although such misrepresentations may on occasions be used for props in games of make-believe they are primarily just that – misrepresentation. As such they are essentially as far removed from fiction as lie, pretence and deceit are.[32]

In fact, there is conflation even in Joseph Garncarz who is among the very rare film scholars who explicitly argue that the category of fiction is context-dependent and that a film can cross the fiction/non-fiction boundary over time.[33] He does not distinguish between 'illusion' ['Illusion'] and the 'as-if-character' ['Als-ob-Charakter'] as his discussion of scenics attests ['Naturaufnahmen']: 'at the end of 1896 the film number [in variety theatre] used … the illusion of taking part. The "as-if-character" of being a part of an event with "borrowed" camera eyes comes as late as … the Biograph recording "Henley", Das Paradies der Rudersports: Die Haupt-Regatta [1901].'[34] And although the imaginative mode of the as-if attitude is at the core of his understanding of scenics, Garncarz still insists that the cited British Mutoscope and Biograph Company's film and the scenics of this type are non-fictions.[35]

Conflating these issues has significant consequences for our understanding of early cinema. Just like all the talk of non-narrative and theatrical cinema precluded us from seeing the specific stylistics of early cinema which was only articulated with the notion of attractions, so do the imprecise invocations of illusions and imaginings make us blind to the nature of early audience's engagement with cinema.

Whether travelogues really do (or, at least, did) invite imagining oneself in the role of the traveller, moreover, remains to be seen. In Peterson the evidence for such a claim revolves primarily around the status of travelogues as forms of ersatz-tourism. The greatest majority of people would not have been to numerous places shown on screen, and the travelogues would have served as substitutes for taking a trip there. The actual substantiations of such imaginings from contemporary catalogues, trade press, advertising strategies and reviews are, however, scant. Even the examples from 'the discourse of armchair travel' that Peterson does cite, moreover, do not articulate any mandates for imaginings. Instead, they focus on the familiarization with the sites, expansion of one's intellectual horizons and the benefits from actually taking the trip:

> Everyone knows the value of travel in broadening the mind and in enlarging the sympathies. To look at good pictures of distant peoples and scenes is to be a stay-at-home traveler, and to enjoy many of the advantages of real travel without its dangers and trials.[36]

When more emphasis is placed on the actual locales, as it is the case in an oft-reproduced advertisement penned by a University of Chicago professor Frederick Starr, there is still no reason to think that any imaginings were involved:

> I have seen Niagara thunder over her gorge in the noblest frenzy ever beheld by man – I have watched a Queensland river under the white light of an Australasian moon go whirling and swirling through strange islands lurking with bandicoot and kangaroo – I have watched an English railroad train draw into a station, take on its passengers and then chug away with its stubby little engine through the Yorkshire Dells, past old Norman Abbeys silhouetted against the skyline, while a cluster of century-aged cottages loomed up in the valley below, through which a yokel drove his flocks of Southdowns. I have been to the Orient and gazed at the water-sellers and beggars and dervishes. I have beheld fat old Rajahs with the price of a thousand lives bejeweled in their monster turbans, and the price of a thousand deaths sewn in their royal nightshirts as they indolently swayed in golden howdahs, borne upon the backs of grunting elephants. I saw a runaway horse play battledoor and shuttlecock with the citizens and traffic of a little Italian village, whose streets had not known so much commotion since the sailing of Columbus. I know how the Chinaman lives and I have been through the homes of the Japanese. I have marveled at the daring of Alpine tobogganists and admired the wonderful skill of Norwegian ski jumpers. I have seen armies upon the battlefield and their return in triumph. I have looked upon weird dances and outlandish frolics in every quarter of the globe, and I didn't have to leave Chicago for a moment.[37]

Starr is here simply listing everything he has seen in such travelogues and he is using the expressions such as 'to see', 'to watch', 'to look upon', 'to marvel' and so on in a perfectly ordinary sense. We regularly say that we see/watch/look/marvel at things in photographs and motion pictures and this does not entail any imaginings so long as the images are of illustrative nature (in the sense specified in the panorama section) as they are here. It is true that on two occasions Starr makes use of 'have been' which, given the fact that he has not actually been in any of these places, might suggest he imagined himself being there. But this is again just a manner of speaking. It is certainly not a hypothetical expression of the 'as though' or 'would' type so it implies no imagination from this perspective. At the end of the paragraph he also makes it clear that he has actually *not* been anywhere given that he never left Chicago. Moreover, there are no markers which would suggest that he imagined himself positioned *within* the locale. Nothing is described as being to his left or right, nothing is in the distance or up close, and everything is simply a subject matter illustrated. It is safe to say, therefore, that no imaginings play a role in Starr's account.

This is further supported by the numerous catalogue entries on scenic subject none of which invite imaginary participation but instead simply articulate the illustrative force of showing. Take, for instance, a typical entry on a title called *Mississippi River*:

> This picture was taken from the Pioneer Limited as it comes along the shores of the Mississippi river. It shows steamboats, small boats and shore line. It is indeed an interesting picture, showing the old river style of travel and the more modern railways.[38]

In contrast with Banvard's *Panorama of the Mississippi River* no imaginings are invoked in this description. This is even more striking because it is clearly stated that the view is taken from a moving ship. Instead, the spectator is simply informed that she is shown images of different types of travel. Another company's catalogue description of the whole scenic category makes my point about the absence of mandates for imagining oneself traveling on a more general level:

> Under this head come many pictures of strong local interest; – street scenes, along the great water highways, in the mountains, and on the plains. Our Niagara Falls series is particularly strong, embracing views of the giant cataract from all of the more interesting points, with several turning panoramas covering the whole extent of this wonderful phenomenon of nature, from the beginning of the rapids, across the Canadian and American Falls and as far down as the cantilever bridge. It will be noted also that the foreign subjects include most of the places visited and admired by tourists. The Chinese Philippine views are all very fine pictorially and photographically. The New York street scenes are without exception very typical of Metropolitan bustle and activity.[39]

Again, there is reference to ersatz-tourism but no actual invitation to imagine oneself a tourist. The Niagara Falls series is singled out, numerous vantage points are described, even panoramic shots are advertised but unlike in Frankenstein's *Panorama of Niagara Falls* there is no call to imagination.[40] None of this should come as a surprise for as we know one important context for early cinema was the illustrated magazine meaning that moving pictures could be easily seen as fulfilling the illustrative function.

Although Peterson does not gather sufficient evidence in favour of the claim that travelogues invited imagining oneself traveling and contemporary accounts and catalogues strongly favour the opposite, this is not to say that no films focusing on representing a place, as Peterson defines travelogues, could not accomplish the mandate envisioned by her. Consider an 1896 description by Vladimir Stasov of a film titled *A Boat Leaving Harbor*:

> Imagine that you suddenly have the open sea in front of you, no shore at all: the shore is the bottom edge of the picture right in front of where we are sitting in our chairs and armchairs ... And the waves are getting bigger and bigger all the time, they are rolling in from far out and coming on right up to you ... on and on, leaping up and crashing down, and the lines of surf are breaking right against the front edge of the picture.[41]

Here, the spectators such as Stasov imagine to be so close to the sea that the waves crash down on them.[42] This is in sharp contrast with how Starr experiences travelogues. Starr simply looks at various locales on the screen. They are locales of foreign lands and Starr is in Chicago while watching them. He does not imagine anything about them but gathers factual information about various local practices and customs. They serve as illustrations of how things actually are. Stasov, by contrast, is doing more than looking at a foreign view on the screen. He is imagining himself to be on the very location that the film represents (on top of clearly being aware that he is actually in front of a screen). He is imagining himself *at* the shore. He is make-believing that the waves roll straight at him and that they will make contact with him. He is imagining that he is in their way. Put simply, he is imagining himself to be watching the locale from *within* the very locale.

And this is not an isolated incident. A contemporary reviewer from Great Britain, similarly, claims that '[t]he motion of treating [sic] waves was so beautifully reproduced that one had an inclination to step backward to avoid getting wet.'[43] In the same vein, in talking about what must be another film focusing on the water subject, Felix Regnault writes in the same year: 'During the bath in the sea, the waves spume and form ridges, children dive in and swim: you'd think you were there.'[44] 'You'd think' – as the analysis in Chapter 1 has shown – embeds the hypothetical inviting imagination.

It seems, however, that these cases were predominantly restricted to the earliest days of cinema and that they mostly had to do with the novelty of the representational medium. Much like how quickly after the initial novelty of the early train films the audiences stopped imagining any threats of onrushing trains and just saw them as motion pictures of trains pulling into the station (as we ourselves do today), reports about imaginary immersions into depicted locales also disappear quickly.[45]

In contrast to numerous moving and 360-degree panoramas, it seems then that there is no concrete evidence that travelogues *in general,* and particularly in the transitional period Peterson focuses on mandated immersive imaginings of the sort she speaks of. And precisely this is the reason Peterson is right in defining them as non-fiction films (but mistaken in invoking any discourse on illusions and fictionalization). There is, however, a special subclass of travelogues which, at least during their initial appearance, went far beyond the illustrative nature of most travelogues – phantom rides.

Phantom rides: From fiction of travel to non-fiction of place

Phantom rides are films taken with the camera mounted in front of the locomotive in motion on its pilot, that is, the cowcatcher (although occasionally these films were also taken from the rear of the train facing the receding background). Although phantom rides fit Peterson's definition of travelogues – they regularly depict places as can be seen from both their catalogue descriptions and titles – their primary appeal derives less from the place they depict and more from the particular experience of travel they convey. It is not only that, as Peterson mistakenly argues for travelogues in general, they mandated spectators imagining themselves traveling, but they mandated spectators imagining themselves traveling *on* the train and imagining themselves *seeing* the views represented. Despite all this, even Garncarz treats phantom rides as non-fictions.[46]

According to Gunning, the first phantom ride ever to be shot was Edison's *View from Gorge Railroad* in June of 1896.[47] The genre, however, seems to have really kicked-off only with American Mutoscope and Biograph Company's *The Haverstraw Tunnel* shot in the summer of 1897.[48] Premiering in London in October of the same year, the film was a great success and produced numerous panegyrics the company was only too happy to include in its Bulletins. The following is a selection from these clippings:

> If you desire a novel experience go to the Palace Theatre any evening at a quarter to ten and travel (in imagination) on the cow-catcher of the locomotive of a West Shore (American) Express through the Haverstraw Tunnel. ... Instead of the scenes and figures coming towards you, as is the case with most of the other pictures, you seem to be going to them, and the effect is decidedly strange.[49]
>
> In all previous instances the audience has sat passive and witnessed scenes in motion, but in the latest example the position is, so to speak, reversed, and the

spectator becomes part and parcel of the picture, for, by the exercise of the very slightest imagination, he can fancy himself perched upon the cow-catcher of an American locomotive tearing along at the rate of sixty miles per hour, with the landscape simply leaping towards him.[50]

You are supposed to witness the surrounding imposing scenery while you are seated on the express train in question. Whereby vast tracks of picturesque country appear to be dashing madly *at* you! Both before and after the train enters the deep, dark gloom of the Haverstraw Tunnel the effect is enough to set all kind brains in front reeling.[51]

Hitherto the audience merely watched moving objects, but in this recent addition the onlooker, by the aid of a little imagination, can fancy himself sitting an [sic] the bogie tracks of an engine travelling at the rate of sixty-five miles an hour with the landscape simply dashing towards him.[52]

As we can readily see, all the accounts in question invoke imaginings either implicitly ('you are supposed to witness') or explicitly ('in imagination', 'slightest imagination', 'little imagination'). The mandate is clearly one of immersive imagining – imagining oneself on the pilot of the rushing locomotive and beholding the view from there. It is precisely imagining oneself as seeing objects from *within* the picture, that is, *on* site while *traveling* that the reviewers recognize as the crucial novelty these films introduce. This type of imagining, we might recall, was also one elicited by moving panoramas.[53] There is space for differentiating between the two, however.

Although both moving panoramas and the earliest phantom rides mandated imaginary travels within the places depicted, the former, as Griffiths informs us, were often criticized for being slow and boring simply due to the speed (i.e. the lack thereof) it took for the canvas to unfurl.[54] Phantom rides, by contrast, were perceived as incredibly fast by their contemporaries ('locomotive tearing along at the rate of sixty-miles per hour', etc.). Whereas moving panoramas, moreover, afforded a lateral (imaginary) view, phantom rides presented a view from in front of the moving vehicle. This novelty the phantom rides introduced was not lost on the contemporary viewers either:

[T]he spectator gets much the same view as he sees from a railway carriage window. It is, however, more extensive, for it includes the track in front as well as the country by the side of the line.[55]

The camera was placed at the front of the engine, pointing straight ont [sic] towards the track, and the resulting picture is most remarkable and unfamiliar, except, of course, to an eye of an engine driver.[56]

A further consequence of this is, of course, that, unlike in moving panoramas, the represented objects could have produced the looming effect ('country ... dashing madly *at* you!' etc.) and would have mandated imaginings about potential crashes. This also means that, as Gunning rightfully points out, the experience was different from what Wolfgang Schivelbusch has called panoramic perception characteristic of actual train travel.[57] From the perspective of imagined experiences of more importance for us here, by extension, the experience would have also been distinguishable from such (almost) contemporary and more advanced panoramas as *Trans-Siberian Panorama* erected for the 1900 Paris Exhibition (Figure 2.2). The lateral view of (imagined) standard railway travel may not only never penetrate directly into the vista but also distinguishes between the various spaces within the vista. As the writer for the *Scientific American* explains:

> To give the visitor the impression of a genuine voyage, there are made to pass before him such remarkable things as he would see upon a journey from Moscow to Pekin ... When a person is on a railway train, he does not see all the points of the landscape with an equal speed. In the foreground, the ballast flies rapidly under his eyes, then the bushes and shrubs at the side of the road move a little less quickly, the more remote houses still less quickly, and finally, the distances unfold themselves quite slowly. ... In a large trench excavated along the entire length of the building is arranged the mechanism that carries along four distances of the landscape at different velocities.[58]

Figure 2.2 Trans-Siberian Panorama (*Scientific American Supplement*, 18 August 1900, p. 20603).

The key points for comparison for contemporary reviewers, however, were not various panoramas discussed here or earlier on in the chapter but other motion pictures. And the reviewers all claim that hitherto no moving pictures afforded the imaginary experience of *traveling within* the image. It is certainly true that no large class of motion pictures authorized imagining *traveling within* the image, but I would also like to emphasize that, with the exception of the earliest surf films such as *A Boat Leaving Harbor* mentioned earlier, no substantial class of films prior to phantom rides mandated imagining *being within* the image.

At this point one might object to this by drawing attention to my discussion of the earliest train films such as *The Arrival of a Train* in Chapter 1. Have I not argued there that these films mandated imagining about the onrushing trains? And have I not claimed in the previous section that the experience was one of imaginary immersion? Does that not mean that the earliest train films already secured the experience I am here alleging appears only with phantom rides – imagining oneself inside the view represented? The objection would indeed be valid if I subscribed to the notion of immersion as being present *within* the image. It is true that Grau defines immersion in this way: 'The quality of apparently being present in the images.'[59] I have, however, spoken only of 'being present'. In Chapter 1 I briefly mentioned the difference between being present *to* the image and being present *within* the image when speaking of imaginary immersion. At this point I need to discuss this distinction in more detail to articulate more precisely the differences in imaginative engagement with films such as *The Arrival of a Train*, on the one hand, and phantom rides, on the other. It is being present *to* the image that describes the experience of early train films. Being present *within the* image is the trait of phantom rides.

In the former case it is the train jumping out of the image that is imagined. The spectator imagines the locomotive invading her space – she does not imagine herself at the train station. Like in Truchet's poster for the Cinématographe Lumière the train is imagined as rupturing the screen and coming to a halt in the screening hall. It is the train that comes to her wherever the auditorium she is in might be. She stays where she is. In phantom rides, by contrast, the spectator imagines she is no longer in the auditorium. Instead, she is whisked away into the very locale that is being screened. She imagines herself to be *within* the image, the sights rushing by her as she rushes through the countryside. Stasov, similarly, does not imagine himself sitting in the auditorium and the waves bursting through the screen. He imagines them crashing down as he imagines himself standing on the beach.

It is also important to recognize that the distinction between these two types of imagining 'being present' is not exactly the one which Gunning emphasizes, that is, the one between things rushing towards you and you rushing towards the objects.[60] Although it is true that in films like *The Arrival of a Train* the spectators only imagined things rushing towards them, once you imagine yourself on a cowcatcher whether you sprint towards the objects or they spring at you is completely interchangeable as the contemporary reports cited above evince ('you seem to be going to them' versus 'the landscape simply dashing towards [you]').

What this distinction between being present *within* the image and *to* the image does articulate is the difference between face-to-face and the modest version of the imagined seeing thesis as elaborated in analytic philosophy circles.[61] Since Walton's account of fiction in terms of make-believe there has been an ongoing debate about what precisely we imagine *seeing* when engaging fiction film. Two of the most influential proposals have been the face-to-face and the modest version of the imagined seeing thesis.[62]

Under the face-to-face version the spectators imagine themselves to be in the space of the things they are imagining seeing. When watching a film like *The Birth of a Nation*, for instance, the viewer imagines to be in the very cabin where the Camerons are hiding. She imagines herself to be inhabiting the camera position exactly like early phantom ride spectator imagined herself to be on the cowcatcher. In the modest version the spectator only imagines to see what is represented without imagining themselves to be on site. In other words, although she imagines seeing the Camerons hiding in the cabin she does not imagine inhabiting the camera position. And this is precisely how the viewers of *The Arrival of a Train* imagined seeing the train – without imagining themselves being at the station. The fact that these two versions of the imagined seeing thesis chime perfectly with the two modes of being imaginatively present demonstrates that the accounts articulated by analytic philosophers interested in film are more than exercises in logical consistency – in fact, they have a historical and empirical reality. This, moreover, means that new film history can go a long way in resolving the current debates in analytic philosophy. In other words, historical data can be used to check which of the versions of the imagined seeing thesis best fits the audience's engagement with the fiction story film. The uniqueness of phantom rides suggests, finally, that there is little reason to believe that the face-to-face view of imagined seeing was ever espoused in fiction story films. Hale's Tours which often embedded such films within their programmes allow us to flesh out this matter.

Before proceeding to the discussion of Hale's Tours, however, we should keep in mind that by 1905 and their first run in Kansas City the novelty of phantom rides as films mandating *imaginary* travel had worn off. As the following catalogue entry for the *Phantom Ride on the Canadian Pacific* (Edison Manufacturing Company, 1903) and typical of phantom ride descriptions in general around 1903 attests, the focus is now on the spectacular place itself and what Peterson refers to as superiority of travelogues over actual travel, rather than on inviting the spectator to imagine herself on the pilot:

> This subject is the most magnificent panoramic view ever taken in the Canadian 'Rockies'. The entire picture of stereoscopic quality which has excited the most enthusiastic praise wherever shown. The scenery is the most magnificent on the North American continent. Innumerable short tunnels are passed, high bridges and many other picturesque effects are shown, and the view, taken from the front of a train running at high speed, is one that even tourists riding over the line are not privileged to enjoy.[63]

From our perspective this means that as more emphasis is placed on the magnificence of locales presented in order to retain the attraction of the genre, the more phantom rides are transformed from fictions about one's own travel into non-fictional representations of a passage through a particular place. They are spectacular illustrations but precisely primarily illustrations – they stop mandating imaginings.

Once the novelty of imagining oneself on the train dissipated, another strategy to resuscitate the phantom ride's attractional promise around 1903 was to emphasize the danger that the very act of recording of the ride presented. In the Selig Polyscope Company Supplement we find the best examples of this approach:

> When this picture [*Panoramic View of Hell Gate*] was made the photographers had a coal ahead of two engines and they were pushed along almost a mile a minute. The experience was so dangerous that it will never again be attempted...[64]

> The danger to the operators in making this negative [*Lava Slides in Red Rock Canyon*] can never be realized yet the picture will give some idea of the risk involved in getting it. To show a set of moving pictures of Colorado without having some of Granite Canyon would be a very serious mistake indeed. Never before has it been possible to get them not only on account of the expenses involved but in the danger and certain death to the operators should there be the slightest hitch in the working in the car in front of the fast train.[65]

In fact, the trend emphasizing *non*-imaginative engagement with phantom rides starts very early on. In the Warwick Trading Company's catalogue from 1897 to 1898, for instance, we expectedly find invitations to mandated imaginings such as: 'The audience is carried, in imagination, over a viaduct across an arm of the sea ...'[66] But on the pages of the Supplement in the 'South Africa' subject section the articulation of the mandate for imaging is downplayed in favour of the illustrative function. A typical description for one of the phantom rides listed there – *South Africa – A Train Ride by the Hex River Mountain* – reads:

> There is no better way of gaining a faithful impression of the natural characteristic of a country than to observe it from a train passing through it. For this reason, if for no other, an animated photograph taken from the back of a moving train affords an excellent idea of the natural formation of the country through which the train is passing.[67]

We can conclude that almost immediately after the initial promotion and reception of *The Haverstraw Tunnel*, phantom rides were advertised in two ways. The first invited imaginary train travel and was dominant at the outset, whereas the other hyped the film's illustrative function (and even the dangers involved in securing the recording) and pushed out the former over the next few years.

Although appeals to imagining traveling on the pilot can still be found here and there in the catalogues in 1903, they are usually just copy-pastes from earlier descriptions. On a rare occasion when, for instance, the 1903 Lubin Manufacturing Company's catalogue cites 'the effect of one sitting in the train and looking out of the window' it turns out that the entry for the whole film – *Railroad Tunnel Scene* – is plagiarized word for word from 1899 F. M. Prescott's catalogue describing Edison Manufacturing Company's film of the same name.[68] What is much more typical for Lubin's 1903 catalogue is the following description: 'The curves in the road shoot past like a cannon ball, fired from a big Krupp gun, and you stand amazed at the ingenuity of the master mind who invented the apparatus for reproducing nature so true and lifelike.'[69] What is advertised as amazing is the power of the apparatus for accurate reproduction and the moving image so produced rather than any imaginary experience potentially mandated by such a reproduction. Crucially, this description is of a sort of a remake of *The Haverstraw Tunnel – Panoramic View of Haverstraw Tunnel, N.Y.* (Lubin Manufacturing Company, 1903) – the phantom ride the premiere of which elicited uniform mandates for imaginings.

It is also worth noting that catalogues are probably to be trusted somewhat less than contemporary reviews when it comes to the reconstruction of historical mandates. The reason is that the catalogues are more inclined to oversell their products as far as their novelty and effect is concerned. In other words, just because a catalogue pitches an imagining it does not mean that it will be taken up by the audience.[70] It is amusing, for instance, to see how many films are described by catalogues as the best ones ever made. With this and the contemporary accounts in mind we can say that the imaginings of travel started losing their mandate as early as in 1899. Consider, for instance, the 1899 Biograph bulletin clippings from the then recent press comments about their latest phantom ride *Brooklyn Bridge*:

> The view starts with a swift rush down the incline from the station on the New York side, shows the Brooklyn trolley cars in motion on either side and pedestrians passing back and forth on the platform in the centre, then takes a plunge in the iron archway which covers the tracks of the electric line for about two-thirds of the distance. ... After spinning through the archway at an almost dizzy speed, the car suddenly rushed out ...[71]

> This picture bewildered the spectators last week, for people who have crossed the bridge one hundred times have never hitherto realized the immensity of the structure.[72]

> The Biograph was more than ordinarily interesting to Brooklyn people, for it represented what is the best thing yet seen here in that line, a complete representation of a trip across the bridge from New York to Brooklyn. The view is from the front end of a fast bridge car and every pillar and joist and trolley car on the trip is faithfully shown.[73]

These are, undeniably, words of praise for the American Mutoscope and Biograph Company's phantom ride but they do not evince any imaginary participation by these critics. In the first case, it is the *car* that plunges into the archway at an almost dizzying speed rather than the spectator. In the second account, the spectators are indeed bewildered, but by the bridge itself rather than the imaginary participation in the travel. The last review, finally, focuses on the faithfulness of representation without invoking any imaginings. Much like with the earliest train and surf films, then, the authority behind imaginings in phantom rides quickly dissipated, first in the viewing context and soon thereafter in the production context as well. The potential discrepancy between the intended engagement and the actual engagement with these films, therefore, is something to keep in mind in the following discussion of Hale's Tours.

Hale's Tours

The myth of a 'demented fellow'

As Raymond Fielding, the first film scholar to devote significant attention to the phenomenon teaches us, Hale's Tours and Scenes of the World presented the movie-going audiences with some of the first specialized motion picture venues and proved to be of great importance for the emergence of the film distribution network.[74]

Although Fielding claims that Hale's Tours were first exhibited at the St. Louis World Fair in 1904, both Musser and Rabinovitz point out that there is no contemporary evidence to back this claim up and that the premiere in fact took place at Kansas City's new Electric Park in May of 1905.[75] The patent for the 'Pleasure Railway', filed on 14 March 1905 and approved on 19 September the same year to George C. Hale and Fred W. Gilford, provides a diagram and specifies the amusement ride in detail (Figure 2.3). The car was mounted on a platform and a system of mechanical levers, shafts and wheels enabled it to vibrate, rock and tilt sideways. With the help of lugs carried by belt mounted on top of said shafts 'sound of wheels of a car going over the rail-joints of a track ... [and] sound like the wheels of a car passing over the railroad-crossings' were also produced.[76] Fielding, further, mentions that the speed of the belt could be regulated to synchronize with the developments on the screen (starting, speeding up, slowing down and stopping). In her analysis of the auditory aspects of Hale's Tours, Rabinovitz also notes the use of steam whistles, bells ringing and other types of clattering sounds.[77] There were also 'means to blow a blast of air into the faces of the occupants' visible in the photograph of the inside of the ride in the form of ventilators (Figure 2.4).[78] As far as the projection apparatus is concerned, the

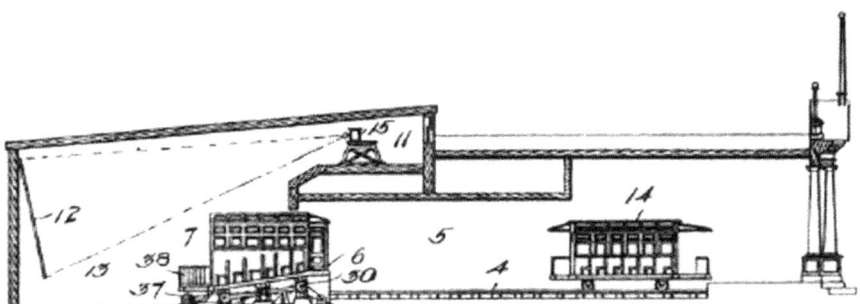

Figure 2.3 Illustration of the 'Pleasure Railway' patented by George C. Hale and Fred W. Gilford (*Official Gazette of the U.S. Patent Office*, 19 September 1905, p. 788).

Figure 2.4 Inside Hale's Tours (*Kinematograph and Lantern Weekly*, 1 October 1908, p. 481).

patent specifies that the projector is to be placed in a gallery above the car though in practice rear-projection was most often used. The screen, which was slightly inclined, was placed in front of the open front of the car 'extending across the field of vision from the vehicle'.[79] The seats in the car, as Figure 2.3 shows, rose upward toward the back. All of this, as the approved patent specifies, 'to give the impression of movement'.[80]

According to Rabinovitz the shows lasted from about ten to twenty minutes (films Selig made especially for Hale's Tours, for instance, average about 600 feet in length which, if the projection speed was eighteen frames per second, equals approximately seven minutes).[81] The car fit about sixty people, and if there were two cars the ride could accommodate up to about 1200 people per hour as one ad claims.[82] Coming at a price of 10 cents some Hale's Tours also included lectures which described the views presented. In the United States Hale's Tours popularity peaked between 1905 and 1907 but the novelty soon dwindled and the proprietors started losing money (trade press starts reporting loses as early as September 1906).[83] By the end of the decade Hale's Tours all but disappeared, though there are reports of some operating as late as 1913 in Butte and Helena, Montana, and Amsterdam, Netherlands.[84]

We cannot be certain where the inspiration for Hale's Tours came from exactly. It is likely that Hale was familiar with phantom rides and perhaps wanted to breathe new life into them. There is also another patent by an inventor William J. Keefe from 1904 for an 'Amusement Device' for which Hale, together with Gilford, came on board as the investor. This 'Amusement Device' is essentially a circular railroad track flanked by walls upon which the images of the passing landscape are thrown from a projector mounted on the train moving on the track 'so as to give the impression to the passenger that they are traveling through the country and visiting the scenes being depicted on the walls ...'.[85] Hale also visited the 1900 Paris Exhibition where he could have seen the aforementioned *Trans-Siberian Panorama* (which was shown in St. Louis in 1904 as well), an updated version of a moving panorama simulating four different levels/distances of the landscape.[86] In Paris he could have also seen two other panoramas which might have stimulated his creativity further – *Cineorama* by Raoul Grimoin-Sanson and *Maréorama* by Hugo d'Alesi.[87] The former simulated a balloon trip by projecting 360-degree images taken from an actual flight on a circular screen using ten synchronized film projectors. The latter imitated a boat ride from Marseille to Yokohama by means of an unfolding canvas, the rocking of the platform representing the ship, sounds of the ship, day- and night-time lighting effects, fans for sea breeze, actors playing hands on deck and even olfactory elements such as seaweed and tar.[88] Regardless of what the direct source of inspiration was, what is certain is that at the time Hale's Tours were the latest addition to a representational cultural series whose goal is to induce the experience of immersion within the image depicted.

Though there is again much interchanging of terms like 'illusion', 'imagination', 'hyper-realism' and 'fantasy' in research on Hale's Tours, the general agreement is that Hale's Tours were effectively cognitive illusions in the sense that I have been talking about. Rabinovitz, for instance, puts it like this: 'Early accounts of these movie rides are reminiscent of the inventive reports regarding the reception of the earliest Lumière films ... [The installation manufacturers] organized a theatrical experience for the cognitive convergence of sensory information as the basis of illusion that "you are really there".'[89] In other words, according to Rabinovitz early accounts of Hale's Tours articulate false beliefs on the part of the audience. In fact, the most notable scholars regularly cite the following report to argue for the ability of Hale's Tours to fool the audience into believing that they were actually taking a ride:

> The illusion was so good that ... members of the audience frequently yelled at pedestrians to get out of the way or be run down.[90]
>
> One demented fellow even kept coming back to the same show, day after day. Sooner or later, he figured, the engineer would make a mistake and he would get to see a train wreck.[91]

The first paragraph supposedly conveys the idea that the cognitive illusion was strong enough for the audiences to believe that they are not only traveling on the cowcatcher but that they could change the behaviour of the people represented in the images. The second paragraph, according to the same argument, highlights the force of cognitive illusion further by homing in on one particular patron who actually believed that one and the same programme presents a new travel experience which eventually has to turn out badly. Let us address the (de)merits of this argument.

First, the fact that the cited report dates from 1916, more than half a decade after the general disappearance of Hale's Tours from North America, is regularly downplayed in this argument. On the example of phantom rides, I have tried to show how even a few years can make a crucial difference for engaging a moving picture genre – there, already two years after the appearance of phantom rides the process of their morphing from fiction into non-fiction began. Given that here we are not dealing with a contemporary account but with an after-the-fact one, there is good reason to give less weight to it than to any contemporary reports we may find (which I discuss below). Second, it is not clear if we are dealing with an account from personal memory or a second-hand report. And finally, even if we choose to ignore the previous two points, what the actual report says does not even necessarily lead us to espouse the view of Hale's Tours as illusions championed by Rabinovitz et al.

Let me explain. That a viewer shouts at the images in front of her does not necessarily mean that she falsely believes something about those images. While watching horror films, people regularly shout things like 'Don't go there!' or 'Look behind!' but that does not mean that they believe there is a person who is actually in danger and whose behaviour they could influence. Instead, they are simply emotionally invested in the game of make-believe they are playing. In other words, they are immersed in the game.[92] As far as the part of the quotation about the 'demented fellow' is concerned, it is true that this chap is completely confused about what is going on. The problem is, however, that the second quoted paragraph above never appears in the 1916 original. The actual quotation from E. C. Thomas, in fact, is as follows:

> [The people of Vancouver, BC] still tell a good story of one depraved individual who became a steady patron in the hope of being present when some such exciting accident should occur, or perhaps even when the well-known Mr. Hale's tour should be brought to a thrilling close through one of those collisions which always seemed to be on the point of happening.[93]

It turns out that both Rabinovitz and Gauthier have mistaken Fielding's *paraphrase*[94] of Thomas's account for the real thing and then erroneously cited the paraphrase as the actual 1916 citation. Unlike the paraphrase, the actual quotation sets up the story of the fellow as precisely a story, an urban myth ('they still tell a good story'). With such a framing we should already be suspect of the veracity of what follows. In this story, moreover, there is no talk of visiting the same show – the fellow does not seem to be fooled into believing that the same show could give a different result. Also, the fellow, who Rabinovitz positions as the exemplary spectator of Hale's Tours, is not 'demented' at all. Rather, he is 'depraved'. And 'depraved' is better understood as a moral failure than as a cognitive one which is closer to the meaning of 'demented'. This is no coincidence for what is depraved about the fellow is actually the hope that he will get to see an accident, that he will witness somebody getting hurt. In other words, the actual quotation seems to be more about the twisted kicks a deprived spectator got out of hoping for an accident than about him confusing the ride for reality.

What seems to be going on in the scholarship is the mythologizing of Hale's Tours of a sort comparable to what happened in the formation of the myth of panicking audience. First, we have a report from *after* the period of Hale's Tours (1916 as opposed to 1905–10) which is presented as contemporary with the events. Then, the first scholar to investigate the phenomenon in detail – Fielding – reads this report as an articulation of illusion rather than of imaginary participation. Fielding's paraphrase of the report, moreover, drops the reference to the urban myth and replaces moral failure with cognitive one. Finally, the paraphrase is mistaken for the original report in Rabinovitz (and Gauthier) giving further credence to the idea that Hale's Tours actually elicited illusions of railway travel.

It is undeniable that the contemporary advertisements from the 1905–1910 period hawk Hale's Tours and a number of imitations and variations they spawned as illusions. The following, for instance, is a fairly typical advertisement:

> Wherever HALE'S TOURS plants have been placed in operation, the unanimous verdict of persons who have attended the exhibition is: 'Greatest thing I have ever seen!' Everyone who witnesses the exhibition is a walking advertisement for HALE'S TOURS. The Public Proclaims it to be the only perfect device giving the illusion of a vehicle ride in existence.[95]

I have already warned, however, that because of their flair to oversell effects we should take advertisements with a grain of salt when it comes to determining whether the product advertised was actually perceived as an illusion. The reports by contemporary audience would be a better guide here and they indeed suggest that it was imagination rather than illusion that played the key role:

> Few nickelodeons, no matter how gaudy or alluring on the outside, can be described as more than puritanically simple within.... Sometimes they are fitted up to look like the interior of a railway car and the workingman may take a quick, imaginative journey into a strange land.[96]

> In the journey through Rome, one could readily believe we were on a tramcar; the rumbling of the wheels, the clanging of the bell to clear the traffic, the motion of the vehicle when rounding corners and the other effects were well-timed, free from exaggeration and as natural as one could desire.[97]

In the first case, the ride is an imaginary one. In the second case, one hypothetically *could* believe being in a tramcar, but of course nobody did. Instead, they imagined this. Even the special supplement to Selig Polyscope Company's catalogue devoted exclusively to Hale's Tours which would be prone to exaggeration puts the matter in terms of imagination rather than illusion: 'The entire picture is filled with hypnotic views that make the beholder steady himself to catch the motion of rounding curves. It is impossible not to imagine that you are actually on the train.'[98] During their heyday, then, Hale's Tours were fiction films much like phantom rides and the earliest train and surf films before them. Unlike the others, they incorporated a number of non-visual means ranging from exhibition venue design to the use of sound and wind, but this did not transform them into full-fledged illusions.

What also sets Hale's Tours apart from these moving pictures is that they often incorporated story films: 'They are beautiful scenic productions taken from all parts of the world. Each has a Comedy Film interspersed, suitable for the Tour'.[99] This has led a number of scholars to view Hale's Tours as a combination of fiction and non-fiction. My point is, however, that Hale's Tours were hybrids only stylistically. Contextually, they mandated imaginings throughout.

The troubles with hybridity

In Chapter 1, I have already referred to Keil's discussion of what he has identified as three hybrid genres in the 1905–7 period – 'motion films with interpolated fictional material, travel films, and fiction films employing scenes of an actuality nature' – in which 'the ratio of fictional to non-fictional material increas[es] with each type'.[100] Exemplary of the first of these genres, according to Keil, are precisely Hale's Tours. Rabinovitz, similarly, claims that Hale's Tours 'allowed the movie spectator to become immersed in a spectacle that combined world of fiction and real and, in the process, to blur the distinction between the two'.[101] Using Keil and Rabinovitz as representatives of the general view of Hale's Tours, I wish to point out the problems such a hybrid model faces in contrast to the one I am proposing.

Both Keil and Rabinovitz base their notion of fiction/non-fiction hybridity on the stylistic distinctiveness of the phantom ride and comedy sections. Keil puts it like this:

> Eventually, the purity of the conceit of the motion film will be disrupted altogether, as the unbroken shots of landscape are deliberately suspended, and staged scenes of action set within constructed train interiors become the structural center of these films.[102]

Clearly, the distinction is between the non-staged on-location shots of the scenery as the camera moves through space and the static shots of vaudeville-like buffoonery performed in a studio and in front of a static camera. It is undeniably difficult to mistake one of these stylistic techniques for the other but, as I have argued in detail in Chapter 1, stylistic features are neither necessary nor sufficient for determining a text's (non-)fictional status. Instead of rehashing the argument made there, moreover, I will demonstrate that in a motion picture that regularly informs the discussions of Hale's Tours – *The Hold-Up of the Rocky Mountain Express* (American Mutoscope and Biograph Company, 1906) – not even the staged/non-staged distinction fits the separation between the phantom ride and comedy segments that well.

The moving picture consists of five shots altogether – three phantom ride sections with one studio section intervening between the first and the second ride and the other between the second and the third ride (Figure 2.5 a-d). There is clearly staging at the end of the second phantom ride when it turns out that it is the robbers who lay the plank on the rails to stop the train as well as throughout the whole third phantom ride which represents the outlaws' flight and their apprehension. But there even seems to be staging at the very opening of the film where an overly animated attempt at catching a soon-to-depart train is depicted. A group of five is cheering on a person who appears running from behind the station in the background and towards the train. That the incident is staged is strongly suggested by the fact that no less than three times he turns around for a brief exchange with the people cheering him on. Barely a few seconds after he exits the screen front left, moreover, all the waving and excitement stops, and the people simply walk out front left as well. If the person really attempted to board

Figure 2.5 (continued)

Figure 2.5 a–d. Stills from the first four shots of *The Hold-Up of the Rocky Mountain Express* (American Mutoscope and Biograph Company, 1906).

the train it is unlikely he would spend so much time going back and forth. And if he really boarded the train one would think the waving goodbye would continue and that the people would face the side of the train as it passes by.[103] Conversely, quite a spontaneous moment takes place during the second interior segment and the robbery of the train as seen from the interior. As the robber exits the car, he brushes against the hat of a lady who, as we are mandated to imagine, just lost consciousness during all the excitement. Due to this inadvertent contact, however, her hat almost falls off and the actress quickly awakes to hold on to it while at the same time retaining the pose of an unconscious woman lying on the edge of her seat.

The other textual criterion for determining (non-)fiction for Keil and Rabinovitz is narrative. Following the claim cited above:

> The latent (but emblematic) narrativity of the train engine gives way to the more obviously fictionalized setting of the passenger car, peopled with stock characters and a site for low comedy. On a formal level, the seductive flow of camera movement is stopped short by a cut to the static framing of the train interior set. But is the latter more inherently narrative than the former? Certainly the emphatic fictionality of the comic hijinks in the train encourages us to enfold the entire film within a fictional framework, but one could argue that the shots of rolling hills and small towns possess their own narrative pull, driven forward by the trains which propel these films.[104]

Keil's first point here is that phantom rides do not necessarily need comic sections to frame them as fictions and this is something with which I certainly agree. But he proposes that the fictionality of phantom ride segments could be derived from their narrative potential, their metaphorical status as narrative. This argument of his is set up through an almost interchangeable use of 'fictionality' and 'narrative'. From the perspective of fiction as mandated imagining advocated here, however, this rhetorical strategy is misplaced. The fictionality of phantom rides derives from the mandate to imagine oneself on the cowcatcher. Whether something is narrative or not is irrelevant to its fictional status and the same holds for any narrative potential in the phantom ride.[105] The better question is whether the phantom rides and comedies make up a single fictional world, whether the train on which one is imagining traveling is the very train in which the comedic sections take part?

There is a good reason to think that is the case. There are certainly precedents in which interior shots flanked by phantom rides are taken to depict the very train. At least as early as 1899 *The Kiss in the Tunnel* (G. A. Smith) makes use of editing and stage design to help mandate imaging a single train across the three shots. The cuts secure that the train has entered and still not left the tunnel while the interior stage design with the black background behind the side of the car confirms that the car is still in the tunnel. Though there are even more cues in *The Hold-Up of the Rocky Mountain Express* that we are dealing with one and the same train (e.g. the exits and entrances of robbers), even before the robbery commences in shot 3, the stage design is used to this end. When the film cuts from the first phantom ride (shot 1) to the first interior scene (shot 2) on both sides of the car we can see moving panoramas depicting that the train is in motion as it was in the previous shot. In the second interior shot (shot 4) following the appearance of the robbers on the rails and the stopping of the train (shot 3), the moving panoramas are stationary as well. The catalogue description of the same film further confirms the singularity of the fictional world:

> The action shows a railroad run, an interior comedy scene, the hold-up as viewed from inside, then on the track, finishing with a race between the train and the bandits, who first take to a hand car trolley and then to a horse and wagon. The robbers are captured at the crossing for an exciting finish.[106]

We are forced to conclude, therefore, that the talk of hybridity and fluidity of non/fiction in early cinema such as Rabinovitz's claim that Hale's Tours 'blurred' the distinction between the real and the fictional world serves less as a stylistic analysis of the general differences between various components of

Hale's Tours and more as a crypto-discourse about the power of cinema to fool. If for Rabinovitz the model spectator of phantom ride sections of Hale's Tours is a 'demented fellow' who mistakes illusion for reality, then the viewing of the whole programme is another confusing experience in which one cannot tell reality apart from fiction. In practice, however, fiction simply supervened on reality. Images of reality were props for mandated imaginings just as they are in all photographic fiction films. The two cannot 'blur'. At most, it may be unclear whether an image ought to be taken as a prop or not. In Hale's Tours, however, there was nothing unclear. All the images were props for imaginary engagement.

Historicizing the imagined seeing thesis

The last thing that remains to be solved about Hale's Tours from the perspective of fiction is the type of imagined seeing they invite. More precisely, do phantom ride segments and the comedy sections invite the same or different kind of imagined seeing? In the section on phantom rides I have already argued that films of this nature mandated imagining seeing from *within* the world, that is, imagining oneself on a cowcatcher and seeing things from there. The same holds for numerous panoramas (both moving and 360-degree ones). By contrast, the earliest travel films simply mandated imagining seeing approaching train without imagining oneself on the track. This, in short, is the difference between the face-to-face and the modest version of the imagined seeing thesis.

It is important to note that, contrary to what analytic philosophers claim on the matter, the face-to-face version does not entail imagining that the objects from within the world will physically interact with the spectator nor does the modest version entail imagining that the objects from within the world cannot make physical contact with the spectator.[107] The latter is demonstrated by the early train films when people readily imagined that the train will break through to the auditorium space and run them over. The former by panoramas, phantom rides and Hale's Tours. For instance, in both 360-degrees and moving panoramas which were perceived as fictions rather than as illusions, only imagining one's own presence and the sight afforded in such a way was cited. Nothing in the image was imagined as a threat. Similarly, although it is true that in the period when they were implicitly perceived and billed as fictions phantom rides were described in terms of imaginings including both objects running at spectators and spectators springing towards those very objects, nothing like the threat similar to the one invoked in the early train films was cited. Even on those occasions when, if an after-the-fact report of Hale's Tours is to be believed, in an imaginative excitement people yelled at the images of passers-by to move out of the way no proper physical contact was imagined. In other words, although one might imagine to be in the presence of other people, she does not necessarily imagine they are in her presence.

All of this is a direct consequence of the nature of make-believe as elaborated in the Introduction. Nothing logically follows from espousing a make-believe.[108] For instance, if one make-believes A and if one make-believes B it does not follow that one also make-believes A *and* B. One is completely free to entertain all sorts of contradictory make-believes like imagining to be present at a place but without imagining any interaction with the people and objects present.

The Hold-Up of the Rocky Mountain Express illustrates this point quite well. At one moment the robbers have the train driver and his partner at gunpoint and one of the robbers starts running down the track directly towards the front of the train (Figure 2.5 c). If make-believes entailed other make-believes, then the spectator would be forced to imagine that the robber is going to do something with the spectator sitting there on the cowcatcher. The robber, however, simply runs below where the camera is placed paying no heed to the position where the spectator imagines herself. In other words, no interaction with diegetic characters follows from imagining oneself to be within the story-world.

What about the interior shots? Is the face-to-face version of the imagined seeing thesis applicable there as well or is a different imaginary regime in operation? It is worth noticing that although the edits in Hale's Tours do cut from shots of movement along the railroad to the shots of the interior, the cuts are not as disruptive as it might look like on first inspection. In other words, there is an argument to be made for retaining the film-internal imaginary position and simply imagining shifting from the cowcatcher to the interior of the car. In a number of Hale's Tours and *The Hold-Up of the Rocky Mountain Express* in particular there is a symmetrical relation that is retained across the shots. The first shot, for example, ends with a quite symmetrical composition in which the railroad track runs from the bottom to the centre along the middle of the image with trees and wooden fences flanking it on both sides (Figure 2.5 a). It is followed by an interior shot where the rug, much like the track, runs across the middle of the screen up to its centre and is flanked by two sets of seats on each side (one behind the other) with two men on the left (in black) and two women (and another behind them) on the right (all in white). On each side there is also a window along which a moving panorama unfolds (Figure 2.5 b). Similar form of symmetry is retained across shots 3 and 4 (Figures 2.5 c & d) and shots

4 and 5 where even an attempt at continuity editing is made (the robber exits shot 3 bottom middle and appears in shot 4 top middle and then finally returns outside in shot 5 from where he exited in shot 3). In the case of interior shots, we could even speak of an additional imaginary symmetry between the Hale's Tours venue (Figure 2.4) and the interior depicted with the screen as the axis of symmetry (Figures 2.5 b & d). If we compare the interior of the Hale's Tours car with the studio shots of the car interior, we can see that they are not that different and that it is possible to imagine that the two make up a single car where one section is facing the other.

Despite these symmetries, however, it is unlikely that comedy segments mandated anything like face-to-face imaginings. First, given that both patents and audience reports focus only on phantom ride segments as inviting imagining of this type we can take the absence of references to the interiors as negative evidence that no such imaginings were mandated in comedy segments. Second, catalogue entries for Hale's Tours films do provide some positive evidence *against* mandates for imagining oneself within the train car. The description of *Grand Hotel to Big Indian* (American Mutoscope and Biograph Company, 1906), for instance, states that '[a]fter a trip down the famous Horseshoe Loop from the Grand Hotel, on the Ulster and Delaware Railway, we show an interior comedy scene...'[109] Whereas there is an implication that the spectator is (supposed to imagine) taking a trip in the first part of the sentence, once it comes to the interior the scene is simply 'shown'. Any you-address is lost. Similarly, separate comedy films – *Deadwood Sleeper* (American Mutoscope and Biograph Company, 1905) and *Quick Lunch* (American Mutoscope and Biograph Company, 1904) – which were part of a Hale's Tours programme with other phantom rides are described in the following fashion:

> [*Deadwood Sleeper*] The greatest comedy picture available for use with any trip. Shows the interior of the sleeping car, with more uproarous [sic] merriment crowded into it than we can describe. Simply a 'corker' for this work. Ends with a burlesque train robbery.[110]
>
> [*Quick Lunch*] Good for use with any trip. A typical station restaurant showing the passengers rushing in, grabbing everything in sight, and mixing things up generally. very funny.[111]

As we can see, the catalogue descriptions do not address the spectator at all, let alone try to invite her to imagine anything about her positioning within what is depicted. This, as I have already mentioned, is in stark contrast with how the phantom ride segments are described in catalogues, patents and contemporary reviews alike. Therefore, there is good reason to conclude that face-to-face imaginings were mandated only for phantom ride segments of Hale's Tours.

Throughout Chapter 2 I have attempted to enrich our understanding of the contemporary experience of early (predominantly) visual immersion techniques. Much like early train films, for instance, I have argued for construing Hale's Tours as imaginary immersion techniques rather than as immersion techniques which produced cognitive illusions. Although some panoramas did fool viewers into believing that they were on site of what was depicted no moving pictures produced any such false beliefs. This chapter also articulated the difference in experiencing travelogues and scenics, on the one hand, and phantom rides and earliest water subjects, on the other. The former provided only visual information and this information, while often cited as superior to actual travel, invited no imagining (seeing or otherwise). The latter, by contrast, mandated spectators to imagine themselves both *seeing* the objects represented and seeing them from *within* the represented locale.

In doing this Chapter 2 further demonstrated how early cinema history can go a long way in resolving important questions regarding the principles of generation behind Walton's mandates. The chapter showed that answers to what precisely we are mandated to imagine cannot be arrived at by conceptual analysis alone. Not only because mandates can change over time but also because they might differ depending on the specific instance of visual fiction. The analysis of contemporary sources for Hale's Tours, early train films and other techniques of visual immersion gives ample evidence that some visual fictions mandated imagining seeing from *within* the represented site whereas others mandated imagining seeing the same *without determining* the spectator's position. In the case of motion pictures, specifically, the face-to-face version of the imagined seeing thesis was reserved for phantom rides. The modest version, by contrast, characterized early train films and the earliest films with water subjects. Moreover, we can take the comedy sections of Hale's Tours to be representative of the transitional narrative fiction cinema as far as imagined seeing is concerned and conclude that the face-to-face version is not in operation there.[112]

The discussion of imagined seeing also provides a bridge to another important question of both analytic philosophy and new film history – the existence/emergence of the filmic narrator or what, following Gregory Currie, I have called the controlling fictional narrator. As I mentioned in the Introduction this fictional agency is the agency we are mandated to imagine as presenting all the information that makes up the actual work. Whereas in literary fiction there are numerous cases which fit the bill (e.g. Charles Kinbote in Vladimir Nabokov's 1962 *Pale Fire*, the anonymous passenger on Captain Marlow's ship in Joseph Conrad's 1899 *Heart of Darkness*), identifying equivalents in fiction film has proved to be more elusive. On the example of early cinema André Gaudreault has, for instance, argued that *all* fiction films have a monstrator – a fictional agency which shows all the (audio)visual information.[113] In an influential proposal in analytic philosophy, George M. Wilson has further argued that controlling fictional narration is a direct consequence of imagined seeing, thereby bringing imagined seeing and fictional showing into immediate interdependence.[114] According to him, if the audience imagines seeing something then the audience also imagines somebody *showing* what is seen. In other words, if there is imagined seeing in cinema there must also be fictional showing. And if there is fictional showing then there must be a fictional narrator. In the last two chapters I will criticize these arguments and offer my own understanding of the birth of fictional narrators in early cinema. Before that, however, I wish to take up the lessons developed in this chapter and disentangle another set of oft conflated concepts – fiction and faking. To do so, I will turn to another early cinema genre which, much like Hale's Tours, is regularly discussed in relation to hybridity – fake or re-enactment.

3

Re-enactments in early cinema: Fake, fiction, fact

In the first two chapters I have attempted to distinguish imaginative engagement from other all-too-often conflated types of participatory experiences. On the example of the train effect, in Chapter 1 I have distinguished between taking evasive actions due to the perceptual illusion of the looming effect and the ones stimulated by mandated imaginings. There I have also emphasized the distinction between the act of make-believe typical of fictions and the feeling of disbelief elicited by magic performances. In Chapter 2 I have disentangled the oft-confused notions of imagination, illusion and immersion on the example of panoramas, phantom rides, travelogues and Hale's Tours. In the case of Hale's Tours, I have, contrary to the received wisdom, argued that extant reports are better described as evoking imaginative train travel than as citing false belief about taking a train ride. As such, I concluded, Hale's Tours are not hybrids of fiction and non-fiction but fictions through and through.

In this chapter I wish to explore yet another popular early film genre which is regularly discussed in terms of hybridity – re-enactment or fake – a genre which stages an event or refashions an existing film as a representation of the event in question. Given that at least since David Levy's article on reconstituted newsreels, re-enactments have been discussed in terms of 'two-way traffic across a weak ontological frontier', the genre gives an excellent opportunity to further elucidate the notion of fiction in relation to early cinema.[1] After reconstructing the historical understanding of fakes with recourse to contemporary sources, my main goal will be to dispel the idea of this genre as hybrid by arguing the following points. First, staging does not amount to fiction. Second, deliberate misrepresentation does not necessarily constitute fiction either. Third, early attempts at narrativization are not equivalent to attempts at fictionalization. Actuality, finally, cannot be defined in terms of indexicality. Faking, therefore, needs to be understood as a predominantly non-fictional film practice whose main problem was that it oftentimes deceived the customers, not that it sold fiction as fact. In other words, both staged representation and outright lie are different from fiction.

What is a fake?

As Frank Kessler reminds us in his elucidating discussion of the genre:

> Film historians ... ought to be very careful when using the term 'fake' and make sure they explicitly state what exactly they wish to refer to.[2]

Up to this point I have been using 're-enactment' and 'fake' interchangeably as a label for a genre that I am yet to outline more precisely but whose first approximation included the staging of actual events or the deliberate mislabelling of existing footage as depicting the event of interest rather than the direct recording of those same events. At first inspection, it might seem that this synonymous use is not the most felicitous because whereas 're-enactment' is neutral 'fake' carries a negative connotation of an intention to deceive. In other words, would it not be more fortunate to reserve 'fake' for a subclass of 're-enactment'? For, as Kessler continues:

> [F]rom the simple fact that an action was staged, one cannot deduce that it was meant to trick audiences into believing they see an authentic record of the event.[3]

Kessler also warns, however, against projecting one's own meaning to past usages. To understand the relationship between intentional deceit and staging in the production, promotion, exhibition and reception of fakes, therefore, it is best to heed his advice and look at how early cinema contemporaries understood the term 'fake'.

One early cinema genre in which fakes played a great role was war films. Driven by curiosity, nationalistic jingoism, imperial pride and the turn-of-the-century audiences were very eager to see moving pictures of various conflicts of the time including those of the Greco-Turkish War (1897), the Spanish-American War (1898), the Second Boer War (1899–1902), the Boxer Rebellion (1899–1901) and the Russo-Japanese War (1904–5).[4] When filmmakers failed to deliver for various reasons – such as war zone dangers, technological problems during shooting, the quality of the image, the non-photogenic nature of contemporary warfare due to the use of smokeless gun powder and the absence of face-to-face combat – fakers filled the demand by staging war films. Warning specifically of fake films about the Boer War, in 1900 'Mr. [Charles] Urban, the managing director of the Warwick Trading Company, Limited … [explained] … that the general understanding of a "fake" film is that of producing a film of a counterfeit representation of an actual event, such as has been practiced extensively with South African war subjects, many of which were made in the suburbs of London, besides France and New Jersey, U.S.A.'[5]

Appeals to diligence about fakes were not reserved for war films alone. We find some of the earliest writings on fakes already in 1897 in the US press in reference to fight films.[6] At the time, boxing had a precarious legal position in the States. Although pugilistic matches themselves were illegal, stage performances, filming and exhibition of the same were not.[7] In other words, the sport elicited great interest but enjoyed very limited spectatorship. Spotting a business opportunity one Dan A. Stuart signed two great heavyweights of the time – Robert Fitzsimmons and James Corbett – for a fight which he would record and distribute widely. In the two months that took Stuart to prepare his films for exhibition, however, another famous film pioneer – Siegmund Lubin – saw his own opportunity and decided to beat Stuart to the punch by re-enacting the fight for his own cameras and offering it to the public.[8]

Speaking of this Lubin's first re-enactment of a boxing match *San Francisco Examiner*, for instance, warned their readers not to fall for the sham and assured them that the genuine recording of the match, the one made by Stuart, is coming to town soon. Titling the article 'Fight Pictures That Are Fake', the journal also explained how a fake is made:

> 'The Examiner' received one of Stuart's telegrams, and Alf Ellinghouse, the well-known theatrical man, received another. In both wires the urgent request is made that the San Francisco public be warned of the attempt to foist 'fake imitations' of the championship fight pictures on it. The assurance is also given that the bona fide kinetoscope views will be in this city shortly, and that they will be introduced in such a manner as to leave no doubt as to their genuineness.
>
> The method of counterfeiting the battle of the champions is simple enough when it is explained. According to Ellinghouse some enterprising Eastern schemers [Lubin] made a careful search through the ranks of the unemployed pugilists until two men bearing reasonable resemblance to Fitzsimmons and Corbett were found. The rest was comparatively easy. One of the impersonators was fitted out with 'a bald wig', the other with a pompadour, and their faces were made up so as to give them as near the appearance of the originals as possible.[9]

As we see the goal of the fake so construed is to present the recording of a staged event as the recording of the actual event. In this case, this is done by staging the event with actors matching the physiques of the spectators as closely as possible. In the case of fake war films, one had to keep an eye on the terrain, military outfits and the like.

Calls for vigilance of the above sort were not without foundation because some producers deliberately muddled the waters and misled their customers if not outright lied when advertising their films. Lubin was in the former camp for he never explicitly claimed that he is in possession of a genuine recording of the match. In fact, he advertised the film as *Corbett and Fitzsimmons Films, in Counterpart of The Great Fight* rather than simply calling it *Corbett and Fitzsimmons*.[10] Albeit in small print, he also used terms such as 'reproduced' and 'fac-simile' which suggested, to anybody who was attentive enough, that this was not a direct recording of the bout.[11] Stuart, however, was far from impressed and started campaigning against Lubin's fake of the Fitzsimmons-Corbett fight and threatening legal action.[12] Lubin responded by putting up ads emphasizing that his films have been copyrighted.[13] This was still not a lie but by focusing on the copyright issues he played footsie and implied that his films were genuine, after all. Only those familiar with the copyright law of the time, however, would have understood that holding a copyright on a film did not mean much beyond vouching that the film in question is not a duplicate of some other copyrighted film – in this case Stuart's recording of the actual match.[14]

On other occasions Lubin was even bolder. In 1898 following another heavyweight bout – the Corbett-Sharkey match – Lubin cited Corbett's trainer in his ads as saying: 'I had the pleasure of seeing your Life Motion Picture of the late Corbett and Sharkey fight, and judge my surprise when I recognized myself jumping into the ring just as it occurred.'[15] Although 'fac-simile' and 'reproduced' are there in fine print again, it is strongly implied that Corbett's trainer recognized himself because Lubin's film allegedly recorded the actual fight. Another strategy involved the speed with which Lubin made his fight films available: 'OUR REPRODUCTION OF THE McGOVERN-DIXON FIGHT WAS READY THE DAY AFTER THE FIGHT TOOK PLACE. DON'T BE A CLAM and buy pictures of a fight which are made four weeks after the fight took place and called original. Which is the fake, the one SHOWN the day after the fight or the one MADE four weeks after?'[16] Such strategies clearly demonstrate the intention to present the films in question as genuine, without ever making the explicit claim that they were direct recordings of the event.

The advertising of a war film exemplifies an even daring misleading strategy bordering on a straightforward lie. The ad for an episode from the Spanish-American War – *Bombardment of Matanzas* (Edward H. Amet, 1898) – all but explicitly states that the recording was taken on location near Matanzas, Cuba at the time of the American navy's shelling of Spanish positions:

> The new TELESCOPIC LENS is a triumph of modern photography. It is possible to obtain accurate pictures at very long range. This is a most marvelous picture. In the distance can be seen the mountains and shore line where are located the Spanish batteries. The flag ship New York and monitor Puritan are in full action pouring tons of iron and steel at the masked batteries on the shore. Volumes of smoke burst from the monster guns, while shot and shell fall thick and fast. Some shells are seen to burst in the air, scattering their deadly missiles in all directions, while others explode in the sea, throwing volumes of water in the air. A final shot from one of the thirteen inch guns of the Puritan lands exactly in the centre of the main battery, completely blowing it out of existence. 600 feet of this engagement was taken and it has been cut down to 100 feet, using only the best and most interesting parts.[17]

It is well known, however, that Amet staged the film using scale models (Figure 3.1).[18]

Contrary to these deceitful strategies there were film producers who tried to be as forthcoming as possible that their films are not genuine. The 1903 Pathé catalogue disclaimer for their 'Historical, Political and Topical Events: Military Scenes' which include 'Episodes of the Transvaal War' states the following:

Figure 3.1 Still from *Bombardment of Matanzas* (Edward H. Amet, 1898).

> We always endeavor to reproduce each event which may interest our customers as it occurs, and with the greatest possible accuracy.
>
> For this purpose, as soon as anything takes place, our operator is at once sent to photograph the scene, whenever that is possible.
>
> We cannot however guarantee that all the views in this series are authentic on account of the many difficulties that arise in taking photographs on the spot.
>
> To supply this want and to keep up to date, we have done our best to reproduce these scenes as near as possible.[19]

Some producers were even more explicit. In its 1900 catalogue, the American Vitagraph Company insisted that all their fake films will be labelled as such:

> Although many of the Boer War Films are taken under trying circumstances, the photography is generally excellent. However, the intense heat of the South African climate and the fine dust which hangs in the air for hours, has in some few instances caused a slight dimness in parts of the views, but this is more than compensated for by the fact that every picture is **absolutely genuine. We will on no condition sell Faked or Pre-arranged War Subjects** unless announced as such, like the following.[20]

Proceeding to cite altogether five such films, the catalogue even divulges their filming location: 'The above five views ... were specifically posed for at an open-air Military Tournament in England by British Infantry and Cavalrymen ...'[21]

Even Lubin, whose initial advertising strategy for his boxing re-enactments deliberately obfuscated the fact that his films were *not* direct recordings of the matches, on some later occasions extensively marketed his fighting films as re-enactments. In 1900, only a few days after another highly publicized boxing fight – the Fitzsimmons-Ruhlin bout – Lubin invited the members of the press to his office in Philadelphia to witness the recording of the re-enactment on his rooftop studio:

> Robert Fitzsimmons and Gus Ruhlin, the principals in Friday night's heavyweight battle in Madison Square Garden; Charley White, referee of the fight; William Madden, manager of Ruhlin, and the seconds of Ruhlin and Fitzsimmons will all be in Philadelphia today to pose for 'fight' pictures.
>
> These men will go to the studio of S. Lubin, photographer of moving pictures, where they will reproduce as nearly as possible Friday's night fight.[22]

Regardless of the transparency and the fact that the actual fighters re-staged their own match, the press remained sceptical and continued calling even such re-enactments fakes. The same article continued: 'The moving pictures thus obtained will be sent all over the country and probably advertised as having been taken at the ring-side.'[23] Although adding the qualifier 'honest', another journal still described the film as a 'fake': '[Fitzsimmons and Ruhlin] were here to enact the scenes of their fight before the camera, so that the public that did not have the chance to see them in the real thing might have the pleasure of looking at an honest fake of the fight.'[24] Complaining about the continuing practice of faking, finally, *Optical Lantern and Kinematograph Journal* argued that the best strategy in promoting such motion pictures is to avoid any deceit. But even for such cases they retained the label 'fake': 'A far wiser plan [than attempting to pass them off as genuine], in our opinion, would have been to make no pretence about reality, show the films as faked and introduce incidents which would be impossible in a genuine picture.'[25]

We can see then that contemporaries understood re-enactments as 'fakes' irrespective of whether the recordings were billed as genuine or not and regardless of whether the films were re-enacted with people who participated in the original event or not. This would seem to make our present use of the term 're-enactment' synonymous with 'fake'. However, it turns out that fake was an even wider category than re-enactment for it included the practice of re-labelling as well.

A British trade journal, for instance, reported how an old fire subject film was re-labelled and sold as new and depicting the Great 1906 San Francisco Earthquake: 'One firm has raked up some fire or another from the dust heap of almost forgotten things, and with perfect *sang-froid* offers it as representing the appalling catastrophe at San Francisco.'[26] What gave the film away as a fake is that it showed firemen at work despite the common knowledge that the quake destroyed the water mains making firefighting impossible.

Up until now I have only discussed the possibility that the filmmakers and distributors deliberately deceived the exhibitors to whom they sold films and the spectators to whom the film was shown. But the exhibitors could also deceive their audiences independently from whatever the producers and distributors did. Stephen Bottomore, for instance, reports a confession of an itinerant Lumière cameraman Francis Doublier who in Russia in 1898 deliberately misrepresented stock footage on hand as genuine shots of Alfred Dreyfus and his jailing on Devil Island.[27] Doublier stopped showing the films only after an audience member objected that the events in question took place in 1894, a year before the Lumière Cinematograph was invented. Another example comes from Germany in 1897 where the same film from the Greco-Turkish War was first presented as *Execution of a Turkish Spy/Erschiessen eines türkischen Spions* and a few months later as *Execution of a Greek Spy/Erschiessen eines griechischen Spions*.[28]

For the contemporaries, then, fakes included both re-enactment and re-labelling. They were a part of different genres: fight films, war films and topical subjects being the most notable ones. Producers, distributors and exhibitors alike faked pictures. In the era of 'fake news' Kessler's advice not to project our own understanding of the fake to past is, therefore, extremely well placed. There is, however, a space for improvement even on Kessler's understanding of the term.

Although Kessler includes both re-enactment and re-labelling among fake films, it seems that the category of fake for contemporaries was potentially even wider than that for trick films sometimes appear to be treated as fakes. In 1900 a notable trade press journal discussed trick films under the heading of 'Fake Cinematograph Pictures' stressing that 'almost any impossible feats can be seen by the use of fake films'.[29] In the next issue the journal appeared to publish a correction in which, prompted by Charles Urban, they admitted that such films are better understood as trick films.[30] But even so the title of the correction remains confusing insofar it uses a disjunction instead of a negation: 'Fake or Trick Cinematograph Pictures'. Moreover, it is unclear that the matter was as unambiguous as Urban makes it to be for there are other reports which interchange trick photography and faking.

One such case concerns the Miles brothers' direct recording of a boxing match between Oscar 'Battling' Nelson and Joe Gans won by Gans – *Gans-Nelson Contest, Goldfield, Nevada, September 3, 1906*. Despite winning the bout because of a Nelson's foul punch under the belt, Gans was not pleased with the film and felt it did not give a representative view of the fight. He repeatedly claimed the film had been 'doctored' in the sense that Nelson's camp modified the actual recording.[31] Nelson's camp responded that 'films are 11,770 feet in length, and contain 180,000 separate photographs ... and it would be impossible to change the films to their own satisfaction even if such a thing were contemplated'.[32] Both are clearly talking about manipulating the frames of direct recordings in same way – essentially doing trick photography. But on at least one occasion this was described as faking:

> Mr. M. C. Coyne, manager of the company showing the pictures here [Fairmont, West Virginia], when questioned about the statement that Joe Gans made to the effect that the pictures were 'doctored' in Nelson's favor, said 'What have we to

gain by "doctoring" or "faking" our pictures, from a business point of view, what difference does it make who had the better of the fight?'[33]

What this demonstrates is that there was some sliding between the notions of doctoring and faking which should not surprise us because doctored photographs were also known as fake photographs at the time.[34] Given that film was a photographic medium back then, it is understandable why some would occasionally call films capitalizing on trick photography fakes.

Another development of Kessler's account of the category pertains to his attempt to distinguish between present and past usages of the term. He gives an example of a German journalist Michael Born who in the 1990s sold staged footage of spectacular non-existent events including, among other things, Kurdish terrorist plots and Ku-Klux-Klan meetings in Germany as actual undercover recordings to a German television channel.[35] To Kessler's mind this is not the type of fakery that characterized film production around 1900. This claim, however, appears to be belied already by some of the earliest fakes.

In 1897 Georges Méliès made four fakes of the Greco-Turkish War including *Mohammedan Inhabitants of Crete Massacring Christian Greeks/Massacres en Crète*.[36] The film is not extant, but according to contemporary reports it depicted Turks and their Albanian allies entering a cottage, dragging a young Greek girl out and decapitating her father. It is undeniable that massacres happened during the war, but this specific beheading appears particularly spectacular and without a clear real-life model. As such, the example is closer to Born's sensational presentation of non-existent events as actual than to re-enactments based on real-life events such as James Williamson's *Attack on a China Mission* (1900).[37]

If this example leaves some doubt, consider the following ad by the Selig Polyscope Company for *Tracked by Bloodhounds* (1904):

THE MOST SENSATIONAL FILM EVER MADE

Tracked by Bloodhounds

Or

A Lynching at Cripple Creek

NEGATIVE ACTUALLY MADE AT COLORADO'S GREAT GOLD CAMP AND OF ACTUAL OCCURRENCE

This is one of the most sensational pictures ever made. Our photographer was in Cripple Creek ready for business when the exciting events occurred. The negative was made in the great gold camp. Dozens of prominent miners and citizens who have since been involved in deportation troubles can easily be recognized in the pictures.

This subject is one of the sensational money-makers. The advertising Cripple Creek has had during the past few months will make the people extremely anxious to see a picture actually made in the Cripple Creek district.[38]

The catalogue description goes on to outline the story in twelve scenes which revolves around a tramp coming to Cripple Creek, strangling a woman to death, being pursued by the titular bloodhounds, and finally getting caught and lynched. The lynching in Scene XI is described thusly:

The captured tramp is rushed up the side of the hill and to the tree. He is hastily arranged for hanging. The rope is thrown over the limb of a tree, where it is caught on the other side by willing hands and strung up with a howling mob of bloodthirsty miners and cowboys surrounding him. Before life is extinct bullets from their revolvers pierce the body.[39]

It is undeniable that lynchings in the late nineteenth- and early twentieth-century United States were not at all uncommon. The practice of photographing actual lynchings as they occurred and even using these photographs as postcards is well documented.[40] Therefore, it is not impossible that there exist genuine film recordings of lynchings from that time.[41] In this particular film, however, we can be certain that the advertised lynching was not of 'actual occurence'.

Cripple Creek that Selig Polyscope Company's catalogue continuously refers to was a mining district in Colorado and one of the centres of union labour strikes in the United States at the beginning of the twentieth century. The district came into national spotlight on 6 June 1904, when an explosion shook the district's Independence depot killing a number of non-union strike breakers.[42] The business-friendly forces supported by the Colorado National Guard immediately started deporting union members – the troubles mentioned in the ad. The locals' intention to lynch the perpetrators assumed to be union workers was reported from coast to coast.[43] There were also reports of titular bloodhounds used to track down those suspected of planting the dynamite.[44] No lynching, however, took place at Cripple Creek.[45] The closest was a threat of lynching to a local sheriff who resigned to save his life (Figure 3.2).[46] And finally, there was no murderous tramp either.

Selig Polyscope Company clearly tried to capitalize on the highly publicized unrests at Cripple Creek. The all-too-common practice of lynching in general and the widely reported threats of lynching and the use of bloodhounds in particular, allowed for a plausible promotion of the film as a direct recording of an extra-legal

Figure 3.2 Colorado National Guard soldiers threaten the local sheriff with lynching.

execution. This tactic, however, is belied by the fact that not only was there no crime at the time involving a tramp and a miner's wife but also that despite the threats there were no lynchings relating to labour unrests either. Clearly then, we are dealing with a presentation of a non-existent event as actually occurring on par with Born's sensationalist 'documentaries' almost a century later. In this sense we could say that fakes also included visual implementations of what we nowadays refer to as 'fake news' – deliberate propagation of fabricated stories. In other words, some fakes were visual enactments of fabricated events where not only the events were presented as factual but also their visual enactments were advertised as direct recordings of those non-existent events.

The last standard question that remains in the attempt to reconstruct the historical understanding of fakes is whether or not the spectators were ever fooled into believing the producers', distributors' and exhibitors' deceitful claims. Views on the matter diverge. Kessler remains relatively agnostic by claiming that catalogues and specialized trade press accounts will not yield desired answers.[47] For the historian of fight films Dan Streible the question is important only for the boxing aficionados and not the general audience.[48] Bottomore includes contemporary reviews to argue that fakes posed a significant problem for contemporaries leaving them fooled on more than one occasion.[49] Film historian Kristen Whissel, finally, has claimed that the audiences discriminated between fakes and actualities perfectly well.[50]

Whissel focuses on war fakes and bases her claims on a couple of related points. The familiarity of the audiences with highly popular stage re-enactments such as 'Buffalo Bill's Wild West' which staged, among other things, battles with Native Americans and preceded cinema would have helped film audiences discern actualities from fakes. The key feature of battle re-enactments – on stage and screen alike – was the ideal positioning of the spectator at the event itself. Once the spectators recognized that the camera is positioned in the middle of the battle it would be easy to perceive such positioning as implausible were it a direct recording of the skirmish. In other words, the film would be immediately recognized as fake. To substantiate this, finally, Whissel cites a contemporary review which makes the very same point.[51]

Bottomore does not deny that plausibility of the camera position served as the main criterion for distinguishing between war fakes and actualities. In fact, he cites a number of contemporary sources which specifically give advice on how to spot a fake along those lines.[52] One example reads:

> You see, you can't take a picture of a battle without getting into the thick of it, – the range of the cinematograph is not large, – and if an enemy saw you turning the handle of a machine on three legs, pointing a long muzzle at them, they, being wholly illogical and unscientific, might conclude that you were practising [sic] with some new kind of Maxim and smokeless powder. The chances that you would be alive to take the pictures back to an admiring British audience would not be hopeful.[53]

But Bottomore emphasizes the point, and rightly so, that the recurrent advice on how to spot a fake must have meant that there were occasions when people were fooled. In fact, he also identifies several such instances. As was already mentioned, it took some time for the spectators to realize that Doublier's films could not have been direct recordings of Dreyfus.[54] Another example concerns a correspondent who wrote to a trade press journal inquiring how to identify a fake: 'A correspondent asks us how he is to know real from sham war films, seeing that several subjects are made at home from life models.'[55] Yet another relates to a certain E. Anderson who wrote to the same journal seemingly believing that he saw a direct recording of the attack on China mission. The journal offered a correction:

> We have received the circular which you enclosed and note that you think it wonderful that some cinematographic artists should be on hand to photograph the attack on a Chinese mission house or station. You appear to take matters too seriously, for the whole thing is a fake picture – a sort of pantomime scene enacted in this country with scenic backgrounds.[56]

We can add to this an example which demonstrates that what might be completely obvious to one person fails to register with another:

> How any person can believe that a motion-picture outfit can be taken on a battlefield and worked directly in front of a lot of riflemen firing directly at the camera, I don't see; but you hear 'Oh!' and 'Ah!' 'Weren't those men *brave*, George, who took that picture at San Juan Hill?' etc., etc., all over theatre when those interesting but fraudulent pictures are being shown.[57]

Whereas the plausibility of the camera position was regularly cited as a litmus test for fake war films, the poor quality of imitation would on most occasions give fake fight films away. During one screening of Lubin's re-enactment of the Corbett-Fitzsimmons match, for instance, the film was immediately recognized as a fake because the protagonists barely resembled the fighters:

> After a delay of several minutes, which seemed hours to the small boy in the gallery, the longlooked for light appeared on the curtain, and on walked three men, who completely filled the space. The audience saw that the picture was a fake in an instant. One of the men wore a wig – plainly visible – imitating Fitzsimmons' bald pate, and the other was made up, pompadour and all, to represent 'Gentleman Jim'.[58]

The fact that this audience felt cheated and successfully demanded their money back also suggests that Streible overstates his case when claiming that 'distinguishing the vile fake from the true document [as an] … evaluative schema was not yet the norm'.[59] For this was not a unique occurrence. The crowd gathered to see the same fight in Canton, South Dakota, was not pleased either:

> The machine performed its duties in a passable manner, but the record of the Corbett-Fitzsimmons fight was a fake pure and simple, it not being a likeness of either one of the men of pugilistic fame that was portrayed on the canvass. It seems that Manager Shaff lets most any old show have the hall, and it will not be long before it will be a difficult task to secure any kind of a Canton audience.[60]

The same can be said of spectators in Jacksonville, Florida, who, spotting a different type of deceit, also demanded their money back:

> [W]hen the fourth round [of the Corbett-Fitzsimmons fight] was announced the same film used in the first and second rounds was used … 'Gin me fo'teen rounds or gimme twenty-five cent!' was the exclamation at this juncture.[61]

It is undeniable that some audiences were more willing to accommodate fakes than others. But even here, the matter seems to have revolved around whether the advertising was clear enough or not:

> An audience that numbered about 2,000 people went to Mozart Park last night to see [Lubin's] Cineograph reproduction of the Corbett-Fitzsimmons fight at Carson. … The audience was rather boisterous at times, and sentiment was divided as to the merit of the production. As it was not advertised as the original Verascope [sic] production, the cry of 'fake' raised by some is uncalled for.[62]

Those who thought the advertising too ambiguous, as we have learnt was often the case when fakes first appeared, felt short-changed.

The same normative concern for the film's potential status as a fake holds for instances when in the absence of the direct recording, as was the case when lighting failure stopped the shooting of the 1899 Fitzsimmons-Jeffries bout, the fake was a useful means of illustration:

> When it is realized that no pictures of the Jeffries-Fitzsimmons fight were taken, the above information becomes truly exciting. The pictures in question are pure fakes. Billy Leedom, in a red wig poses as Fitzsimmons, while Jack McCormick tries to act as Jeffries did.[63]

In other words, it was not only boxing aficionados who were worried about fakes – the matter was important to the public at large. Or, put in yet another way, a direct recording of a boxing match was preferable to a fake as soon as fakes started appearing. In fact, sometimes the concern went as far as to colour the reception of genuine films. More than one report of a screening of the already mentioned lightweight championship match between Nelson and Gans claimed that the films were fake:

> The pictures of the Battling Nelson-Joe Gans fight, shown for the first time in this city at the New York Theater Roof last night, are somewhat of a disappointment, to put it mildly.
>
> In the first place, they are not good clear pictures; in the second place only twenty-six of the forty-two rounds are given – the first twenty and the last six rounds – and, what's more, the last six rounds are so unlike the rest of the fight in environment and action that there is a strong smell, as of cheese burning, noticeable even from the films.
>
> In plain English, we are compelled to the belief that these final six rounds are especially posed and not the real result of the battle.[64]

It is likely, however, that the reporter is mistaken. The reason the film was shorter is because the filmmakers – the Miles brothers – edited the forty-two round long film to a manageable size.[65] The fact that the fight lasted so long also meant that the lighting conditions were deteriorating as the match progressed.[66] By the time of last rounds, the lighting would have been so bad to explain why 'the last six rounds are so unlike the rest of the fight', especially if there was a sharp transition from the twentieth to the thirty-seventh round.[67] Interestingly then, the category of fake was of such importance that the concern for failing to spot a fake occasionally led audiences to report genuine films as fakes. This was not lost on the contemporaries either:

> [W]e have recently seen a number of subjects, purporting to be records of real events, but palpably fakes, in which the aim of the makers has been to conceal their nature. … excesses in the past have led to an excess of incredulity to-day, and many a genuine subject is regarded as a 'stage managed' one.[68]

Finally, there is also good reason to believe that the obverse failures of discrimination on par with those reported for fake war films – confusing fakes for direct recordings of events – took place in the case of fake fight films as well. The above film by Miles brothers was also cited as a fight film which is likely to cause epistemic problems for at least one group of viewers: 'the ladies who prefer to see the prize fight on canvas instead of at the ringside … will not know whether the end of the fight is faked in the picture or not'.[69] The remark is undoubtedly sexist because, among other things, it misrepresents patriarchal norms precluding women from attending live bouts as female preferences. But it still allows us to extract the articulation of the litmus test for spotting fake fight films – a level of familiarity with live matches. Its non-sexist version can be found already in the commentaries of the Fitzsimmons-Jeffries fight that Streible himself cites:

> [U]nfortunately there are thousands of people who did not see the actual fight, and who, for that matter, never saw either of the fighters, and it is upon the credulity of these unfortunates that the promoters of the 'fake' pictures depend for the success of their questionable scheme.[70]

Some commentators went even further by claiming that even people familiar with the actual ringside matches could be fooled.

> Whether the pictures were those of the originals or only substitutes requires an expert's eagle eye for the mill is so clever and so much like the original that the average person would be inclined to think the Fitzsimmons and Jeffries really were pictured.[71]

That distinguishing fakes and direct recordings was of no small importance to the contemporaries is also in line with the fact that genuine films were generally preferable to fakes all things being equal. If this is the evaluative preference, then it makes sense that ads would internalize the evaluative criterion and either obfuscate the promotional message in the hope of increasing sales or come clean beforehand to pre-empt any criticism concerning fakery. We have seen both strategies on the preceding pages. And we have also seen that the spectators oftentimes demanded their money back upon discovering false advertising.

Although the above preference was a general rule, Bottomore reminds us that occasionally fakes were preferred to direct recordings. The same year that Méliès made the first war fakes, the war correspondent Frederic Villiers made the first genuine war films on location. One would think that the first war pictures ever taken would have caused a sensation but Bottomore has demonstrated that whereas Villiers's films had only enjoyed a limited run in the UK, Méliès's fakes were distributed all around the world.[72] Unlike Méliès's war films, none of Villiers's survives so we cannot be exactly sure why Méliès's were much more successful. Some of the possible reasons include the potential poor quality of Villiers's films and their relative uneventfulness when compared to action-packed Méliès's offerings.

We see then that when a plethora of contemporary records is examined – trade press, catalogues, ads, newspaper reports, recollections, memoirs and the like – it is possible to glean a relatively clear picture of both the understanding and the reception of fakes. Contemporaries understood fakes to include re-enactments of events that took place, stagings of non-existent events, re-labelling of existing footage and on occasions even trick films.[73] Regardless of the intentions of the filmmakers and exhibitors to deceive or not such films were regularly labelled as fakes. Although generally direct recordings were preferable to fakes, there were occasions when fakes overshadowed genuine films in popularity. Moreover, many fakes were, undoubtedly, immediately spotted as fakes because of their quality of impersonation or the implausible camera positioning. But some managed to fool their audiences. And determining whether something was a fake or not was no academic matter reserved for a small number of spectators with special interests but of importance for the public at large. In fact, spotting a fake constituted such an epistemic concern that it could lead to overcorrections – misidentification of genuine films as fakes.

Fakes, indexicality and fictionality

Having outlined how contemporaries produced, advertised, exhibited and understood fakes, it is worth inspecting the recurrent conflations that nowadays take place in the scholarship on fakes. These concern how staging, deception, narrative and indexicality are related to fiction.

We have learnt that all other things being equal, genuine films were preferred to fakes. In other words, fakes had an advantage only when no direct recording of the event existed, was of low quality or when such a recording was particularly uneventful. The term 'fake' already articulates why in general the audiences favoured genuine recordings – fakes are not the real thing. But a genuine recording is not the real thing either in the sense that it is not the thing that it represents. It is only a recording of that thing. The question, therefore, comes down to why prefer one representation over the other. Among film historians who have tried to explain this general favouritism of genuine films, the notion of indexicality often does the heavy lifting. Bottomore, for instance, claims:

> [E]arly producers and showmen, in making a selection of actuality films to represent a war, would try to commission or select shots which had some kind of indexical connection with the events.[74]

Re-enactments, by contrast, also 'had a "connection" to the war, but it was a different kind of connection, of an "iconic" or "symbolic" kind'.[75]

Since Peter Wollen's reading of C. S. Peirce in the late 1960s, film scholars have regularly used one of Peirce's trichotomies of signs to distinguish analogue photographs from hand-made visual representations such as paintings and drawings.[76] In this trichotomy, signs can be icons, indices or symbols. Icons represent by way of similarity – a drawing of a dog is an icon of that dog because it resembles the animal. The word 'dog' is a symbol because the connection between the word and its referent is arbitrary. Depending on the language, words as different as 'Hund', 'canis' or 'pas', represent the same thing by convention. Dog's pawprint, finally, is an index because there is a direct existential link between the dog and the pattern in the sand. Under this model photographs are generally icons – a photograph of a dog will usually resemble the dog. But what is more important is that photographs are indices because, to it put in Wollen's terms, they signify 'by virtue of an existential bond' between themselves and their objects.[77]

Within this framework, indexicality describes the special ontological relationship between the representation and its object. The reason genuine films are preferred over fakes for Bottomore, then, is because the latter lack that special ontological link. He does not mean that fakes are not indices at all – they are undoubtedly indices of whatever is in front of the camera. But, according to Bottomore they are not indices of the event in question. So, for instance, although the *Battle of Matanzas* is both an icon and an index of the model ships used in staging the battle, Amet's film is only an icon of the shelling. The problem with this account, however, is twofold. First, Peirce's indexicality is a broader concept from how it is usually construed in film studies and, therefore, not a good description for the special relationship said to obtain in genuine films. Second, indexicality in the narrower sense amounts to a direct causal link and, therefore, applies to at most photographic negatives.

Peirce's definition of indices certainly includes signs which, like photographs, are automatic causal outcomes of what they represent – for example, an instrument for measuring humidity or a medical symptom. But it also includes proper names:

> I define an Index as a sign determined by its dynamic object by virtue of being in a real relation to it. Such is a Proper Name (a legisign); such is the occurrence of a symptom of a disease.[78]

Film scholars, however, have either missed or neglected this passage in Peirce. For them a proper name like 'Theresa May' is a typical example of a symbol. It is only because the former UK prime minister was named Theresa by her parents that we use this specific name to refer to her. There is no relation between how the name sounds or how its graphic form looks like to who Theresa May is. Her parents could have easily named her Margaret.

But in Peirce's understanding the class of index comprises even more than automatic causal effects and proper names. Some hand-made visual representations also make the cut. Consider the following clarification of his definition:

> An *index* is a representamen which fulfils the function of a representamen by virtue of a character which it could not have if its object did not exist, but which it will continue to have just the same whether it be interpreted as a representamen or not. For instance, an old-fashioned hygrometer is an *index*. For it is so contrived as to have a physical reaction with dryness and moisture in the air, so that the little man will come out if it is wet, and this would happen just the same if the use of the instrument should be entirely forgotten, so that it ceased actually to convey any information.[79]

We have already learnt that the index guarantees the existence of an object it represents. The existential connection is based on the causal connection between the index and its object rather than on an automatic causal connection. There is a causal link between a proper name and a person as much as there is one between the little man in the hygrometer and humidity. But it is only in the latter that the causal connection is automatic.

If the sufficient condition of indexicality is to guarantee the existence of the represented object, then hand-made visual representations of objects made with those objects as models also count as indices. If I paint a dog while looking at that dog, there is a casual link between the painting and the dog. Because of this connection the painting guarantees that there is a dog who served as the model. It is true that just by looking at the painting we cannot tell if it was made with an actual dog as a model. But the same is true of a photograph. A photograph could be made by exposing a square millimetre at a time in such a way that the final outcome has the appearance of a dog without there ever being a dog in front of the camera. What is important is only whether there is a link between the sign and its object – not whether we can reconstruct the link. Peirce's explanation that even if we lost the ability to reconstruct the casual link between the little man in the old hygrometer and humidity the appearance of the little man will still count as an index, makes this point clear.

The response might be that it does not matter if Peirce's original account of indexicality does not allow for distinguishing between painting and photographs or even photographs and some words for that matter. Wollen was relating indexicality to André Bazin's idea of automatic reproduction and moulding by light so we should focus on Wollen's understanding rather than Peirce's.[80] In this narrower understanding of indexicality typical of film studies, the index is produced automatically by direct contact with its object.[81] When a dog's paw touches the sand a pawprint is made. An analogue photograph, similarly, is made by light coming from the model and reaching the photosensitive emulsion. The light from the object literally touches the photograph. By this logic the image that was fixed in Villiers's films bore a direct link to war events reproduced. Méliès's war films only bear a direct link to the studio set and the actors on it.

Unfortunately, this account does not work either. It is true that in recording analogue film the light coming from the object reaches the photosensitive emulsion and instigates the photochemical reaction which gives rise to the image. But this holds only for the negative. The audiences would have hardly ever seen a negative – rather, what was screened in early cinema exhibition venues were copies of that original print, at least one step removed from the original. The copies themselves are produced by photographic printing where light is shone through the original onto the new film strip. The crucial point to note here is that the light that ends up on the new film strip and produces the image that is the copy is the new light – not the light coming from the original object. The direct contact between the object and the image the audiences saw, in other words, is lost. Or put in yet another way, indexicality understood narrowly as the relationship in which the index and its object were in direct contact at one point in time obtains only for initial photographic products such as negatives.

In fact, scholars invested in the notion of indexicality for explaining the preference for genuine film are faced with an additional problem. The direct contact obtains only for negatives of light-emitting objects such as stars, fire or bioluminescent beings. Standard objects of early cinema recordings covered in this chapter such as military personnel or boxers only *reflect* light – they do not emit their own light. If somebody sprayed water on my car and I got wet in the process because some of that water bounced off the car soaking me, we would not say that I was in *direct* contact with the car. Although the water was in direct contact with both me and the car I was in direct contact only with the water. In this analogy, most objects of analogue photography and film behave like the car whereas light functions like the water. In most genuine war and boxing films the indexicality, therefore, does not even hold for negatives.[82]

How then do we distinguish between fakes and genuine films if both are representations and practically neither are indices in the narrow sense of what they represent? In the previous section I was using 'direct recording' interchangeably with 'genuine films'. But we have seen that this cannot mean direct contact. Instead, it can only mean that the negative was made at the time of the event on location with the event taking place in front of the camera. As one catalogue puts it: 'The "WARWICK" WAR AND FILMS OF TOPICAL EVENTS FROM ALL PARTS OF THE WORLD ARE TAKEN ON THE SPOT, and are not made on Hampstead Heath, New Jersey, France, or in somebody's back Garden.'[83] I am obviously not claiming that film historians are unaware of where and how genuine films were made. I am just proposing that using the theoretical framework of indexicality is helpful neither for delineating fakes from genuine recordings nor for explaining why the latter were preferred to the former. In other words, theorizing contemporary accounts here obfuscates far more than it elucidates.

Next to the problematic appeal to indexicality, film scholars are also quick to treat various features usually connected to fakes – staging, deception and narrative – in terms of fictionality. One commonplace, for instance, has been to conflate staging with fiction. Under this account any staging necessarily entails introduction of fictional elements into the film.

In the introduction to a widely cited volume on the intersections between narrative fiction and documentary filmmaking, for instance, the editors state the following:

For the authors in this collection, these intersections begin literally at the beginning of the cinema, blurring the lines between fact and fiction. *Blacksmith Scene* (1893), Edison and Dickson's first publicly exhibited film, purports to show exactly that: three blacksmiths working and enjoying a beer. But of course the men captured on film were not professional blacksmiths but Edison employees, and the film was staged and shot at the Edison laboratory. Examples of such fabrications continue famously through a series of the then-popular Spanish-American War films that used miniatures sets and model ships to recreate sea battles, which were vigorously marketed as authentic depictions.[84]

Another pair of notable film historians discusses fakes in the following fashion:

> The sophistication of audiences allowed film-makers to blend representations of 'real' people and situations with 'unreal' or fictional contexts. Audiences became adept at distinguishing between scenarios that had been elaborately staged for the benefit of the camera and films that depicted real events.[85]

Even as diligent an historian as Bottomore conflates staging and fiction when he writes:

> [W]hy did staged representations of war become such a common genre in early cinema? My answer was that they answered a need, which non-fiction could not meet, for a more dramatic representation of war.[86]

> [T]he films made by Villiers and Méliès seem to offer a strong contrast – a binary opposition, in the jargon – between the straight recording of war as pioneered by Villiers, and the unashamed faking/fictionalisation as practiced by Méliès.[87]

That something is staged, however, does not mean that it is fictional. In Chapter 1 I have argued that magic theatre performances test credulity rather than mandate imaginings.[88] Such performances are undoubtedly staged for they are prepared in advance in front of an audience on stage. Executions, similarly, be they legal or extra-legal, as we have learnt, were also often carefully pre-arranged events with the deed itself often taking place on a scaffold to provide as clear a view as possible for as many people as possible.[89] Consider a coronation or a royal wedding as another example where staging is understood somewhat more broadly to include highly choreographed events where there is a strict protocol guiding the partakers' behaviour but which do not take place on stage in a narrow sense. To argue with a straight face that such a staging makes the event fictional seems absurd. Whoever was invited to the royal wedding in St George's Chapel at Windsor Castle in 2018 did not make-believe Prince Harry and Meghan Markle walking down the aisle. Rather, they witnessed the couple exchanging vows and being pronounced man and wife. The same is true of, say, Queen Elizabeth II's coronation. Therefore, there are numerous events which are staged either on a literal stage or in some other venue that do not constitute fictions.

The objection might be that fakes stage something for the camera while the examples in the previous paragraph concern highly choreographed events which may but need not be recorded. But consider TV interviews as a counterexample to this rejoinder. The subject of the talk might not be rehearsed in advance but there is a significant amount of mise-en-scène work going into the production of a TV interview – lighting is set-up, the wardrobe is chosen, the make-up is applied, the studio is set and so on. It is hardly the case that interviews on *60 Minutes* or *HARDtalk* are fictions just because they are recorded on camera.

Perhaps the issue is that I have been misconstruing the notion of staging all along. I have been talking about events which involve a lot of stagecraft and preparation, be they for camera or not. The point of staging under this objection, however, is that fakes, at least of the re-enactment variety discussed in the above citations, stage in order to represent something else. TV interviews, coronations, royal weddings and so on do not represent some other event that has already taken place or is about to. Re-enactments, as the word clearly implies, enact something anew. Staging in such films produces a performance which stands for something else. The miniature sets and ship models in Amet's film and Lubin's staging of a boxing match represent an episode from the Spanish-American War and a famous championship match, respectively.

The answer to this retort is that staging so construed is essentially representation. But representation – that something stands for something else – is not necessarily fictional. The utterance 'Yesterday I took a train to the university' is a representation of how I go to work and one that does not mandate any imaginings. A recording of me embarking at my local train station, reading something for half an hour and disembarking at the station in the neighbouring city is the same. A comic strip of me doing the same is again a representation of my commute. None of these representations are fictional because they stand for my actual train ride, that is, they only ask the hearer/viewer/reader to believe that this is how I got to work yesterday.

This does not yet resolve the matter completely for representations in fakes are not just any representations but staged representations. Though representations need not be fictional I still need to demonstrate that *staged* representations are not necessarily fictional in the sense that I argued that photographic representations do not necessarily entail imaginings. To do this consider impressions.

An impressionist mimics the voices, the sounds and mannerisms of other people, most often celebrities and public personages. For the most part such performances are staged in front of the audience. A necessary condition for doing a minimally successful impression of a person, moreover, is the ability to convey the idea of who the impression of it is. In other words, one of the things that the impressionist is doing while performing is representing the person he or she is mimicking. A successful impressionist like Kevin Spacey will enthuse the audience by how exactly alike he sounds to Marlon Brando or how uncannily his gestures resemble those of Al Pacino. What strikes us in such a performance is how much like Brando Spacey sounds and behaves – their intonations, speech patterns, prosody, movements being virtually indistinguishable. There is no default mandate to make-believe that Kevin Spacey is Marlon Brando. Rather, the point is to appreciate the impressionist's vocal and mimicking skills in achieving his target's likeness.

There are, undoubtedly, impressions where in addition to being enthralled by the impressionist's skills we are also mandated to imagine the scenario played out. For instance, when on the TV-show *Saturday Night Live* Kate McKinnon impersonates Angela Merkel as being romantically infatuated with Barack Obama. There next to delighting in, say, how McKinnon's facial expressions resemble those of the German Chancellor we are also mandated to make-believe that the German Chancellor is trying to make the 44th President of the United States jealous. But this only means that impressions can be embedded within games of make-believe. It does not change the fact that there are some staged representations – namely impressions like Spacey's outlined above – which do not mandate imaginings on their own.

This was not lost on the contemporaries either. One British film production and distribution company's catalogue, for instance, describes a film of a famous impressionist of the time as follows:

IMPERSONATIONS BY HARRY TATE

This clever mimic impersonates six well-known favourites of the music-hall stage ... The make-ups, costumes, facial expressions and entire deportment are most faithful impersonations of the originals. When accompanied by suitable music the exhibition of this subject is most enthusiastically received by all audiences where these artists are known.[90]

As we can see, the ad does not in any way imply that the spectator should make-believe that Harry Tate is any of the 'six well-known favourites of the music-hall stage'. Rather, the audiences are to revel at how much alike in appearance and behaviour he is to all of them.

That the people appearing in boxing films standing in for the actual pugilists were often described as impersonators or imitators also did not lead the press to conclude that the matches were fictional. Instead, as the accounts of Lubin's reproduction of the Fitzsimmons-Corbett match cited in the previous section demonstrate, the recognition of such impersonators or imitators was one of the main criteria for identifying a fake. Another example reads:

> The views were decidedly on the fake order, being unrecognizable by people who are familiar with the ring and who know pictures of Corbett and Fitz. The first round was so tame that the lovers of the manly art could not restrain the disgust they felt at the palpable fakeness of the alleged representation.[91]

Moreover, what concerned the author of the cited text was precisely what we have identified as the key criterion for the success of impersonations and impressions – the likeness to the subject in question. The reporter concludes the piece with the following remark:

> The management of the machine represented the pictures to be a fac-simile of the Corbett-Fitzsimmons fight.
>
> The definition of the word fac-simile is 'An exact copy, or likeness,' etc.
>
> Was the exhibition last night an exact likeness of the fight, which took place at Carson on St. Patrick's day?[92]

Although the commentator does not provide an explicit answer, an implicit one can be found earlier in the text: 'The "fight" became such a farce that the audience left the theatre in a laughing disgust, as it were.'[93] Nobody failed to recognize that the two people on screen were representing Corbett and Fitzsimmons. And as soon as the screening started it was clear to the spectators that the two men appearing on the curtain were impersonators. But this did not lead the viewers to uncover any mandated imaginings. Rather, they saw the film for what it was – a recording of a staged impersonation of the match where the success hinges on its likeness to the actual match.

Yet another example of the meaning of 'staging' concerns deception. It is possible to stage an event and deceptively present it as real. Fakes included both films like *Bombardment of Matanzas* where deception revolved around the fact that the film was not a direct recording of the represented event and those like *Tracked by Bloodhounds* where events that never took place were deceptively presented as actually having occurred and been recorded. When staging is understood in this sense, present-day scholars again often make conflations – this time between deception and fiction. When talking about fakes, Jonathan Auerbach, holds, for instance:

> As with other faked actualities, many of these war scenes were openly advertised as 'counterfeit presentments,' and even if they weren't billed as such, their veracity or authenticity was less an issue than how thrilling they seemed. For both audience and makers, in other words, the quest for sensation tended to render the opposition between fact and fiction relatively moot.[94]

In a reference to Michael Born's practice of staging and selling fake documentaries, a notable film theorist uses the same contrast equating deception with fiction: 'a respected director of upwards of thirty programmes for Stern TV, was recently jailed for four years as a common criminal for having allegedly passed off fiction as fact'.[95]

But why would deception necessarily constitute fiction? As I have already argued in Chapter 2 on the example of one form of deception – illusion – deception is a matter of (false) belief rather than make-believe. In the specific cases of concern to us in this chapter, that an ad strongly suggests that the *Bombardment of Matanzas* was shot on location does not mandate a make-believe that Spanish position at Matanzas are shelled or that a camera recorded the naval battle on location. Instead, the ad instils a false belief that the film is a direct telescopic lens recording of the shelling. Similarly, the point of the catalogue description for *Tracked by Bloodhounds* is for the reader to falsely believe that a tramp was lynched in Cripple Creek. It is not to serve as a prop for make-believing the same. If successful, both types of texts will deceive the potential viewer into believing that she is witnessing a direct recording of an actual event. The already mentioned E. Anderson falsely believed that he was in the possession of a direct recording of the attack on a China mission. He did not treat the film as fictional. If, by contrast, the viewer sees through the deception in one way or another, she will not start treating the film as fictional either. Rather, she will recognize it as an especially affronting type of fake. During the heyday of fakes, as we have seen, the typical response was to hiss, jeer, demand one's money back and, on occasions, even to call the police.

The last conflation which makes a regular appearance in the discussion of early cinema that I wish to discuss here is that of narrative with fiction. A typical formulation reads:

> By placing film within the purview of narrative a purely iconic cinema was partially abandoned in favor of a visual discourse that encouraged a certain

connotative looseness in regards to the image. Within narrative cinema waves and trains could have additional, thematic and cultural meanings beyond their iconic value, and thus the introduction of narrative revealed a fundamental ambiguity implicit in the cinema: The tension between the photographic literalness of its mode of representation and the fabricated, invented, and often conventionalized view of the world found in its fictional elements and devices.[96]

In Chapters 1 and 2 I have argued that already outside of narrative cinema recorded trains and waves had 'additional, thematic and cultural meanings beyond their iconic value' – namely, for a few years they mandated imaginings about vehicles crashing into the auditorium and being transported to the beach, respectively. Furthermore, there is no reason to claim that the introduction of narrative into early cinema also entailed the introduction of fictional elements.

Consider, for instance, Edison Manufacturing Company's *Capture of Boer Battery by the British* (1900) – a fake shot in the Orange Mountains at New Jersey. The catalogue gives no hint that the film is staged so there is a good reason to believe that some deception was involved on the part of the producer. The camera position just behind the Boer lines, however, would reveal to those attentive enough that the film is a fake. So those who, on the one hand, were deceived by the film would have falsely believed that they witnessed a charged in the fashion of those exclaiming 'Oh!' and 'Ah!' cited above. Those who, on the other hand, recognized the film for what it was would have, depending on how the exhibitor presented the film, either used the film as an illustration of the war events or taken the exhibitor to task for false advertising. In neither case, however, would the film have mandated any imaginings.

But the role of deception is not what interests us here. It is primarily the relation of narrative structure to fiction in cinema that is of concern. Albeit minimal, there is a storyline to Edison's film: the British are attacking the Boer position, the Boer hold on for a while, but eventually are either killed off or run away. There is even closure: in the end the British capture the battery. The description of the film in narrative terms is not only mine but appears in the catalogue ad as well:

> Nothing can exceed the stubborn resistance shown by the Gordon Highlanders, as we see them steadily advancing in the face of a murderous fire of the Boers, who are making their guns speak with rapid volleys. One by one the gunners fall beside their guns, and as the smoke clears for an instant the Highlanders are seen gaining nearer and nearer the disputed ground. Finally, a grand charge is

made, the siege is carried, and amid cheers they plant the colors on the spot they have so dearly earned.[97]

In other words, the catalogue suggests that the film was intended to be understood as a brief story by the contemporaries. A story without individualized characters but a story nevertheless.

That something constitutes a story, however, does not mean that in engaging it we are mandated to imagine the story in question. My earlier statement 'Yesterday I took a train to the university' could be easily expanded into a short story: 'The train was late. I thought I will not make it to my appointment in time. But it was pushed back so I made it after all.' The story is far less exciting than the one conveyed by the Edison Manufacturing Company's film, but it is nevertheless a story. Moreover, there is no reason to treat my story as fictional in a normal context in which I am trying to convey what happened to me yesterday.

Visual stories also need not entail any mandated imaginings. Documentaries regularly tell stories, yet the audiences are not supposed to make-believe them. When watching the first episode of the first season of *Making a Murderer* (Laura Ricciardi and Moira Demos, 2015 –) we are not supposed to imagine that Steven Avery was jailed for a rape he did not commit – we are supposed to believe it. Similarly, when viewing *Citizenfour* (Laura Poitras, 2014) we are supposed to ask ourselves whether the film accurately depicts Edward Snowden's story as it unfolds and not to make-believe it. We see then that narrative representations – verbal and visual alike – need not be fictional.

We have previously concluded that staged representations need not be fictional either. What remains is to demonstrate that staged narrative representations also do not entail fiction. For this we can return to our example with impressions. If Kevin Spacey impersonated more than just a few lines or gestures and re-enacted an episode from Marlon Brando's life – say, him running up the aisle to accept his 1955 Oscar, getting a kiss from Bette Davis, saying a few words and leaving the stage with the statue in hand – we would have no reason to treat the impersonation as fiction. In the sense that Spacey's hypothetical impersonation is a staged narrative representation of a short event that has a beginning, a middle and an end, so is *Capture of a Boer Battery by the British* in a proper sense a staged narrative representation of a capture of a battery during the Transvaal War. The representation that is Edison Manufacturing Company's film may be lacking in likeness to what it represents when compared to Spacey's bravura performances. But there is no necessary link between the representation's likeness and whether the representation mandates imaginings or not. My brief verbal account of the capture of a Boer battery film or the catalogue ad are both much less alike to how an actual capture would have looked like than Edison Manufacturing Company's fake. Yet they all represent the capture and none of them mandates imaginings about the skirmish.

Fakes and imaginary participation

We have seen that the features often characteristic of fakes – staging, deception and narrative – do not entail that the film which exhibits them is fictional. Although they were non-fictional in general, this does not mean that some fakes could not be fictional. In fact, there is evidence that during the earliest days of war fakes some distributors intended the films to be seen as mandating imaginary participation on par with that of the earliest surf films mentioned in previous chapters. Whissel, for instance, cites an 1899 description of the 'War films' section of F. M. Prescott's catalogue:

> In these superior films can be seen the dead and wounded and the dismantled cannon lying on the field of battle. The men are seen struggling for their lives, and the American flag proudly waves over them and can be plainly seen through the dense smoke. The brave American and Cuban soldiers show their valor and superiority in fighting the hated Spaniards. You think you can hear the huge cannon belch forth their death-dealing missiles, and can really imagine yourself on the field witnessing the actual battle.[98]

For Whissel the passage evinces that it was precisely the ability to position the spectator as an ideal participant-observer that is the crucial trait of war fakes. The very feature that allowed informed spectators to distinguish between fake and genuine war films – the impossible camera position – was the reason war fakes enjoyed popularity for a time. In fact, re-enactments, according to Whissel, informed the audience's expectations of how the battle should look like so that genuine war films strived to replicate the mode of address used in re-enactments.

What is of most concern to us is how widespread the intended mandate articulated above was and what was its reception? Is the mandate discernible elsewhere or is this a lone example? Did the audiences report imaginary participation with the films in question thereby producing a feedback loop like the one identified in the descriptions of train films and Hale's Tours or did the intention fall flat?

By claiming that while watching war fakes spectators were regularly supposed to imagine themselves on location, Whissel is effectively suggesting that the intended mandate was typical. Next to the catalogue, as further evidence she cites the context of a hugely popular contemporary live re-enactment – William F. Cody's traveling show 'Buffalo Bill's Wild West'. Cody's shows, according to Whissel, positioned spectators as ideal participant-observers and even seated some of them in a stagecoach while a re-enacted attack and rescue took place around them. She argues that 'the particular visual pleasure and peculiar authenticity of "Wild West" re-enactments derived from their power to endow audiences with an imaginary presence at historically significant and highly sensational moments'.[99]

The first problem with Whissel's outline is her conflation of imaginary participation with willing suspension of disbelief, on the one hand, and, illusion, on the other. According to her, 'the pleasure of "Wild West" re-enactments depended upon the amusement-seeker's *willing* and temporary suspension of disbelief'.[100] Although she is clear to say that such spectators were never fooled into believing they were on the frontier, the notion of 'willing suspension of disbelief', as I argued in Chapter 2, still connotes illusion as false belief which is distinct from imagination. When connecting the experience of live and film re-enactments, similarly, Whissel is claiming that imaginary participation is the definitive trait of re-enactments. But she regularly substitutes 'imaginary' for 'illusory'. To give just two examples:

> [In 'Buffalo Bill's Wild West'] the audience saw the event repeated as it was originally perceived by the agent-observer and thereby took up a position of (illusory) 'presence' unique to the 'genuine frontiersman' that was rendered available to (and made safe for) urban consumers en masse.[101]
>
> ... film reenactments carved out the imaginary position of the agent-witness for their audiences by creating the illusion of being 'embedded' within imperial traffic, and in so doing they created the pleasurable illusion of presence 'on the scene' of history.[102]

All of this does less damage to her argument than it evinces that even in as thoughtful a scholar as Whissel the notions of willing suspension of disbelief, illusion and imagination are not sufficiently demarcated. As such the conflations still stand in the way of a more precise understanding of historical audiences. In fact, Whissel treats re-enactments as hybrid films in the tradition of David Levy.[103] But if both live and filmed re-enactments regularly invited audiences to imagine themselves on location and the audiences responded appropriately, as she claims they did, then both should have constituted fictions through and through. This, however, is belied by the very materials that Whissel quotes in support of her view.

In the case of live re-enactments, both the actual quotations from the programme and the reception of Cody's show that she cites give no credence to the claim that mandated imaginings about one's own positioning on the frontier were either intended or uncovered by contemporaries. Instead, as she herself quotes, the point was to 'illustrate life as it is witnessed on the plains'.[104] Illustrations, as I have argued in the Introduction and Chapter 2, do not entail any mandated imaginings. Rather, illustrations serve as verisimilar representations which allow the spectator to generate accurate beliefs about the object of illustration. This much is clear from the very passages Whissel chooses to cite from:

> Our aim is to make the public acquainted with the manners and customs of the daily life of the dwellers in the far West of the United States through the means of actual and realistic scenes from life. ... We assure the auditor that each scene presents a faithful picture of the habits of these folk, down to the smallest detail.[105]
>
> ... Hon. Wm. F. Cody ('Buffalo Bill') gives us at the Wild West Exhibition, which every man, woman and child the world over should see and study as realistic fact.[106]

The programme itself, moreover, regularly invokes illustration as the show's main function (Figure 3.3). For the second number of the 1893 show, for instance, the programme states that certain Miss Annie Oakley 'will illustrate her dexterity in the use of Fire-arms'.[107] The fifth scene will be 'illustrating prairie emigrant train crossing the plains' followed by 'a group of Syrian and Arabian horsemen [who] will illustrate their style of Horsemanship'.[108] Later on, 'a group of Mexicans from Old Mexico, will illustrate the use of the Lasso, and perform various Feats of Horsemanship'.[109] Even the part of the programme potentially most conducive of imaginary participation – titled 'Capture of the Deadwood Mail Coach by the Indians' during the 1893 season – is articulated in terms of illustration rather than imagination:

> Among the most stirring episodes in the life of the Western pioneer are those connected with the opening of new lines of travel, for it is here, among the trails and canyons, where lurk the desperadoes of both races, that he is brought face to face with danger in its deadliest forms. No better illustration of this fact is furnished than in the history of the famous Deadwood Coach, the scarred and weather-beaten veteran of the original 'star route' line of stages, established at a

CONGRESS OF ROUGH RIDERS OF THE WORLD.

Programme

OVERTURE, "Star Spangled Banner"   COWBOY BAND, WM. SWEENY, Leader
1 GRAND REVIEW introducing the Rough Riders of the World and Fully Equipped Regular Soldiers of the Armies of America, England, France, Germany, and Russia.
2 MISS ANNIE OAKLEY, Celebrated Shot, who will illustrate her dexterity in the use of Fire-arms.
3 HORSE RACE between a Cowboy, a Cossack, a Mexican, an Arab, and an Indian, on Spanish-Mexican, Broncho, Russian, Indian and Arabian Horses.
4 PONY EXPRESS. The Former Pony Post Rider will show how the Letters and Telegrams of the Republic were distributed across the immense Continent previous to the Railways and the Telegraph.
5 ILLUSTRATING A PRAIRIE EMIGRANT TRAIN CROSSING THE PLAINS. Attack by marauding Indians repulsed by "Buffalo Bill," with Scouts and Cowboys.
   N. B.—The Wagons are the same as used 35 years ago.
6 A GROUP OF SYRIAN AND ARABIAN HORSEMEN will illustrate their style of Horsemanship, with Native Sports and Pastimes.
7 COSSACKS, of the Caucasus of Russia, in Feats of Horsemanship, Native Dances, etc.
8 JOHNNY BAKER, Celebrated Young American Marksman.
9 A GROUP OF MEXICANS from Old Mexico, will illustrate the use of the Lasso, and perform various Feats of Horsemanship.
10 RACING BETWEEN PRAIRIE, SPANISH AND INDIAN GIRLS.
11 COWBOY FUN. Picking Objects from the Ground, Lassoing Wild Horses, Riding the Buckers.
12 MILITARY EVOLUTIONS by a Company of the Sixth Cavalry of the United States Army; a Company of the First Guard Uhlan Regiment of His Majesty King William II, German Emperor, popularly known as the "Potsdamer Reds"; a Company of French Chasseurs (Chasseurs a Cheval de la Garde Republique Francaise); and a Company of the 12th Lancers (Prince of Wales' Regiment) of the British Army.
13 CAPTURE OF THE DEADWOOD MAIL COACH BY THE INDIANS, which will be rescued by "Buffalo Bill" and his attendant Cowboys.
   N. B. This is the identical old Deadwood Coach, called the Mail Coach, which is famous on account of having ruined the great number of people who lost their lives on the road between Deadwood and Cheyenne, 30 years ago. Now the most famed vehicle extant.
14 RACING BETWEEN INDIAN BOYS ON BAREBACK HORSES.
15 LIFE CUSTOMS OF THE INDIANS. Indian Settlement on the Field and "Path."
16 COL. W. F. CODY, ("Buffalo Bill"), in his Unique Feats of Sharpshooting.
17 BUFFALO HUNT, as it is in the Far West of North America—"Buffalo Bill" and Indians. The last of the only known Native Herd.
18 THE BATTLE OF THE LITTLE BIG HORN, Showing with Historical Accuracy the scene of CUSTER'S LAST CHARGE.
19 SALUTE.   CONCLUSION.

Figure 3.3 The 1893 programme for Buffalo Bill's Wild West.

time when it was worth a man's life to sit on its box and journey from one end of its destination to the other. The accompanying picture affords an idea of the old relic, and it is because of its many associations with his own life that it has been purchased by 'Buffalo Bill,' and added to the attractions of his 'Great Realistic Exhibition of Western Novelties'.[110]

Figure 3.4 An illustration of the Deadwood Coach.

'The accompanying picture', furthermore, in the attempt to depict the drama of the attack, does not position the observer within the coach but rather well outside (Figure 3.4). If the intention was to mandate imaginary participation in the event, one suspects a picture with a different composition and an implicit observer position would have been chosen.

The reception of Cody's show tells a similar story. In an endorsement which reappears in all four versions of the programme from 1887 to 1907 consulted here, W. T. Sherman writes: 'so far as I can make out you have been modest, graceful, and dignified in all you have done to illustrate the history of civilization on this Continent during the past century.'[111] Or as a review also included in different versions of the programme puts it: 'The reception accorded to his "show [is] that [it] is not a show, but an illustration".'[112]

These findings make it difficult to accept Whissel's argument that there was an underlying mandate in fakes coming from live re-enactments such as the 'Buffalo Bill's Wild West'. But they still do not invalidate the catalogue description from F. M. Prescott and the intended mandate to imagine oneself on the battlefield articulated therein. In other words, there is at least one catalogue where the whole war film category is described in terms of imaginary participation. This, however, is as far as the evidence for intended mandates goes. The existing American and British catalogues overwhelmingly describe both war actualities and re-enactments in terms of illustration and/or accurate representation rather than invoke imaginary engagement in either.

Edison's War Extra about the Spanish-American War, for instance, states that the films 'are sure to satisfy the craving of the general public for absolutely true and accurate details regarding the movements of the United States Army getting ready for the invasion of Cuba'.[113] In their general description of 'Military' films which include actualities and re-enactments alike American Mutoscope and Biograph boasts of how illustrative their films are: 'Every possible phase of military life and activity has been portrayed by us in the following views ... showing in the most faithful manner, the troops and manoeuvres of all the countries of the world.'[114] In their account of the 'Spanish-American War Subjects' the last three films – *A Call to Arms on Board Ship. Firing* (1898), *Landing of an Attacking Squad of Marines* (1898) and *Marines Retreating to their Ships* (1898) – are described as follows: 'These three Photographs, joined and shown consecutively, form a very interesting and effective picture, which illustrated one complete episode in the War.'[115] The descriptions of R. W. Paul's series 'Army Life' advertised over a few years read: '[A] series of Animated Photographs illustrating the life and career of a soldier, and the work of each branch of the Service' and 'This series is the first successful attempt to illustrate in animated pictures the life and career of a soldier in the British Army.'[116]

When the ads focus exclusively on re-enactments like the R. W. Paul's series titled 'Reproductions of Incidents of the Boer War' it is, for instance, only described as '[a]rranged under the supervision of an experienced military officer from the front'.[117] In the case of a film depicting a re-enacted battle such as *Wrecking an Armoured Train* (Sir Robert Ashe, 1899) again no imaginary participatory engagement is intended either: 'A graphic and complete reproduction of the armoured train incident at Mafeking. The British are seen defending the train and firing on the Boers. Several are wounded, and at last the British soldiers hoist a white flag in token of surrender.'[118] In Lubin's catalogue entry for war films the following representative accounts of films depicting the action in the Spanish-American War can be found:

Death of Macao and his Followers, 50 feet.   Naiad.

This is a memorable occurrence, and one that created indignation throughout the civilized world. The poor Cubans are caught in ambush, and although they defend themselves, are mercilessly shot down in their tracks. The film is as true to the actual scenes and your audience will be thoroughly aroused.[119]

Repulse of Spanish Trops [sic] at Santiago by the American Forces, 60 feet.   Name.

Here is an exciting picture where the Spaniards are repulsed with great loss by the Volunteer Army of the United States. This is an exact reproduction of the fight as it occurred, and it inspires you to see how bravely our soldier boys drive the Spaniards from their position and shoot them down as they try to escape.[120]

Even when the ideal position of the camera is highlighted as it is often the case in films representing battle charges, the call for imagining oneself in the middle of the battlefield is an exception rather than the norm in American and British catalogues alike:[121]

309   Indian Charge.   Indian

This scene shows 30 Pawnee and Sioux Indians headed by the famous scout and Indian fighter Pawnee Bill, mounted on mustangs making one of the fastest charges ever executed. At first they appear but small specks on the horizon, but soon grow into a dashing, surging group of indians and halt when close to camera making them appear life size. The speed at which this charge was made is something terrific, and never fails to thrill and inspire the audience. Sharp and clear, showing distinctly the war painted faces of the indians.[122]

The Defence of the Flag – Camp Meade, Pa. – 28 feet.   Ennuvear

This is another arranged picture in which the Charleston Cadets of Boston illustrate a manoeuvre employed in modern warfare. The soldiers are seen coming up a hill in short rushes and firing as they approach, and finally planting the flag on the crest of the hill.[123]

1182	Currasiers Mounting	Doll
1183	" " Departing	Dome
1604	" " Charging	Record
1485	" " Skirmishing	Drab

The above four scenes are among the best Military subjects ever photographed, the Cavalry Charge in particular being remarkably exciting. It shows a complete squadron of regular cavalry approaching the camera at full gallop and coming to a sudden halt immediately in the foreground.[124]

All the cited entries describe re-enactments which boast charges straight at the camera, yet none of the verbal accounts invokes any imaginary participation. In other words, although war re-enactments often capitalized on charges towards the camera the producers and distributors rarely invited the audiences to imagine themselves caught up in the battle.

On even rarer occasions genuine films were made during the skirmish and on the battlefield itself – the ideal that, as Whissel explains, the camera positioning in re-enactments was pushing the actualities towards. Within Whissel's framework, this would be a perfect opportunity to invite the audience to imaginary participation, yet catalogues reveal no such intention:

> 5772 a THE 4.7–INCH NAVAL GUN IN ACTION at the Battle of Pretoria
>
> This and the following films are the *only subjects yet photographed* while the guns were in action (not pre-arranged for the occasion). It shows a 4.7-inch gun firing at the Boers outside Pretoria on June 4th, 1900. Mr. Rosenthal photographed this incident in company with several London War Correspondents while bullets fell thick and fast, and these gentlemen were almost smothered twice by the dirt thrown up by bursting shells, which fell in rather too close proximity for comfort. Commander De Horsey, R.N., within 30 feet of our photographer, was wounded in this battle, and several mules were killed. A shell is seen bursting to the right of the gunners.
>
> 5723 b THE 5-INCH SIEGE GUNS IN ACTION at the Battle of Pretoria
>
> ... Mr. Rosenthal, referring to the taking of the film, writes that Boer shells were bursting all around and overhead, and that but very few of the thousands of people who will see the reproductions of these films 'will think of the poor devil who turned the handle of the camera'.[125]

Most people, according to the producers, will be thrilled to see a genuine film shot in the heat of the battle. But what they should really consider, the description implies, is the risk taken by the cameraman to secure the shot. Put differently, they should awe at the cameraman's resolve rather than imagine themselves in his shoes.

Not only were the mandates for imagining oneself on location articulated very rarely in contemporary war re-enactments and virtually never in genuine war films, but the reception also shows no concrete signs that the audiences uncovered any mandates of the type in war films in general. Reviews typical of the reception of R. W. Paul's films of 'Army Life' and included in his catalogue, for instance, read:

> There are also very realistic photographs of cavalry charges, of the firing of mines, the building of bridges by engineers; and, generally speaking, the spectator obtains from the representation an idea of Army life that he could not get from a most extensive reading of Army literature.[126]

A review included in Gaumont's special on the Russo-Japanese War writes, similarly: 'As vivid and realistic illustrations of events of the day, it would be impossible to find anything better than the living pictures now being shown on the bioscope at the Palace [Theatre, London].'[127] In the same vein, a news report about a motion picture re-enactment of The Battle of Chemulpo Bay from the same war states: 'The battle of Chemulpo will be illustrated [tonight] and other war scenes presented.'[128]

The conclusion that presents itself, then, is that although the producers of war re-enactments often positioned the camera in what Whissel describes as the ideal position there were very limited articulations of the mandate to imagine oneself inhabiting that camera position. And even on those rare occasions the audiences did not respond in kind. This is quite different from the promotion and reception of early train films described in Chapter 1 which also capitalized on movement towards the camera but which, at least for a short time, both invited and secured imaginary participation. The other difference, of course, is that that imaginary engagement was about trains bursting into the auditorium rather than spectators transporting themselves on location. The relationship of promotion and reception of war re-enactments is also quite distinct from the feedback loop that we have seen in the promotion and reception of Hale's Tours discussed in Chapter 2. There the intended mandates about imaging oneself on the train were picked up by the audiences whose reviews were again included in the promotional materials to strengthen the mandates. The feedback loop in war films as exemplified by the R. W. Paul's catalogue, instead, emphasized the films' illustrative nature.

4

The lecturer and make-believe: The borders of the text and explicit mandates

In the first three chapters I argued for an institutional approach to fiction. Rather than insisting on either stylistic features or authorial intentions as constitutive of fiction, I proposed an alternative to construing mandated imaginings. According to my model, mandates derive from a complex negotiation among key aspects of cinema as an institution – production, distribution, exhibition and reception. No single aspect suffices to give a full account of how the historically specific imaginative engagement with the earliest film genres came about. Moreover, given the cinema's relative youth in comparison to other arts and the related availability of material documenting contemporary institutional discourses, the institution of early cinema presents a unique case-study for how a representational art learns to perform the task of fictional representation. In other words, early cinema allows us to historicize Kendall L. Walton's notion of mandate by providing crucial insights into how mandates arise, are negotiated, turn into conventions and eventually become so transparent that it is difficult to give satisfactory answers to question about why some films are fictional and others not, despite both using actual footage.

By focusing on the period from roughly between 1880 and 1915, in this chapter I trace the relation between the institutions of lecturing and early cinema fiction making, arguing for an important connection between them. The lecturing practices developed during this period are of particular importance for understanding imaginative engagement with early cinema for at least four reasons. First, recurrent trade press advice favouring particular lecturing styles evinces concern with the intelligibility and clarity of mandates for the audience. By examining these instructions, we can gain further understanding of why particular mandates were preferred over others. Second, lecturing practices demonstrate another important way of how to transform actual footage into props for imaginative engagement. Whereas the first three chapters revealed a network of contemporary anxieties and responses, filmmaking intentions, and marketing and exhibition strategies as constitutive of this transformation, here it is a specific style of performance – namely, the specific use of markers of enunciation – that is decisive. Third, the transformation in question is a product of lecturing practices preceding the appearance of cinema. In other words, cinema owes a number of strategies for transforming actual footage into fictions to prior practices. Finally, these practices provide the earliest model for the film narrator whom we are mandated to imagine as responsible for all the imaginings the text prompts – the controlling fictional narrator. Put differently, the lecturer allows us both to better understand the subsequent use of voice-over in narrative cinema and to re-evaluate influential accounts of the birth of film narrators.

For a long time, it was forgotten that the lecturer ever even existed. Over the last three and a half decades it took the combined efforts of Noël Burch, Norman King, Charles Musser, André Gaudreault and Germain Lacasse, and Tom Gunning among others to rescue him (the lecturer was most often male[1]) from historical oblivion.[2] A resurgence of interest into this figure has revealed his institutional and historical background, geographical presence and documented various roles he fulfilled ranging from bombastic showmanship to didactic tutelage.

Institutionally speaking, magic lantern shows are usually considered to be one of the key precursors to cinema lecturing practices.[3] The magic lanterns themselves were invented around 1660 and became a part of the repertoire of itinerant showmen by the eighteenth century. A particularly popular form of the show in the late eighteenth century was the Phantasmagoria which sought to conjure up supernatural and frightful images. The nineteenth century with its zeal for popular education saw a rise of charismatic lecturers such as John Tyndall who combined spectacular effects with the principles of enlightenment at metropolitan institutions specializing in dissemination of knowledge. With the advent of cinema in the late nineteenth century numerous lecturers heralded by E. Burton Holmes would combine lantern slides and moving pictures in their travelogues.

Magic lantern lectures, however, were certainly not the only precursor to cinema lecturing. As Joe Kember has pointed out on the example of Victorian Britain, there were other forms of illustrated lectures which were accompanied by panoramas and dioramas rather than by magic lanterns but which should also be understood as an important institutional and historical context for early cinema lecturing.[4] Not even illustrated lecturing in general, however, gives us the full institutional context. Fairground, music hall and vaudeville house were some of the key venues for early cinema but little or no illustrated lecturing took place there.[5] Therefore, fairground and related showmanship (including town-hall, store-front and street performances) present another context for early cinema lecturing practices.[6] Whereas the dialectics of uplifting edification and spectacular hype informed both illustrated lecturing and fairground showmanship, it can be said that lecturing gravitated more towards the former and showmanship more towards the latter. In other words, we can follow Kember in establishing a relatively fuzzy line between 'lecturers' who mostly presented themselves in an enlightening capacity and 'showmen' whose performance primarily rested on exaggeration and duplicitousness. Indeed, scholars have recognized the *negative* influence a performance style typical of 'showmen' – the barker style – exercised on film lecturing practices, that is, as a manner of presentation officially to be renounced by the contemporary trade press dispensing advice on film lecturing.[7]

The presence of the film lecturer has been documented in numerous countries and regions including Belgium,[8] Germany,[9] the Netherlands,[10] Quebec,[11] Spain,[12] the UK,[13] the United States[14] and, of course, Japan.[15] There has also been work on the life, careers and practices of individual lecturers such as Stephen W. Bush,[16] E. Burton Holmes,[17] Lyman H. Howe,[18] Peter Marzen,[19] Cor Schuring,[20] John L. Stoddard,[21] Eric Williams[22] and James Williamson[23].

Film lecturers were, to put it in Germain Lacasse's words, 'the intermediary for two kinds of encounters: that between the audience in general and a revolutionary technology, and that between specific audiences and the film'.[24] They not only afforded narrative clarity by providing running commentary and story context, performing dialogue lines and otherwise dramatizing the action, or translating foreign intertitles,[25] but also mediated the cultural specificities by pointing out the national particularities of the country of production, or sought to produce a particular impression on the audience by emphasizing certain attractions or disseminating propaganda on the behalf of, say, the Communist Party. Though much work has been dedicated to film lecturer's narrative role, with the exception of Rick Altman's research no study has been devoted to the immediate concern of this chapter – the detailed articulation of the film lecturer's role in the imaginative engagement the audience was mandated to espouse.[26]

To undertake this analysis, it is imperative to approach the film lecturer from the perspective of the function underlying the whole range of roles from tutelage to political agitation and showmanship – namely the comprehensibility of images. In other words, regardless of whether the lecturer performed as an over-the-top showman or an edifying guide, in both cases he would still have needed to secure the comprehension of screened images by means of verbal accompaniment. The standard strategy for affording such comprehension was to frame the information into a story. From this perspective, we can regard film lecturers as a sort of Western counterparts to benshi, performers in charge of securing the same type of narrative comprehension in Japanese cinema. Although the film lecturer never reached the cultural relevance his Japanese colleague did nor did he play as important a role in the exhibition practices as long as benshi did,[27] even in the United States there was a period in which film lecturers enjoyed great popularity as they were perceived as a solution to the problem of narrative complexity preferable to the use of intertitles. According to Gunning and Altman, the importance of nickelodeon's lecturer peaked in 1907–9 and again in 1911-12 – coinciding with the changes in film narrative structure and length – and the problems the new form caused for narrative comprehension.[28] Gaudreault adds that the film lecturer also played an important role between 1902 and 1904 when developments in editing allowed for the chase film.[29] We can also note that lecturers were a key component of some of the most notable earliest film genres including travelogues, passion plays and boxing films.

The first question that arises concerns the relation between the film lecturer and the film text. Whereas it is clear that illustrated lectures were intermedial texts made up of both the lecture *and* images, this is far from obvious in the case of early cinema. In fact, some scholars have suggested that the lecturer was not a part of the text during that period.[30] Miriam Hansen, for instance, argues the following:

> If the lecturer eventually followed other nonfilmic activities into oblivion, it was not just because of an undoubtedly operative tendency of linearization, but because he remained adjunct to a particular show, a live performance, the local sphere of exhibition.[31]

Moreover, early films need not have been accompanied by lecturers and were often not. An illustrated lecture, by contrast, would simply not be an illustrated lecture if either the lecture or the images were missing. The question is further complicated by the problem of the early film text itself. While we nowadays routinely identify single films as film texts, we often forget that we do so because of the present-day institutional context. Simply put, individual films are nowadays regularly screened as single units. This, however, was not the case during early cinema when single motion pictures were regularly embedded within larger film programmes and performative contexts. In the following section, therefore, I will argue against the view that the lecturer was perceived to be external to the text and attempt to articulate what precisely constituted the text during this period. More precisely, I will claim that both explicit and implicit arguments against film lecturer's intratextuality are invalid. Whereas the former conflate evaluative criteria with those of intra- and extratextual demarcation, the latter hinge on the restrictive view which sees the early film text as exclusively defined by the recording. Finally, given that these arguments revolve around what has traditionally been understood as narrative fiction film, I will propose that to understand the film lecturer's role in the imaginative engagement with the film text we need to look not only at other contemporary and preceding film genres but at the previous illustrated lecturing practices as well.

The relation of the film lecturer to the text

There is certainly precedent that agents responsible for narrative comprehension of early cinema were construed as a part of the text. A case in point are benshi – Japanese orators who for more than four decades introduced and explained films, translated intertitles, spoke dialogue lines, provided poetic commentary and on occasions even transformed the meaning of the screened images. During the first decade benshi standardly gave *maesetsu* – detailed accounts of films to be shown – describing, at first, exotic Western locales and places (as most of films at the time were foreign imports) and, as more narrative films started appearing, summarizing plot and character traits. In the wake of Russo-Japanese War (1904–5) benshi started developing the art of concurrent vocal narration – *setsumei* – which quickly displaced *maesetsu* in importance. By mid-teens, moreover, two types of *setsumei* arose – a solo performance reserved for foreign films and explaining the ongoing action, and *kowairo setsumei* accompanying Japanese films in which dialogue lines were spoken (by one or more benshi). Under the ensuing attack of Pure Film Movement only the form of solo *setsumei* survived but such a style combining narration, commentary, and mimetic dialogue also succeeded in ushering in the Golden Age of benshi between 1925 and 1932 and in establishing the audio and visual tracks as equals. Regardless of whether they imitated character voices as in *kowairo*, or narrated and commented on the action as in solo *setsumei*, Jeffrey A. Dym and Andrew Aaron Gerow have convincingly argued that benshi were a key ingredient in Japanese cinema experience from 1896 to 1939. Crucially, at least since the Russo-Japanese War, their *setsumei* performance *together* with the images screened constituted the intermedial film text.[32]

We cannot, however, simply use Dym's and Gerow's findings to decide on the potential intermediality of film exhibition in American and European contexts. First, benshi enjoyed a far stronger institutional position in Japanese cinema than their Western counterparts ever did. For example, benshi were one of the crucial factors for why the conversion to sound in Japan took far longer than in America and Europe. Second, unlike in America and Europe, Japan had a longer and stronger tradition of various intermedial forms in which two simultaneous media (most often visual and verbal) conveyed narrative information. Though both the West and Japan shared the institution of magic lantern, in Japan there was also a number of other commingled forms – *etoki* where Buddhist inflected stories were accompanied by pictures and music, *kabuki* theatre, and *bunraku* puppet theatre where the oral component was in fact primary. Finally, even Dym claims that the condition of intermediality is not the one that obtained in the West.[33]

This view seems to be endorsed, if only implicitly, in the work of some highly influential film historians. Tom Gunning writes:

> As Noel Burch indicates, the film lecturer endowed the film image with narrative order and legibility, a reading at the service of linear storytelling.
>
> But, as Burch also points out, providing added realism and narrative clarity through an *exterior* supplement contradicted the traditional diegetic realism to which American film aspired. The lecturer could supply such values only as a supplement, an additional aid, rather than as an inherent organic unity. A lecturer's commentary undermined an experience of the screen as the site of a coherent imaginary world in which narrative took place . ...
>
> Within the narrator system, narrative clarity and spectator empathy could not be achieved at the expense of diegetic illusionism.[34]

Gunning, Burch and Hansen, then, all see the film lecturer as a performer apart from the film text. This is not a matter of extradiegesis – a property that is, following Gérard Genette's narratological work, generally imputed to entities which, though outside of the story in a certain sense, still remain a part of the text.[35] Lecturers are not extradiegetic narrators in the sense the filmic narrator that Gunning argues D. W. Griffith ushers in is.[36] Instead, in Burch, Gunning and Hansen there appears to be a textual border separating the screen from the verbal performance. The question that presents itself is whether the reason for the lecturer's externality is simply a consequence of an a priori understanding of film as defined by its recording medium or whether other criteria are crucial for this verdict. Given that these historians were among the first to emphasize the importance of production, distribution and exhibition contexts for the history of cinema as opposed to simply focusing on specific moving pictures, let us address the second option first.

What Gunning and Burch highlight as explicit contrast to the lecturer's 'exteriority' are in fact general textual features rather than properties of a recording – namely 'an inherent organic unity' and 'a coherent imaginary world'. The problem is that 'an inherent organic unity' and 'a coherent imaginary world' are very unlikely candidates for defining whether an element is intratextual or not. Numerous films represent incoherent imaginary worlds but that is not used as a reason for claiming that an element contributing to this incoherence is extratextual. Similarly, if the point is that the narrative spoken by the lecturer and the one unfolding on screen do not coincide, then, were the same divergences to occur in sound film, we would also be forced to say that one of the tracks is extratextual. At most, the failure to represent a coherent imaginary world may result in an evaluative dismissal of the film. In the same vein, inherent organic unity is a criterion of evaluation and not of intra- or extratextuality. That rather than representing a unified story from the novel of the same name, *Uncle Tom's Cabin* (Edwin S. Porter, 1903), only picks out the most dramatic scenes without much concern for the causal connections between them, does not mean that any part of the film is extratextual because of that.

If their arguments are to be taken at face value then, at best, Gunning and Burch appear to be claiming that *at the time* the criteria of evaluation functioned as criteria of textual demarcation. At worst, they are confusing the former with the latter. The problem with the first scenario is that no contemporary sources are given in favour of the claim that audiences in the transitional era used evaluative criteria to demarcate among exhibition elements. Moreover, the very reason behind the surge in the film lecturer's popularity at the time was precisely the perceived disunity, incomprehensibility and incoherence of the films shown. Yet, for all the complaints about such films in the trade press at the time there is no evidence that anybody expresses the view that some parts of these films are extratextual.[37] In the second scenario, to assume that an exhibition element could undermine inherent organic unity and the coherent imaginary world that element would in fact need to be understood as internal rather than as external to the text. The occasional broken filmstrip, the time it takes to change the reels, the loud projection noise, the potentially distracting chatter, all these factors would have influenced the viewing experience, but they could not make a dent in the organic unity and diegetic coherence of the film screened. The reason is that all these projection circumstances are properly external to the text. The only thing these projection aspects could have done is to influence the level of spectators' *immersion*.[38] To put it more precisely and in Walton's terms, these aspects could either stop the game of make-believe (e.g. the break in the filmstrip and between reels), distract our attention from the game (e.g. noise) or modulate the level of our engagement with the game. They could not change what was to be imagined, the level of its coherence or whether it was inherently unified or not.

Perhaps I have been misrepresenting Gunning and Burch, and they really are trying to articulate the notion of immersion understood as the level of engagement with the game of make-believe here. Perhaps this is implied in the phrase 'diegetic illusion'. In other words, perhaps the reason the film lecturer for them is external is because he fails to secure 'diegetic illusion'. Hansen's thoughts on the matter might also be construed as pointing in this direction:

> Paradoxically, while aiming to clarify the narrative and enhance the viewer's absorption, the lecture effectively undermined an emerging sense of diegetic illusion; the presence of a human voice inhibited closure of the fictional world on screen and thus the perceptual segregation from theater space essential to the diegetic effect.[39]

If that indeed is the case, then a number of qualifications need to be made. First, when it comes to 'diegetic illusion' as a concept in film studies, the recourse to 'illusion' is particularly loaded and carries with it extremely problematic connotations. As Gregory Currie and Walton have pointed out on numerous occasions, whereas illusion entails false beliefs make-believe does not.[40] It is the former that informed much of post-classical film theory. Furthermore, the re-articulation of the train-effect in terms of make-believe as opposed to illusion (and attraction) as well as the dismissal of illusion as an explanatory model for the immersive experience of phantom rides and Hale's Tours in previous chapters should have also demonstrated that the distinction between the two is no nit-picking matter but an important addition to the understanding of the phenomenology of early audiences. Second, if 'diegetic illusion' really does attempt to get at immersion, then there is still too much equivocation between diegetic illusion, diegetic realism, narrative coherence, closed fictional worlds and organic unity in these passages. As I explain above, narrative coherence and organic unity are by no means one and the same. Similarly, closed fictional worlds (taking place in one medium only) can be narratively both coherent and incoherent, diegetically both realistic and unrealistic. The same holds for fictional worlds which are not defined by a single medium. Finally, contrary to Hansen's assertion, there is neither an a priori nor a historical reason that 'the perceptual segregation from theater space [is] essential to the diegetic effect'. That in the Japanese tradition there are various intermedial forms which allow for immersion takes the thrust out of the a priori version of her argument. From a historical perspective, Hansen's claim holds only if the bourgeois theatre is construed as the main institutional context for early cinema. It is clear, however, that illustrated lecturing and other forms of showmanship which invited no segregation of the theatre space played as important a role.

Given that none of these historians would deny the importance of these contexts (for they were among the first ones to point them out), the likelier reason for why Burch, Gunning and Hansen see the lecturer as extratextual appears to be implicit rather than explicit. It seems that in the end they all fall back onto the recording medium as the key criterion for textual demarcation. We can flesh out this implication by comparing their claims to those of another author who has significantly contributed to our understanding of the lecturer – André Gaudreault:

> [O]ne of the principle concerns of producers of the day [between 1908 and 1909] was to encourage filmmakers to find a way to create ambitious narratives that could dispense with the service of the lecturer … In fact, there was a solution … : intertitles … [T]his solution had an advantage of rendering the narration *external* to the images uniform … In the end, the solution that won out over all others, as film history has shown, was to incorporate the film narrator *into the film itself*.[41]

Gaudreault seems to say that both the lecturer's interventions and clarification through intertitles share the feature of extratextuality. Burch, Gunning and Hansen reserve the trait for the lecturer only. In a later piece Gaudreault bases the claim about the intertitle's (in his more specific vocabulary this time around, subtitle's) externality on the fact that for a while in the United States each scene was copyrighted separately with the intertitle serving as the title in the copyright:

> It's as if the written remarks were seen as something outside the trade in images, something apart from them that overdetermined them as well as commented on, qualified, and identified them, *but from without*. It's as if title cards were an element definitively exogenous to the scene, completely extraneous and heterogeneous elements with respect to the images.[42]

Although the copyright practice Gaudreault mentions undoubtedly took place, it is unlikely that once projected the intertitles would have been perceived as external to the film for by the same logic the discrete scenes would have to have been treated as separate films. Certainly, not much research has been done on intertitles but the rare and more detailed studies of the practice until 1915 – Eileen Bowser's, Claire Dupré La Tour's and Katherine Nagels's– give credence to Burch, Gunning and Hansen's view rather than Gaudreault's.[43] Though intertitles were used as sparingly as possible at the time, this was not because they were perceived to be external to the text, but because they hampered suspense, broke the continuity in the game of make-believe and impinged on the 'reality effect' – effectively much of what the lecturer was criticized for doing. In other words, however disruptive of an inherent organic unity intertitles might have been, they were a part of the visual sequence screened and as such a part of the text.[44] In this sense, it is still the filmstrip that implicitly defines the borders of the text for Burch, Gunning and Hansen rather than their nominal conditions of organic unity, fictional coherence and/or diegetic illusion which are more open to intermedial notions of the text.[45] Under the implicit logic, by contrast, the film text appears to be constituted exclusively by what was recorded on the filmstrip. We might take this discussion then as a lesson that even when non-restrictive articulations of the film text are attempted, the present-day understanding of it as defined by the recording medium still very much informs the criteria for textual demarcation. The discussion also demonstrates that to identify an element as contributing to or detracting from organic unity and fictional coherence entails that we categorize the element as intratextual.

It is also important to note that Burch, Gunning, Hansen and Gaudreault discuss the lecturer's narrative comprehension function in relation to what has traditionally been understood as narrative fiction cinema. The lecturer, however, could also play this role in other early cinema genres which are traditionally understood as non-narrative such as scenics, actualities, phantom rides and the like. There were, moreover, traditionally understood non-fiction genres which were narrative such as war panoramas, travelogues, passion plays and boxing films. Furthermore, given the complex nature of mandated imaginings in relation to the earliest cinema genres I argued for up to now, we cannot focus only on the transitional period to understand the lecturer's narrative role in relation to make-believe and in relation to the text. As we will quickly see on the example of E. Burton Holmes, lecturers could transform actual footage into props for games of make-believe.

The lack of historical evidence for the idea that criteria of evaluation served as criteria of textual demarcation and the theoretical indefensibility of using the former as the latter provides us with an argument against the claim that film lecturers were perceived as extratextual exhibition elements. The focus on the lectures of the transitional period, moreover, does not only overlook the possibility that the range of fictional texts in which lecturers played a role was far wider than what traditionally understood fiction genres allows for. It also neglects the importance of the pre-transitional lecturing practices for construing the relationship between the text and the lecturer. To push the argument in favour of the lecturer's intratextuality even further both a model of the text which does not a priori dismiss intermediality and historical data which evince this view are required.

An inclusive model of textuality may be found in the writings of Seymour Chatman who defines the text as 'any communication that *temporally* controls its reception by the audience' and which has a beginning and an end.[46] It not only accommodates intermedial practices of crucial importance for the pre-history of cinema and projected entertainment, but is still compatible with present-day understanding of film texts as individual films. Finally, it also allows for the possibility, opened up already by the notion of film as defined by the recording medium, that it is the film programmes rather than single films which represented the film text for the early audiences.

Musser was one of the first to point out that the early film exhibition venues such as the late 1890s Eden Musée in New York capitalized on structured programmes rather than on random strings of individual films.[47] In other words, occasions where discrete films were subjugated to 'unified programs built around a single event, theme or narrative' were quite common as the huge popularity of passion play, boxing match and travelogue programmes at the same time evinces.[48] In the German variety theatre context, similarly, film programmes also revolved around a single theme with the depictions of the Imperial fleet constituting one important example.[49] Such programmes, interestingly, meet both the explicit and implicit criteria articulated by Burch et al. – they are defined by the filmstrip and exhibit a unity. But this does not mean that the text is simply expanded 'horizontally' to include a number of reels projected in sequence.[50] On numerous occasions, according to Musser, it was the resulting programme with *all* of its performance aspects that constituted the text and not what could have been found on the reel(s) at the time. And this is the very 'vertical' or multi-track expansion that Chatman's definition of the text allows for. For instance, passion plays were regularly accompanied by lectures, boxing matches enjoyed a running commentary not unlike the one by present-day sports commentators, and travelogues essentially hinged not only on verbal accounts of voyage in question but on the persona of a specific lecturer. In Musser's own words relating to another popular early genre:

A lecture was almost certainly an integral part of many of the Musee's programs, particularly Panorama of the War. This program, in particular, is comparable in many respects to more modern documentaries using silent stock footage, although the modes of production and exhibition are radically different.[51]

The comparison with 'modern documentaries' is particularly apt because it allows us to construe the lecturer as a voice-over narrator whose crucial property for our purposes is that he is internal to the text. As Sarah Kozloff has argued, lecturers were the key model for the implementation of voice-over narrators shortly following the advent of the sound era.[52]

Contemporary accounts also speak in favour of the lecturer's intertextuality. First, earliest film lectures are regularly placed in the tradition of illustrated lecturing strongly suggesting that they were perceived as intermedial forms. Consider, for instance, a contemporary reviewer's report on Horitz *Passion Play* (Marc Klaw and Abraham L. Erlanger, 1897) – the first passion play to be recorded on film for American audiences – which uses Stoddard's lectures (Figure 4.1) as context:

> One of the most attractive of Mr. John L. Stoddard's lectures was that on the 'Passion Play' at Ober-Ammergau. It was illustrated by magnificent photographs, and yet, … [a] painting or a photograph can only partly convey the thought of movement and action, while, by the other means, the spectator is able to judge of the dramatic character of the works of these mountain peasants, and the imagination is only slightly called upon to picture the scenes in their complete reality.[53]

Similarly, a reviewer of another Passion Play – *Passion Play of Oberammergau* (1898) produced by Eden Musée – comments on how the moving images illustrate the lecture even making a point about the relative importance of sound within such intermedial texts: '[the full evening's entertainment] began by showing a map of the Holy Land and then takes the listener on an imaginary journey detailing the many events in the life of Christ and the most important of which were illustrated by the cinematograph.'[54]

Second, these earliest lectures were also regularly perceived to have a crucial narrative role and to be executed with such high quality that they could have even been performed as stand-alone acts. Returning to Horitz *Passion Play* again:

> Mr. Lacy's lecture was well studied and effectively delivered. He … accompanied the presentation of the illustrations by a running commentary couched in graceful language, and telling fittingly the story which was being pictured. It may, in fact, be said, that had the lecture been the only attraction of the evening it would have been enjoyed by thoughtful people, and it certainly helped to a more thorough understanding of the movements in the various tableaux.[55]

Figure 4.1 The Passion Play (*John L. Stoddard's Lectures*, Vol. 4, Boston, 1890, p. 326).

The lecture, finally, not only contributes to narrative comprehension of moving images but also comes across as unified with the visual track ('telling fittingly the story which was being pictured').

Third, though references to the institutional context of illustrated lecturing disappear in the transitional era, the recognition of intermediality remains a feature of the writings on film. In Germany, for instance, 'der Erkläerer' or 'der Rezitator' – as the lecturer was known there – is regularly seen as not only contributing to narrative clarity but amplifying the viewer's experience through emphasis on sensational story elements and even taking over the reins of the story:

> The lecturer sobbed, the audience clenched their fists, a completely, completely different tragedy than the one the film producer had imagined rushed by. As the reputable workman pushed back the prostitute both necessities were present in this movement: attitude of high rank and a brutal act. 'The man of work does not want what was thrown out of the palaces, the woman without a heart, he throws her out of his simple room …' evokes the lecturer. The audience boils.[56]

The power of the lecturer was such that the reviewer concludes with, within German circles, an oft-remarked fear of the revolutionary potential of cinema: 'The revolutions of tomorrow will come from the cinema.'[57]

It is true that unified programmes were not the only organizing principle that guided exhibition. The other route was to produce a variety show, and showmen like Eberhard Schneider clearly preferred this approach. This does not change the fact, however, that there were programmes which capitalized on thematic unity and which made use of lecturers as their integral and internal part. Yuri Tsivian's work on early Russian film audiences, moreover, goes even further than Musser's in claiming that it was the overall exhibition rather than single films that constituted the text for early spectators.[58] For Tsivian even the programmes that appealed to greatest variety as their organizing principle could often not avoid producing 'phantom narratives' which exhibited 'the semblance of a causally motivated narrative' across films which, taken individually, would have diegetically had nothing to do with each other.[59] Musser's and Tsivian's work, then, allows us to recognize that the application of the principle of unity and diegetic coherence as a guidance for delimiting what a text is does not make discrete films its only viable candidate. By that token, programmes with accompanying performances are as good a contender for the status of the text as discrete films are. Combined with the preceding analysis of the necessary textual status of the elements contributing to or disappointing these two principles and with excerpts from contemporary accounts, we have strong evidence for the claim that lecturers constituted a separate but intratextual track.

There are, moreover, examples where, by the very nature of the format, it seems undeniable that at least one aspect of the lecturer's performance was a part of the text. Lecturers, for instance, spoke dialogue lines – a practice relatively common as attested by W. Stephen Bush's lectures on *Enoch Arden* (D. W. Griffith, 1911) and *Faust* published in trade press.[60] Therefore, however poorly the lines might have been delivered, and however much this 'might [have] undermine[d] film's illusionism', there is no denying that audiences were often mandated to imagine at least what the lecturer was saying to be a part of the text.[61] In fact, it might be argued that the audiences were also mandated to imagine the manner of delivery, for the condition of undermining film's 'diegetic illusionism' is precisely to perform in the fashion which does not cohere with what has been mandated to imagine about the character hitherto. If, for instance, Marguerite's lines from the second reel of scene 8 from *Faust* ('To die so young . . .') were to have been performed jocularly instead of broodingly as her captivity demands, then narrative coherence and 'diegetic illusionism' would have been at risk. Stephen Bottomore, furthermore, cites at least one occasion where not only the content and fashion of the delivery but the whole lecturer's performance must have been construed as a part of the text if misunderstanding of the show were to be avoided – Harry Hemsley's act in *In and Out of Picture* in October of 1914 in London.⁶² In it, Hemsley not only lip-syncs characters but also choreographs action between on-screen and off-screen by passing objects from his screen version to himself on stage. Finally, even Richard Crangle who warns against uncritical extrapolation of findings on magic lantern practices – American and European intermedial texts par excellence – to film lecturing finds that one of the key similarities between the two is their status as intermedial texts:

> [T]he verbal element [of both lantern and moving picture practices] could not logically function without the visual element, and the visual element was perceived to be not fully delivered without some form of additional explication.⁶³

There are, therefore, numerous highly popular genres such as passion plays, fight films, travelogues, panoramas of the war and performances by famous lecturers in which lectures were not only a part but an important part of the text for early audiences. This, moreover, was not only a feature of the earliest years but extended into the transitional era as well. And even in those cases where lecturers performed under par, that they were perceived as undermining 'diegetic illusion' and 'inherent organic unity' is in fact evidence of their intratextuality rather than extratextuality.

Ideal, printed and delivered lectures

Although, as I have demonstrated, we have good reasons to doubt descriptions of lecturers as external to the text, Gunning is certainly right to point out that lecturing often impeded what he calls 'film illusionism' – so long as we take him to be referring to a smoothly running game of make-believe. Gunning is also correct to emphasize the importance film trade press had in regulating cinema lecture practices and promoting some styles of performance over others after the nickelodeon boom.⁶⁴ This was nothing new, for, as Altman and Kember have demonstrated, similar concern for performance style could be read on the pages of magic lantern manuals and periodicals between 1888 and 1905 at a time when cinema and magic lantern shared the trade press.⁶⁵ Interestingly, a set of instructions was repeated with striking regularity,

1. The lecturer should give an air of mastery over his subject matter.
2. Although the slides should explain him and not vice-versa, the images should not dominate over his lecture.
3. His voice should be sufficiently loud.

4. He should prepare a written lecture but instead of reading it aloud he should learn it by heart and vary it if necessary.
5. There should not be too many slides nor should there be too much time devoted to a single slide (approximately hour-long lectures with one slide per minute are advised).
6. The lecture should be executed in an articulate, professional, and fluent manner.
7. The lecturer should limit his movement on the stage, face the audience and, when necessary, draw attention to crucial details of the slides.
8. The apparatus should never be acknowledged and any visual or verbal ostentation is prohibited.
9. He should use jokes sparingly.
10. He should deal with apparatus breakdown calmly.[66]

From the perspective of an illustrated lecture as an intermedial text consisting of two tracks – verbal and visual – these rules allow us to deepen our understanding of the workings of mandated imaginings.[67] Two of the rules are mostly concerned with either preparations (4) or non-verbal performance (7) so I will bracket them off in the following discussion. The remaining eight do, however, inform the content and the form of game of make-believe in a more tangible fashion. Some of these prescriptions appear to be more concerned with the 'genre' of the game of make-believe to be played, while others bear directly on the constant threat that a game of make-believe may be impeded or interrupted.

Concerning questions of 'genre', instructions (1), (2), (5), (6) and (9) easily make the list. We are invited to play a game for about an hour (5) in which the oral component is the dominant track of the intermedial text (2), is performed by a knowing agent (1), is presented in a clear rather than staccato or monotonous manner (6) and where coarse jokes should be avoided at all cost (9). I am disinclined to count rule (4) here because whether something is read or recited from memory it does not determine the style of execution dealt with in more detail in (6). In other words, I take 'genre' here to be informative of the duration of the text and its segments, of the relationship between its tracks, of the type of language employed and of the 'narrator's' epistemic traits.

Regarding how smooth the game of make-believe runs (3), (8) and (10) appear to be crucial. Rule (10), for instance, deals with an occasion where the visual track is simply decommissioned and the game of make-believe is severely hampered if not discontinued. Such occurrence, I trust, is not unlike the disappearance of the sound track from a contemporary screen (given that the sound track is the subordinate track in sound cinema, whereas in illustrated lectures the subordinate track is the visual one). Though we could continue watching the film we would most probably miss a number of props necessary to build a fully intelligible fiction. The rule regarding the volume of the lecturer's voice (3) essentially tackles the same problem concerning legibility of props. If audience members are unable to hear what the lecturer is saying, then they simply do not have sufficient props to participate in the game of make-believe in an appropriate fashion.

Instruction (8) seems to present a different type of concern. It is not a worry that some parts of the text – that is, the props in the game of make-believe – might be lost, rather that some parts of the text might cause problems in construing what is being mandated to imagine. Take, for instance, the imperative 'never [to] acknowledge the existence of the operator or of the lantern'.[68] Such acknowledgements significantly complicate the task of what to make-believe for historical audiences. Are they to imagine the operator and the lantern to be a part of fiction much like the characters in the story the slides show and the lecturer's voice informs of? Or is this an instance where the game is temporarily suspended and additional information about the exhibition given? For us, these references might be a question of 'genre' in the sense elaborated above. In this particular case the references might be a matter of identifying what Linda Hutcheon refers to as a genre of metafiction as opposed to that of regular fiction – texts which ruminate on their own status as texts by means of text-internal calling of attention to conditions of production and/or exhibition.[69] Metafiction, however, was far from a common genre at the period in question (or in any representational medium for that matter). Therefore, what for present-day audiences might constitute a revelation that they are encountered with a specific 'genre', for the audiences at the end of nineteenth and the beginning of twentieth century would constitute an obtrusive glitch in a game of make-believe best to be avoided if possible.

One might object that films like *The Big Swallow* (James Williamson, 1901) and *Uncle Josh at the Moving Picture Show* (Porter, 1902) demonstrate that early film-going audience and, by extension, magic lantern audiences had no problem understanding embedded fictions which depicted the apparatus. I am not denying that. These films, regarded as individual texts, however, never pose a problem whether the apparatus which is projecting *the films themselves* (*The Big Swallow* and *Uncle Josh at the Moving Picture Show*) and shares the auditorium space with spectators is part of fiction or not. It is clearly not. The level of metafictional complexity is far lower in this case.

The second part of provision (8) pertains to 'ostentatious verbal and visual effects'.[70] This means that the lecturer is strongly encouraged never to use demonstratives when speaking of images. This may include anything ranging from the use of perceptual imperatives (e.g. 'Look!') and bodily demonstratives (e.g. pointing one's finger in a direction of an object) to spatial deictics (e.g. 'here/this is x'). All these acts are either instances of direct spatial ostentation or of *discourse* – statements which cannot be fully understood without the context in which they were made. To understand what 'here' or 'this' refers to we need to know where the utterance was made. Similarly, to understand what 'look!' draws attention to we need to know who issued the command to whom and where. In other words, we are dealing with actions which cannot be understood without reference to the immediate spatial context of their performance. Any action of this sort raises questions about the fictional status of either the lecturer or the audience. In cases of bodily demonstratives and spatial deictics problems arise in reference to the lecturer's status in the game of make-believe. At this point we are no longer speaking only of the manner and content of his delivery as props in the game. We are called to consider his whole bodily presence. Is he positioning himself spatially within the fictional world? Are we to imagine him physically sharing the world with the characters? Or is this a momentary suspension of the game in which ostentations of the sort 'this is x' are supposed to be construed as merely a shorthand for 'this is an image of x'? In cases of perceptual imperatives, the status of the audience is similarly called into question. Is the audience to imagine themselves as beckoned to inhabit a spatial position within the fictional world? Should they imagine themselves as being face to face with the imaginary x in question? Or is this simply a cry to direct attention and as such a fleeting glitch in the game of make-believe?[71] Both options are open, and it seems that trade journal commentators preferred the issue not to be raised at all, not least because both of them would have hindered the smooth running of the game.

A concern very similar to the one embedded in (8) was expressed at the time of the increased lecturer's popularity in cinema during the nickelodeon boom. Regular calls for the avoidance of the barker style can be found on the pages of the contemporary film trade press. The barker, a figure most closely associated with the fairground and store shop theatre exhibition, was usually stationed in front of the attraction venue and tasked with hyping the attraction that lay within and rounding up as many patrons as possible. Essentially a peddler of visual delights, the barker relied on his vocal sales pitch to bring customers in. By addressing the potential audience directly, his primary function was to enhance the lure of the attraction and to accentuate the wonders of spectatorship, rather than smoothly guide the would-be patrons into a diegetic world. In other words, barker did everything that the rule (8) advised against.

Concerns about the barker's ostentatious performance style were at the core of much of the arguments launched by the cinema trade press against the use of his style. For instance, calls by Bush 'never [to] shout, and [to] avoid as the most fatal of all the 'barker' style: '*Here we* see on the *left*.' 'In *this picture* we behold on the *left* the beautiful heroine,'[72] and similar warnings by a certain A. S. that 'audiences do not tolerate any admixture of personality'[73] suggest that an unskilled (or an unfocused) lecturer could easily disrupt the game of make-believe. There is a reference in these admonitions not only to the spatial deictics and parts of the apparatus – both marked in italics – but also to problems of ostentation implied in the phrase 'admixture of personality'.

An extract from one of the rare surviving transcripts made by a certain Professor Sellmann of a lecture as it was *actually* delivered in Berlin in 1912 demonstrates that these worries were well founded:

> Othello, a Moor, has made a great conquest and comes home again. Here he finds that his beloved, – please, gentleman in the second row, stand up and allow the lovely lady to pass, – so, he finds that a certain Sir Rodrigo chases after her what induces the black one to go into rage and become jealous. – You little lady, keep that child a bit quieter.[74]

What seems to be the problem is not so much that the whole verbal accompaniment was outside the text as Burch, Gunning and Gaudreault would suggest, but that the text itself and the respective aspects of the mandated game of make-believe is repeatedly being broken on the verbal track. If the former were the case, what need is there for Sellmann to produce a lengthy transcript of an actual lecture in the discussion of artistic traits of a photoplay? What can be gained by smugly remarking on the use of dialect, grammatical errors and discrepancy between the spoken word and the projected image if it is not the notion of organic unity that is really at stake? And indeed, 'speech', Sellmann concludes thereafter, 'is not organically bound up with the film play. It is nothing but an explanation which can naturally always be represented differently by another reciter.'[75] Such criticism, as I argued, speaks in favour of the lecturer's intermediality rather than externality. But even more importantly, Sellmann never remarks on the direct addresses to the audiences, that is, 'admixtures of personality' as the ones contributing to disunity. It is the dialect, grammatical errors and narrative discrepancies that are his concern. This gives further credence to my claim that nothing extratextual could be seen as contributing to or detracting from organic unity. A good comparison with such intermittent actual lectures, therefore, might be to think of projection issues and how audiences dealt with them. For instance, because of the limited capacity of the reels they would have often had to be changed and if the cinema had only one projector this would regularly turn games of make-believe into intermittent activities. Similarly, we may think of the above actual lecturing practices as a particularly annoying example of this kind of intermittent game of make-believe. Lecturers could have been especially susceptible to this type of incompetence given the performative nature of the job and the relatively lax norms guiding audience behaviour at the time.

There were also practices which deliberately diverged from advice of Bush and others subscribing instead to the barker style. Lectures printed and distributed by the Kalem Company and Lubin were regularly willing to pay no heed to the instructions in the trade press. Kalem Company, for instance, opted for some good-old fashioned marketing which, interspersed with ostentations, directly addressed the audience and heightened the awareness of the apparatus: 'Ladies and Gentlemen: You will see in the screen before you a picture of unusual interest.'[76] This practice cannot be subsumed simply under the show's introductory remarks for it reoccurs throughout the lecture: 'We are at Queenie's home again. ... Notice the preciousness of these animals.'[77] All of these then, as I have demonstrated above, must have made it problematic to grasp what was to be imagined.

A variation on this point arises, for example, in the lecture Siegmund Lubin published as an accompaniment to his *The Passion Play* (1898):

1. THE ANNUNCIATION – In this Film Mary is seen seated at a rough table in deep meditation. The angel appears at her side, coming slowly with outstretched arms ...
2. SHEPHERDS WATCHING THEIR FLOCK BY NIGHT – This scene represents the plains near the city and opens with the shepherds guarding their flocks, as the youthful David did a thousand years before. Suddenly the angel appears by their side. ...
3. THE BIRTH OF CHRIST – Joseph and Mary are here seen at the rude manger within the stable. By their side stands a faithful ass.[78]

The lecture opens with an ostentation – 'in this film' – which mandates no imaginings. There is simply a representation of Mary in front of the audience. The game of make-believe – at least for the minority atheist audience if we follow the argument from Chapter 1 – starts with the lecture's second sentence which, insofar it eliminates ostentations, invites imagining the appearance of an angel. As the scene and the lecture unfold more and more props appear and the game of make-believe appears to be running smoothly. At least until the remarks accompanying the second scene take place – 'this scene represents …'. The game is broken only to be picked up again in the same utterance which supplies props about shepherds and David. The opening of scene 3 presents a more equivocal intrusion. Is 'here' meant to be a shorthand for 'here in the picture' or has the lecturer mandated us to imagine him witnessing the birth? The use of passive 'seen' (also appearing in the first sentence of the lecture) would suggest the former. This is further supported by the recurrence of passive forms of perceptual verbs pertaining to the audience when the apparatus is not explicitly invoked: 'It will be noticed …', 'Herod's terrible vengeance is here shown', 'Joseph is here seen' and so on. Lubin's lecture is, therefore, somewhere between Kalem's and the above cited actual lecture of *Othello* (Henri Andréani and David Barnett, 1910). More than raising doubts about how to play the game of make-believe appropriately, it regularly interrupts and restarts the game. Unlike our German lecturer, however, Lubin's lecture is intentionally disruptive, disappointing trade press' implicit demands for the game of make-believe to be a continuous experience.

If the delivery was well prepared and executed in the style of Bush's printed lectures, it is reasonable to assume that the whole of the lecturer's voice would have been perceived as a non-diegetic part of the text, much like that of the voice-over narrator in later films analysed by Kozloff.[79] In other words, such 'voice-over' would have continuously been perceived as contributing to the game of make-believe. This much is suggested by the following lines from a lecture Bush prepared for *Enoch Arden* in which ostentations are eliminated:

> Scene 2. – Philip Ray, the miller's only son, and
>
> Scene 3. – Enoch Arden, a rough sailor's lad, made orphan by a winter shipwreck, had built their castles on dissolving sand, but
>
> Scene 4. – when the dawn of rosy childhood past and the new warmth of life's ascending sun was felt by either,
>
> Scene 5. – either fixed his heart on that one girl and Enoch spoke his love.[80]

Next to the elimination of ostentation, special attention is paid to the synchronization between the visual transitions and the tale told. As we can see, continuous long sentences run over multiple shots and the cuts between shots are verbally marked by either conjunctions or commas. This must have further contributed to the unity and diegetic coherence of the intermedial text.

To be completely fair, not all markers of enunciation are gone even in this exemplary lecture by Bush:

> Scene 1. – Here on this beach, a hundred years ago, three children of three houses. Annie Lee, the prettiest damsel in the port, and[81]

There are both spatial ('here' and 'this') and temporal ('ago') deictics. There is, however, no reason to think they could cause interference of the sort those employed in barker-like lectures would. First, there are no bodily demonstratives or ostentations revealing the apparatus so there is no reason to include the lecturer's body into the intermedial text. Second, the use of temporal deictics precludes us from reading the spatial ones as shorthand for implicit ostentations which imply the presence of the apparatus ('this is an image/picture/film/representation of x'). The reason is that the temporal deictic necessarily informs us of the temporal position the source of the voice inhabits in relation to the fictional world. The source of the voice is hundred years in the future from the events taking place in *Enoch Arden*. In other words, it would be mistaken to construe the opening sentence of the lecture as breaking the game of make-believe and saying something like 'This is an image of a beach from a hundred years ago.' Such a statement simply invites us to recognize the recording as hundred years old, rather than mandate us to imagine anything. In fact, at the time of the lecture this would have been a factually incorrect statement for the beach presented was shot in 1911 (Figure 4.2). This leads us to read the spatial deictics as informative of the source of the voice as well – present on the beach in question, hundred years after the events of the story. In other words, such use of deictics is clearly a part of the game of make-believe and would not have caused trouble for the game's continuity.

Broadly speaking, then, whereas the trade press implicitly advocated for a lecturing style that would afford uniform mandates for imaginings and continuous games of make-believe, the actual lecturing practice ranged from games plagued by persistent and oftentimes annoying pauses to those which accomplished the ideal of organic unity between the visual and the verbal track. As we have seen from the preceding examples, moreover, deictics as markers of enunciation played a crucial role in mandating imaginings. A good part of the problem with the barker style, as I have suggested, was the use of various ostentations (including deictics) which generated uncertainties as far as what imaginings the intermedial text mandated. At the same time, as the example of Bush demonstrates, a disciplined lecturer could have made use of deictics (either by avoiding or deploying them) to mandate uniform and specific imaginings.

Figure 4.2 Still from *Enoch Arden* (D. W. Griffith, 1911).

The next section will show how a systematic deployment of deixis not only transformed another genre that is traditionally understood as documentary into fictions – travelogues – but also managed to produce an agent the audiences were mandated to imagine as responsible for all the information that makes up the text. In other words, I will argue that the appearance of the film narrator preceded both what Gunning terms the 'Cinema of Narrative Integration' and what Gaudreault investigates in relation to legal decisions on the nature of story in cinema.[82] The specific brand of a film narrator who is in control of all of the images (and sounds) in the film, in fact, appears with at least the illustrated lectures of E. Burton Holmes. It is with a simple turn of a phrase that he transformed non-staged recordings into props for imagining and ushered in the controlling fictional narrator.

The lecturer and the performance of the film narrator through deixis

Holmes started his career as an illustrated lecturer in 1890 at the Chicago Camera Club where he presented photographs from his recent trip to Europe. From 1893 Holmes started lecturing on a regular basis presenting on journeys he made all around the world. By 1897 he was among the first lecturers to start to add motion pictures to his repertoire of photographs and hand-coloured slides. Holmes would continue to lecture well into the twentieth century retiring only after World War II (he even received a star on Hollywood Boulevard).

Altman's study is the only detailed narratological discussion of Holmes's performance style in relation to make-believe.[83] In fact, it is a comparative analysis one of whose main goals is to flesh out the difference between Holmes's signifying practices and those of another key lecturer – John L. Stoddard (who, retiring in 1897, hand-picked Holmes as his successor). Stoddard started lecturing in 1876 in Boston but only later introduced lantern slides to his lectures. As Altman points out, Stoddard's lecturing practices were a prime example of implementing Kember's rule (2) articulated by T. C. Hepworth's as follows: 'The views should be the best of their kind, but must be altogether subservient to the text.'[84]

Stoddard's lectures combine the matter-of-fact present tense which informs us of the states of affairs regarding the region visited and personal past of Stoddard's own lived experience of the travels undertaken:

> Of all the countries on our globe, Norway, in some respects, must rank as the most wonderful. From the North Cape to its most southern limit the distance is about eleven hundred miles. ...
>
> There have been few experiences in my life more joyous and exhilarating than my arrival in Christiania. It was six o'clock in the morning as our steamer glided up its noble harbor.[85]

As far as make-believe is concerned, the verbal component of Stoddard's lecture does not produce any props. We are not invited to imagine that Norway is wonderful, rather we are invited to recognize and accept this fact (along with numerous other facts). We are, furthermore, not mandated to imagine that it was six o'clock in the morning when Stoddard landed in Christiania. He simply informs us of the fact that he did so some time ago. Stoddard does not shy away from using deictics (here 'my' appears twice and 'our' once) but these could not have posed any problems for the audience for Stoddard's lectures were never conceived as games of make-believe to begin with. They were simply a combination of factual statements about visited regions seasoned with a touch of past first-hand experiences.

Unlike Holmes, Stoddard never took any of the images himself, so he relied exclusively on photographs derived from other sources, hand-painted slides and reproductions of existing drawings and etchings. Given that the function of these images was primarily illustrative we can safely say that the image track of his intermedial texts, precisely like his verbal performance, mandated no imaginings.

Holmes, as I already mentioned, used both photographs and motion pictures in his lectures.[86] The fact that the material was no less documentary than photographs Stoddard used, however, does not mean that the intermedial text they were a part of – Holmes's illustrated lecture – did not mandate any imaginings. This should come as no surprise for, as I argued at length in Chapter 1, it is the institutional and/or performative context that determines whether a recording of the world props up a game of make-believe or not. A lecturer can transform a recording of the actual world into an image of a fictional world simply by mandating us to make-believe certain things about the image. A recording of Elsinore can be momentarily transformed into (a prop for how to imagine) Hamlet's court when accompanied by a recital from Shakespeare's play. A recording of practically any building, for that matter, can be instantaneously transmuted into Hamlet's court if the lecturer instructs us to do so. In what follows, and building on Altman's work, I will argue that Holmes similarly integrates the image track into his intermedial fictional text and, in doing so, provides perhaps the earliest models for the film narrator.

Starting with an analysis of the printed version of Holmes's first lecture – 'Through Europe with a Camera' from volume seven of his *Lectures* published in 1901 – Altman identifies the key traits that would prove to be the mainstay of Holmes's style. These include the persistent use of narrative present and first-person plural. A typical section from the lecture (and his overall oeuvre) reads as follows:

> The first event of interest after passing Sandy Hook is the departure of the pilot. We all rush to the rail to see him clamber down the ship's side and tumble himself into a little row-boat, which immediately puts off.[87]

The combination of 'we' and narrative present conspires to evoke a sense of comradeship between Holmes and the audience. Holmes appears to invite the audience to embark on the journey with him. The first-person plural can be read as addressing the actual passengers on the ship or as simply referring to oneself, but it can also be understood as mandating the audience to imagine themselves accompanying Holmes on the voyage. The use of the present tense makes for the coincidence of: (1) the imagined time of the story, (2) the time of narration of the story, (3) the time of hearing the story and (4) the time of perceiving the images. All of this coaxes the audience to identify a mandate to join Holmes. As Altman observes, moreover, the features of the image track work in tandem with the verbal track to secure this mandate. Holmes's lectures regularly position the images with reference to the observers and their movements. For instance, the above cited departure of the pilot is accompanied by a high-angle photograph positioned above the hand rail. In another example, the sequence of a closer shot of the Tower of Pisa which is followed by a wider shot of it (Figure 4.3) is motivated by a verbal account of departing Pisa and looking back at the tower:

> [As we stand] it is difficult to realize that the tower is really thirteen feet out of the perpendicular. But if we glance toward the base, one hundred and seventy-nine feet below, the fact is at once startlingly apparent. Descending, then, before the tower shall decide to topple over, let us leave the city by the Porta Nova, glancing back ... for another look at our old friend.[88]

In other words, verbal track secures the continuity and spatial overlapping of the elements in the image track making the latter appear as the visual representation of the observers' point of view.

Though Altman's astute narratological analysis illuminates a number of key features of Holmes's lecturing style, there is one crucial problem with Altman's account – his understanding of fiction. Near the end of his chapter on lecture logic, Altman considers what the unacknowledged use of other people's photographs means for Holmes's work. In other words, Altman is concerned with

Figure 4.3 Moving away from the Tower of Pisa. E. Burton Holmes (*The Burton Holmes Lectures*, Vol. 7, New York, 1901, pp. 20–1).

the fact that Holmes incorporates photographs he did not take himself into his lecture. He believes that this practice brings two meaning systems operating in Holmes's lectures into sharp relief: 'While the first system is purely documentary or *mimetic* in nature, the second establishes a fiction and its supporting *diegetic* world.'[89] He claims, moreover, that 'one becom[es] visible only because of the temporary failure of the other'[90] and that 'we learn that diegetic coherence has actually taken precedence over mimetic accuracy'.[91]

The crux of the problem is an untenable binary opposition that Altman appears to construct – factual validity, documentary practice and mimesis, on the one hand, are contrasted to narrative coherence, fiction and diegesis, on the other. A representation of a story, however, is not necessarily fiction for documentary practice regularly includes story-telling. Similarly, that a story is coherent does not mean it is fictional or vice versa. It is true that borrowing another photographer's image of the Museum of Olympia makes for a smoother transition from the exterior to the interior of the museum in Holmes's story. It is also true that blowing up and cropping one and the same photograph instead of producing another one taken closer chimes well with the narrative of moving away from the Leaning Tower depicted in that image. And, to address Altman's final example, it is no less true that Holmes suggests in both word and image sequence that the Roman Forum is far closer to St. Peter's Cathedral than the actual 4 km of walking that separates them: 'Leaving these ruins, once the very center of the ancient world, we turn to a temple grander than any ever built in the ancient days – St. Peter's.'[92] But none of these deceptions, as we have learnt in the previous chapter, necessarily makes the story which refers to these images fictional.

What is crucial to grasp here, and this also pertains directly to Altman's claims that the visibility of fiction allegedly hinges on the failure of mimesis, is that the propositional content of Holmes's claims on its own does *not* mandate us to imagine anything. This propositional content does not mandate us to imagine that Holmes stood where the borrowed shot of the Museum of Olympia was made, that he moved away from the Leaning Tower of Pisa or that Roman Forum and St. Peter's Cathedral are right next to each other. Or, to put it more precisely, the propositional content mandates us to do so only because there is another marker in Holmes's lecture style that necessarily makes us construe the intermedial text as authorizing a game of make-believe to begin with. The *precondition* for such a mandate is Holmes's use of narrative present (rather than the use of 'we'). Given that the voyage (the story) is clearly not taking place at the time of Holmes's lecture, the narrative present forces the audience to *imagine* it is taking place now. In other words, all tales which recount past but actual events in the present tense are at the same time instances of fiction. Holmes's game of make-believe is visible from the get-go. Not because Holmes tampered with the photographs making up the image track but because he uses present tense. If Holmes were lecturing in the past tense, then the audience would be perfectly legitimate to dismiss the call to imagine themselves as participating in the voyage. They could take 'we' to refer to Holmes's actual entourage, and construe all of his statements as claims to factuality. Some of them, that is, the claims that Altman focuses on, would then under closer scrutiny be revealed as instances of pretence or lie.

Altman also appears to conflate different aspects of make-believe when he claims that '[o]ur ability to identify with Holmes depends on his ability to create a continuous and believable representation of space and time'.[93] First, it should be noted that the verb 'to identify' is rather unfortunate when speaking of games of make-believe in general. Although we do on occasions identify with fictional characters – in the sense that we wish to be like them – Altman here is speaking of something else. I take it he means that we imagine ourselves to be sharing Holmes's visual perspective and, by extension, accompanying him on his voyage and having essentially the same visual experiences as he is. This, however, has nothing to do with 'a continuous and believable representation of space and time'. Imagining ourselves as sharing in Holmes's visual perspective hinges exclusively on his use of first-person plural. Only Holmes's 'we', when understood as a prop in a game of make-believe and not (only) as a reference to his entourage or as a reference to oneself, allows this. Not even the use of present tense, moreover, is crucial here for the story could be told in the past tense and still allow for audience to imagine themselves as participants in the journey. The only difference would be that they would have to imagine themselves *having seen* the sights in question rather than *seeing* them at this very moment. (The exclusive use of past tense in Holmes's lecture would, of course, make it perfectly legitimate to read the intermedial text merely as a factual report on his voyage where 'we' refers either to the passengers or to oneself.)

All of this leads us to the conclusion that in the intermedial text that is Holmes's lecture, Holmes is the fictional narrator who is responsible for all the images we see and sounds we hear. Moreover, it is important to note that whether the audience imagined themselves as accompanying Holmes or not does not make a difference regarding his status as a fictional narrator. Even if they did not, they were still mandated to imagine that the story is taking place in the present – this fact already suffices for us to call Holmes's verbal performance a game of make-believe. He is not *claiming* that he is travelling at this very moment; rather he is *mandating* us to imagine that (at least) he is travelling at this very moment. This, it is worth emphasizing again, is not to say that the audiences were mandated to imagine only the story as coming from Holmes. They were also mandated to imagine him as responsible for the image track. One of the key findings of Altman's analysis strongly speaks in favour of this conclusion. As he notes, relating images to observers and their movements regularly sets up images as point-of-view shots: 'Holmes' photographs are described not as "location y" but as "location y seen from location x".'[94] These, in turn, mandate us to imagine that what is shown on screen is what (at least) Holmes is showing/seeing as he explores the sight in question.

As we have seen, a turn of phrase can easily transform non-staged recordings into props for imaginings. Here, it falls to some of the subtlest means – deictics, that is, the markers of enunciation present in pronouns and verb tenses – to do so. The fact that the audience is mandated to play a game of make-believe does not mean that the factuality (and occasional pretence) of the verbal propositional content and pictorial referential content is eliminated no more than it means that the profilmic referential content is lost in photographic fiction films. Contrary to what Altman claims, imagination *supervenes* on the documentary system and no failure of one is necessary to spot the other. What is important, as Altman rightly points out, is that already practices older than fiction film managed to transform photographic representations into props. Crucially, this was accomplished using the verbal rather than the visual track. Moreover, the lecturer was not only the key figure for this feat but also the first agent to inhabit the role of the *controlling* film narrator. Such narrators are entities mandated to be *imagined* as responsible for *all* the mandates and props that make up the text. In other words, these narrators mandate imaginings about themselves as agents to whom all the information that makes up the intermedial text can be attributed and/or who dispense that information. In Holmes's case, to repeat (on top of believing), we are mandated to imagine Holmes as telling the tale and showing/seeing all the images.

This chapter has tried to articulate one part of the history of Walton's mandates for imagining on the example of lecturers by placing them within the larger institutional context of illustrated lecturing. I argued, moreover, that lecturers not only shed light on how specific control was mandated over images but also how actual recordings were transformed into props for imaginative engagement in the first place. In other words, lecturers present the earliest instance in the history of photographic film where textual parameters alone mandated the film's fictional status.

In the remainder of the book I wish to zero in on a specific type of mandate I already started exploring here – controlling narration. The model of the (controlling) film narrator, for Holmes used both photographic stills and motion pictures in his travelogues, differs significantly from the ones proposed by Gunning and Gaudreault.[95] Their models revolve around the use of the visual track, whereas the model ushered in by lecturers hinges on the importance of the verbal track. Moreover, their model identifies implicit narrators, whereas Holmes's establishes explicit ones. Whether or not Gunning and Gaudreault are correct to identify the mandate for imaging a narrator in early cinema is a matter I take up in the final chapter.

Before tackling the debate on controlling fictional narrators head on, however, it will be necessary to turn our attention to institutional discourses at the moment when narrative cinema becomes the dominant. Screenwriting manuals construed as pre-theoretical narratological discourse provide a historical introduction into the discussion of mandates concerning potential narrator figures.

5

Implicit mandates and fictional narrators

In this chapter I bring the investigation of implicit mandates and what counts as a prop for imaginings to a close. On the example of a crucial issue within Kendall L. Walton's model – controlling narration – I articulate in detail what it means to implicitly mandate an agency presenting all the narrative information. Whereas in literary fiction such mandates hinge on deictic properties of language, their absence in film leads to the conclusion that there are no similar implicit mandates in fiction film. This proves to be of direct relevance for film studies because the finding gives us further reasons to abandon linguistic models when speaking of narrators in fiction film. It allows us to construe the early development of narrative cinema without any such agency and to recognize that contemporary practitioners and contributors to developments in story-telling saw the absence of narrators precisely as one of the key differences between literary and film fiction. In other words, the final chapter forces us to take contemporary narratological discourse seriously when attempting to give an account of what it meant to imaginatively engage the telling of a film story.

Specifically, I argue against the thesis generally accepted in non-analytic film narratology circles, namely the one popularized by Christian Metz which assigns the control over the whole of the audio-visual track to an entity dubbed 'the great image-maker'. By drawing on both new film history and analytic philosophy I demonstrate that whereas on most occasions there are mandates for a fictional narrator in literary fiction, in fiction film this is so only in exceptional cases. I refer to this thesis as the asymmetry between fictional narrator in literary and film fiction, and I argue that this asymmetry was already well known to commentators during the early cinema period.

It must be admitted that there is uncertainty about what narrative role the great image-maker exactly has. Metz's initial formulation from the 1960s allows for at least three different readings of the role in question: the author, the implied author and the narrator.

Every narrative is ... a discourse ... In Jakobsonian terms, one would say that a discourse, being a statement or sequence of statements, refers necessarily to a subject of the statement. ... Albert Laffay ... has shown this to be true of film narrative. The spectator perceives images which have obviously been selected (they could have been other images) and arranged (their order could have been different). In a sense, he is leafing through an album of predetermined pictures, and it is not he who is turning the pages but some 'master of ceremonies,' some 'grand image-maker' (*grand imagier*) who (before being recognized as author, if it is an *auteur* film, or, if not, in the absence of an author) is first and foremost the film itself as a linguistic object (since the spectator always knows that what he is seeing is a film), or more precisely a sort of 'potential linguistic focus' ('*foyer linguistique virtuel*') situated somewhere behind the film, and representing the basis that makes the film possible. That is the filmic form of the narrative instance, which is necessarily present, and is necessarily perceived, in any narrative.[1]

Considering the developments of narrative theory in Europe of the time and the fact that the wide use of the notion of the 'implied author' that Wayne C. Booth introduced in 1961 was for the most part still reserved for the United States, it is safe to assume that the great image-maker was initially thought of as a narrator figure much like Gérard Genette's later extradiegetic narrator who was assumed to be in control of the whole of the text.[2] This much is certainly strongly implied in *The Imaginary Signifier* where Metz compares films to dreams and lists the absence of the narrator in dreams as one of the main distinctions between the two.[3] The identification of the great image-maker with the filmic narrator can be seen in a number of prominent scholars' work including those of Sarah Kozloff, André Gaudreault and François Jost as well.[4]

The translation of Genette's seminal *Narrative Discourse* into English in 1980 has, starting with Brian Henderson's 1983 'Tense, Mood and Voice in Film', prompted a number of film scholars to apply Genette's categories to film.[5] Henderson found the category of voice to be the most problematic for direct application to film especially because he felt that the voice-over narrator ought not to be thought of as an equivalent to the extradiegetic narrator. Later narratological studies, however, would have far less reservations about appropriating the category. Kozloff would identify the great image-maker with the extradiegetic narrator and Tom Gunning would understand the ushering in of narrative cinema in the work of D. W. Griffith as the birth of 'the narrator system' which he also construed along Genettian categories.[6] Other prominent narratologists who have identified a filmic narrator in fiction film equivalent to the extradiegetic narrator include David A. Black, Seymour Chatman and

Peter Verstraten.⁷ Either explicitly or implicitly much of this work has hinged on the allegedly analytic premise that 'there cannot be a narrative work without a narrator' identifiable in the above citation from Metz as well.

To engage the question of filmic narrator, therefore, it will be necessary to address the notion of the literary narrator in general and Genette's model in particular. Given that the goal of this chapter is, moreover, to spell out the necessary and sufficient conditions for the existence of controlling fictional narrators in general I will also articulate my understanding of narrative. Early cinema again provides unique insights for it is during this period that the story-films establish themselves as the industry and the stylistic dominant. If Metz is correct that all narrative fiction films necessarily entail the existence of a narrator, then articulations of such an entity should be found already in that period. In other words, if story films started appearing already during the cinema of attractions period and if the transitional period ushered in 'the narrator system' then it is reasonable to assume that the contemporary discourse on cinema would exhibit at least some signs of interest in the narrator figure. Up to this point I demonstrated that 'fictional showing', although present in specific lecturing practices, was generally absent from fiction film during early cinema. This includes both fiction films which hinged on imagining seeing from within the world like phantom rides and those which mandated no imagining seeing of the sort such as comic parts of Hale's Tours. Let us consider if the changes in the telling of the fictional story which took place roughly up to 1915 ushered in any controlling 'fictional showing' comparable to that of E. Burton Holmes.

Narrative and narrator in early cinema

Narrative

To speak of a narrator there of course must be a narrative (though, as I will demonstrate, the obverse does not hold). A narrative, as I define it, is a text with a beginning and an end, and out of which a chronological sequence of events (story) may be inferred. More specifically, adapting an account given by Marie-Laure Ryan, narrative is a representation of a story (itself a mental representation) which is (1) populated by agents who play a role in (2) causal and non-deterministic changes in states of affairs of the story-world which (3) are sufficiently distinguished to count as disturbances in equilibrium.⁸ These conditions do important work of exclusion. The first condition excludes representations of non-anthropomorphized entities from the class of narratives (e.g. 'The door opened and then closed'). The second condition dismisses representations of deterministic processes (e.g. 'The ball was falling toward the ground at a constant rate of acceleration'). Representations of general causal but non-deterministic processes such as evolution (e.g. 'Life developed, first, out of inorganic matter, and then from a common ancestor'), natural cycles (e.g. 'Having fallen in autumn leaves will reappear come springtime') and chronologies (e.g. '1895: Cinématographe at Grand Café; 1896: Kinetoscope in Messina, Italy, etc.') are eliminated by the first and the second condition in tandem. Representations based on historical causality such as Hegel's *Phenomenology of Spirit* would, under this framework, still count among narratives – for Hegel's Spirit is essentially an anthropomorphic agent which brings about change. The second condition eliminates representations which do not represent sequences of events. Finally, the third condition bars representations which do not appear to elicit much expectation for narrative closure from narratives (e.g. 'Mark entered the kitchen wondering about life'). The list of conditions is meant as a fuzzy-set definition in the sense that there will always be border-line cases in which we will not be able to agree whether one or any of the conditions are met or not.

From these parameters it follows that there are a number of representations (and even representations of temporally unfolding events) that are not narratives. For instance, none of the following is a narrative: propositions, mathematical proofs, logical arguments, recipes, maps, questions, imperatives, conditionals, hypotheticals, databases, computer programs, various types of laws (religious, natural, legal, etc.), legal judgements, chronologies, abstract paintings, this sentence and the like. Closer to our field of interest, in representational art a painting such as Paul Cézanne's *Still Life with Apples* is not a narrative for it fails to meet not only one but all the criteria specified. The second and the third condition are absent in virtually all photographs and panoramas such as 1893 *The Battle of Sedan* (traveling panoramas, by contrast, were most often narratives). In early cinema, furthermore, numerous scenics are not narratives for they regularly lack agents playing a role in changes of states of affair. Edison Manufacturing Company films of George Sandow, for instance, also fail to be narratives despite satisfying the first two conditions – they lack any concrete departure from the state of equilibrium.

There is at least one prominent film historian who disagrees with this account of narrative – André Gaudreault. For him the very existence of a minimal temporal transformation is sufficient for something to count as narrative. Apart from shots where there is no change (freeze frames and motionless shots) and shots composed of images which are completely distinct 'every shot would be either a narrative or a segment of a possible narrative'.⁹ For him, Sandow films are narratives because we can clearly register changes – Sandow flexing his muscles in different ways.

The problem with Gaudreault's minimal definition of narrative is that were we to apply it we would be forced to call all film representations of any dynamic temporal developments narratives. In that sense any two adjacent frames from Sandow films or from any other film regarded on their own (so long as they depict dynamic temporal development) would count as a narrative. There is, however, little value in calling a change which occurs in a fraction of a second a narrative. Such changes would not even allow for the understanding of what kind of action is taking place. In fact, when presented with any two adjacent frames shots from a Sandow film it is unlikely we could even register change let alone comprehend that Sandow is flexing his muscles. And even if we did register the change across the two frames it is unlikely these would hold any kind of information of interest to narrative analysis.

The definition I propose above, by contrast, can easily dismiss these examples from the class of narratives. At the same time, it does allow for early film narratives such as *The Waterer Watered/L'Arroseur arrosé* (Louis Lumière, 1895) where two agents (the gardener and the troublemaker) engage in an altercation which ends in gardener spanking the boy. Not only is there a sufficient disturbance in the equilibrium – there is even narrative closure. This much is attested by a contemporary catalogue description: '[the film] shows the bad boy playing practical jokes on the gardener. It ends in a thorough wetting for the both, and the total defeat of the mischievous urchin.'¹⁰

My proposed definition also provides an insight about the relation of fiction film to narrative – it is not only that narrative films need not be fiction films, but fiction films need not be narratives either. Consider early films treating water subjects discussed in Chapter 2. Although these films mandate imagining oneself at the beach this imagining hardly involves oneself playing any significant role in the events taking place. At most, as one reviewer noticed, 'one ha[s] an inclination to step backward to avoid getting wet'. Moreover, the events which do unfold – the waves rising and crashing down, the lines of the surf breaking – do not only introduce any disruptions in the equilibrium but are also causally deterministic. Gaudreault would be forced to call such films narratives simply because they represent natural phenomena as they unfold over time.

At this point we might inquire whether early train films such as *The Arrival of a Train/L'Arrivée d'un train en gare de La Ciotat* and phantom rides constitute narratives. *The Arrival of a Train* does appear to be a narrative both from the perspective of mandated imaginings and actual representational content. In the former case, we are dealing with a suspense story in which a train is threatening to jump from the screen directly into the auditorium only to swerve at the last moment. Gorky, for instance, after inviting us to imagine the collision and ripped sacks of lacerated flesh concludes: 'But this, too, is but a train of shadows. Noiselessly, the locomotive disappears beyond the edge of the screen.'[11] If we focus on actual representational content, we identify numerous agents (people in the train and on the station) who play a role in the events (disembarking and boarding) which are sufficiently distinguished to count as disturbances in the equilibrium.[12] Gorky's account can again serve as evidence: 'The train comes to a stop, and grey figures silently emerge from the car, soundlessly great their friends laugh, walk, run, bustle, and ... are gone.'[13]

In the case of phantom rides which mandate no imaginings – as they did in the period between following their early heyday and their later revival in Hale's Tours – it is difficult to speak of any narrative form. As the commentators of *Brooklyn Bridge* (American Mutoscope and Biograph Company, 1899) cited at length in Chapter 2 attest, we are only dealing with a representation of crossing the bridge from Manhattan to Brooklyn. There are no anthropomorphic agents – only cars – and the pedestrians who can be seen on either side do not play a role in this passage. When phantom rides do mandate imaginings, the matter is different.

It might be assumed that I already decided in favour of phantom rides as narratives in Chapter 2 when I claimed that phantom rides present part and parcel of the overall fiction that is the Hale's Tours show. Given that the interpolated segment is narrative in form we can also say that the phantom rides preceding and following the segment present temporal developments in that fictional world, and as such add to the film's narrative content. At the same time, however, I criticized Charlie Keil's interchangeable use of 'fictionality' and 'narrativity' by arguing that mandates to imagine do not necessarily invite imagining stories – imagining proposition-like states of affairs do not either. This is effectively another way of saying what I have claimed above – that the category of fiction and narrative are independent. In other words, I have said nothing about whether phantom rides are narratives when appearing outside of Hale's Tours context as they originally did with the premiere of *The Haverstraw Tunnel* (American Mutoscope and Biograph Company, 1897).

From the perspective of phantom rides as stand-alone mandated imaginings the matter seems to come down to whether the excitement they undoubtedly evoked amounts to anything like the narrative arch of suspense that was reported for *The Arrival of the Train*. The resolution of the issue, in other words, seems to hinge on whether this imaginary participation in the form of an exhilarating experience amounts to imagining a story. Or, to put it more precisely, does the content of this imaginary experience constitute a sufficient departure from the equilibrium? In Lumière brothers there is not only a sudden realization that there is a train in motion but also that, as Stasov cited in Chapter 1 puts it, this train is on a collision course and 'get[ing] bigger and bigger'. In other words, there is an imaginary threat which demands resolution (and affords it with a sigh of relief). And indeed, in the accounts of *The Haverstraw Tunnel* something similar is the case:

> The train is invisible, and yet the landscape sweeps remorselessly, and far away the bright day becomes a spot of darkness. That is the mouth of the tunnel, and towards it the spectator is hurled as if a fate was behind him. The spot of darkness becomes a canopy of gloom. The darkness closes around, and the spectator is being flung through that cavern with demoniac energy behind him. The shadows, the rush of the invisible force, and the uncertainty of the issues makes one instinctively hold one's breath as when on the edge of a crisis that might become a catastrophe.
>
> But the daylight shines ahead, and again the spectator is being swept through the fields and amid a fair country. The audience half-reels as it catches itself, exhausted from the sensation of travelling on the front of an express at lightning speed.[14]

As the spectator imagines traveling through the countryside something appears on the horizon, something which at first looks merely like a black speck but rapidly transforms into a shroud of darkness. This veil engulfs the viewer causing concern that something terrible might happen, some unknown catastrophe. But just as the spectator braces herself for the impending doom, the darkness disappears as quickly as it appeared, and the viewer finds herself safe again in the sunlit horizon. As we can see, there is an emotional arch here which spells out a narrative quite like the one experienced when imaginatively engaging *The Arrival of a Train* – a threat avoided at the last moment, a minimal narrative satisfying all three conditions spelled out above.

Contemporary reports, therefore, demonstrate that even some prime examples of what Gunning has dubbed the cinema of attractions were accounted for in narrative terms. This of course does not mean that the formal traits usually associated with the cinema of attractions such as the direct address to the spectator, temporal punctuality and the highlighting of the power of display disappear. But it does mean that temporal punctuality can go hand in hand with chronological development and that the power of display can be a part of the construction of diegesis as early as in train film and phantom ride genres. In other words, this finding expands the category of double nature films – films combining both attractions and stories – from trick films, chase films and passion plays to include some train films and phantom rides as well. It also demonstrates that key examples of Gunning's cinema of attractions were described in terms of both attraction *and* narrative by their contemporaries. Crucially, this conclusion offers itself once the films in question are treated as fiction, that is, when the role of imagination is examined in detail.

Narrator

If the existence of a narrative in film is a necessary criterion for the existence of a film narrator can we say that the latter appears immediately with the appearance of the former? In other words, do all film narratives have a film narrator by definition? With some notable exceptions this is indeed the prevalent view among film scholars. For a standard articulation of this position as it pertains to the period under scrutiny we can turn to two key book-length studies of narration in early cinema – Gunning's *D. W. Griffith and the Origins of American Narrative Film* and Gaudreault's *From Plato to Lumière*:

> Because film's narrative discourse represents the actual text of a film – its existence as a series of filmic images – no narrative film can exist except through its narrative discourse. It logically follows that every narrative film has a filmic narrator embodied by this discourse.[15]
>
> A narrative work (a film, a novel, or another work) would thus be the result of a tension between two poles: on the one hand, the diegetic universe (the story told), and on the other, the agent that organizes this world (the storyteller). ... Every narrative is simultaneously a discourse (the discourse of the storyteller) and a story (the story told).[16]

When it comes to fictional narratives to which both devote most of their attention, it is crucial to understand that both Gunning and Gaudreault emphasize that the narrator is *not* the flesh and blood author but an entity internal to the text. In other words, in fiction film the narrator is fictional and as such distinct from the actual author. In this Gunning and Gaudreault are fully in line with Genette's key articulation of the distinction between the narrator and the author:

It is not Abbé Prévost who tells of the love of Manon and Des Grieux, it is not even the Marquis de Renoncourt, supposed author of the *Mémoires d'un homme de qualité*; it is Des Grieux himself, in an oral narrative where 'I' can designate only him, and where 'here' and 'now' refer to the spatiotemporal circumstances of that narrating and in no way to the circumstances of the writing of *Manon Lescaut* by its real author. And even the references in *Tristram Shandy* to the situation of writing speak to the (fictive) act of Tristram and not the (real) one of Sterne; but in a more subtle and also more radical way, the narrator of *Père Goriot* 'is' not Balzac, even if here and there he expresses Balzac's opinions, for this author-narrator is someone who 'knows' the Vauquer boardinghouse, its landlady and its lodgers, whereas all Balzac himself does is imagine them; and in this sense, of course, the narrating situation is never *reduced* to its situation of writing.[17]

The logic behind Gunning's and Gaudreault's arguments is essentially that of Metz and Laffay – because narrative discourse, that is, the presentation of a story, is nothing but the narrative text itself, there necessarily needs to be an agent doing this presenting, that is, the narrator.[18] In other words, because every narrative work is a product of narrating there needs to be a narrator. There is certainly nothing problematic in claiming with Gaudreault and Gunning that if there is narrating then there needs to be a narrator. In fact, this is a tautology. The problem arises because at the same time they mean that if there is narrating of a *fictional* story then there needs to be a *fictional* narrator. But this is as formally valid as saying that if there is narrating of a brief story then there needs to be a brief narrator. It is true that, as Gunning points out, if there is a message then there is also a sender.[19] But if the message has a content which mandates specific imaginings it does not follow that these mandates also include *imagining* a sender. The same is especially true of visual messages.

This, however, does not necessarily preclude the possibility that the specific narrative films that Gaudreault and Gunning focus on mandate imagining narrators. Gaudreault, for instance, distinguishes between two agents of narrative discourse in film – the monstrator and the narrator proper. Whereas the latter appears only with editing and oversees the concatenation of shots into a sequence the former is ushered into existence with the earliest film narratives and controls the *showing* of the content of single-shot films. In other words, for Gaudreault a specific form of the narrator – the monstrator – should already be present in *The Arrival of a Train* or *The Haverstraw Tunnel*. The contemporary accounts, however, do not provide the slightest shred of evidence that the mandates to imagine a train were accompanied by mandates to imagine that the train was shown let alone to imagine somebody showing it. It is clear that who is *actually* showing the film is the projectionist – but no mandated imaginings apply to her.

Logically speaking, as we have learnt earlier, no imagining entails any other imagining. We can imagine two contradictory things without a problem as much as we can imagine something without imagining any of its entailments. I can imagine touching an object, for instance, without also imagining being in the object's presence. Therefore, *nothing* follows from imagining seeing. And *nothing* follows from fictional showing either. This much is corroborated by historical evidence as well. In the accounts of train films and phantom rides cited in the previous chapters there is no suggestion that there is any showing from *within* the diegetic world, let alone that the showing should be *imagined* as performed by somebody either. In fact, there are contemporary reports which, like the one following the screening of *The Haverstraw Tunnel*, clearly state that the only showing is the actual one taking place in the music hall:

> The Palace Theatre is now showing by the Biograph the most remarkable film ever exhibited in England.[20]
>
> The most recent addition to the series of animated photographs now being shown at the Palace Theatre represents the scene from the footplate of a locomotive running 60 miles an hour.[21]

Both logic and empirical evidence, then, attest that monstration understood as fictional showing is independent from imagined seeing.

While Gaudreault does not consider contemporary reviews in his discussion of early film monstrators and narrators, he does cite another contemporary discourse as proof of his claims – judicial decisions. Specifically, two copyright lawsuits and their accompanying decisions from 1902 and 1905, according to Gaudreault, present the first pre-theoretical articulations of the concepts of monstrator and narrator proper, respectively. The first lawsuit concerns an actuality film, so the conclusions he draws from that cannot be applied to the discussion of fictional narrators. But his discussion of 1904 *Personal* originally shot by American Mutoscope and Biograph Company and quickly remade by the Edison Manufacturing Company under the title *How a French Nobleman Got a Wife through the 'New York Herald' Personal Columns* clearly can.

The 1902 lawsuit determined that it is sufficient to copyright only one photograph from a single-shot film to copyright the whole film and thus articulated film not as a mere amalgam of photographs but as a unity of these photographs. For Gaudreault this means that it has been recognized that the photographs are linked together through a discourse whose agent is none other than the monstrator. Once Porter remade American Mutoscope and Biograph Company's *Personal* in 1904, Biograph quickly sued the Edison Manufacturing

Company arguing that given that Biograph had copyrighted one photograph from their film the whole film is copyrighted which means that Edison has infringed on their copyright. Porter and Edison's lawyers retorted that in order to copyright the whole film American Mutoscope and Biograph Company had to have copyrighted eight photographs – one from each of the film's eight shots – because the film is merely an agglomerate of eight distinct and separate films. According to Gaudreault, whereas Biograph effectively argued that the film was narrated by combining shots into a unity, Edison claimed that no such narrating is taking place and that the film is simply a sequence of disparate shots. In the end Judge Lanning sided with the former view stating:

> I am unable to see why, if a series of pictures of a moving object taken by a pivoted camera may be copyrighted as a photograph, a series of pictures telling a single story like that of the complainant in this case, even though the camera be placed at different points, may also not be copyrighted as a photograph ... In that story, it is true, there are different scenes. But no one has ever suggested that a story told in written words may not be copyrighted merely because, in unfolding its incidents, the reader is carried from one scene to another.[22]

To Gaudreault's mind '[t]his recognition of the *film narrator* ... [establishes] the *film* equivalent of the *textual* narrator'.[23] But as we can see from Genette's quotation above the textual narrator is a fictional entity engaged in a fictional activity – we are mandated to imagine that Tristram is writing the book which consists of exactly the same words as Sterne's book. Are we mandated to imagine anything similar in *Personal* or its remake? A *fictional* agency in control of combining the shots and presenting them as a story? Nothing of the sort exists. I am not denying that there is an equivalence between different camera placements and carrying the reader from one scene to another, as Gaudreault puts it, but this equivalence is only on the level of narrating and not on the level of *fictional* narrating. Gaudreault's narratology, in other words, can only provide theoretical models for distinguishing the forms of narrative discourse but, unlike Genette's, it can tell us little about the fictional status of narrators.

The situation is similar with Gunning's study. Gunning distinguishes three aspects of narrative discourse – the profilmic, enframing and editing. Whereas the profilmic concerns mise-en-scène in the theatrical sense of the word and enframing pertains to the manipulations of camera and film stock, editing is a matter of joining enframed shots together. In Gaudreault's vocabulary the first two aspects of narrative discourse are the monstrator's responsibility and the last one that of the narrator proper. Gunning, by contrast, prefers to speak of a single filmic narrator embodied by narrative discourse overall because the last aspect need not be necessarily present.[24] Gunning's point is that the filmic narrator becomes truly visible only with the developments taking place between 1908 and 1913 in what he dubs 'the narrator system' when moral commentary, characterization and the formation of unambiguous temporal relations become more pronounced.

Gunning's analysis of Griffith's early films at Biograph is an extremely detailed and nuanced study of how each of the aspects of narrative discourse contributed to conveying moral commentary, characterization and temporal relations in narrative fiction film. In other words, it is an unparalleled investigation of how early narrative fiction films were narrated. The problems arise, however, when the role of imagination is taken into consideration because these very films are at the same time understood to be narrated not only by Griffith the author but *fictionally* as well. For want of space I cannot consider all of Gunning's examples so I will only tackle *The Song of the Shirt* (1908) which, as Gunning himself puts it, 'exemplifies Griffith's work in Genette's category of voice, expressing the filmic narrator's judgments about characters or actions through contrast edits'.[25] 'For Genette,' Gunning continues, 'voice refers to the act of narrating the story and to the elements in the text which refer to this act'.[26] And, to be perfectly clear, under Genette's model this act of narrating as well as its agent are necessarily fictional:

> [A] confusion [between the author and the narrator] is perhaps legitimate in the case of a historical narrative or a real autobiography, but not when we are dealing with a narrative of fiction, where the role of narrator is itself fictive ...
>
> So it is this narrating instance that we have still to look at [under the category of voice], according to the traces it has left – the traces so it is considered to have left – in the narrative discourse it is considered to have produced.[27]

The Song of the Shirt is a story of a seamstress who tries to find work in order to provide for her sick sister but once she does and completes the task she is refused payment. Her subsequent pleas with the factory owner and the foreman fall on barren ground and upon her return home her sister dies in front of her eyes.

Gunning perceptively identifies the final three shots as the core of the film's social commentary – while in the first shot the factory owner dances merrily with two girls and in the second the foreman wines and dines in the same upscale restaurant, in the last shot the seamstress' sister finally succumbs to her affliction in a shabby room. And Gunning also eloquently articulates the key role that editing has in this process distinguishing between contrast editing whose primary concern is the juxtaposition of the lives of the wealthy and the poor and parallel editing which is mainly motivated by temporal relations and deadlines. In other words, it is undeniable that the story is a social critique and that this critique has been articulated through narrative discourse. But this does not mean that anybody from the story world is responsible for this narrative discourse. As this typical entry from the catalogue attests, the story is simply shown without any fictional showing taking place: 'In this Biograph story are shown two orphaned sisters, in poverty and sickness, struggling to eke an existence, frugal though it be.'[28] We are not mandated to imagine anybody juxtaposing these shots in the way that we are mandated to imagine Tristram writing the story of his life or, to recall the example from Chapter 4, to imagine anybody like Holmes showing us all of the sights on the screen. Nor are we mandated to imagine anybody like the anonymous narrator in *Père Goriot* (1835) who 'knows' the sisters and their plight and controls these shots because, as we have learnt above, showing a fiction does not entail fictional showing.[29]

If there is an early film which at least approaches what it would mean for there to be a fictional filmic narrator, then it is *The Big Swallow* (James Williamson, 1901). The film depicts a man angered to find himself to be an object of a camera. To this he reacts by walking up to the camera so close that only his mouth can be seen. At this point he swallows both the camera and the operator upon which he moves back to a close-up of his face in which he expresses his great satisfaction with the snack. But even in this film the audience is mandated to imagine somebody showing the film only to the point where the man's mouth covers the screen. In the remainder of the film there is no additional camera and no additional operator within the diegetic world standing at the very spot where the gobbled-up camera and operator stood and showing us the film's second part. And there is again nobody on par with Genette's narrator in Balzac's *Père Goriot* who 'knows' both the gentleman and the cameraman and who we should imagine narrating the whole story (before *and* after the swallow).

The catalogue entry for Williamson's film is also clear that there is fictional showing going on, albeit only halfway:

'I won't! I won't! I'll eat the camera first!' Gentleman reading, finds a camera fiend with his head under a cloth, focusing him up. He orders him off, approaching nearer and nearer, gesticulating and ordering the photographer off, until his head fills the picture, and finally his mouth only occupies the screen. He opens it, and first the camera, then the operator disappear inside. He retires munching him up and expressing his great satisfaction.[30]

In contrast to typical catalogue articulations of 'showing' discussed here and at the end of Chapter 2 which all refer to actual showing even in the cases of phantom rides, in *The Big Swallow* it is clear that we are mandated to imagine 'a camera fiend' 'focusing [the gentleman] up'. In other words, on those rare occasions when fictional showing in early cinema is mandated, it is likely to be recognized as such by contemporaries. Therefore, let us turn to the contemporary discourse which, given that it was directed at aspiring story-tellers and practicing filmmakers, arguably has the highest chance of identifying the fictional narrator in early cinema – screenwriting manuals and the discussions of narrative clarity in the trade press.

Contemporary narratological discourse

As I already noted in the chapter on lecturers, narrative clarity was one of the key concerns in the transitional era when it comes to film's narrative function. Although in the United States this demand for comprehensibility saw the renewed popularity of lecturers between 1908 and 1912, the ideal solution to meeting this demand was always with recourse to the visual track alone. The idea that the spectator should be able to reconstruct the story by simply looking at the screen appears at least as early as 1906 – in an Edison Manufacturing Company's advertisement we read that their 'latest dramatic success ... *Kathleen Mavourneen* ... tells its own story – plainer than words'.[31] By 1908 the issue of narrative comprehension arose to such prominence in the trade press that the following correspondence appeared in the *Moving Picture World*:

> Many a time I have watched a new film subject projected on the screen and thought to myself: If I only knew what this or that part of the picture meant, then I could get very much more enjoyment out of the entertainment. But how would it be possible for the theater manager to explain the film subjects unless the film manufacturer furnishes a printed description of each picture when they are sent out? I think that half of the time the theater manager himself does not understand the picture as it is projected on the canvas. If some film manufacturer would make every one of his film subjects explain themselves as they pass through the machine he would soon have all the business he could attend to. If instead of having a few words of explanation on his film about every 100 feet, as most of them do, they would have these explanations come in at every 20 or 30 feet (or at every place on film wherein an explanation was necessary), then the theater manager would have no use for a lecturer. ... W. M. RHOADS.

In reply: The idea of a lecturette is a good one, but one that few proprietors will take the trouble to arrange. For instance, Kalem Company arranged a lecturette or resume of the story of Evangeline to go with that film; we understand that so few exhibitors applied for it that the company abandoned the idea of reprinting.

To issue titles every 100 feet would unnecessarily add to the cost of the film and is a little too much to ask renters to pay 12 cents per foot for title. We would blame the actors inasmuch as they did not render the story intelligently. A perfectly thought out plot, well put together, should tell its own story.[32]

We are dealing with a crisis of narrative comprehensibility here and although various solutions are proposed in both the letter and the response to it – providing a synopsis to the audiences in the form of printed material, increasing the number of intertitles, and using lecturers – the ideal solution that crystallizes is that the film 'should tell its own story'. This notion would remain the mainstay of thinking about the matter throughout the transitional era.

To put it in Gunning's terms, the film learning to tell its own story amounts to developments in narrative discourse such as those he describes in his book on Griffith. So, for Gunning learning to tell its own story essentially translates to introducing the narrator who tells the story. My argument, however, is that these developments introduce no such mandates. Next to analytic arguments introduced above and negative evidence of the absence of narrators in contemporary catalogues and reviews the positive historical proof for my claim can be found in the screenwriting manuals and instructions for screenwriters which start appearing with regularity around 1910.

By this time the conditions in the American film industry led to such a demand for original fiction story films – or photoplays as they were called then – that the demand could not be met by the production companies' creative staff alone. To address this need the producers turned to the open market and started soliciting scripts. This, in turn, opened a market for columns advising aspiring screenwriters, screenwriting textbooks and even film magazines devoted exclusively to 'photoplaywrights'. For instance, as early as 20 August 1910 *Film Index* devoted a full page to the 'Tribulations of a Scenario Writer'.[33] William Lord Wright wrote columns 'For Those Who Worry O'er Plots and Plays' and 'For Photoplay Authors' for *Motion Picture World* (from March 1912) and *New York Dramatic Mirror* (from March 1913), respectively. Similarly, specialized magazines such as *Photo Playwright* and *Photoplay Author* appeared in April 1912 and January 1913, respectively (Figure 5.1). By 1915 Clarence J. Caine could publish a book-length collection of his writings on the topic originally appearing in *Picture-Play Weekly* and *Picture-Play Magazine*.[34]

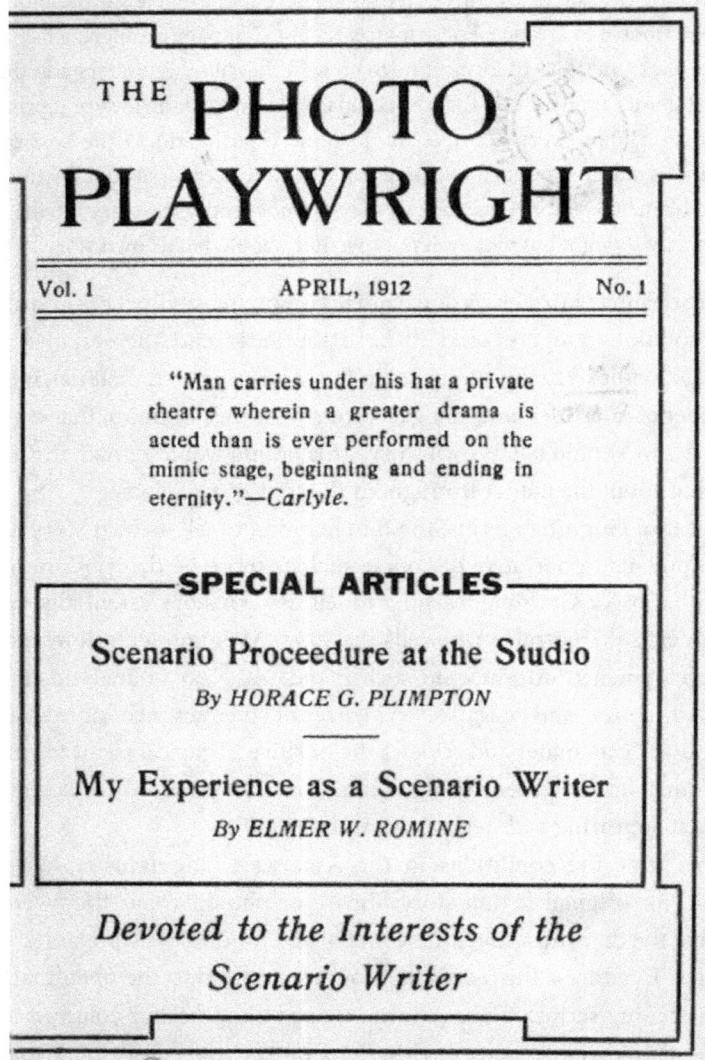

Figure 5.1 The first issue of *Photo Playwright*, April 1912.

The first textbooks such as E. J. Muddle's *Picture Plays and How to Write Them* and Ralph P. Stoddard's *The Photo-Play* can be tracked to at least 1911 and, much like other commentary, readily promulgate the ideal of narrative clarity adopted from the preceding trade press commentary:[35]

> The story must be told by a series of happenings. While titles and sub-titles are used, and often strengthen the interest in the story, no manufacturer would buy

a Scenario which would not stand alone or carry its story to the audience by the pictures, regardless of the title.[36]

The idea that the story tells itself or, as we read here, that it is 'told by a series of happenings' strongly suggests the view that for contemporaries there is no unitary agent within this world of events that tells the story. Rather, based on the events that unfold in front of the spectator's eyes she can reconstruct the story. And the following analogy should explain why this should come as no surprise. Consider a sports event of your own choosing. Regardless of the event you pick it turns out that you are dealing with a series of happenings which meets all the requirements of Ryan's narrative text in the same sense that a story on the screen does. The sports event has a clearly defined beginning and an end, it temporally controls its own reception meaning there is a temporal dimension internal to the event and a story can be reconstructed out of it with agents (players) having a role in non-deterministic events counting as disturbances in the equilibrium (playing the game). The story could go something like this: the reigning boxing champion is dominating through most of the fight but in the fifth round he is knocked out by a punch to the solar plexus. In fact, a boxing match was accounted for in narrative terms much like this in R. W. Paul's catalogue:

> [The match] opens with the referee bringing the gloves into the ring … In the second round [Johnny] Hughes [the light weight-champion of England] is seen to get the better of his opponent [Dido Plumb] … In the fifth and last round … [Plumb] hits him [Hughes] under his heart, which brings Hughes to the ground. He struggles hard to get up, but the blow has been too hard for him, and he is counted out, and the prize is awarded to Dido Plumb…[37]

But is there anybody telling or, better yet, *showing* this story over and beyond the happenings on the sports arena themselves? Not the recording of the match, but the match itself? There might be a commentator near the ring, of course, but she cannot be the narrator in our sense of the term for she simply reports what she sees and is in principle in no more a privileged position to do so than we are. And even if the commentator was the narrator there are certainly sports events without commentators. There are happenings, therefore, which amount to narratives but have no narrators.

Another example of such narratorless happenings which are nevertheless narratives are fictional happenings in plays. Just transfer the hypothetical boxing match on stage, have the actors make-believe they are boxing and the result is again a narratorless narrative but this time a *fictional* narratorless narrative. We are mandated to imagine the same story as above and at the same time we are *not* mandated to imagine anybody showing the story. On a more general level, in plays there are again imaginary agents (characters) who interact in non-deterministic manner which brings them out of the initial equilibrium and supplies the content for imaginary story but provides no mandates for narrators of such stories. Importantly for us, the property of narratorial absence in plays was not lost to the contemporaries who advised on writing 'plays in photographs'.

Plays were seen to share much with the photoplays – certainly more than verbal narratives – because it was precisely the presentation of a story through visual action that was seen as common to both. Standard definitions of photoplay, for instance, put it like this: 'A photoplay is a play which is acted before the camera, and is shown to an audience by means of the moving picture';[38] 'the photoplay is nothing but a series of scenes *in action* which make up a story';[39] or 'it is a story told in pictured action instead of being described in words'.[40] Verbal narratives, by contrast, were seen as having the luxury of long descriptions and slow developments as opposed to the immediacy of visual action. In fact, the photoplaywrights were often faulted for confusing written stories with photoplays. As a typical passage from the *Photo Playwright* attests: 'Most of the amateur scenario writers tell only a story – always write stories, and use long leaders, etc. A photoplay is an action-story. The action is the essential thing.'[41] Crucially for us, this distinction between verbal recounting and visual action translated into seeing plays and photoplays as sharing the absence of narratorial control. As the manual by Howard T. Dimick explicitly states:

> [C]ompulsory and self-explanatory causes and effects move the play without visible agency, save the cumulative circumstances which react upon the characters; in a [verbal] story the plot is frequently a matter of the author's will alone, and of his obtruding personality, which we feel to control the events.[42]

Given that at the time 'author' as a term was used to denote both the author and the narrator – the separation would fully happen only with Genette's narratology – the idea here is that verbal fiction in general mandates *imagining* somebody telling the story on top of somebody actually telling it.[43] This is so because on most occasions in written fiction there is some attitude taken towards the events, some running commentary on the events and this commentary amounts to a part of the narrative discourse. Given that verbal fiction invites us to imagine not only the content of narrative discourse (the story) but the narrative discourse itself (the narrating) and given that this narrative discourse reveals some characteristics of the speaker behind it ('obtruding personality'), Dimick finds it that we are mandated to imagine a narrator which has those traits. Plays and photoplays, by contrast, although they are clearly artefacts as much as verbal fictions do not mandate us to *imagine* any personality behind their narrative discourse – there is an asymmetry between them and written fiction.[44] It is clear to Dimick that there is a team actually responsible for the narrative discourse – cameraman, director, actors, playwright and so on – but by no means should anybody be imagined as behind the discourse:

> [A]ll the devices of the camera and its accessories are aimed at conveying through the medium of a sequence of pictures and pictured events a complete and self-explanatory, dramatic action, which shall, by its appeal chiefly to the eye, unfold in the mind of the spectator satisfying effects and results of the playwright's labors.[45]

There is undoubtedly a message and a sender responsible for it, but the content of the message does not mandate us to *imagine* a sender on top of the actual team behind the film.

What does distinguish plays from photoplays (next to the use of film recording technology and film specific devices, of course) is the absence of the screen actors' voices and the recourse to written material such as titles, intertitles and other types of inserts: '*A photoplay is a story told largely in pantomime by players, whose words are suggested by their actions, assisted by certain descriptive words thrown on the screen, and the whole produced by a moving-picture machine.*'[46] Perhaps it is these verbal additions that might have revealed some fictional personality telling the story to the contemporaries after all?

Screenwriting manuals virtually never speak of lecturers attesting to their decline by 1912 so we are definitely not dealing with any narrators of the Holmes-type. It is the intertitles and various other forms of written text that appear on the *image* track that are the necessary evil in the pursuit of narrative clarity. Although the manuals make a recurrent point that '*[t]he perfect motion picture has no subtitles and needs none*'[47] they also readily admit that in practice there is no getting around them:

> [W]hen this [the complete elimination of leaders] is attempted, the lucidity of the story is too liable to suffer, whereas an occasional leader of a few words will bridge over a certain combination of events, giving the story a clearness quickly grasped by the audience, and perhaps avoid the introduction of several minor scenes otherwise necessary to make the story intelligible.[48]

Berg J. Esenwein and Arhur Leeds are most systematic among authors or manuals when it comes to clarifying four main functions of intertitles: (1) highlighting the passage of time, (2) explaining on-screen action when the profilmic and filmic events do not provide sufficient representational clarity, (3) 'breaking' a scene to shorten the on-screen time of a given action, and (4) guiding the spectator's reception of the following scene.[49]

Much like other authors, Esenwein and Leeds also distinguish between intertitles proper and 'letters, clippings, and similar interests' where a typical example of the former is 'After three years' and a typical example of the latter 'Darling John, I am forever yours – Mary.' In our vocabulary the distinction is between the two is one of non-diegetic as opposed to diegetic material. The former is somehow 'outside' the story-proper: 'the use of a leader is a frank confession that you [the photoplaywright] are incapable of "putting over" a point in the development of your plot solely by the action in the scenes – you must call in outside assistance, as it were'.[50] From the perspective of mandated imaginings, furthermore, whereas the former mandates us only to imagine the content of the sentence – that three years have passed – the latter mandates not only to imagine that Mary is in love with John but that she also wrote the letter to John comprising these very words.

Contemporary authors of screenwriting manuals were fully aware of this because they clearly felt that the latter types of inserts, due to their specific narratological properties, presented less of an aesthetic problem than the former ones. As Esenwein and Leeds put it: 'no matter what other kind of insert you employ, it will doubtless seem to be more a part of the action than will a plain leader. For this reason it is best, whenever possible, to use a letter, telegram, news item, or some similar insert, in place of a leader.'[51] Caine similarly advises to 'try to make leaders word pictures, so that the cut-ins will be part of the scenes themselves'.[52] In a description of a typical film, Epes Winthrop Sargent even explicitly states that we are supposed to imagine the picture of the letter on screen as the *visual appearance* of the letter itself: 'in the library in the heroine's home. The girl goes to the table and sits down to write. ... a written letter blots out the library. It is just as though we read the letter over her shoulder.'[53] Esenwein and Leeds add that there is a 'ridiculous practice of many studios in having all their letters in films written in the same handwriting. A note written by a schoolboy, another penned by a society woman, and a letter laboriously spelled out by a tramp, all appear, to judge by the handwriting, to have been written by the same person.'[54] The suggestion is that the letters written by different people should be graphically distinguishable because we are mandated to imagine that the graphemes in question not only represents the content of the letter but also the visual appearance of the letter.

Why does all this matter to our discussion of narrators? Because although contemporaries recognized the distinction between written inserts that are a part of the imaginary world (letters, clippings, etc.) and those which only describe that imaginary world being only a part of the film's visual track (intertitles proper), neither were seen as mandating any imaginings about the narrator:

> Few in an audience will object to the introduction of letters, telegrams, newspaper items, and the like – provided there are not too many such inserts – because these seem to fit into the picture as a part of the action, and are not, like leaders, plainly artificial interpolations by the author.[55]

The artificial-looking intertitles are not signs of some imaginary narrator but simply marks of the director's and the photoplaywright's failure to convey the story through action (and occasional letter, clipping, etc.) alone. Despite the fact that, as I mentioned earlier, the term 'author' denoted both the author and the narrator at the time, Esenwein and Leeds are not talking about the author as the fictional narrator here for, unlike Dimick, there is no reference to anything like 'obtruding personality'. Dimick's point is that in verbal fiction it is *often* but not always the case that there is some running commentary which is indicative of personal traits of the narrator to be imagined. A good example of this is *Tristram Shandy* (1759–67). But on other occasions like Arthur Schnitzler's *Rhapsody: A Dream Novel* (1926) where the information is conveyed in a matter-of-fact style no such personality comes forth. In these cases, Dimick denies the presence of an obtruding personality – a distinguishable narrator – but in saying so clearly does not suggest that this means that the stories in question have no authors. In other words, the difference between the author and the narrator is sufficiently clear. The 'artificial interpolations by the author' are interpolations of the *actual* agent of narrative discourse.

It is true that the notion of 'obtruding personality' is not identical to what Genette has in mind when he speaks of narrators. For him every narrative, regardless of whether it is told by an imaginary character with a name such as Tristram Shandy or anonymously 'in third person' (as it is often mistakenly said), has a fictional narrator.[56] 'Obtruding personality', moreover, is not the most fortunate way to approach the figure of the narrator in fiction film not least of all because the camera and the operator in *The Big Swallow* are not identifiable to the spectator during the first half of the film at all – their presence is revealed only retroactively and after they have been robbed of the narratorial role. The following sections offer a more precise discussion of the narrator in both film and literature. This is not to deny, however, that for the contemporaries the notion of 'obtruding personality' did important work. It contributed to a greater understanding of literary and film fiction insofar it distinguished the two from the perspective of narratorial control and implicit mandates behind this control.

Genette's theory of voice

Let us briefly return to the already cited passage from Genette: '"I" can designate only him [Des Grieux], and … "here" and "now" refer to the spatiotemporal circumstances of that narrating and in no way to the circumstances of the writing of *Manon Lescaut* by its real author.'[57] The key point here is that in literary narratives deictic terms (e.g. 'I', 'here', 'now') used fictionally refer to the agent of fictional narration (fictional speaker) and not to the agent of actual narration (actual author).[58] In other words, the real proof of the existence of narrators in literary fiction for Genette is not some vague notion of an 'obtruding personality' but something more precise. It is the fact that language is replete with deictics – words whose meaning can be fathomed only with the knowledge of the circumstances in which they were uttered. If we come across a sentence like 'I was in Paris' or 'it is nice here' we can understand the sentences in full only if we know who wrote them and where, respectively. Put differently, by drawing attention to the very act of speaking deictics serve as markers of subjectivity in language.

When the deictics appear in the fictional context then, Genette reasons, we are mandated to *imagine* that they are markers of some character and/or narrator in the story-world rather than take them as markers of the author's subjectivity. And indeed, when Tristram Shandy begins his tale by saying 'I wish either my father or my mother … had minded what they were about when they beget me' we are mandated to imagine that 'I' refers to Tristram. We are neither mandated to imagine nor are we supposed to construe that 'I' is referring to the actual author – Laurence Sterne. Let us call this property the intra-ontological reference of deictics.

Now, there are special cases such as *In Search of Lost Time* (1913–27) – the novel that serves as a case-study for Genette's monograph – where the author and the fictional narrator appear to coincide – the novel authored by Marcel Proust is narrated by certain Marcel. Genette has insisted that even in narratives such as these we still need to refer to the narrator as an entity ontologically distinct from Proust. To emphasize this difference Genette proposes to refer to narrators by using scare quotes whenever their name coincides with the author's or whenever they are anonymous. Thus, we should speak of 'Marcel' rather than Marcel and of 'Homer' rather than Homer when talking about fictional narrators of *In Search of Lost Time* and *Odyssey*, respectively. In the literature such a stance is usually referred to as the ontological gap argument and hinges on the implicit understanding of fiction in terms of separate fictional worlds.

Building on Walton's work George M. Wilson has produced a convincing argument against such a view.[59] According to Wilson there is nothing curious about engaging actual authors as fictional narrators. In the case of *In Search of Lost Time*, he has argued, we are mandated to imagine Marcel Proust to be narrating the events of the novel and this makes him the fictional narrator. There is no need to posit a fictional entity bearing the name 'Marcel' (which is supposed to invoke actual Proust) as the one who narrates. In Walton's terminology Proust is simply a prop to whom we attribute certain imaginary properties – in our case the fact that he is narrating. This is no different from imagining that, in a recent film, Abraham Lincoln is a president by day and a vampire hunter by night. It is also no different from imagining that London is the city where Sherlock Holmes lives. In other words, we need not postulate some fictional 'Lincoln' or fictional 'London' to imagine the stories in question.[60] All of this does not, however, mean that Genette's claim about the intra-ontological reference of deixis is invalid. It simply means that although it is often the case that we are authorized to imagine the actual author as the fictional narrator even on those occasions the deictics still refer to the fictional narrator, and not to the actual writing. And it also explains why in Dimick's and in other people's writing at the time 'author' can denote both the author and the narrator.

At this point we might simply want to use what Genette calls extradiegetic narrator as our model for the film narrator. With Wilson's modification in mind that authors can serve as fictional narrators it certainly fits the bill of the only real film narrator we have identified up to now – E. Burton Holmes. This is best avoided, however, because the typology of narrators as described by Genette – one based on the distinction between narrative levels and the relation to the story – introduces some confusion as to what the term 'diegesis' in 'extradiegetic' stands for. This in turn allows for issues what precisely we are mandated to imagine to creep in.

Originally, the extradiegetic narrator, as opposed to the intradiegetic one, stands for the narrator on the narrative level zero from whence all the events are narrated. In that sense, any fictional narrative has at least the extradiegetic narrator occupying level zero with the story itself (e.g. characters, events, etc.) – the diegesis – occupying level one. Further embedded narration by the characters produces metadiegetic levels two, three and so on. Attributes 'homodiegtic' and 'heterodiegetic', on the other hand, are used to denote that the narrator is or is not a character in the story narrated by the narrator. Once examples of such narrators are presented in a two by two matrix, problems arise for the implication here is that extra/intra and hetero/homo axes are mutually independent (Table 5.1). A look at the 'intra' column, however, reveals noteworthy discrepancies.

Scheherazade is the key problem here for when she is described as both intradiegetic and heterodiegetic what 'diegetic' stands for is not the same in both cases. Insofar she is heterodiegetic, 'diegetic' refers to the stories she tells – those on level two (for she plays no role in them). Insofar she is intradiegetic, 'diegetic' stands for the story she is a part of – the one on level one told by an unnamed extradiegetic narrator in which she postpones her execution for 1001 nights by means of story-telling. The same relations hold for Odysseus when described as both intradiegetic and homodiegetic narrator. He is intradiegetic for he is a part of the level one story 'Homer' – the extradiegetic narrator of *Odysseus* – tells.[61] But Odysseus is homodiegetic from the viewpoint of the level two story he tells in chapters ix–xii. Genette implicitly admits of this problem when he says that the narrative level is a property of the narrators and not that of characters. Therefore, he later does away with the misleading tabular representation and replaces it with the comic-strip one embedding stick-figures within balloons denoting narrating acts.[62] This, however, does not resolve all of the problems. Further problems pertain to what type of story Scheherazade is telling and the relation within the extra/intra pair.

Genette is explicit that the narrative level is not an ontological dimension, that is, that the stories within stories may but need not be fictional in relation to the story they are embedded in. For Genette then, there is no difference between the internally actual story Odysseus recounts about his adventures and

Table 5.1 A typology of narrators based on their narrative levels ('extra-' or 'intradiegetic') and relation to the story ('hetero-' or 'homodiegetic').*

	Extradiegetic	Intradiegetic
Heterodiegetic	'Homer'	Scheherazade
Homodiegetic	'Marcel'	Odysseus

*Adapted from Genette, *Narrative Discourse*, p. 248.

the internally fictional stories Scheherazade tells to postpone her execution – they are all level two stories. Though it is not a matter of an ontological gap, the question, however, of how exactly the extradiegetic narrator is 'outside' of the story it recounts still remains unanswered. Interestingly, there is an asymmetry in the relation between 'extra' and 'intra', on the one hand, and 'homo' and 'hetero', on the other. Whereas the prefix 'extra' is reserved for the narrative level zero, 'intra' is reserved for all other narrative levels. In contrast, narrators may be either homo- or heterodiegetic regardless of the plane, including the zero level. In other words, Genette does not allow for the existence of extradiegetic narrators in the chain of embedded narratives, they are all intradiegetic.

There are two problems here. First, this asymmetry between 'extra' and 'intra' destabilizes Genette's claim that narrative levels have nothing to do with ontological barriers for the position of the extradiegetic narrator is reserved exclusively for the border between the author and his or her fictional narrative. Second, if every narrating act produces a meta-narrative level, should Odysseus not, although intradiegetic with reference to what 'Homer' recounts, be extradiegetic in reference to what he (Odysseus) recounts? And given that no such thing is allowed for in Genette's outline does that not imply that 'Homer', the extradiegetic narrator of the whole of *Odyssey*, is somehow differently 'outside' the story than Odysseus, the extradiegetic narrator of chapters ix–xii, is? And does that not further suggest that 'Homer' might not only not be a part of the story (for he is heterodiegetic unlike Odysseus) but not even of the story-world? But there must be a contradiction here for Genette clearly states that the narrator is never the author and that, unlike the author, there is always a spatiotemporal relation between her and the story she relates. In other words, although extra-heterodiegetic narrators are not strictly speaking part of the story they are a part of the story-world, that is, they share the same fictional world (though they are, most often, temporally apart). This is no different from the fact that I am a part of the story-world (i.e. the world) of an actual story I recount about my friend although I took no part in the story myself. It seems then that there is a tension in how 'diegetic' is read when prefixed by the pair 'extra' and 'intra'. It shifts between denoting the story and denoting the story-world and as such ushers in more ontological confusion.

Another ontological confusion can be illustrated more clearly on the example of Scheherazade. Given that Genette's balloon representations do not distinguish between fictional and non-fictional metadiegetic stories relative to the diegetic level, Scheherazade is represented as though she has an ontological relation to her stories no different from the one 'Homer' does to *Odyssey*. However, Scheherazade produces a fictional story within the fictional one which further complicates the picture. From the perspective of the story on the level one, Scheherazade is undoubtedly intradiegetic but that is not the problem. The problem is the attribute 'heterodiegetic' which, playing on the similarity with the special type of 'outside' 'extradiegetic' implies, masks the fact that Scheherazade is no more heterodiegetic (or homodiegetic for that matter) to the story she tells than Proust is heterodiegetic (or homodiegetic) to the story of *In Search of Lost Time*. Moreover, unlike Odysseus, Scheherazade cannot even be extradiegetic from this perspective for the same reason Proust, at least in Genette's view as opposed to that of Wilson's, is not the extradiegetic narrator of *In Search of Lost Time*.

Simply put, Genette fails to see that under his model the deictics in these particular narratives do not refer to Scheherazade's time-space (with the maharaja during a given night) but to the extradiegetic narrator ontologically distinct from Scheherazade. Scheherazade is a not a fictional extradiegetic narrator in the sense she is a fictional intradiegetic one, she is the fictional author.[63] To put it in Genette's terms, the fictional extradiegetic narrator for each of these 1001 stories can only be 'Scheherazade' and not Scheherazade. Narrative levels, so long as they are presented with balloons, still fail to account for this.

There are further concerns with Genette's account. It seems to be implied that Odysseus is awarded his own voice in chapters ix–xii somewhat differently than he is in his other dialogue lines. It is also unclear whether in Genette's account epistolary and dialogue-only novels have extradiegetic narrators or not. Moreover, the key question for identifying the narrator for Genette is 'who is speaking?' The question, however, does not appear to be the most felicitous one even in the case of literary narratives. The reason is that there are numerous literary fictions in which there is, strictly speaking, no speaking. For instance, in Sue Townsend's *The Secret Diary of Adrian Mole, Aged 13 ¾* (1982) Adrian the narrator does not speak but writes entries into his diary. And to take another Genette's example it is fictionally indeterminate whether the manner in which the narrative in *Père Goriot* is conveyed is spoken, written or perhaps even thought.

Because of all these concerns, instead of speaking of the extradiegetic narrator I will use a term introduced by Gregory Currie – the controlling fictional narrator. Currie defines the controlling narrator as one whose fictional utterances 'coincide with the text we are reading when we read the work'.[64] In the above scheme 'Homer' is the controlling narrator and so is the extradiegetic narrator fictionally recounting the story of Scheherazade. It is important to note that although Odysseus and Scheherazade perform further intradiegetic story-telling, on this view they are embedded narrators to whom the controlling narrator borrows the voice only temporarily in a fashion no different from how the voice is borrowed in the instances of dialogue.

Currie's term, moreover, paves the way to a more felicitous question for identifying narrators, for it denotes a fictional narrator who is the *source* for the whole of the text and not merely part of it (admittedly, on most occasions paratextual information need to be bracketed off). As such, it allows us to use the same term in constructing narratological models for different media of fiction. It is certainly as applicable to audio-visual forms as much as it is to literature. In the question of audio-visual fiction narratives, for instance, in order to identify the narrator, we can ask 'who is the source of the polyphonic track?' More precisely: is there an agency for which we can say that it is fictional that *all* but paratextual audio-visual information can be attributed to? In the case of illustrated lectures explored in Chapter 4 we have already seen that Holmes's performances made use of such a figure. Before giving an answer to this question on the example of film, I first wish to address literary fiction given that a number of theories of film narrators rest on theories of literary narrators.

The near-ubiquity thesis for literary fiction

I will be referring to the claim that controlling narrators are indeed a property of, if not all, then at least the greatest bulk of literary narrative production as the near-ubiquity thesis for literary fiction. (In the discussion of fiction film, I will produce an obverse thesis – the near-absence thesis.) Therefore, I will briefly sketch out the problems with previous claims to ubiquity or near-ubiquity and propose my own argument for near-ubiquity.

For a period of time, a key narratological assumption was that there could not be a narrative without a narrator. Since Genette's description of the extradiegetic narrator in *Narrative Discourse* this has been implicitly transformed into the assumption that there cannot be a fictional narrative without a fictional narrator. Later, accomplished narratologists such as Seymour Chatman, Mieke Bal and Shlomith Rimmon-Kenan would explicitly support this thesis.[65] It took analytic philosophers rather than scholars from literary departments to point that the thesis, as has been shown in the first section of the chapter, is formally invalid. At the same time, however, Genette's claim is a more complex one because for him it is the presence of deixis that entails the existence of a fictional narrator not the fictional narrative itself.

Recently, analytic philosophers such as Noël Carroll, Gregory Currie, Berys Gaut and Andrew Kania have garnered much attention by claiming that no fictional narrators but explicit ones such as Ishmael from Hermann Melville's *Moby Dick* (1851) or 'Marcel'/Marcel from *In Search of Lost Time* exist.[66] In other words, there is no such thing as 'Homer' in *Odysseus* regardless of whether he is a distinct fictional entity or the author Homer imagined as the narrator. George M. Wilson responded.[67] In what follows, I will argue in more detail against Carroll, Currie and Kania but for reasons different from Wilson's. Moreover, I will demonstrate that my argument for near-ubiquity is stronger than Wilson's. Finally, I will tackle some of the points Gaut raises and rearticulate my own argument for the near-ubiquity of fictional narrators in fictional literary narratives.[68]

Wilson's response to Carroll and Kania concerns their proposal that we need not imagine fictional declarative sentences as assertions. In other words, Carroll and Kania have claimed that we need not imagine any narrative agency making those assertions, rather that they may be understood as containers for propositional content. Thus, sentences like 'Katie loves Hubbell' need merely express the proposition 'that Katie loves Hubbell'. Even if that were the case, Wilson argues, there are sentences in literature such as conditionals and questions which often employ illocutionary force over and beyond pure declaratives. Wilson asks us to consider the following sentences: 'Katie loves Hubbell. Many people thought so. But was it true?' He concludes that the additional illocutionary force found in the question is a sufficient marker of some internal minimal narrating agency. Currie and Gaut replied that both utterances following the initial declarative 'Katie loves Hubbell' can be thought of as issuing from the actual author and not the fictional narrator. From the perspective of Dimick's 'obtruding personality', Currie's and Gaut's answer here is to claim that any such personality is only the actual author's. Finding no definite answer to these objections, Wilson concludes that 'these considerations rest finally on claims about the phenomenology of our imaginative engagement with novels and kindred works of literary fiction'.[69]

In contrast to Wilson, my claim is that there is a way to determine that sentences such as 'Katie loves Hubbell' are fictional assertions and not merely containers of propositional content as Carroll et al. would have it. It is precisely with recourse to Genette's understanding of intra-ontological reference of deixis that this can be done. Propositional content in analytic philosophy is usually discussed in the form 'x does y' or 'x is y'. The present simple in these sentences is not used for an action occurring at the moment of speaking but for expressing a fact, a state of affairs or a generalization. These sentences are easily understood without any recourse to temporality. Literary narratives, on the other hand, regularly employ verb tenses to express the time, however imprecisely, of a particular event or state of affairs. In the case of 'Katie loves Hubbell' the present simple verb does not merely express a state of affairs or generalization as it does in sentence like 'humans are mammals'. It says more. It says that with respect to the 'present' Katie was in love with Hubbell and still is. To make the point clearer consider the same sentence in the past simple tense: 'Katie loved Hubbell'. This sentence means that with respect to the 'present' Katie was in love with Hubbell *and* that she may or may not still be in love with him. Thus, and this is the crucial moment in my argument, we cannot simply translate sentences which use verbs narratively into propositional content of the form 'at one point in time x does/is y' without losing relevant temporal information. The propositional content must keep a reference to the 'present'. But then, how can we fully imaginatively engage propositional content p such as 'x was y' without recourse to a 'present' temporal position at which x might no longer be y? This 'present' temporal position, moreover, as the eminent linguist Émile Benveniste elaborates, can be understood only as the moment of speaking about the event contained in p.[70] Thus, thinking of literary narrative sentences in terms of containers of propositional content, if the chain of reasoning is followed through, establishes a controlling fictional narrator no different from the one introduced by imagining sentences as fictional assertions. In other words, we are mandated to imagine a controlling fictional narrator irrespective of differences in imaginative engagement.

The argument – the linguistic version of the ontological gap argument (henceforth LOGA) – may be formalized as follows:[71]

(1) 'Present' can only be understood by positing a speaker/writer cotemporaneous with it;[72]
(2) The temporal dimension of tensed verbs can only be fully understood with reference to the present tense, that is, the 'present';[73]
(3) (1) and (2) entail that the temporal dimension of tensed verbs can only be understood by positing a speaker/writer contemporaneous with the 'present' which they refer to;
(4) Temporal deictic terms such as 'now', 'yesterday', 'tomorrow' can only be understood by positing a speaker contemporaneous with the 'present' which they refer to;
(5) (3) and (4) entail that tensed verbs behave like temporal deictic terms as far as the understanding of their temporal dimension is concerned;

(6) Intra-ontological reference of deixis: In literary narratives deictic terms used fictionally refer to the agent of fictional narration (fictional speaker)[74] who may at the same time be the actual author;[75]

(7) (5) and (6) entail that any text of literary fiction in which: (a) there is no explicit controlling fictional narrator, (b) there is at least a single narrative usage of a tensed verb and (c) this use cannot be ascribed to any particular character (meaning it is on level zero), has an implicit controlling narrator, that is, the agent contemporaneous with the 'present' referred to in the tensed verb.

If this argument is sound then we can assign controlling narrators to a huge subclass of literary fiction.[76] Not only to all of the novels which have explicit narrators such as *Moby Dick* and *In Search of Lost Time* but also to those which we ordinarily say are recounted in 'third person' – for example, Balzac's *Père Goriot*, Dostoevsky's *Crime and Punishment* (1866), Albert Camus's *Stranger* (1942) and Franz Kafka's *The Trial* (1925). Subclasses which need to be left out include pieces written exclusively in the form of direct speech and epistolary novels without an explicit 'editor'.[77] It is true that all the words in such novels can be attributed to one of the diegetic characters. But none of these characters is responsible for all the utterances that make up the novel. In other words, these novels lack narrative level zero where controlling narration takes place.

The near-absence thesis for fiction film

The enunciator as the filmic narrator

The chapter opened with an overview of the idea of the great image-maker and filmic narrators modelled on Genette's extradiegetic narrator and the premise thought to guarantee their existence – there cannot be a narrative without a narrator. By now, I demonstrated that not only is the version of this premise pertaining to fictional narratives invalid, but there are also representations which fit a broad definition of narrative yet have no narrators. This should suffice to dismiss standard articulations of filmic narrators as unwarranted.[78]

A somewhat different approach to vindicating filmic narrator's existence was espoused by a group of theorists who, again building on Metz's work, set out to apply Benveniste's distinction between *histoire* and *discourse* in his analysis of enunciation.[79] Based on the analysis of French spoken and written language,

Benveniste concluded that there are two types of enunciation, that is, linguistic acts: (1) those which mark the presence of the enunciator, that is, the utterer – *discourse* – and (2) those which lack clear markers of her presence – *histoire*. Put differently, *discourse* can be identified by the presence of deixis, that is, words such as 'here', 'now' and 'I' all of which refer to the context of enunciation. (The types of words around which LOGA revolves.) The consequence is that, as I already said, without the knowledge about the context of enunciation we cannot fully comprehended *discourse* sentences such as, 'I am standing here now.' Such sentences shed no light on the identity of the speaker and her exact time and location. *Histoire*, on the other hand, lacks such markers of enunciation and the complete understanding of the utterance is afforded without recourse to the context of its enunciation. For instance, 'Romeo and Juliet are star-crossed lovers.' In Benveniste's words, *histoire* appears to recount itself. This analysis was particularly appealing to the enunciation theorists for they argued that narrative cinema, by passing itself as *histoire* whereas it was in fact *discourse*, propagated various ideological tasks.[80]

The argument for the ubiquity of filmic narrators that the enunciation theorists espouse follows the same logic as my argument for the existence of controlling fictional narrators in literary fiction. In short, according to the enunciation theorists, in narrative fiction film it is possible to identify filmic analogues to linguistic deixis on the lowest diegetic level which mandates us to imagine the existence of an agent responsible for all the audio-visual information presented. Indeed, Gaudreault and Jost give the most extensive list of such markers: exaggerated foreground, low angle point of view shot, framing devices such as keyhole image, types of camera movement which makes us aware of its presence, artificial make up, montage jump cuts, punctuations such as superimpositions and look at the camera.[81]

Metz brings all of the devices listed above under a common denominator: 'Enunciation is the semiologic act by which some parts of a text talk to us about this text as an act …. All figures of enunciation consist in metadiscursive folds of cinematic instances piled on top of each other.'[82] The use of the term 'metadiscursive' should not fool us here. Metz assumes filmic narrative is already discursive insofar it is *discourse*, that is, insofar it regularly employs filmic versions of linguistic deixis. This can be read from his famous statement that the filmic shot resembles enunciation more than it does a word (e.g. picture of x ought to be understood as saying 'Here is x'). Even in his last work Metz notes that '[f]ilm does not contain any deictic equivalents, with the exception, ... of one sort of global permanent deictic – a very atypical one, ... "*There is*" [Voici], which is always tacit and always present...'[83] Following this logic, because figures Gaudreault and Jost refer to are both discursive and reflexive, they must be metadiscursive.

First, there is no reason to think of film as *discourse* to begin with.[84] As Edward Branigan and David Bordwell remind us, the only reason why Metz is comfortable with identifying narrative fiction film with *discourse* is because under his linguistic model of film analysis, film, although comprising various semiotic systems, is processed in linguistic terms on the level of spectator's comprehension.[85] Thus an image of x comes across as 'Here is x' for the spectator. Branigan and Bordwell list a number of experiments from cognitive psychology which suggest that this need not be the case and that in fact there is much more reason to believe that we do not analyse images linguistically. Given that this list is now more than 30 years old, I will add that even if the spectator did analyse the images in linguistic terms and did so in the manner Metz proposes this would still warrant no inference about the existence of the fictional narrator. The reason for this can be understood with recourse to the notion of ontological fallacy. Arguably, the linguistic processing is one of what images stand for in the real world, that is, what we recognize and not one of what these images mandate us to make-believe. In other words, the image of Humphrey Bogart in *Casablanca* (Michael Curtiz, 1942) is initially processed as 'Here is Humphrey Bogart' and not as 'Here is Rick'. Therefore, the deixis in 'Here is x' refers to the spectator and not to the fictional world the filmic text conveys or to the alleged narrator. Strictly speaking, there is no deictic or tense in the fictional world, there is just an image of x, and this image gets cognitively translated into a linguistic statement which is (mentally) uttered exclusively on the spectator's end. In other words, even if an image were to be processed linguistically such a processing would not constitute a mandate to imagine anything.

This still does not mean that the devices listed by Gaudreault and Jost do not allow for some other types of inferences about the existence of a narrator. If we unpack Metz's statement, however, we will see that enunciation so conceived is a perfect fit with Linda Hutcheon's understanding of 'metanarrative' as a text which 'provides, within itself, a commentary on its own status as fiction and as language, and also on its own processes of production and reception'.[86] This, in turn, is a subclass of Viktor Shklovsky's concept of defamiliarization and Bertolt Brecht's notion of estrangement. The crucial point to note here is that metanarrative moments are often metadiscursive *only* in oral and especially in written narratives, because they relate to the narrator's subjectivity in one way or another. The most famous example is, of course, the controlling fictional narrator in *Tristram Shandy* who regularly addresses the audience and comments on the process of writing.

Metanarrative moments, however, need not produce fictional truths about the existence of a narrator. If a character who is not a narrator addresses an actual reader by saying: 'Dear sir, you should not think of me as a mere character' – arguably an analogue to a character's look at the camera – this statement mandates no imaginings about the narrator. The only 'I' that 'you' entails is the character uttering the sentence. And this can be informative of the controlling fictional narrator only if the character is the controlling fictional narrator. By way of analogy, the only 'I' a look at the camera entails is the character doing the looking. A similar argument applies to other devices listed above. Consider the use of hand-held camera and editing in the work of Lars von Trier. There is no more reason to assume that these devices generate any fictional truths about the existence of a fictional narrator than there is to think that two different copies of *Gulliver's Travels* (1726) printed using two different font types and sizes generate two distinct fictional truths about what the font type and size of Gulliver's entries into ship's log were. It is true that von Trier's use of these devices produces various effects important for the appreciation of his films including the attention drawn to the fact that we are not watching a classical Hollywood film. Although this could be understood as the 'text talk[ing] to us about this text as an act' the act referred to is, however, not an act of a fictional narrator but an act of an actual (be it the author, the cameraman, the editor or whoever). There is nobody in the work-fiction of von Trier's films to whom we are mandated to attribute such an act. The key point is to understand that even in literary fiction it is not the type of style that Shklovsky is interested in and that draws the attention to itself that which guarantees the existence of the narrator. *Ulysses* (1922) does not have a fictional narrator because of the range of unconventional narrative styles employed there but because there are deictics in the novel which establish a (spatio)temporal link to the fictional narrator. Furthermore, a hypothetical novel which uses no verbs or deictics would definitively draw attention to itself but would not have a fictional narrator precisely because there are no deictics in it. Simply put, it is the deictics that usher in an *implicit* fictional narrator in both literature and film fiction. Insisting that devices Gaudreault and Jost list or Gunning's 'narrator system' establish a fictional narrator only introduces unnecessary ontological entities whose main purpose appears only to retain the applicability of a concept derived from literary theory to film at all cost.

Perhaps an even better way to demonstrate why none of the above devices amounts to a case for the existence of the controlling fictional narrator is to draw attention to how it would look like if a fictional agency were in control of the audio-visuals presented. Consider mockumentaries such as *Zelig* (Woody Allen, 1983) and *This Is Spinal Tap* (Rob Rainer, 1984) in which we are prompted to imagine that everything we see and hear on screen was recorded by a crew of fictional filmmakers. *This Is Spinal Tap*, for instance, opens with a 'behind the scenes' shot of the director Marty DiBergi (played by Rob Rainer) introducing us to the film we are about to see. In it DiBergi gives a brief account of his motives for making a film about the famous *Spinal Tap* rock band. DiBergi is clearly the fictional director and, in turn, the controlling fictional narrator who is responsible for whole of the film we see in front of us (including the 'behind the scenes' shot). A variation on the theme obtains in recent horror films in which the camera and its crew are swooped up into the action: consider, for example, *[Rec]* (Jaume Belagueró and Paco Plaza, 2007), *Paranormal Activity* (Oren Peli, 2007) or *Cloverfield* (Matt Reeves, 2008). The roots of somebody recording from within the fictional world can, as we have seen, be traced to at least *The Big Swallow*.

Recent sitcoms such as *The Office* (2001–3) and *Parks and Recreation* (2009–15) also seem to suggest a fictional crew filming the characters. The presence of the crew is implied through the characters' addresses at the camera. Moreover, sometimes the characters appear to answer questions posed by the personnel behind the camera. The crew's identities and reasons for filming are, however, left indeterminate. What all these films and TV shows have in common is that they prompt us to imagine that they have been recorded from within the fictional world. So, at the very least we can identify the fictional recording as the source of all of the audio-visual information we are presented with. Although these examples testify to occasional appearance of controlling fictional narrators in fiction film, their existence is secured through markers substantially different from those listed by Gaudreault and Jost. These markers, unlike those of Gaudreault and Jost, do authorize us to imagine some subjectivity behind the camera – the documentary context in *This Is Spinal Tap* and the Q&A form (without the explicit recording of the question, admittedly) in *The Office*. To conclude then, there is no reason to think that metanarrative *necessarily* ushers a narrator into existence or that it is informative of the narrator figure in any way.

The return of the great image-maker

A notable exception among film narratologists is David Bordwell. In his *Narration in Fiction Film* he has explicitly denied the existence of controlling fictional narrators and has instead advocated for a model of impersonal narration. As his critics rightly point out, Bordwell's account becomes plagued with anthropomorphisms once he starts discussing narration's key attributes – knowledge, self-consciousness and communicativeness.[87] Bordwell discusses various situations in which it is clear that particular pieces of information are deliberately withheld from the viewer for, as he puts it, narration has to know them. Thus, supposedly non-anthropomorphic narration is endowed with attributes only a narrating agent can have. Although the criticism is valid it is far less effective as a demonstration of the existence of the narrator than as one of the difficulties of articulating the effect of the narratorless narrative without recourse to anthropomorphic metaphors.

Analytic philosophers, who have also tended to discount controlling fictional narrators, were more careful in staying away from anthropomorphisms in their accounts.[88] It would appear that the lone voice arguing extensively in favour of the narrator's existence among analytic philosophers is George M. Wilson.[89] His indebtedness to the notion of the great image-maker is clear from the title of the first of his three pieces referenced: '*Le Grand Imagier* Steps Out'.

Wilson begins by criticizing what he calls the face-to-face version of the fictional showing hypothesis, advocated by Chatman and Jerrold Levinson, for confusing 'showing the fictional' with 'fictional showing'.[90] He invokes the example of a shadow play to demonstrate how a fictional story of a hawk attacking a mole can be told in shadows by an actual person using her hands without there being any fictional showing from within the fictional world by some fictional agent. Indeed, it is sufficient to actually present a series of images in which it is fictional that the envisaged events take place in order to show those events as fictional. In other words, the shadows which represent a hawk attacking a mole are understood as props and mandate us to imagine that a hawk is attacking a mole. Although there clearly is a person responsible for the shadows, there is nothing in the shadows that mandates us to *imagine* somebody presenting us with these shadows. Here we have another variation then on the claim that messages mandating imaginings need not mandate any imaginings about the sender.

Wilson's next step is to construct a more complex variant of the fictional showing hypothesis in order to establish a way in which a viewer could coherently imagine fiction films as being fictionally narrated. The mediated fictional showing hypothesis states that fictional showing in filmic texts boils down to 'the fictional exhibition and sequential arrangement, by means of editing, of *motion picture shots* of the occurrences that constitute the story'.[91] Here, motion picture shots should be understood as naturally iconic images which like photographs exhibit natural counterfactual dependence on the array of elements and features present in the photographed situation, but unlike them are not produced by a camera. Their crucial characteristic is that although they are produced from within the fiction, the exact manner of their production is left indeterminate in our imaginative engagement with them.[92] In other words, Wilson holds that when watching a film, we regularly imagine that we are shown edited images of fictional events by a controlling fictional narrator.

Note two crucial steps in Wilson's argument for the existence of the controlling fictional narrator: (1) the images constituting the filmic text are made within the fictional world, and (2) there is an agent in this fictional world who arranges and shows them. The issue is that step 2 can rest solely on what can be dubbed 'the material' version of the ontological-gap argument. Naturally iconic images are fictional material artefacts, and these can, according to the material version of the argument, be handled exclusively by fictional entities. Thus, according to Wilson, it is safe to assume a fictional agent is doing the handling. This, however, is problematic. If Wilson goes to such pains to construct an indeterminate conception of the production of naturally iconic images, would it not also make sense to claim that their arrangement and exhibition are indeterminate as well? Why do we have to posit a sort of a great image-maker doing the editing if we do not have to imagine her producing the shots as well? Even if Wilson resolved this issue, the crucial problem of the argument is step 1. There is no reason to suppose that what we are shown in the filmic text are naturally iconic images to begin with. As Carroll argues, given the ontological and technological complexity of naturally iconic images, it is unlikely that regular audiences entertain these concepts at all.[93] In addition, there are no textual clues to engender such concepts. There is nothing in the visuals of almost any fictional film that would suggest the postulation of naturally iconic images. And in fact, the discussion of actual reception and promotion of films throughout this monograph demonstrates that no audience imagined such a thing.

In his latest work, Wilson notes that the fictional showing hypothesis rests on the imagined seeing thesis.[94] Therefore, the fictional showing hypothesis is invalid if the imagined seeing thesis is. Although I have already argued that fictional seeing does not entail fictional showing and even that actual seeing does not entail actual showing let us entertain Wilson's argument for a moment to point out another weakness even if this point is bracketed off.

According to the imagined seeing thesis the viewers imagine seeing slices of the fictional world from a string of precisely determined visual perspectives.

Depending on the variant, they imagine seeing the slices of the fictional world either from a vista within the fictional world – face-to-face version – or through naturally iconic images – mediated version. Although Wilson's thesis is clearly of relevance for the epistemology of film, it is inapplicable to the discussion of controlling fictional narrators.[95] This is so because Wilson confuses what Walton refers to as work-worlds and game-worlds. According to Wilson, it is work-fictional that spectators are both shown and see cinematic images:

> [I]t is a standard function of a cinematic work of fiction to prompt viewers to imagine – to make believe – themselves being shown the narrative events and circumstances of successive shots. Moreover … it is fictional in the movie … Since 'fictional showing' is putatively what the movie's images are meant to achieve, and 'imagined seeing' is putatively what movie viewers do in response to those images, it is often easier to formulate certain points in terms of one thesis rather than the other. But, to repeat, the two theses are utterly interdependent, although, of the two, the Imagined Seeing Thesis is probably the more fundamental.[96]

It is important to remember, however, that for Walton something is work-fictional if and only if it holds for *any* game that the work prompts and game-fictional, otherwise.[97] Consider Sandro Botticelli's *The Birth of Venus* again. It is both work- and game-fictional that Venus is standing on a shell. But it is only game-fictional that George, standing in front of the painting in the Uffizi Gallery in Florence, is seeing her standing on a shell. Put otherwise, the painting prompts a game of make-believe in which, among other things, Venus is standing on a shell for *any* viewer. But when it comes to *seeing* Venus standing on a shell, it is only game-fictional that *he* is seeing her. For when Julia, another visitor at the Gallery, regards the painting, it is *Julia* who imagines seeing Venus on a shell.[98] It is clear then that Wilson's imagined seeing thesis and fictional showing hypothesis are both game-fictional. Given that claims about the narrator's presence are work-fictional, neither can tell us anything about the controlling fictional narrator.[99]

Exceptions to near-absence thesis for fiction film

The results of the previous section, of course, do not imply that there are no paintings whose representations fully coincide with the view of a work-fictional character. A classic example is Jan van Eyck's *Arnolfini Portrait* in which the convex mirror in the background reveals two figures whose position coincides with the vista from which the newly-weds are represented. In other words, this is an instance analogous to a point of view shot in cinema. Similarly, the outlined results should also not lead us to completely reject the idea of controlling fictional narrators, for there are several distinct categories of films in which we can identify the source of all sounds and images as fictional.

I have already spoken of some of them: mockumentaries such as *This Is Spinal Tap*, sitcoms in the vein of *The Office* or recent horror films such as *Paranormal Activity* and *[Rec]* make it work-fictional that there is a fictional recording of fictional events identical to the actual recording we see. I could also imagine a film, say of a bank robbery, in which all the shots are identified as belonging to one of the cameras of an intelligent surveillance system. All of these in one way or another continue the legacy of *The Big Swallow*. These examples also demonstrate that, contrary to Wilson's claims about naturally iconic images, we need strong markers within the fictional world to prompt us to imagine that the world in question is mediated through some sort of fictionally produced images.

There are also films in which all the film's sights and sounds (minus the paratextual ones) are attributable to a fictional character who is *not* recording the events in front of him: the stranger in *Russian Ark/Russkii kovcheg* (Alexander Sokurov, 2002). The whole film is an exquisitely choreographed 99-minute-long point of view shot. Moreover, unlike in films such as *Lady in the Lake* (Robert Montgomery, 1947) and *Blue* (Derek Jarman, 1993), there is not even a single non-diegetic sound in the film which could wrest control over even a part of the audio-visual track away from the stranger. As such, the stranger could be compared to literary first-person narrators, such as Katniss Everdeen from *The Hunger Games* (2008), who speaks in the present tense about the events unfolding in front of them. This example also illustrates that there are instances of controlling fictional narration which invoke neither the imagined seeing thesis nor the fictional showing hypothesis. *Russian Ark* neither mandates us to imagine ourselves seeing anything (as is the case with the earliest audiences of train films and phantom rides) nor does it mandate us to imagine being shown anything (as is the case with Holmes's lectures) – the mandate is simply to imagine that whatever is seen on screen is seen by someone from within the fictional world.

The same irrelevance of imagined seeing thesis and fictional showing hypothesis for controlling fictional narrators is demonstrated in situations in which it is fictional that somebody orally recounts the story but the person in control of the images and corresponding sounds is the *addressee* rather than the teller. A localized example may be found in *The Fall* (Tarsem Singh, 2006). The girl who is listening to Roy's story, Alexandria, visually imagines one of the characters – 'The Indian' – to be from the Asian subcontinent when he is in fact

Native American. The discrepancy is revealed by the fact that Roy refers to the 'Indian's' wife as a 'squaw' and to his dwelling as a 'wigwam'.

Finally, there are examples where control over images, at least local, is explicitly awarded to a character. Consider the rewind sequence in Michael Haneke's *Funny Games* (1997, 2007). After Anna has managed to shoot Peter with a shotgun, Paul searches frantically for the remote control and, having found it, pushes the rewind button. What follows is the whole sequence played out in reverse.

Although generally absent from fiction film then, there are some ways in which controlling narrators may appear: (1) sustained point of view shots without non-diegetic elements (e.g. *Russian Ark*), (2) fictionally determinate motion pictures shots (e.g. mockumentaries, implicit fictional shooting in sitcoms such as *The Office*, and horrors influenced by Daniel Myrick and Eduardo Sánchez's 1999 *The Blair Witch Project*), (3) events depicted as fictional characters' own imaginings (e.g. representations of dreams and local examples in *The Fall*) and (4) control proper, persistently marked by salient cues (e.g. *Funny Games*).

What all these examples illustrate is that, because of the current conventions in film fiction, we need the continuous appearance of salient intradiegetic cues to fictionally assign narrative control to a fictional agent or device. In other words, clear and unequivocal work-imaginings about this control need to be mandated. Therefore, although in principle there is nothing that would constrain the existence of controlling fictional narrators in fiction film, in practice strong and reoccurring markers of control are necessary to any attribution of such to a particular narrator. In other words, all these examples illustrate that controlling fictional narrators in film are always explicit and that in film there is no analogue to implicit markers in literary fiction, that is, deictics.

Importantly, this has been the case since the earliest days of cinema. As the analysis of contemporary narratological discussions during the transitional era has demonstrated, the very fact of a fictional narrative does not entail a fictional narrator. For contemporaries of early narrative cinema there is nothing problematic about a story recounting itself in images. This is simply a feature of story-telling in a new medium. Later theoretical constructs beginning with Laffay and Metz are just that – constructs or what Walton would call gameworlds. They start their analyses from an essentially linguistic position, so it is no wonder that they end up misidentifying various filmic features for deictics. Or, like Wilson, they produce extravagant accounts of what spectators imagine without looking at historical data. People contributing to screenwriting manuals and thinking about the principles of visual story-telling during the transitional era did not imagine any 'naturally iconic images'. And they would have found the idea of film images as a form of discourse which asserts 'This is x' equally exotic. Instead, contemporaries were faced with a decidedly novel form of story-telling and attempted to articulate its principles in its own terms. We would do well to do likewise.

Conclusion

On the preceding pages I have attempted to articulate the importance of imagination for the understanding of the experience of early cinema. I argued that imagination allows us to rethink the train effect over and above the existing accounts based on the looming effect and the incredulity of magic tricks. I proposed that the analysis of make-believe contributes to the debate on whether early cinema was primarily construed in terms of attractions or narratives by supplying the arguments in favour of the latter. I claimed that in the case of the earliest narrative films including both adaptations and trick films the imaginative engagement with these films was significantly different from the games of make-believe the films prop today. I offered evidence that various (predominantly) visual immersion techniques can be distinguished in terms of whether they elicited imaginings or whether they actually fooled people into believing something that was not the case. In the case of film immersion techniques, I articulated the differences between what people imagined when watching train films and when viewing phantom rides and Hale's Tours. I invoked imagination to dispel the lingering myths about the allegedly illusory nature of Hale's Tours. I demonstrated the distinction between illustration and serving as a prop for imaginary engagement in fake films. I claimed that lectures could not only modify specific imaginings in fiction films but also transform otherwise dominantly illustrative travelogues into imaginary voyages. And I reasoned that audiences imagined early story films as recounting themselves without invoking any ancillary entities like narrators.

I have tried to put forward as nuanced an account of imaginative engagement with early cinema as possible. In the case of films like *Uncle Tom's Cabin* (Edwin S. Porter, 1903) and *The Astronomer's Dream or the Man on the Moon/La Lune à un mètre* (Georges Méliès, 1898), I claimed that it was the actors' performance rather than the film itself that was the prop. When it comes to techniques of visual immersion, I argued that phantom rides invited the spectator to imagine herself within the world screened while early train films saw spectators imagining the threat bursting out of the screen and rushing to meet them in the space of the auditorium. On the example of fakes, I demonstrated how intentions by filmmakers to mandate similar imaginings could fall flat among spectators. The subtlest use of the present tense, I demonstrated, allowed travel lecture attendees to imagine themselves whisked away to foreign lands in the company of the lecturer. And in the case of narrative fiction film, contemporaries even objected to uniform fonts used in letter inserts because they imaginatively engaged these inserts as visual rather than as merely propositional representations.

From this perspective imaginative engagement, like the appeal of attractions, played an important role in early train and surf films, phantom rides, narrative trick films, Hale's Tours and the like. Unlike attractions, however, the scope of imaginative engagement with cinema only increased as time passed. It is true that relatively quickly a number of films like train films were no longer engaged with imaginatively, but they were immediately supplanted with an even greater number of productions that were. Imaginative engagement with cinema, therefore, provides an uninterrupted thread from the earliest days of cinema until today and well into the foreseeable future. Moreover, the history of such engagement, unlike the history of attractions, follows a thread that never yields to another dominant that is narrative cinema. Unlike the history of narrative cinema, furthermore, the history of imaginative engagement can accommodate both the cinema of attractions and later experimental genres.

One such line of inquiry could follow the genre of historical films with Alfred Clark's *The Execution of Mary, Queen of the Scots* (1895) as one of its earliest examples. The representation of beheading, undeniably, presents a great attraction. But what of other aspects of the film – particularly its indebtedness to a historical event? How much would the audiences have cared about the veracity of the representation? Or would they have been more invested in the images as props for make-believe? For instance, would they have been interested in whether the costumes worn by the actors accurately represent those of the time depicted? Or would they have instead imagined these costumes as worn in Mary's time without much consideration of historical accuracy?

Another potential investigation might tackle the advertising film genre. In Edison Manufacturing Company's *Admiral Cigarette* (1897), for instance, we could reasonably argue that the admiral jumping out of the box is an attraction that would have appealed to the audience. But the admiral's sudden appearance does not seem to be culmination of the film *qua* advertisement. Instead, he proceeds to shower the other four characters who were on screen even before his appearance with cigarettes and then moves to the edge of the frame to allow them to unfurl the banner reading 'We all smoke'. The banner clearly refers to the background writing 'Admiral Cigarette'. Given that the other characters have distinct costumes depicting a generic American, Native American, Uncle Sam, and an oriental character, respectively, we might wonder whether the audiences would have taken the content of the advertisement as a game of make-believe or whether they would have taken these people as flesh and blood advocates of smoking the Admiral Cigarette brand. In other words, do advertising film actually claim things about their product or do they put the audience in an imaginary relationship towards it? This line of inquiry, I believe, might also shed some light on imaginative engagement with the early experimental film given that the pioneers of experimental cinema such as Walter Ruttmann come with a pedigree in advertising. I suspect, then, that the investigation of these and many other early cinema genres from the perspective of imaginings might reveal that make-believe organized the early viewing experience in as unexpected ways as it did in early train, surf and trick films.

To articulate the theoretical importance of imagination in the early cinema period I have drawn on Kendall L. Walton's theory which identifies make-believe as constitutive of fiction. This led me to revise the taxonomy new film history inherited from earlier scholarship. It allowed me to call into question standard models from both analytic philosophy and film studies which determine a film's fictional status according to authorial and/or textual features alone. It aided me in clearly delineating mandated imagining from illusion, immersion and illustration. It helped me to distinguish fiction from various forms of faking – staging, deliberate misrepresentation and narrativization. The analysis of historical data permitted me to contribute to debates on the nature of imagined seeing. It paved the way for an argument for the asymmetry of controlling fictional narrators in literature and film. It also allowed me to articulate the difference between explicit and implicit mandates for imaginings. Perhaps most importantly, the discussion of imagination in early cinema enabled me to emphasize the fact that fictional status may change over (a very brief period of) time irrespective of the filmmakers' initial intentions.

I proposed that we should treat the earliest train, surf and phantom ride films as fictions while recasting numerous trick films as actualities of (magic) theatre performances, thereby further dismantling the Lumière/Méliès dichotomy. I argued that through catalogues, posters, advertisements, organization of film programmes, verbal performances, reviews, editorials and so on, producers, distributors, exhibitors, lecturers and commentators of film all played a role in fixing and changing a film's fictional status. I demonstrated that the talk of 'willing suspension of disbelief' and 'diegetic illusionism' comes with a terminological baggage of illusion as false belief which has no place in discussions of fiction as make-believe. I pointed out that immersion does not necessarily entail either fiction or illusion or any transformation between the two. I clarified that illustration in its visual form (photographic or otherwise) does not entail any imagining either. I marshalled contemporary discussions of phantom rides and Hale's Tours to give further credence to the idea that the face-to-face version of the imagined seeing thesis is in operation only in exceptional cases. I argued that the variability in presentational strategies in a given film does not necessarily entail the film's non/fictional hybridity. I built on discussions from screenwriting manuals to argue that there is nothing contradictory about eliminating controlling fictional narrators from the majority of fiction film. I specified that deixis as a prop for implicit imaginings in literature has no equivalent in film. And finally, I proposed that from the perspective of imaginative engagement with early cinema the myth of the birth of cinema also obscures the fact that films like *Arrival of a Train/L'Arrivée d'un train en gare de La Ciotat* migrated from fiction to non-fiction in a matter of decade or two.

According to this model which allows for migration from and into fiction over time, the mandates for imaginings do not fluctuate as much as they get completely activated or deactivated. It is not that after a while the viewers of *Uncle Tom's Cabin* start, say, engaging one of the actors pretending to hit the other as something other than a prop for imagining that Legree is going to kill Uncle Tom. Instead, over time, the spectators stop using only the actors' performances as props and apply the status of the prop to the film image itself. In the case of train films, similarly, it is not that the audiences start to imagine that the train is going to stop at the station instead of crash into the auditorium. Rather, they stop imagining things altogether and start seeing such films as recordings of everyday events.

Although I have argued that with time a number of films crossed fiction/non-fiction boundaries I have stopped short of describing the cognitive and cultural reasons behind the process in detail. This is another line of inquiry worth pursuing. I suspect that we might start off from the notion of the novel representational medium and argue that as soon as the spectators get accustomed to the medium, they stop imagining any threats from the screened trains. In the case *Uncle Tom's Cabin* and *The Astronomer's Dream or the Man in the Moon*, similarly, we could conjecture that as soon as the novelty of the film's reproductive faculty wears off the audiences proceed to imaginatively engage the film image itself. And perhaps we could also say that phantom rides get another boost to imaginative engagement because they are placed into a novel exhibition context. In other words, it might not be strictly a matter of medium novelty but rather a question of novelty within a broader institutional context. But what of biblical films whose non-fictional status hinges on a larger set of cultural beliefs? And what of the fact that these beliefs differ across both religious and national borders? All these questions feed into the broader questions of the notions of history which, I trust, only adds to their importance.

I am also confident that a robust understanding of fiction can contribute to film theory. Since its classical incarnations film theory has privileged narrative fiction film but has, at the same time, disregarded what the notion of fiction does to the theories' logical coherence. For instance, given André Bazin's investment in the ontological properties of the photographic image and its relation to the object photographed he should be forced to say that what is represented in *Casablanca* (Michael Curtiz, 1942) is first and foremost Humphrey Bogart rather than Rick. At the very least, however, this ignores the fact that on many occasions of watching photographic narrative fiction films it is the fiction that interests us more than the actors. In other words, Bazin's theoretical commitments downplay the importance of make-believe when engaging films based on the photographic image in favour of the profilmic.

To give an example from 'contemporary theory', Christian Metz has claimed that the crucial characteristic of the film medium is that its signifiers, unlike all other non-photographic media, are imaginary. Metz understands the signifiers as the objects and actors we see in the image, and the signifieds as the fictional objects and characters. More generally, the profilmic would be the signifier and the fictional world the signified. One of the problems here is the unwarranted use of the term 'imaginary' to describe 'a certain presence and a certain absence' of the signifier, and to, on the basis of that, claim that 'every film is a fiction film'. It is unwarranted because if the signifier is the profilmic then the profilmic is clearly absent (in the sense of not being physically present and more precisely, in the sense of us not being able to orientate ourselves towards it based only on the information in the image). What is present is the image of the profilmic. And to claim that the profilmic is both absent and present is to conflate the representation and the represented. A more precise way of describing the film within Metz's own framework would be to say that the image (the array of visual data) is the first signifier which signifies the profilmic. And then it could be said for the profilmic that at the same time as being the first signified it is also the second signifier which in turn signifies the fictional world. The fact that the second signifier is embedded, however, does not make such a signifier either imaginary or fictional. In other words, a precise analysis of the notion of imaginary demystifies some of Metz's key theoretical claims and invalidates his general claim that all films are fiction.

Finally, the most recent theories focusing on digital developments in cinema have insisted that the nature of the medium has radically changed because the relation between the image and its referent is no longer indexical. It is not only that the images of objects can be manipulated at will but also that given that the technology is becoming increasingly advanced it becomes impossible to say with certainty if the images were even taken with any actual objects in front of the camera. But the theoretical impetus which starts from the fact that the referent (the primary signified and the second signifier) was potentially never there can have little bearing on fiction film because the referents in fiction film (the second signified) were never there to begin with. It is impossible to record fictions in the first place – film can only record props. In other words, whatever consequences follow from these considerations they can have far less bearing on fiction than on documentary film.

Fiction construed as mandated imagining, therefore, can contribute to film theory and new film history as much as focus on imagination in early cinema can add to elucidating concepts in philosophical aesthetics and to better understanding the contemporary experience of early cinema. This monograph has been an attempt at pointing in the direction of how this can be done.

Notes

Introduction

1 'Theatrical Chat', *Grand Forks Daily Herald*, 20 December 1903, p. 5.
2 'Vaudeville and Minstrels', *Philadelphia Inquirer*, Second Section, April 9, 1899, p. 10.
3 I use the term 'new film history' in the sense it appears in Thomas Elsaesser, 'The New Film History as Media Archeology', *Cinémas: revue d'études cinématographiques/Cinémas: Journal of Film Studies* 14.2-3 (2004), pp. 75–117. There, as in this monograph, the term refers to the work of film scholars who, starting with Noël Burch and Barry Salt in the 1970s, began rethinking early cinema and challenging the teleological, linear and great men models of film history. This use, however, requires some further justification because the term has been employed in other ways as well. In fact, when Elsaesser originally coined 'new film history' in his review of the then recent scholarship on film history, the term did not focus on early cinema alone. See Thomas Elsaesser, 'The New Film History', *Sight and Sound* 55.4 (1986), pp. 246–51. This broader understanding which derives its meaning from the opposition to the 'old film history' while leaving the time frame studied open also has significant overlap with another recently minted term – 'new cinema history'. See Richard Maltby, 'New Cinema Histories', in R. Maltby, D. Biltereyst and Philippe Meers (eds), *Explorations in New Cinema History: Approaches and Case Studies* (Chichester, 2011), pp. 3–40. This should come as no surprise because already in his piece from 1986 Elsaesser states that 'New Film History ... should really be called New History of the Cinema.' Elsaesser, 'The New Film History', p. 247. Next to opposing the linearity and teleology of 'old film history' the key trait that 'new cinema history' shares with 'new film history' as originally conceived by Elsaesser is that they both share the idea initially suggested by Robert C. Allen and Douglas Gomery that it is non-filmic material that often teaches us more about film history than films. See Robert C. Allen and Douglas Gomery, *Film History: Theory and Practice* (London, 1985). It is undeniable that many historians of early cinema – who I refer to as 'new film historians' – have over the years used new cinema history methods in their work. But given that many works on early cinema have also focused more on single authors and films, I will use 'new film history' in the sense specified by Elsaesser in 2004 to highlight that some of the work discussed predates and/or does not necessarily involve a new cinema history approach.
4 Siegfried Kracauer, *Theory of Film: The Redemption of Physical Reality* (New York, 1960), p. 30.

5   Richard Abel (ed.), *Encyclopedia of Early Cinema* (London, 2005), pp. liii–liv.
6   For the discussion of the myth of the panicking audience, see Chapter 1.
7   Such terms are described best in John Searle, 'The Logical Status of Fictional Discourse', *New Literary History* 6.2 (1975), p. 321: 'Every subject matter has its catchphrases to enable us to stop thinking before we have got a solution to our problems.'
8   Kendall L. Walton, *Mimesis as Make-Believe: On the Foundations of the Representational Arts* (Cambridge, MA, 1990).
9   Gregory Currie, *The Nature of Fiction* (Cambridge, 1990); David Davies, *Aesthetics and Literature* (London, 2007); David Davies, 'Fiction', in B. Gaut and D. McIver Lopes (eds), *The Routledge Companion to Aesthetics*, 3rd edn (New York, 2013), pp. 330–9; Peter Lamarque and Stein Haugom Olsen, *Truth, Fiction, and Literature: A Philosophical Perspective* (Oxford, 1994); Kathleen Stock, 'Imagination and Fiction', in A. Kind (ed.) *The Routledge Handbook of Philosophy of Imagination* (New York, 2016), pp. 204–16. Some dissent has come from Stacie Friend, 'Imagination, Fact and Fiction', in K. Stock and K. Thomson-Jones (eds), *New Waves in Aesthetics* (Basingstoke, 2008), pp. 150–69; Stacie Friend, 'Fictive Utterance and Imagining II', *Aristotelian Society Supplementary Volume* 85.1 (2011), pp. 163–80; Stacie Friend, 'Fiction as a Genre', *Proceedings of the Aristotelian Society* 112.2 (2012), pp. 179–209. She has argued that although most of fiction rests on imagination, imagination still fails to provide a definition of fiction in sufficient and/or necessary terms. Only recently Derek Matravers has been bold enough to claim that imagination informs fiction no more than it does non-fiction: Derek Matravers, *Fiction and Narrative* (Oxford, 2014). For a rebuttal see Stock, 'Imagination and Fiction'.
10 Stock, 'Imagination and Fiction', p. 215.
11 Gregory Currie and Anna Ichino, 'Imagination and Make-Believe', in *The Routledge Companion to Aesthetics*, p. 320.
12 David Lewis, 'Truth in Fiction', *American Philosophical Quarterly* 15.1 (1978), pp. 37–46; Saul Kripke, *Naming and Necessity* (Cambridge, MA, 1980); Thomas Pavel, *Fictional Worlds* (Cambridge, MA, 1986); Lubomír Doležel, *Heterocosmica: Fiction and Possible Worlds* (Baltimore, 1998).
13 Bertrand Russell, 'On Denoting', *Mind* 14.56 (1905), pp. 479–93.
14 Cf. Currie, *The Nature of Fiction*, pp. 62–70.
15 Walton, *Mimesis as Make-Believe*, p. 5.
16 Searle, 'The Logical Status of Fictional Discourse'.
17 Nicholas Wolterstorff, *Works and Worlds of Art* (New York, 1980), pp. 219–34; Currie, *The Nature of Fiction*, pp. 52–98.
18 Currie, *The Nature of Fiction*; Lamarque and Olsen, *Truth, Fiction, and Literature*; Davies, 'Fiction'.

19 Currie, *The Nature of Fiction*, pp. 92–8.
20 Walton, *Mimesis as Make-Believe*, p. 69, italics in the original.
21 Gregory Currie, *Image and Mind: Film, Philosophy and Cognitive Science* (Cambridge, 1995), p. 267.
22 Tom Gunning, *D. W. Griffith and the Origins of American Narrative Film: The Early Years at Biograph* (Urbana, 1991); André Gaudreault, *From Plato to Lumière: Narration and Monstration in Literature and Cinema*, trans. T. Barnard (Toronto, 2009).
23 George M. Wilson, *Seeing Fictions in Film: The Epistemology of Movies* (Oxford, 2011).
24 Cf. ibid.
25 Quoted in Stephen Bottomore, 'The Panicking Audience?: Early Cinema and the "Train Effect"', *Historical Journal of Film, Radio and Television* 19.2 (1999), p. 194.
26 Cf. Robert C. Allen, 'Contra the Chaser Theory', *Wide Angle* 3.1 (1979), pp. 4–11; Robert C. Allen, 'From Exhibition to Reception: Reflections on the Audience in Film History', *Screen* 31.4 (1990), pp. 347–56; Daniël Biltereyst, Richard Maltby and Philippe Meers (eds), *Cinema, Audiences and Modernity: New Perspectives on European Cinema History* (Abingdon, 2011); Ian Christie (ed.), *Audiences: Defining and Researching Screen Entertainment Reception* (Amsterdam, 2012).
27 Cf. Lauren Rabinovitz, *For the Love of Pleasure: Women, Movies, and the Culture in Turn-of-the-Century Chicago* (New Brunswick, NJ, 1998); Gregory A. Waller, *Main Street Amusements: Movies and Commercial Entertainment in a Southern City, 1896–1930* (Washington, 1995); Melvyn Stokes and Richard Maltby (eds), *American Movie Audiences: From the Turn of the Century to the Early Sound Era* (London, 1999); Shelley Stamp, *Movie-Struck Girls: Women and Motion Picture Culture after the Nickelodeon* (Princeton, 2000); Jacqueline Najuma Stewart, *Migrating to the Movies: Cinema and Black Urban Modernity* (Berkeley, 2005); Biltereyst, Maltby and Meers (eds), *Cinema, Audiences and Modernity*. For a pioneering contemporary sociological study see Emilie Altenloh, *Zur Soziologie des Kino: Die Kino-Unternehmung und die sozialen Schichten ihrer Besucher* (Jena, 1914).
28 Miriam Hansen, *Babel and Babylon: Spectatorship in American Silent Film* (Cambridge, MA, 1991), p. 1.
29 Dan Streible, *Fight Pictures: A History of Boxing and Early Cinema* (Berkeley, 2008), pp. 52–95.
30 Denis Condon, 'Irish Audiences Watch Their First US Feature: *The Corbett-Fitzsimmons Fight* (1897)', in R. Barton (ed.), *Screening Irish-America: Representing Irish-America in Film and Television* (Dublin, 2009), pp. 135–47.
31 As Janet Staiger reminds us, we should also be careful not to replace a general spectator with a general female/black/working-class, etc. spectator. Janet Staiger, *Interpreting Films: Studies in the Historical Reception of American Cinema* (Princeton, 1992), p. 13.
32 Kendall L. Walton, 'Transparent Pictures: On the Nature of Photographic Realism', in *Marvelous Images: On Values and the Arts* (Oxford, 2008), p. 88.

33 Ibid., 89, italics in the original.
34 Ibid., 90, italics in the original.
35 André Bazin, 'Theater and Cinema – Part Two', in *What Is Cinema? Vol. 1*, ed. and trans. H. Gray (Berkeley, 2004), p. 97.
36 In analytic circles the idea that we see through photographs much like through mirrors is known as the 'transparency thesis'. It hinges on the claim that 'the "slope" descending from direct, face-to-face seeing is "slippery" all the way to (what I call) seeing through photographs'. Kendall L. Walton, 'On Photographs and Pictures: Objections Answered', in *Marvelous Images*, p. 122. Noël Carroll, for instance, disagrees with Walton by claiming that photographs, unlike mirrors, do not provide egocentric information – information about the position of the observer's body in relation to the object of. For Carroll, to see an object (through something) means to be able to determine one's own spatial relation to that object. Cf. Noël Carroll, *The Philosophy of Motion Pictures* (Malden, 2008), pp. 93–102. Notice that for my argument it is irrelevant whether the transparency thesis holds or not – it is only important that Walton subscribes to it. My own view is that Walton's thesis is invalid because there is 'a significant stopping place' (different from Carroll's) on the 'slippery slope' – viz. whether the very light reflecting of the surface of the object is the light that reaches our eyes. This is so in the case of mirrors and binoculars but not in the case of photographs. This also means that Bazin mistakenly compares photographs to mirrors, but this again does not impinge on my argument. I only needed to demonstrate that for him the idea of presence rests on the properties he believes photography to share with mirrors. For more on the importance of the physics of light for Bazin's ontology of photography see Mario Slugan, 'Taking Bazin Literally', *Projections: The Journal for Movies and Mind* 11.1 (2017), pp. 63–82.

1 The status of fiction in early cinema: Train and trick films

1 Charlie Keil, 'Steel Engines and Cardboard Rockets: The Status of Fiction and Nonfiction in Early Cinema', in A. Juhasz and J. Lerner (eds), *F Is for Phony: Fake Documentary and Truth's Undoing* (Minneapolis, 2006), p. 39.
2 Tom Gunning, 'Early American Film in J. Hill and P. Church Gibson (eds), *The Oxford Guide to Film Studies* (Oxford, 1997), pp. 255–71.
3 Keil, 'Steel Engines and Cardboard Rockets'.
4 Kendall L. Walton, *Mimesis as Make-Believe: On the Foundations of the Representational Arts* (Cambridge, MA, 1990).
5 André Gaudreault and Tom Gunning, 'Introduction: American Cinema Emerges (1890–1909)', in A. Gaudrault (ed.), *American cinema, 1890–1909: Themes and Variations* (New Brunswick, NJ, 2009), p. 18.

6 Richard Abel (ed.), *Encyclopedia of Early Cinema* (London, 2005), pp. liii–liv.
7 Keil, 'Steel Engines and Cardboard Rockets', pp. 39–41.
8 Martin Loiperdinger reminds us that there were three versions of the film; two from 1896, and one from 1897, with the last version being the one we are nowadays familiar with. In this section I will be speaking of the 1897 version but in the rest of the monograph the film will be a short-hand for a number of train films like it. Also, given its production date it is clear that not even the first version of the film could have been shown during the first screening at Grand Café on 28 December, 1895. See Martin Loiperdinger, 'Lumière's Arrival of the Train: Cinema's Founding Myth', *The Moving Image* 4.1 (2004), p. 103.
9 Keil, 'Steel Engines and Cardboard Rockets', p. 39.
10 Ibid., p. 40.
11 Admittedly, in the case of travelogues Keil mentions lecturing accompaniments as an extratextual feature which could influence the film's fictional status. In Chapter 4, however, I argue that such lectures should be understood as textual properties.
12 Tom Gunning, 'Before Documentary: Early Nonfiction Films and the "View" Aesthetic', in D. Hertogs and N. de Klerk (eds), *Uncharted Territory: Essays on Early Nonfiction Film* (Amsterdam, 1997), pp. 9–24.
13 Loiperdinger has argued by identifying members of the Lumière's family among the cast and by pointing to relative dearth of looks at the camera that the film is, in fact, staged. Staging is, however, neither a sufficient nor necessary condition for a film to be fictional because it is a presentational technique, that is, a textual feature. Loiperdinger correctly points out that staging in *The Arrival of a Train* has only to do with deception and our willingness to see the film as a precursor to direct cinema. See Loiperdinger, 'Lumière's Arrival of the Train', pp. 107–14. For more on the conflation of staging and fiction see Chapter 3.
14 I discuss the relationship between narrative and fiction in more detail in Chapters 3, 4 and 5.
15 André Bazin, 'Every Film Is a Social Documentary', *Film Comment* 44.6 (2008), pp. 40–1. I take titles to be features external to films as long as they cannot be found projected on the screen – something typical of many early films including *The Arrival of a Train* and *A Trip to the Moon*.
16 Cf. Jacques Malthête, *Méliès: Images et illusions* (Paris, 1996).
17 Tom Gunning, 'Colorful Metaphors: The Attraction of Color in Early Silent Cinema', *Fotogenia* 1.1 (1994), pp. 249–55; Joshua Yumibe, *Moving Color: Early Film, Mass Culture, Modernism* (New Brunswick, NJ, 2012).
18 Keil, 'Steel Engines and Cardboard Rockets', pp. 40, 42, italics in the original.
19 Ibid., p. 40.
20 If we downplayed the representational nature of the film, we could speak of it in terms of visual arrays and sounds changing over time.

21 There are, admittedly, sounds in the film which are recordings of actual actors speaking their lines. This might prompt us to think of *Toy Story* as a digitally animated illustration of verbal performances of Tom Hanks, Tim Allen and others. This, however, confuses the illustrations of performances themselves for illustrations of what they are performing. If we insist on talking of illustrations it is the latter that the film does. But even then these illustrations are to be engaged imaginatively no less than, say, illustrations in children's books.

22 Hannah Frank catalogues a number of visual imperfections which alleviate this task – fingerprints, camera apparatus reflections, particles of dust and dirt, etc.: Hannah Frank, 'Traces of the World: Cel Animation and Photography', *Animation* 11.1 (2016), pp. 23–39.

23 This is not to say that we are necessarily *not* mandated to imagine the representational content of these films based on their textual features alone. The point here is just to demonstrate that, unlike films such as *Toy Story*, we can engage some digitally animated cinema as non-fictional and that the flight-announcement context makes these specific films non-fictional.

24 It is possible that what is now thought of as not populating the actual world in fact is a part of it (or at least was at some time). If it turns out that one of the entities previously thought not to populate the actual world in fact exists or that it at least existed – for instance, fossils of unicorns are uncovered – this affects the fictional status of direct representations of such entities. However, the status is changed only for the audiences engaging these texts *after* the discovery. No changes are made retroactively.

25 In Christian Metz's vocabulary the direct representations in photographs would be imaginary signifiers. Christian Metz, *The Imaginary Signifier: Psychoanalysis and the Cinema*, trans. C. Britton (Bloomington, 1982). I avoid the term because of its manifold problems. Some of the most relevant ones include: (1) Metz uses the notion of the imaginary signifier to claim that every film is fiction: cf. ibid., p. 44. This claim is persuasively refuted by Noël Carroll, 'From Real to Reel: Entangled in Nonfiction Film', *Philosophic Exchange* 14.1 (1983), pp. 4–45. (2) The description of imaginary signifier as the presence of absence mystifies the fact that *all* representations stand for something that is not actually there. (3) Embedded representation implied in imaginary signification is not specific to film but is a property of all recordings (e.g. audio recordings).

26 Noël Carroll, 'Fiction, Non-Fiction, and the Film of Presumptive Assertion: A Conceptual Analysis', in R. Allen and M. Smith (eds), *Film Theory and Philosophy* (Oxford, 1997), pp. 173–202.

27 Trevor Ponech, 'What Is Non-Fiction Cinema?' in *Film Theory and Philosophy*, pp. 203–20; Carl Plantinga, 'What a Documentary Is, after All', *The Journal of Aesthetics and Art Criticism* 63.2 (2005), pp. 105–17.

28 For book-length discussions of biblical themes in silent cinema see David J. Shepherd, *The Bible on Silent Film: Spectacle, Story and Scripture in the Early*

Cinema (Cambridge, 2013); and David J. Shepherd, *The Silents of Jesus in the Cinema (1897–1927)* (New York, 2016). For an account of the early passion plays in the United States see Charles Musser, 'Passions and the Passion Play: Theatre, Film and Religion in America, 1880–1900', *Film History* 5.4 (1993), pp. 419–56.

29 Lubin Manufacturing Company Catalogue Special, 'The Passion Play', 1905, p. 2, block capitals in the original, in C. Musser et al. (eds), *Motion Picture Catalogs by American Producers and Distributors, 1894–1908* (Baltimore, 1984).

30 In the next section and on the example of train film I will be arguing that transformation in cinema can take place in the opposite direction as well – from fiction to non-fiction.

31 In an earlier essay, Carroll, admittedly, does allow for a more institutional view of fiction according to which films are indexed as fictions or non-fictions by '[p]roducers writers, directors, distributors, and exhibitors': Carroll, 'From Real to Reel', p. 24. Even under this broader account, however, audience does not get a say in determining the status of films – an element which plays an important role under my proposal. Moreover, given that in his latest essay on the subject he explicitly espouses an intentionalist account I take it this is his most-up-to-date view on the matter. See Carroll, 'Fiction, Non-Fiction, and the Film of Presumptive Assertion'.

32 'All persons fictitious' disclaimer appears as a consequence of a libel suit against MGM's *Rasputin and the Empress* (Richard Boleslawski, 1932). The term 'film documentaire' meaning 'factual, meant to provide a record of something' appears to have been used widely already in 1920s France. In English, John Grierson described the traits of Robert Flaherty's *Moana* (1925) as 'documentary' in his contemporary review: John Grierson, 'Moana', *New York Sun*, 8 February 1926.

33 For a recent book-length study of early travelogues and non-fiction cinema see Jennifer Lynn Peterson, *Education in the School of Dreams: Travelogues and Early Nonfiction Film* (Durham, 2013). Chapter 2 discusses the book in more detail.

34 Yuri Tsivian, *Early Cinema in Russia and Its Cultural Reception*, trans. A. Bodger (London, 1994); Stephen Bottomore, 'The Panicking Audience?: Early Cinema and the "Train Effect"', *Historical Journal of Film, Radio and Television* 19.2 (1999), p. 177.

35 Gregory Currie, 'Film, Reality, and Illusion', in N. Carroll and D. Bordwell (eds), *Post-Theory: Reconstructing Film Studies* (Madison, 1996), p. 333.

36 For the most recent reappraisal of 'the train effect' which is not interested in its veracity but instead in the role that the bourgeois discourse on it had in propagating class distinction in Britain see Rebecca Harrison, *From Steam to Screen: Cinema, the Railways, and Modernity* (London, 2018), loc. 663–1409.

37 Loiperdinger, 'Lumière's Arrival of the Train'.

38 Tom Gunning, 'An Aesthetic of Astonishment: Early Film and the (In)credulous Spectator', *Art and Text* 34.1 (1989), pp. 31–45; Tom Gunning, '"Primitive" Cinema: A Frame-Up? Or the Trick's on Us', *Cinema Journal* 28.2 (1989), pp. 3–12.

39 Quoted in Bottomore, 'The Panicking Audience?', p. 213.
40 Ben Singer, 'Modernity, Hyperstimulus, and the Rise of Popular Sensationalism', in L. Charney and V. R. Schwartz (eds), *Cinema and the Invention of Modern Life* (Berkeley, 1995), pp. 72–99; Ben Singer, *Melodrama and Modernity: Early Sensational Cinema and Its Contexts* (New York, 2001).
41 Cy Warman, 'Ringtown Put out the Light', *Omaha Daily Bee*, 26 September 1897, p. 17.
42 Quoted in Bottomore, 'The Panicking Audience?', p. 213.
43 Quoted in Loiperdinger, 'Lumière's Arrival of the Train', p. 97.
44 Quoted in ibid., p. 98.
45 Quoted in Bottomore, 'The Panicking Audience?', p. 194.
46 Quoted in ibid., pp. 192–3.
47 Quoted in ibid., p. 194.
48 Cf. David Lewis, *Counterfactuals* (Oxford, 1973).
49 Quoted in Bottomore, 'The Panicking Audience?', p. 213.
50 It might be objected that imaginings cannot serve as explanations for actual behaviour – for how can something non-existent bring about any actual effect? But using imaginings as explanations for actual behaviour is no more mysterious than using thoughts for the same. Moreover, there clearly are examples when imaginings prompt certain bodily responses. Try, for instance, imagining a delightful dessert made of fish dressed with chocolate ice-cream and dipped into excrement of your choosing and see if it causes no actual reaction. Or consider the fact that sexual imaginings are known to cause actual arousal. There is, therefore, no reason why imagining a violent and impeding crash could not make one turn nervous.
51 The key criterion for distinguishing unimaginative and the imaginative viewer here is undeniably made along gender lines, with men identified as the former and women as the latter. There are gender stereotypes clearly at play here, but I would suggest that the reviewer's (who is probable a male) stance is more ambiguous than it might seem at first. On the one hand, there seems to be a slight negative connotation in the very term 'unimaginative' as describing somebody missing a valuable ability. After all, such a man is incapable of partaking in the film fully. He only 'kind of' shivers. On the other hand, although being imaginative is implied to be a positive trait, women in this account clearly tend to be too imaginative. This, in the long tradition of women being presented as irrational, hysterical and overly emotional, leads to excessive reactions such as screaming and fainting. Although the review implies that the optimal stance would be an imaginative albeit a more restrained one, the question remains: who, in the reviewer's eyes, enjoyed the film more?
52 Loiperdinger, 'Lumière's Arrival of the Train', p. 99.
53 Quoted in ibid., p. 101.
54 Ibid., p. 102, italics in the original.

55 Gunning, 'An Aesthetic of Astonishment'.
56 Ibid., p. 35.
57 Ibid., p. 43.
58 For a study of the notion of 'willing suspension of disbelief' see Anthony J. Ferri, *Willing Suspension of Disbelief: Poetic Faith in Film* (Lanham, 2007). For the continuing importance of apparatus theory and its place in textbooks see Susan Hayward, *Cinema Studies: The Key Concepts*, 5th edn (Abingdon, 2018). For a recent revival of apparatus theory see François Albera and Maria Tortajada (eds), *Cinema beyond Film: Media Epistemology in the Modern Era* (Amsterdam, 2010).
59 Gunning, 'An Aesthetic of Astonishment', p. 34.
60 Ibid., p. 33.
61 Quoted in Tsivian, *Early Cinema in Russia*, p. 111.
62 Gunning, 'An Aesthetic of Astonishment', p. 34.
63 Ibid.
64 Miriam Rosen, 'Méliès, Georges', in J. Wakeman (ed.), *World Film Directors: Volume I, 1890-1945* (New York, 1987), pp. 747-65.
65 Ibid.
66 André Gaudreault and Philippe Marion, *The End of Cinema?: A Medium in Crisis in the Digital Age,* trans. T. Barnard (New York, 2015), p. 92; André Gaudreault, 'La cinématographie-attraction chez Méliès: Une conception durable', in A. Gaudreault and L. Le Forestier (eds), *Méliès, carrefour des attractions: Suivi de Correspondance de Georges Méliès (1904-1937)* (Rennes, 2014), pp. 27-43.
67 Richard Abel, '*A Trip to the Moon* as an American Phenomenon', in M. Solomon (ed.), *Fantastic Voyages of the Cinematic Imagination: Georges Méliès's Trip to the Moon* (Albany, 2011), pp. 129-42.
68 'Vaudeville and Minstrels', *Philadelphia Inquirer*, Second Section, 9 April 1899, p. 10.
69 Tom Gunning, 'A Trip to the Moon (1902)', in J. Geiger and R. L. Rutsky (eds), *Film Analysis: A Norton Reader*, 2nd edn (New York, 2013), p. 42.
70 Turquety Benoit, 'Tricks and Effects: Introduction', *Early Popular Visual Culture* 13.2 (2015), p. 104.
71 Frank Kessler, '*A Trip to the Moon* as *Féerie*', in *Fantastic Voyages of the Cinematic Imagination*, p. 115.
72 Ian Christie, 'First Footing on the Moon: Méliès's Debt to Verne and Wells and His Influence in Great Britain', in *Fantastic Voyages of the Cinematic Imagination*, pp. 65-80.
73 Abel, '*A Trip to the Moon* as an American Phenomenon'.
74 Ibid.
75 For more on the notion of cultural series see Nicolas Dulac and André Gaudreault, 'Circularity and Repetition at the Heart of the Attraction: Optical Toys and the Emergence of a New Cultural Series', in W. Strauven (ed.), *The Cinema of Attractions Reloaded* (Amsterdam, 2006), pp. 227-44.

76 *Omaha World Herald*, 13 September 1903, p. 22.
77 *Omaha World Herald*, 1 November 1903, p. 18.
78 *Daily Picayune*, 19 December 1902, p. 4.
79 *Baltimore American*, 27 December 1903, p. 30.
80 Anton Kaes (ed), *Kino-Debatte: Texte zum Verhältnis von Literatur und Film 1909–1929* (München; Tübingen, 1978); Richard Abel (ed.), *French Film Theory and Criticism: A History/Anthology, 1907–1939. Vol. 1* (Princeton, 1988).
81 Max Beer, 'Film, Theater und Roman', *Frankfurter Zeitung*, 1 July 1913, my translation. Similar criticism was used to dismiss *The Cabinet of Dr. Caligari* in 1922: 'There is not a single refinement of director's craft; all the effects are obtained with the help of means belonging to painting, music, literature, etc. Nowhere does one see [the contribution of] the camera': quoted in Abel, *French Film Theory and Criticism*, p. 271.
82 *Lincoln (Neb.) Evening News*, 18 May 1903, p. 7.
83 *Times Picayune*, 29 March 1903, p. 36.
84 *Morning Olympian*, 29 November 1903, p. 3.
85 *Trenton Evening Times*, 18 October 1903, p. 11. Abel has documented in detail how in the US Méliès's film was regularly perceived to be an American, namely Edison's, production; Abel, '*A Trip to the Moon* as an American Phenomenon'. The first two quotations above present *A Trip to the Moon* as an American film whereas the last one is a rare occasion of the proper identification of the film's actual author.
86 Tsivian, *Early Cinema in Russia*, p. 109.
87 Loiperdinger, 'Lumière's Arrival of the Train', pp. 93–4.
88 For the reproduction see Laurent Mannoni, Donata Pesenti Campagnoni, Donata and David Robinson, *Light and Movement: Incunabula of the Motion Picture, 1420–1896 = Luce e movimento: incunaboli dell'immagine animata, 1420–1896* (Gemona; Paris; Torino, 1995), p. 401.
89 American Mutoscope and Biograph Company Catalogue, 1897, p. 1, in *Motion Picture Catalogs*.
90 American Mutoscope and Biograph Company Catalogue, 1902, p. 122, in *Motion Picture Catalogs*.
91 F. M. Prescott Catalogue of New Films, 1899, p. 9, in *Motion Picture Catalogs*.
92 Lubin Manufacturing Company Catalog, 1903, p. 64, in *Motion Picture Catalogs*.
93 Ibid.
94 American Mutoscope and Biograph Company Catalogue, 1902, p. 66, in *Motion Picture Catalogs*.
95 Ibid.
96 'Star' Films Catalogue, 1903, p. 18, in *Motion Picture Catalogs*. The same description of the same film, but now billed as *Four Heads Are Better Than One* because it has been duped, also appears in Lubin Manufacturing Company Catalogue, 1903, p. 25, in *Motion Picture Catalogs*.

97 Gunning, 'An Aesthetic of Astonishment'; Matthew Solomon, *Disappearing Tricks: Silent Film, Houdini, and the New Magic of the Twentieth Century* (Urbana, 2010).
98 Edison Manufacturing Company Catalogue, 1901, p. 82, in *Motion Picture Catalogs*; Selig Polyscope Company Catalogue, 1903, p. 14, in *Motion Picture Catalogs*.
99 Lubin Manufacturing Company Catalogue, 1903, pp. 16–17, in *Motion Picture Catalogs*.
100 American Vitagraph Company Catalogue, 1903–4, p. 4, in *Motion Picture Catalogs*.
101 Edison Manufacturing Company Catalogue, February 1903, 4, p. in *Motion Picture Catalogs*.
102 Méliès's catalogue is reproduced in Jacques Malthete, *Méliès: Images et illusions* (Paris, 1996), pp. 222–4; Warwick Trading Company Catalogue Supplement 2, 1902, pp. 1–6, in *Early Filmmakers' Catalogues*, British Film Institute (London, 1983); Lubin Manufacturing Company Catalogue, 1903, pp. 7–9, in *Motion Picture Catalogs*.
103 In the first season the text continues: 'The events depicted took place in Minnesota in 2006. At the request of the survivors, the names have been changed. Out of respect for the dead, the rest has been told exactly as it occurred.'
104 Maguire and Baucus Catalogue of Edison Films, 20 January 1897, in *Motion Picture Catalogs*.
105 Prestwich Manufacturing Company Catalogue, 1898, in *Early Filmmakers' Catalogues*.
106 Maguire and Baucus Catalogue, Fall 1897, in *Motion Picture Catalogs*.
107 Warwick Trading Company Catalogue, 1898–7, in *Motion Picture Catalogs*.
108 Ibid., pp. 6, 38.
109 American Vitagraph Company Catalogue, 1900, pp. 2–3, 5, in *Motion Picture Catalogs*.
110 Ibid., 6.
111 Edison Manufacturing Company Catalogue, 1901, pp. 93–4, in *Motion Picture Catalogs*.
112 Ibid., pp. 81–8.
113 Warwick Trading Company Catalogue, 1901, pp. 54–5, in *Early Filmmakers' Catalogues*.
114 American Mutoscope and Biograph Company Catalogue, 1902, pp. 65, 119, in *Motion Picture Catalogs*.
115 Lubin Manufacturing Company Catalogue, 1903, pp. 16–29, 63–5, in *Motion Picture Catalogs*.
116 Selig Polyscope Company Catalogue, 1903, pp. 14–20, 29–30, in *Motion Picture Catalogs*.
117 R. W. Paul's Catalogue, 1902, no pagination, in *Early Filmmakers' Catalogues*; Hepworth & Co Catalogue, 1903, pp. 4–5, in *Motion Picture Catalogs*.

118 American Mutoscope and Biograph Company Catalogue, 1902, p. 119, in *Motion Picture Catalogs*.
119 American Mutoscope and Bioscope Company Catalogue, 1901, p. 3, in *Motion Picture Catalogs*.
120 American Mutoscope and Biograph Company Catalogue, 1902, p. 65, in *Motion Picture Catalogs*.
121 Ibid., p. 72.
122 Ibid., p. 68.
123 Ibid., p. 73.
124 Gunning, 'An Aesthetic Astonishment'; Gunning, 'Primitive Cinema'; Tom Gunning, *D. W. Griffith and the Origins of American Narrative Film: The Early Years at Biograph* (Urbana, 1991); Tom Gunning, '"Now You See It, Now You Don't": The Temporality of the Cinema of Attractions', *Velvet Light Trap* 32 (1993), pp. 3–12; Tom Gunning, 'The Whole Town's Gawking: Early Cinema and the Visual Experience of Modernity', *Yale Journal of Criticism* 7.2 (1994), pp. 189–202; Gunning, 'Early American Cinema'.
125 Charles Musser, 'Rethinking Early Cinema: Cinema of Attractions and Narrativity', *Yale Journal of Criticism* 7.2 (1994), pp. 203–32; Charles Musser, 'A Cinema of Contemplation, a Cinema of Discernment: Spectatorship, Intertextuality and Attractions in the 1890s', in Strauven, *The Cinema of Attractions Reloaded*, pp. 159–80.
126 *Baltimore American*, 27 December 1903, p. 30.
127 *Trenton Evening Times*, 18 October 1903, p. 11.
128 Gunning, 'A Trip to the Moon (1902)', p. 48.

2 Hale's Tours and adjacent cultural series: Illusion, immersion, imagination

1 Cf. Noël Burch, *Life to Those Shadows* (Berkeley, 1990); Raymond Fielding, 'Hale's Tours: Ultrarealism in the Pre-1910 Motion Picture', in J. Fell (ed.), *Film Before Griffith* (Berkeley, 1983), pp. 116–30; Philippe Gauthier, 'The Movie Theater as an Institutional Space and Framework of Signification: Hale's Tours and Film Historiography', *Film History* 21.4 (2009), pp. 326–35; Lynne Kirby, *Parallel Tracks: The Railroad and the Silent Cinema* (Durham, 1997), pp. 46–7; Jennifer Lynn Peterson, *Education in the School of Dreams: Travelogues and Early Nonfiction Film* (Durham, 2013), p. 226; Lauren Rabinovitz, '"Bells and Whistles": The Sound of Meaning in Train Travel Film Rides', in R. Abel and R. Altman (eds), *The Sounds of Early Cinema* (Bloomington, 2001), pp. 167–80; Lauren Rabinovitz, 'More Than the Movies: A History of Somatic Visual Culture through *Hale's Tours*, Imax, and Motion Simulation Rides', in L. Rabinovitz and A. Geil (eds), *Memory Bytes: History,*

Technology and Digital Culture (Durham, 2004), pp. 99–125; Lauren Rabinovitz, 'From *Hale's Tours* to *Star Tours:* Virtual Voyages, Travel Rides, and the Delirium of the Hyper-Real,' in J. Ruoff (ed.), *Virtual Voyages: Cinema and Travel* (Durham, 2006), pp. 42–60; Lauren Rabinovitz, 'Thrill Ride Cinema: *Hale's Tours and Scenes of the World*', in *Electric Dreamland: Amusement Parks, Movies and American Modernity* (New York, 2012), pp. 67–94.

2 Cf. Charlie Keil, 'Steel Engines and Cardboard Rockets: The Status of Fiction and Nonfiction in Early Cinema', in A. Juhasz and J. Lerner (eds), *F Is for Phony: Fake Documentary and Truth's Undoing* (Minneapolis, 2006), pp. 39–49; Rabinovitz, 'Thrill Ride Cinema'.

3 Vsevolod Pudovkin, *Film Technique and Film Acting*. Trans. I. Montagu (London, 1958).

4 Cf. George M. Wilson, *Seeing Fictions in Film: The Epistemology of Movies* (Oxford, 2011).

5 Cf. Jeffrey Ruoff (ed.), *Virtual Voyages: Cinema and Travel* (Durham, 2006); Peterson, *Education in the School of Dreams*.

6 Frank Gray, '*The Kiss in the Tunnel* (1899), G. A. Smith and the Emergence of the Edited Film in England', in L. Grieveson and P. Krämer (eds), *The Silent Cinema Reader* (London, 2004), pp. 51–62; Tom Gunning, 'The Attraction of Motion: Modern Representation and the Image of Movement', in A. Ligensa and K. Kreimeier (eds), *Film 1900: Technology, Perception, Culture* (Bloomington, 2009), pp. 165–73.

7 Stephan Oettermann, *The Panorama: History of a Mass Medium* (New York, 1997); Alison Griffiths, *Shivers Down Your Spine: Cinema, Museums, and the Immersive View* (New York, 2008); Erkki Huhtamo, *Illusions in Motion: Media Archaeology of the Moving Panorama and Related Spectacles* (Cambridge, MA, 2013).

8 Oliver Grau, *Virtual Art: From Illusion to Immersion*. Trans. G. Custance (Cambridge, MA, 2003), pp. 25–9.

9 For a view that movement in cinema is no illusion see Christian Metz, *Film Language: A Semiotics of the Cinema*, trans. M. Taylor (New York, 1974), p. 315; Gregory Currie, 'Film, Reality, and Illusion', in N. Carroll and D. Bordwell (eds), *Post-Theory: Reconstructing Film Studies* (Madison, 1996), pp. 325–44; Tom Gunning, 'Moving Away from the Index: Cinema and the Impression of Reality', *differences* 18.1 (2007), pp. 29–52.

10 Noël Burch, 'Narrative/Diegesis – Thresholds, Limits', *Screen* 23.2 (1982), pp. 16–33; Noël Burch, 'Passion, poursuite: la linéarisation', *Communications* 38.1 (1983), pp. 30–50; Tom Gunning, *D. W. Griffith and the Origins of American Narrative Film: The Early Years at Biograph* (Urbana, 1991); Miriam Hansen, *Babel and Babylon: Spectatorship in American Silent Film* (Cambridge, MA, 1991).

11 Samuel Taylor Coleridge, *Biographia Literaria* (New York, 1884), pp. 364–5.

12 Noël Carroll, *Mystifying Movies: Fads & Fallacies in Contemporary Film Theory* (New York, 1988).
13 Grau, *Virtual Art*, pp. 13–14.
14 Ibid., p. 17.
15 In an article focusing on early cinema, one film historian introduces the concept with reference to computer games to make the same point: '[While playing *Max Payne*] I had obviously encountered a kind of immersion, an experience of realism so vivid that I momentarily lost the distinction between fiction and reality.' Jan Holmberg, 'Ideals of Immersion in Early Cinema', *Cinémas: Revue d'études cinématographiques/Cinémas: Journal of Film Studies* 14.1 (2003), p. 130.
16 Grau, *Virtual Art*, p. 56.
17 Quoted in ibid., p. 98.
18 Quoted in ibid.
19 Quoted in ibid.
20 Quoted in ibid.
21 Quoted in Griffiths, *Shivers Down Your Spine*, p. 73.
22 Griffiths, *Shivers Down Your Spine*, pp. 37–78.
23 Quoted in ibid, p. 59, italics in the original.
24 Quoted in ibid, pp. 60–1.
25 Quoted in ibid, p. 47.
26 It is important to keep in mind that moving panoramas were often accompanied by a lecture so the lecture could have played an important role in effecting immersion. In the chapter on lecturers (Chapter 4) I discuss in some detail how one such example of illustrated lecturing played out.
27 Griffiths, *Shivers Down Your Spine*, p. 73.
28 Peterson, *Education in the School of Dreams*.
29 Ibid., p. 54, italics in the original.
30 Ibid., p. 60.
31 Ibid., p. 25.
32 I discuss the relationship between deception and fiction in detail in Chapter 3.
33 Joseph Garncarz, 'Nicht-fiktionale Filmformen in Varietés und Wanderkinos', in U. Jung and M. Loiperdinger (eds), *Geschichte des dokumentarischen Films in Deutschland. Vol. 1. Kaiserreich, 1895–1918* (Stuttgart, 2005), pp. 71–4.
34 Joseph Garncarz, 'Filmprogramm im Varietés: Die "Optische Berichterstattung"', in *Geschichte*, p. 80.
35 Ibid; Joseph Garncarz, 'Der nicht-fiktionale Film im Programm der Wanderkinos', in *Geschichte*, p. 117.
36 F. H. M., 'In the Mississippi Valley,' *Moving Picture World*, 20 January 1912, p. 216.
37 Frederick Starr, 'Prof' Starr's Valuable Contribution', *Nickelodeon* 1.3 (1909), p. 64.
38 Selig Polyscope Company Catalogue, 1903, p. 31, in C. Musser et al. (eds), *Motion Picture Catalogs by American Producers and Distributors, 1894–1908* (Baltimore, 1984).

39 American Mutoscope and Biograph Company Catalogue, 1902, p. 130, in *Motion Picture Catalogs*.
40 This is in line with Peterson's idea that travel films can constitute a superior experience to the one of actually traveling, because they can provide a view of the site which would most often be inaccessible to an ordinary traveler. The important thing for my investigation is the relationship such 'ideal' views have to imagination. Here, they clearly invite no imaginings. This will be an important result for the discussions of the idea of the imagined seeing thesis.
41 Quoted in Yuri Tsivian, *Early Cinema in Russia and Its Cultural Reception*, trans. A. Bodger (London, 1994), p. 124.
42 They are clearly aware of the frame but that has no effect on the mandate to imagine. It might well be of importance for the level of engagement with the imagined, that is, immersion.
43 Quoted in Stephen Bottomore, 'The Panicking Audience?: Early Cinema and the "Train Effect"', *Historical Journal of Film, Radio and Television* 19.2 (1999), p. 212, [sic] in the original.
44 Quoted in Martin Loiperdinger 'Lumière's Arrival of the Train: Cinema's Founding Myth', *The Moving Image* 4.1 (2004), p. 97.
45 Bottomore, 'The Panicking Audience?'.
46 Garncarz, 'Filmprogramm im Varieté', pp. 84–5.
47 Gunning, 'The Attraction of Motion', p. 168.
48 *The Haverstraw Tunnel* is identified as the first phantom ride by Gray, 'The Kiss in the Tunnel (1899)', p. 55.
49 Quoted in Kemp R. Niver, *Biograph Bulletins, 1896–1908* (Los Angeles, 1971), p. 35.
50 Quoted in ibid., p. 36.
51 Quoted in ibid., italics in the original.
52 Quoted in ibid.
53 Although a number of phantom rides have 'panorama' or some derivative of it in their title, it would be mistaken to think the term was applied exclusively to them. It was used both to label and describe numerous scenics as well. In other words, we cannot conclude anything about the film's potential for imaginary immersion on the basis of the term 'panorama' either in its title or its description. That the term appears also does not mean that the film in question includes any camera pans.
54 Griffiths, *Shivers Down Your Spine*, p. 68.
55 Quoted in Niver, *Biograph Bulletins*, p. 36.
56 Quoted in ibid., p. 35.
57 Gunning, 'The Attraction of Motion', pp. 169, 171; Wolfgang Schivelbusch, *The Railway Journey: The Industrialization of Time and Space in the Nineteenth Century* (Berkeley, 2014).
58 'The Panoramas of the Exposition of 1900', *Scientific American Supplement*, 18 August 1900, p. 20603.

59 Grau, *Virtual Art*, p. 14.
60 Gunning, 'The Attraction of Motion', p. 168.
61 Wilson, *Seeing Fictions in Film*; Paisley Livingston, 'The Imagined Seeing Thesis', *Projections: The Journal for Movies and Mind* 7.1 (2013), pp. 139–46.
62 An alternative to the imagined seeing thesis has been proposed by Gregory Currie, *Image and Mind: Film, Philosophy and Cognitive Science* (Cambridge, 1995), pp. 164–97. According to him, when watching film, we do not imagine *seeing* anything – rather based on images we imagine propositions that such and such is the case. Richard Moran also points out that imagining seeing is not the same as imagining visually, insofar one can imagine objects visually without imagining seeing them. Richard Moran, 'The Expression of Feeling in Imagination', *The Philosophical Review* 103.1 (1994), pp. 75–106.
63 Edison Manufacturing Company Catalogue Supplement, May 1903, p. 13, in *Motion Picture Catalogs*.
64 Selig Polyscope Company Supplement, November 1902, no pagination, in *Motion Picture Catalogs*.
65 Ibid.
66 Warwick Trading Company Catalogue, 1897–8, p. 8, in *Early Filmmakers' Catalogues*.
67 Warwick Trading Company Catalogue Supplement, 1897–8, p. 4, in *Early Filmmakers' Catalogues*.
68 F. M. Prescott Catalogue of New Films, 1899, p. 13, in *Motion Picture Catalogs*; Lubin Manufacturing Company's Catalogue, 1903, p. 63, in *Motion Picture Catalogs*.
69 Ibid.
70 A point explored further in Chapter 3.
71 Quoted in Niver, *Biograph Bulletins*, p. 42.
72 Quoted in ibid.
73 Quoted in ibid.
74 Fielding, 'Hale's Tours'. They also gave early taste of the business to a number of people like Adolph Zukor who would go on to become key players in the industry later on.
75 Charles Musser, *The Emergence of Cinema: The American Screen to 1907* (New York 1990), p. 429; Rabinovitz, 'Thrill Ride Cinema', p. 68.
76 *Official Gazette of the U.S. Patent Office*, 19 September 1905, p. 788.
77 Rabinovitz, 'Bells and Whistles'.
78 *Official Gazette of the U.S. Patent Office*, 19 September 1905, p. 788.
79 Ibid.
80 Ibid. According to the patent, there was another car which carried the passengers to the car in which they watched the projection. In practice, however, it seems that this 'transit' car was seldom used.

81 Rabinovitz, 'Thrill Ride Cinema', p. 77; Selig Polyscope Company Catalogue, 'Hales' Tours films', Supplement 44, August 1906.
82 *Billboard*, 17 February 1906, p. 19.
83 *Variety*, 22 September 1906, p. 11.
84 'Features at Montana State Fair', *Billboard*, 19 July 1913, p. 30; Ivo Blom, 'Chapters from the Life of a Camera-Operator. The Recollections of Anton Nöggerath: Filming News and Non-Fiction, 1897–1908', *Film History* 11.3 (1999), pp. 262–81.
85 *Official Gazette of the U.S. Patent Office*, 9 August 1904, p. 1577.
86 For a description see 'The Panoramas of the Exposition of 1900', pp. 20602–3.
87 Ibid.
88 'The Maréorama at the Paris Exposition', *Scientific American*, 29 September 1900, p. 198.
89 Rabinovitz, 'Thrill Ride Cinema', pp. 84, 86.
90 Fielding, 'Hale's Tours', pp. 123–4; Rabinovitz, 'From *Hale's Tours* to *Star Tours*', p. 49; Rabinovitz, 'More Than Movies', p. 110; Rabinovitz, 'Thrill Ride Cinema', p. 84.
91 Fielding, 'Hale's Tours', p. 124; Gauthier, 'Movie Theater', pp. 327–8; Rabinovitz, 'More Than Movies', p. 111; Rabinovitz, 'From *Hale's Tours* to *Star Tours*', p. 49; Rabinovitz, 'Thrill Ride Cinema', p. 85.
92 Here, immersed is meant in the ordinary sense which covers more than the immersion of being present, that is, in the general sense of immersion in an experience.
93 E. C. Thomas, 'Vancouver, B.C., Started with "Hale's Tours" in 1905', *Moving Picture World*, 15 July 1916, p. 373.
94 Fielding, 'Hale's Tours', p. 123. In fact, Fielding's piece is available in three more places but they all paraphrase E. C. Thomas the same: Raymond Fielding, 'Hale's Tours: Ultrarealism in the Pre-1910 Motion Picture', *Smithsonian Journal of History* 3.4 (1968–9), pp. 101–21; Raymond Fielding, 'Hale's Tours: Ultrarealism in the Pre-1910 Motion Picture', *Cinema Journal* 10.1 (1970), pp. 34–47; and Raymond Fielding, 'Hale's Tours: Ultra-Realism in the Pre-1910 Motion Picture', in D. E. Staples (ed.), *The American Cinema* (Washington, 1973).
95 *Billboard*, 7 April 1906, p. 11, block capitals in the original.
96 Lucy France Pierce, 'The Nickelodeon', in G. Mast (ed.), *The Movies in Our Midst: Documents in the Cultural History of Film in America* (Chicago, 1982), p. 53. Published originally in 1908.
97 *Kinematograph and Lantern Weekly*, 1 October 1908, p. 481.
98 Selig Polyscope Company Catalogue, 'Hales' Tours Films', Supplement 44, August 1906, no pagination.
99 Ibid.

100 Keil, 'Steel Engines and Cardboard Rockets', p. 42.
101 Rabinovitz, 'Thrill Ride Cinema', p. 90.
102 Keil, 'Steel Engines and Cardboard Rockets', p. 44.
103 There is even more staging if misrepresentation is understood as staging. In the opening of the film we can also discern that the station is Phoenicia on the Delaware Railroad – a long way from Rocky Mountains in the film's title. I discuss various meanings of the term 'staging' in the next chapter.
104 Keil, 'Steel Engines and Cardboard Rockets', p. 44.
105 For a more detailed discussion of why narrative does not amount to fiction see Chapters 3 and 4.
106 Quoted in Niver, *Biograph Bulletins*, p. 252.
107 Cf. Wilson, *Seeing Fictions in Film*.
108 Gregory Currie, *The Nature of Fiction* (Cambridge, 1990), pp. 74–5.
109 Quoted in Niver, *Biograph Bulletins*, 1971, p. 252.
110 Quoted in ibid.
111 Quoted in ibid.
112 I examine this problem in the final chapter. It is true that at present I have not determined with certainty that the *modest* version of the imagined seeing thesis is applicable to comedy sections. An alternative could be that people simply imagined certain events on the basis of the moving pictures without imagining *seeing* them. That something 'shows the interior of the sleeping car' or that there is a 'showing [of] the passengers' does not provide definite clues on how to resolve the issue. Given that comedy sections of Hale's Tours belong to the category of fictional narratives one way to resolve this is to look at fictional narratives in general and particularly information we can glean from screenwriting manuals that start appearing around the time – an analysis I undertake in the final chapter.
113 André Gaudreault, *From Plato to Lumière: Narration and Monstration in Literature and Cinema*, trans. T. Barnard (Toronto, 2009).
114 Wilson, *Seeing Fictions in Film*, p. 55.

3 Re-enactments in early cinema: Fake, fiction, fact

1 David Levy, 'Re-Constituted Newsreels, Re-Enactments and the American Narrative Film', in R. Holman (ed.), *Cinema 1900–1906: An Analytical Study* (Brussels, 1982), pp. 243–58.
2 Frank Kessler, '"Fake" in Early Non-Fiction', *KINtop* 14/15 (2006), p. 92.
3 Ibid.

4   For an unparalleled account of the history of early war films, including the earliest war fakes see Stephen Bottomore, *Filming, Faking, and Propaganda: The Origins of the War Film, 1897–1902* (Utrecht, 2007). For an illuminating account of the Spanish-American War from the American film-industry perspective consult Charles Musser, *The Emergence of Cinema: American Screen to 1907* (New York, 1990), pp. 225–62. For more on the Boer War and film faking see Andrew Shail, 'The Great American Kinetograph: News, Fakery and the Boer War', in A. Shail (ed.), *Reading the Cinematograph: The Cinema in Short Fiction, 1896–1912* (Exeter, 2011), pp. 104–28.
5   'Fake or Trick Cinematograph Pictures', *Optical Magic Lantern Journal and Photographic Enlarger*, December 1900, pp. 153–4.
6   For a comprehensive study of boxing films in the silent era see Dan Streible, *Fight Pictures: A History of Boxing and Early Cinema* (Berkeley, 2008).
7   Musser, *The Emergence of Cinema*, p. 195.
8   For an account of the filming and faking of the Corbett-Fitzsimmons match see Streible, *Fight Pictures*, pp. 52–95; Musser, *The Emergence of Cinema*, pp. 194–208.
9   'Fight Pictures That Are Fake: Clever Schemers Working San Francisco with a Counterfeit Kinetoscope', *San Francisco Examiner*, 22 May 1897.
10 *New York Clipper*, 17 April 1897, p. 115.
11 *New York Clipper*, 15 May 1897, p. 180. It also must be noted that the meaning of these terms might have been lost on some. A projection of Lubin's film in Elizabeth, NJ, which culminated in customers demanding their money back was commented upon thusly: 'It was surprising to see how many people there were who did not know the meaning of the compound word fac-simile. They know it, however, now.' 'Exhibition of Corbett-Fitzsimmons Fight at the Lyceum Causes a Riot', *Phonoscope* 1.9 (1897), p. 8.
12 *New York Clipper*, 24 April 1897, p. 134.
13 *New York Clipper*, 15 May 1897, p. 180.
14 This strategy did not always work. Newspaper articles report that Huber's dime museum in New York and a certain Marion S. Robinson of Toronto, were slapped with an injunction for screening Lubin's re-enactment of the 1899 Jeffries-Sharkey fight. The reason was not copyright but property right. William A. Brady's lawyer successfully argued that because Brady went to great lengths to secure the match and its filming (by American Mutoscope and Biograph Company), Brady held the property right over the 'reproduction of the fight'. 'Pictures Pay Well', *Topeka State Journal*, 26 December 1899, p. 2; 'Fake Photos Stopped in Canada', *Morning Telegraph*, 14 January 1900, p. 3.
15 *New York Clipper*, 17 December 1898, p. 718; 24 December 1898, p. 734; and 31 December 1898, p. 750.

16 *New York Clipper,* 17 February 1900, p. 1092; and 24 February 1900, p. 1113, block capitals in the original.
17 *New York Clipper*, 2 July 1898, p. 302, block capitals in the original.
18 Kirk J. Kekatos, 'Edward H. Amet and the Spanish-American War Film', *Film History* 14.3/4 (2002), pp. 405–17; Bottomore, *Filming, Faking, and Propaganda*, Chapter 3, pp. 10–15.
19 Pathé Catalogue, 1903, p. 60, in Charles Musser et al. (eds), *Motion Picture Catalogs by American Producers and Distributors, 1894–1908* (Baltimore, 1984). Interestingly, in a later catalogue the disclaimer is dropped and many of the same films are advertised as 'Historical, Political & Genuine Military Scenes', Pathé Catalogue, 1905, pp. 92–93, in British Film Institute, *Early Filmmakers' Catalogues* (London, 1983).
20 American Vitagraph Company Catalogue, 1900, p. 4, italics and bold in the original, in *Motion Picture Catalogs*.
21 Ibid.
22 'To Take Fight Pictures', *Topeka State Journal*, 15 August 1900, p. 2. The article misreports the date of the re-enactment – the correct date is 13 August.
23 'To Take Fight Pictures', p. 2.
24 'Fitz and Ruhlin Fight the Fight Over Again', *Philadelphia Inquirer*, 14 August 1900, p. 6.
25 *Optical Magic Lantern and Kinematograph Journal*, September 1906, p. 199.
26 Quoted in Kessler, '"Fake" in Early Non-Fiction', p. 88, italics in the original.
27 Stephen Bottomore, 'Dreyfus and Documentary', *Sight and Sound* 53.4 (1984), p. 290.
28 Herbert Birett, *Lichtspiele: Der Kino in Deutschland bis 1914* (Munich, 1994), p. 39.
29 'Fake Cinematograph Pictures', *Optical Magic Lantern Journal and Photographic Enlarger*, November 1900, p. 138.
30 'Fake or Trick Cinematograph Pictures', *Optical Magic Lantern Journal and Photographic Enlarger*, December 1900, pp. 153–4.
31 'Joe Gans Tells His Side of Fight', *Evening Star*, 31 October 1906, p. 9.
32 *Fergus County Argus*, 30 November 1906, p. 8.
33 'The Real Thing', *Fairmont West Virginian*, 19 December 1906, p. 10.
34 Cf. 'Experiences of a Newspaper Photographer', *Photographic Times* 37 (1905), pp. 201–5.
35 Kessler, '"Fake" in Early Non-Fiction', p. 87.
36 Bottomore, *Filming, Faking, and Propaganda*, Chapter 3, pp. 9–13.
37 Williamson's film was based on the Siege of the International Legations in Peking that took place in the summer of 1900 during the Boxer Rebellion. For more on the film see Frank Gray, 'James Williamson's "Composed Picture": *Attack on a China Mission – Bluejackets to the Rescue*', in J. Fullerton (ed.), *Celebrating 1895: The Centenary of Cinema* (Sydney, 1998), pp. 203–11; For more on the fakes portraying the Boxer Rebellion see Bottomore, *Filming, Faking, and Propaganda*, Chapter 13, pp. 1–26.

38 Selig Polyscope Company Catalogue, 'Tracked by Bloodhounds', Supplement 17, 1905, pp. 1, 3, block capitals in the original in *Motion Picture Catalogs*.
39 Ibid., p. 7.
40 James Allen, *Without Sanctuary: Lynching Photography in America* (Santa Fe, 2004); Amy Woods, *Lynching and Spectacle: Witnessing Racial Violence in America, 1890–1940* (Chapel Hill, 2009).
41 There is an advertisement for a film titled *Lynching Scene* (1897) which claims that this is '[a] genuine Lynching Scene' and adds: 'By our contract with the authorities names of party and place cannot be given' – International Film Company Catalogue, 1897–8, p. 18, in *Motion Picture Catalogs*. As the film is only 75 feet long it seems unlikely that all of the following happened within the equivalent short time frame: 'angry mob overpowering the sheriff, storming the jail, and dragging their prisoner to the nearest telegraph pole, from which he is immediately swung into eternity, as bullet after bullet is fired into his swinging and writhing body', ibid. However, because lynchings were sometimes pre-arranged and photographers pre-invited to document the deed, there is still a non-negligible chance that this is '[a] genuine Lynching Scene'. Moreover, given that the film refuses to specify the victim's name and location it is impossible to disprove that the lynching it depicts (either directly or as a re-enactment) did *not* take place.
42 Tim Blevins, Chris Nicholl and Calvin P. Otto (eds), *The Colorado Labor Wars: Cripple Creek 1903–1904, A Centennial Commemoration* (Colorado Springs, 2006).
43 'Photographs of Men Marked for Assassination Are Found in the Victor Strikers' Headquarters', *San Francisco Call*, 8 June 1904, p. 2; 'Threaten Lynching', *Evening Times-Republican*, 7 June 1904, p. 1; 'Every Man Walking Arsenal', *Washington Times*, 8 June 1904, p. 3.
44 'Troops to Save Town from Torch of Mob', *Evening World*, 7 June 1904, p. 3.
45 'Sherman Bell's Story of Colorado Disorder', *Washington Times*, 21 August 1904, p. 2.
46 'With Threats of Violence, Citizens Alliance Force City Officials to Resign', *Bisbee Daily Review*, 8 June 1904, p. 1.
47 Kessler, '"Fake" in Early Non-Fiction', p. 92.
48 Streible, *Fight Pictures*, p. 140.
49 Bottomore, *Filming, Faking, and Propaganda*, Chapter 2, pp. 10–15.
50 Kristen Whissel, 'Placing the Spectator on the Scene of History: The Battle Re-Enactment at the Turn of the Century, from Buffalo Bill's Wild West to the Early Cinema', *Historical Journal of Film, Radio and Television* 22.3 (2002), p. 236; Kristen Whissel, *Picturing American Modernity: Traffic, Technology, and the Silent Cinema* (Durham, 2008), p. 95.
51 F. M. Prescott Catalogue of New Films, 1899, p. 22, in *Motion Picture Catalogs*; Quoted in Whissel, *Picturing American Modernity*, p. 87.

52 Bottomore, *Filming, Faking, and Propaganda*, Chapter 2, pp. 12–13.
53 Quoted in ibid., Chapter 2, p. 12, [sic] in the original.
54 Bottomore, 'Dreyfus and Documentary', p. 290.
55 'Sham War Cinematograph Films', *Optical Magic Lantern Journal and Photographic Enlarger*, March 1900, p. 30.
56 *Optical Magic Lantern Journal and Photographic Enlarger*, December 1900, p. 168.
57 'Experiences of a Newspaper Photographer', *Photographic Times* 37 (1905), p. 203, italics in the original.
58 'Exhibition of Corbett-Fitzsimmons Fight at the Lyceum Causes a Riot', p. 8.
59 Streible, *Fight Pictures*, p. 140.
60 *Dakota Farmers' Leader*, 16 July 1897, p. 5.
61 'Our Tattler', *Phonoscope* 1.7 (1897), p. 7.
62 'Two Thousand People', *Wheeling Daily Intelligencer*, 21 June 1897, p. 5.
63 'Fake Fight Pictures', *Waterbury Evening Democrat*, 3 August 1899, p. 6.
64 'May Be Fight Films Have Been Faked', *Washington Times*, 9 October 1906, p. 8.
65 Streible, *Fight Pictures*, p. 174.
66 Ibid.
67 The mistaken reports 'that the last four or five rounds of the great battle were not caught by the machine, because it ran out of film', together with the aforementioned Gans's complaints, must have also added to the confusion. *Evening Times*, 27 September 1906, p. 4.
68 *Optical Magic Lantern Journal and Photographic Enlarger*, September 1906, p. 199.
69 'A Filmy Story', *Daily Appeal*, 18 September 1906, p. 1.
70 Quoted in Streible, *Fight Pictures*, p. 141.
71 Quoted in ibid., pp. 139–40.
72 Bottomore, *Filming, Faking, and Propaganda*, Chapter 3, pp. 6–16.
73 It should be noted that the event could also be pre-staged as is the case with Georges Méliès's *The Coronation of King Edward VII/Le Sacre d'Édouard VII* (1902).
74 Bottomore, *Filming, Faking, and Propaganda*, Chapter 2, p. 7.
75 Ibid.
76 Peter Wollen, *Signs and Meaning in the Cinema* (Bloomington, 1969).
77 Ibid., p. 122.
78 Charles S. Peirce, 'Letter to Lady Welby', in A. W. Burks (ed.), *The Collected Papers of Charles Sanders Peirce, Vols. 7–8* (Cambridge, MA, 1966), p. 228.
79 Charles S. Peirce, 'Harvard Lectures on Pragmatism', in C. Hartshorne and P. Weiss (eds), *The Collected Papers of Charles Sanders Peirce, Vol. 5–6* (Cambridge, MA, 1974), pp, 50–1, italics in the original.
80 Cf. André Bazin, 'The Ontology of the Photographic Image', in H. Gray (ed. and trans.), *What Is Cinema? Vol. 1* (Berkeley, 2004), pp. 9–16.
81 Cf. Mary Ann Doane, 'The Indexical and the Concept of Medium Specificity.' *differences* 18.1 (2007), pp. 140–2.

82. For more on this point and a wider critique of indexicality and how it relates to Wollen's reading of one of Bazin's classic papers see Mario Slugan, 'Taking Bazin Literally', *Projections: The Journal for Movies and Mind* 11.1 (2017), pp. 63–82.
83. Warwick Trading Company, 1901, p. 52, in *Early Filmmakers' Catalogues*, block capitals in the original.
84. John Parris Springer and Gary D. Rhodes, 'Introduction', in G. D. Rhodes and J. P. Springer (eds), *Docufictions: Essays on the Intersection of Documentary and Fictional Filmmaking* (Jefferson, 2006), p. 6.
85. Simon Popple and Joe Kember, *Early Cinema: From Factory Gate to Dream Factory* (London, 2004), p. 60.
86. Bottomore, *Filming, Faking, and Propaganda*, Chapter 2, p. 15.
87. Ibid., Chapter 3, p. 19.
88. Shail has perhaps the most nuanced view on the relationship between staging and fiction. He identifies the films about the Boer War as those which made British audiences come to appreciate staging as a part of filmmaking. Prior to this, films involving staging were seen as illustrations of theatrical performances, or, as I argue in Chapter 1, as recordings of games of make-believe rather than games of make-believe in themselves. So Shail does recognize that staging does not necessarily entail fiction. But he also claims that prior to Boer War film in Britain was incapable of fictional utterances which is belied by my analysis of train films and phantom rides. Cf. Shail, 'The Great American Kinetograph'.
89. Cf. Wood, *Lynching and Spectacle*, pp. 71–111.
90. Warwick Trading Company, 1901, p. 93, in *Early Filmmakers' Catalogues*.
91. 'Fake Fight Pictures', *Phonoscope* 1.7 (1897), p. 12.
92. 'Exhibition of Corbett-Fitzsimmons Fight at the Lyceum Causes a Riot', p. 8.
93. Ibid.
94. Jonathan Auerbach, *Body Shots: Early Cinema's Incarnations* (Berkeley, 2007), p. 32.
95. Derek Paget, *No Other Way to Tell It: Dramadoc/Docudrama on Television* (Manchester, 1998), p. 1.
96. John Parris Springer, 'The Newspaper Meets the Dime Novel: Docudrama in Early Cinema', in *Docufictions*, pp. 27–8.
97. Edison Manufacturing Company Catalogue, July 1901, pp. 28–9, in *Motion Picture Catalogs*.
98. F. M. Prescott Catalogue of New Films, 1899, p. 22, in *Motion Picture Catalogs*; Quoted in Whissel, *Picturing American Modernity*, p. 87.
99. Ibid., p. 74.
100. Ibid., p. 79, italics in the original.
101. Ibid., p. 81.
102. Ibid., p. 93.

103 Whissel, 'Placing the Spectator on the Scene of History', p. 226.
104 Ibid., p. 228; Whissel, *Picturing American Modernity*, p. 72.
105 Whissel, *Picturing American Modernity*, p. 70.
106 Quoted in ibid., p. 73.
107 William F. Cody, *Buffalo Bill's Wild West: Historical Sketches & Programme* (Chicago, 1893), p. 2.
108 Ibid.
109 Ibid.
110 Ibid., p. 23.
111 Ibid., p. 15. Other programmes include William F. Cody, *Buffalo Bill's Wild West, America's National Entertainment: An Illustrated Treaties of Historical Facts and Sketches* (London, 1887), p. 28; William F. Cody, *Buffalo Bill's Wild West: Historical Sketches and Daily Review* (Cincinnati, 1907), no pagination; *Buffalo Bill's Wild West: Historical Sketches and Daily Review* (Buffalo, 1907), no pagination.
112 William F. Cody, *Buffalo Bill's Wild West: Historical Sketches & Programme* (Chicago, 1893), p. 11.
113 Edison Manufacturing Company Catalogue, 'War Incidents', Supplement 4, 20 May 1898, p. 2, in *Motion Picture Catalogs*.
114 American Mutoscope and Biograph Company Catalogue, 1902, p. 156, in *Motion Picture Catalogs*.
115 Warwick Trading Company, 1897-8, p. 54, in *Early Filmmakers' Catalogues*.
116 'Army Life', R. W. Paul Film Catalogue, 1900, p. 2, in *Early Filmmakers' Catalogues*; 'Army Life', R. W. Paul Film Catalogue, 1902, no pagination, in *Early Filmmakers' Catalogues*.
117 'Reproductions of Incidents of Boer War', R. W. Paul Film Catalogue, 1903, in *Early Filmmakers' Catalogues*.
118 Ibid.
119 Complete Catalogue of Lubin's Films, 1903, p. 75, in *Motion Picture Catalogs*.
120 Ibid.
121 The only catalogue entry outside of F. M. Prescott's that supports Whissel's thesis of imaginary participation is the ad for *American Cavalry Charging with Drawn Sabres* which, next to Prescott's catalogue, also makes an appearance in Lubin's. There, however, the ad is only one among twenty-seven in the 'War Films' section. The rest mandate no imagining: *Motion Picture Catalogs*, pp. 74-8.
122 International Film Company Catalogue, 1897-8, p. 8, in *Motion Picture Catalogs*.
123 American Mutoscope and Biograph Company Catalogue, 1902 p. 173, in *Motion Picture Catalogs*.
124 Warwick Trading Company, 1897-8, p. 20, in *Early Filmmakers' Catalogues*.
125 Warwick Trading Company, 1901, pp. 159-60, in *Early Filmmakers' Catalogues*, italics in the original.

126 'Opinions of the London Press', R.W. Paul Catalogue, 1900, p. 26, in *Early Filmmakers' Catalogues*.
127 The 'Elge' List, June 1904, p. 4, in *Early Filmmakers' Catalogues*.
128 'Good House at the Moving Pictures', *Daily Alaskan*, 2 August 1905, p. 2. The review does not specify which production company's the film is.

4 The lecturer and make-believe: The borders of the text and explicit mandates

1 There are, however, examples when female lecturers were explicitly sought after: *Der Kinematograph*, 30 August 1911, no pagination; *Das Lichtbild-Bühne*, 9 December 1911, p. 26. There are also lecturers who explicitly stated their gender in the ads: *Der Kinematograph*, 29 January 1913, no pagination; *Der Kinematograph*, 5 March 1913, no pagination.
2 Noël Burch, *To the Distant Observer: Form and Meaning in the Japanese Cinema* (Berkeley, 1979); Noël Burch, 'Passion, poursuite: la linéarisation', *Communications* 38.1 (1983), pp. 30–50; Norman King, 'The Sound of Silents', *Screen* 25.3 (1984), pp. 2–15; Charles Musser, 'The Eden Musée in 1898: The Exhibitor as Creator', *Film & History: An Interdisciplinary Journal of Film and Television Studies* 11.4 (1981), pp. 73–96; Charles Musser and Carol Nelson, *High-Class Moving Pictures: Lyman Howe and the Forgotten Era of Traveling Exhibition, 1880–1920* (Princeton, 1991); André Gaudreault and Germain Lacasse (eds), 'Le bonimenteur de vues animées/The Moving Picture Lecturer', *Iris* 22 (1996); Tom Gunning, *D. W. Griffith and the Origins of American Narrative Film: The Early Years at Biograph* (Urbana, 1991); Tom Gunning, 'The Scene of Speaking: Two Decades of Discovering the Film Lecturer', *Iris* 27 (1999), pp. 67–80.
3 Laurent Mannoni, *The Great Art of Light and Shadow: Archaeology of the Cinema*, ed. and trans. R. Crangle (Exeter, 2000); Richard Crangle, Stephen Herbert and David Robinson (eds), *Encyclopaedia of the Magic Lantern* (London, 2001).
4 Joe Kember, *Marketing Modernity: Victorian Popular Shows and Early Cinema* (Exeter, 2009).
5 David Robinson, 'Magic Lantern Shows', in R. Abel (ed.), *Encyclopedia of Early Cinema* (London, 2005), p. 583.
6 Kember, *Marketing Modernity*, pp. 84–112.
7 Gunning, *D. W. Griffith*, p. 91.
8 Pascale Bertolini and Jacques Polet, 'Boniments, explications et autres bruits de scène: les accompagnements de spectacles cinématographiques muets en Belgique', *Iris* 22 (1996), pp. 145–60.

9 Judith Buchanan, '"Now, Where Were We?" Ideal and Actual Early Cinema Lecturing Practices in Britain, Germany and the United States', in J. Brown and A. Davison (eds), *The Sounds of the Silents in Britain* (New York, 2013), pp. 38–54; Martin Loiperdinger, 'Missing Believed Lost: The Film Narrator, Then and Now', in K. Askari, S. Curtis, F. Gray, L. Pelletier, T. Williams and J. Yumibe (eds), *Performing New Media, 1890–1915* (New Barnet, 2014), pp. 87–94.

10 Ivo Blom and Ine van Dooren, '"Ladies and Gentlemen, Hats Off, Please!": Dutch Film Lecturing and the Case of Cor Schuring', *Iris* 22 (1996), pp. 81–102; Ansje van Beusekom, 'The Rise and Fall of the Lecturer as Entertainer in the Netherlands: Exhibition-Practices in Transition Related to Local Circumstances', *Iris* 22 (1996), pp. 131–44.

11 Germain Lacasse, 'Du bonimenteur québécois comme pratique resistante', *Iris* 22 (1996), pp. 53–66; Germain Lacasse, *Le bonimenteur de vues animées: Le cinéma muet entre tradition et modernité* (Québec, 2000).

12 Daniel Sánchez Salas, 'A History of the Lecturer in Spanish Silent Cinema', *Iris* 22 (1996), pp. 171–82.

13 King, 'The Sound of Silents'; Vanessa Toulmin, 'The Fairground Bioscope', in C. Harding and S. Popple (eds), *In the Kingdom of Shadows: A Companion to the Early Cinema* (London, 1996), pp. 191–206; Vanessa Toulmin, *Electric Edwardians: The Story of the Mitchell & Kenyon Collection* (London, 2006); Joe Kember, '"It Was Not the Show, It Was the Tale That You Told": Film Lecturing on the British Fairground', in S. Popple and V. Toulmin (eds), *Visual Delights: Essays on the Popular and Projected Image in the Nineteenth Century* (Trowbridge, 2000), pp. 61–70; Kember, *Marketing Modernity*.

14 Musser, 'The Eden Musée in 1898'; Musser and Nelson, *High-Class Moving Pictures*; Gunning, *D. W. Griffith*; Rick Altman, *Silent Film Sound* (New York, 2004).

15 Burch, *To the Distant Observer*; Aaron Andrew Gerow, *Visions of Japanese Modernity: Articulations of Cinema, Nation, and Spectatorship, 1895–1925* (Berkeley, 2010); Jeffrey A. Dym, *Benshi, Japanese Silent Film Narrators, and Their Forgotten Narrative Art of Setsumei: A History of Japanese Silent Film Narration* (Lewiston, NY, 2003).

16 Richard L. Stromgren, 'The Moving Picture World of W. Stephen Bush', *Film History* 2.1 (1998), pp. 13–22.

17 Altman, *Silent Film Sound*, pp. 58–72.

18 Musser and Nelson, *High Class Moving Picture*.

19 Martin Loiperdinger, '"The Audience Feels Rather at Home…": Peter Marzen's "Localisation" of Film Exhibition in Tier', in F. Kessler and N. Verhoeff (eds), *Networks of Entertainment: Early Film Distribution 1895–1915* (Eastleigh, 2007), pp. 123–30.

20 Blom and van Dooren, 'Ladies and Gentlemen, Hats Off, Please!'

21 Altman, *Silent Film Sound*, pp. 56–8.

22 Stephen Bottomore, 'Eric Williams: Speaking to Pictures', in J. Brown and A. Davison (eds), *The Sounds of the Silents in Britain* (New York, 2013), pp. 55–71.
23 Martin Sopocy, *James Williamson: Studies and Documents of a Pioneer of the Film Narrative* (Madison, NJ, 1998).
24 Germain Lacasse, 'The Film Lecturer', in A. Gaudreault, N. Dulac and S. Hidalgo (eds), *A Companion to Early Cinema* (Malden, MA, 2012), p. 487.
25 As Katherine Nagels reminds us 'intertitle' is not the contemporary term: 'intertitles were known by a variety of names, including *leaders*, *titles*, *captions*, *headings*, and *sub(-)titles*'. Katherine Nagels, '"Those Funny Subtitles": Silent film Intertitles in Exhibition and Discourse', *Early Popular Visual Culture* 10.4 (2012), p. 368, italics in the original. For a terminological point which sees 'intertitle' as anachronistic for the titling practices until around 1912 see André Gaudreault, 'Titles, Subtitles, and Intertitles: Factors of Autonomy, Factors of Concatenation', *Film History*, 25.1–2 (2013), pp. 81–94.
26 Cf. Altman, *Silent Film Sound*, pp. 55–72.
27 Cf. Dym, *Benshi*.
28 Gunning, *D. W. Griffith*; Altman, *Silent Film Sound*.
29 André Gaudreault, *From Plato to Lumière: Narration and Monstration in Literature and Cinema,* trans. T. Barnard (Toronto, 2009).
30 Burch, 'Passion, poursuite'; Gunning, *D. W. Griffith*; Gaudreault, *From Plato to Lumière*.
31 Miriam Hansen, *Babel and Babylon: Spectatorship in American Silent Film* (Cambridge, MA, 1991), p. 97.
32 Cf. Dym, *Benshi*; Gerow, *Visions of Japanese Modernity*.
33 Dym, *Benshi*, pp. 7–8.
34 Gunning, *D. W. Griffith*, pp. 92–3, my italics.
35 Gérard Genette, *Narrative Discourse: An Essay in Method*, trans. J. E. Lewin (Ithaca, NY, 1980). I discuss problems concerning Genette's notion in detail in the chapter on fictional narrators. The issues raised there do not change the thrust of the argument here because extradiegetic for Gunning remains an intratextual phenomenon.
36 Gunning, *D. W. Griffith*. In the final chapter I will be arguing that no fictional narrator is present either in D. W. Griffith's or later classical Hollywood films.
37 For typical complaints see Van C. Lee, 'The Value of a Lecture', *Moving Picture World*, 8 February, 1908, pp, 93–4; and E. Esther Owen, 'The Value of a Lecture with the Show', *Moving Picture World*, 22 February, 1908, p. 143.
38 Immersion can, admittedly, be broken by intratextual elements as well. *Uncle Tom's Cabin* causes problems for immersion as much as it does for coherent imagination and the impression of unity. To repeat, however, immersion is distinct from both coherent imagination and the impression of unity.
39 Hansen, *Babel and Babylon*, p. 97.

40 Gregory Currie, *The Nature of Fiction* (Cambridge, 1990); Kendall L. Walton, *Mimesis as Make-Believe: On the Foundations of the Representational Arts* (Cambridge, MA, 1990).
41 Gaudreault, *From Plato to Lumière*, p. 132, my italics.
42 Gaudreault, 'Titles, Subtitles, and Intertitles', p. 90, italics in original.
43 Eileen Bowser, *The Transformation of Cinema, 1907–1915* (New York, 1993), pp. 139–45; Claire Dupré la Tour, 'Intertitles and Titles', in *Encyclopedia of Early Cinema*, pp. 471–6; Nagels, 'Those Funny Subtitles'.
44 I discuss intertitles in more detail in Chapter 5.
45 Their nominal condition seems to be the implicit one in Gaudreault's account.
46 Seymour Chatman, *Coming to Terms: The Rhetoric of Narrative in Fiction and Film* (Ithaca, NY, 1990), p. 7, italics in the original.
47 Musser, 'The Eden Musée in 1898'.
48 Ibid., p. 82; Charles Musser, *The Emergence of Cinema: The American Screen to 1907* (New York, 1990), pp. 193–224.
49 Joseph Garncarz, 'Filmprogramm im Variéte: Die "Optische Berichterstattung"', in U. Jung and M. Loiperdinger (eds), *Geschichte des dokumentarischen Films in Deutschland. Vol. 1. Kaiserreich, 1895–1918* (Stuttgart, 2005), pp. 93–100; Martin Loiperdinger, 'Filmpropaganda des Deutschen Flottenvereins', in *Geschichte*, pp. 121–48.
50 As Garncararz has demonstrated sometimes the whole programme was spliced together on a single reel. Garncarz, 'Filmprogramm im Variéte', pp. 96–7.
51 Musser, 'The Eden Musée in 1898', p. 82.
52 Sarah Kozloff, *Invisible Storytellers: Voice-Over Narration in American Fiction Film* (Berkeley, 1988).
53 'The Passion Play', *Philadelphia Inquirer*, 23 November 1897, p. 5.
54 *New Haven Journal-Courier*, 15 March 1898, p. 5.
55 'The Passion Play', p. 5.
56 Ulrich Rauscher, 'Die Welt im Film', *Frankfurter Zeitung*, 31 December 1912, my translation.
57 Ibid.
58 Yuri Tsivian, *Early Cinema in Russia and Its Cultural Reception*, trans. A. Bodger (London, 1994), pp. 100–3.
59 Ibid., p. 102. One of Tsivian's key arguments in favour of this view are the very strict censorship rules informing the exhibition of films of the Imperial Family in Tsarist Russia. These rules go at great lengths to avoid evocation of any inappropriate narratives that the adjacent films in the program might elicit.
60 W. Stephen Bush, 'Lectures on Notable Reels', *Moving Picture World*, 24 June 1911, pp. 1430–1. Given that *Enoch Arden* appeared on 12 June and 15 June, respectively, it is most likely that the version of *Faust* Bush is referring to is the one by Henri Andréani and David Barnett from Pathé which, although from 1910, premiered in the United States on 16 June 1911.

61 Gunning, *D. W. Griffith*, p. 93. A good analogy might be issues spectators unaccustomed to dubbing have when watching dubbed films. It is difficult to deny dubbed speech as a part of the text but for these viewers such speech simply hampers diegetic realism.
62 Bottomore, 'Eric Williams', p. 57.
63 Richard Crangle, '"Next Slide Please": The Lantern Lecture in Britain, 1890–1910', in R. Abel and R. Altman (eds), *The Sounds of Early Cinema* (Bloomington, 2001), p. 45.
64 Gunning, *D. W. Griffith*, p. 91.
65 Altman, *Silent Film Sounds*, p. 134; Kember, *Marketing Modernity*.
66 Adapted from Kember, *Marketing Modernity*, p. 66.
67 For an easily accessible resource of both reading and visual material see http://www.magiclantern.org.uk (accessed 20 February 2019).
68 Kember, *Marketing Modernity*, p. 66.
69 Linda Hutcheon, *Narcissistic Narrative: The Metafictional Paradox* (Waterloo, 1980).
70 Kember, *Marketing Modernity*, p. 66.
71 Note the difference from direct addresses in fiction film. There the addresses by characters cannot be but construed as a part of the text and, therefore, we must imagine ourselves as being addressed. In these lecturing instances, however, we may legitimately read the address as a temporary break in the game.
72 W. Stephen Bush, 'Lectures on Moving Pictures', *Moving Picture World*, 22 August 1908, p. 137, my italics.
73 A. S., 'Explain the Pictures! The Most Pressing Need of the Day Is an Intelligent Description of Film Plots and Travel Pictures', *The Bioscope*, 10 December 1908, p. 5.
74 Hagen Sellmann, 'Literatur und Kinematograph', *Eckart*, January 1913, pp. 256–7, my translation.
75 Ibid, p. 258.
76 *Moving Picture World*, 2 May 1908, p. 400.
77 Ibid., p. 401.
78 Lubin Manufacturing Company Catalogue Special, 'The Passion Play', 1905, p. 13, in Charles Musser et al. (eds), *Motion Picture Catalogs by American Producers and Distributors, 1894–1908* (Baltimore, 1984). Thirty-one discrete films making up the play could have been bought separately and/or with an assortment of any number of about 100 stereopticon slides.
79 Kozloff, *Invisible Storytellers*.
80 Bush, 'Lectures on Notable Reels', p. 1430.
81 In his lecture Bush borrows heavily from Alfred Tennyson's poem of the same name (the film also clearly signals its source in its opening intertitle: 'From the Poem by Alfred Lord Tennyson'). This was, however, no simple borrowing because Bush deliberately organized his lecture in such a way that shot transitions

are accompanied by conjunctions (e.g. 'but', 'and', etc.). This part of the poem is originally organized in following verses:

> Here on this beach a hundred years ago,
> Three children of three houses, Annie Lee,
> The prettiest little damsel in the port,
> And Philip Ray the miller's only son,
> And Enoch Arden, a rough sailor's lad ...'

The lecture, by contrast, transforms the first three lines into a single shot account and, crucially, does not end it with 'The prettiest little damsel in the port' but adds an 'and' to it to smooth out the shot transition. Similarly with the second shot description where the fourth verse becomes 'Phillip Ray, the miller's only son, and'.

82 Gunning, *D. W. Griffith*; Gaudreault, *From Plato to Lumière*.
83 Altman, *Silent Film Sounds*, pp. 58–72.
84 Quoted in ibid., p. 58.
85 John L. Stoddard, *John L. Stoddard's Lectures. Vol. 1* (Boston, 1897), pp. 11, 12.
86 In late 2003 a number of films shot by Holmes (and thought lost) were discovered. They are housed in the George Eastman museum and awaiting restoration.
87 E. Burton Holmes, *The Burton Holmes Lectures. Vol. 7* (Battle Creek, 1901), pp. 6–7.
88 Ibid., pp. 18–20.
89 Altman, *Silent Film Sounds*, p. 69, italics in the original.
90 Ibid.
91 Ibid., pp. 69–70.
92 Holmes, *The Burton Holmes Lectures*, p. 27.
93 Altman, *Silent Film Sounds*, p. 69.
94 Ibid., p. 62.
95 Gunning, *D. W. Griffith*; Gaudreault, *From Plato to Lumière*.

5 Implicit mandates and fictional narrators

1 Christian Metz, *Film Language: A Semiotics of the Cinema*, trans. M. Taylor (New York, 1974), pp. 20–1, italics in the original.
2 Wayne C. Booth, *The Rhetoric of Fiction* (Chicago, 1961); Gérard Genette, *Narrative Discourse: An Essay in Method*, trans. J. E. Lewin (Ithaca, NY, 1980).
3 Christian Metz, *The Imaginary Signifier: Psychoanalysis and the Cinema*, trans. C. Britton (Bloomington, 1982), p. 125.
4 Sarah Kozloff, *Invisible Storytellers* (Berkeley, 1988), p. 44; André Gaudreault, *From Plato to Lumière: Narration and Monstration in Literature and Cinema*, trans. T. Barnard (Toronto, 2009), p. 89; André Gaudreault and François Jost, 'Enunciation

and Narration', in T. Miller and R. Stam, *A Companion to Film Theory* (Malden, MA, 1999), p. 58.
5   Brian Henderson, 'Tense, Mood and Voice in Film (Notes after Genette)', *Film Quarterly* 36.4 (1983), pp. 4–17.
6   Kozloff, *Invisible Storytellers*; Tom Gunning, *D. W. Griffith and the Origins of American Narrative Film: The Early Years at Biograph* (Urbana, 1991).
7   David Alan Black, 'Genette and Film: Narrative Level in the Fiction Cinema', *Wide Angle* 8.3/4 (1986), pp. 19–26; Seymour Chatman, *Coming to Terms: The Rhetoric of Narrative in Fiction and Film* (Ithaca, NY, 1990); Peter Verstraten, *Film Narratology* (Toronto, 2009).
8   Marie-Laure Ryan, 'Toward a Definition of Narrative', in D. Herman (ed.), *The Cambridge Companion to Narrative* (Cambridge, 2007), p. 29.
9   Gaudreault, *From Plato to Lumière*, p. 34.
10 Maguire and Baucus Catalogue, Fall 1897, p. 2, in Charles Musser et al. (eds), *Motion Picture Catalogs by American Producers and Distributors, 1894–1908* (Baltimore, 1984).
11 Quoted in C. Harding and S. Popple (eds), *In the Kingdom of Shadows: A Companion to the Early Cinema* (London, 1996), p. 5.
12 I admit that whether all this counts as a sufficient divergence from equilibrium might be contentious – this is hallmark of fuzzy definitions.
13 Quoted in Harding and Popple, *In the Kingdom of Shadows*, p. 5.
14 Quoted in Kemp R. Niver, *Biograph Bulletins, 1896–1908* (Los Angeles, 1971), p. 36.
15 Gunning, *D. W. Griffith*, p. 21.
16 Gaudreault, *From Plato to Lumière*, p. 58.
17 Genette, *Narrative Discourse*, p. 214, italics in the original.
18 Genette's logic is somewhat different as it hinges on properties of deixis – I address his argument for the separation of narrators and authors in literary fiction in detail below. Importantly, Genette focuses only on linguistic narratives.
19 The assumption here is that messages are intentional artefacts (and that narrative works are messages). This is not to deny that we cannot misconstrue something as a message (say a constellation of the stars as a sign from the gods) but this, strictly speaking, would not be a message.
20 Quoted in Niver, *Biograph Bulletins*, p. 36.
21 Ibid.
22 Quoted in Gaudreault, *From Plato to Lumière*, p. 112.
23 Gaudreault, *From Plato to Lumière*, p. 112.
24 This approach also has an added benefit on minimizing the number of theoretical entities – in Gaudreault there is a proliferation of film narrators which include profilmic monstrator, filmographic monstrator, filmographic mega-monstrator, filmographic narrator and film mega-narrator (the great image-maker).
25 Gunning, *D. W. Griffith*, p. 134.
26 Ibid.

27 Genette, *Narrative Discourse*, pp. 213–14.
28 Quoted in Niver, *Biograph Bulletins*, p. 403.
29 The underlying reason for this, as I elaborate in more detail below, is that, unlike in Balzac's novel, in Griffith's film there are no deictics.
30 Quoted in Michael Chanan, *The Dream That Kicks: The Prehistory and Early Years of Cinema in Britain*. 2nd edn (London, 1996), p. 186.
31 *New York Clipper*, 8 September 1906, p. 766.
32 *Moving Picture World*, 22 February 1908, p. 143.
33 William H. Kitchell, 'Tribulations of a Scenario Writer', *Film Index*, 20 August 1910, p. 6.
34 Clarence J. Caine, *How to Write Photoplays* (Philadelphia, 1915). For an in-depth history of screenwriting see Edward Azlant, *The Theory, History, and Practice of Screenwriting, 1897–1920* (Madison, 1980); Edward Azlant, 'Screenwriting for the Early Silent Film: Forgotten Pioneers, 1897–1911', *Film History* 9.3 (1997), pp. 228–56.
35 E. J. Muddle, *Picture Plays and How to Write Them* (London, 1911); Ralph P. Stoddard, *The Photo-Play, a Book of Valuable Information for Those Who Would Enter a Field of Unlimited Endeavor* (Cleveland, 1911).
36 Ibid., no pagination.
37 R. W. Paul Film Catalogue, 1903, p. 19, in British Film Institute, *Early Filmmakers' Catalogues* (London, 1983).
38 Elbert Moore, *Elbert Moore's Text Book on Writing the Photoplay* (Chicago, 1915), p. 18.
39 Berg J. Esenwein and Arthur Leeds, *Writing the Photoplay* (Springfield, MA, 1913), p. 27, italics in the original.
40 Epes Winthrop Sargent, *The Technique of the Photoplay* (New York, 1913), p. 7.
41 'The Clearing House', *Photo Playwright* 1.4 (1912), p. 15.
42 Howard T. Dimick, *Photoplay Making; A Handbook Devoted to the Application of Dramatic Principles to the Writing of Plays for Picture Production* (Ridgewood, NJ, 1915), p. 20.
43 As I show below following George M. Wilson's work it will become clear that, contrary to Genette, there is nothing essentially mistaken in *imagining* the real author as the narrator. Then the author is simply the fictional narrator. There are a number of narratives which mandate us to do so and Holmes's narratives are one of the examples we have already seen.
44 Gaudreault insists that there is an agent responsible for showing the happenings on stage – the monstrator. Although generally invisible the traces of his activity, according to Gaudreault, can be seen in the use of techniques such as prologue and epilogue as well as devices characteristic of epic and expressionist theatre (placards, voice-off, gestus, etc.). We are again dealing with a formally invalid argument which claims that the presence of a narrative discourse conveying a fictional story

necessary entails the existence of a fictional narrator. Cf. Gaudreault, *From Plato to Lumière*, pp. 72–80.
45 Dimick, *Photoplay Making*, p. 67.
46 Esenwein and Leeds, *Writing the Photoplay*, p. 1, italics in the original.
47 Herbert Case Hoagland, *How to Write a Photoplay* (New York, 1912), p. 14, italics in the original.
48 William Lewis Gordon, *How to Write Moving Picture Plays* (Cincinnati, 1914), p. 17.
49 Esenwein and Leeds, *Writing the Photoplay*, pp. 180–5.
50 Ibid., p. 171.
51 Ibid., p. 187.
52 Caine, *How to Write Photoplays*, p. 196.
53 Sargent, *The Technique of the Photoplay*, p. 13.
54 Esenwein and Leeds, *Writing the Photoplay*, p. 190.
55 Ibid.
56 Although we regularly speak of other people as him or her doing this or that, strictly speaking it is impossible to speak in third person. Speaking is always in the first person in the sense that it always implies a speaking 'I' and not a speaking 'he' or 'she'.
57 Genette, *Narrative Discourse*, p. 214.
58 This also holds for instances of oral narration because of the properties of deixis discussed below.
59 Kendall L. Walton, *Mimesis as Make-Believe: On the Foundations of the Representational Arts* (Cambridge, MA, 1990); George M. Wilson, *Seeing Fictions in Film: The Epistemology of Movies* (Oxford, 2011).
60 Some analytic philosophers and literary theorists object and claim that this still does not settle the status of the textual element in question and that the use of actual people, places and times does pose a problem as far as the semantics of fiction is concerned. For them the problem appears to be how to account for fictional truths of sentences which are populated by both actual and fictional entities if only the former properly denote. Various solutions next to Walton's have been proposed. Some have tried to give an account of fictional worlds in terms of possible worlds (David Lewis most notably), whereas others have sought to construe fictional worlds as domains performed by fictional agents relating information as actual (the approach favoured by Gregory Currie). For a good recent summary of the problems and possible solutions to the ontology of fictional entities see Amie L. Thomasson, 'Fictional Entities', in J. Kim, E. Sosa and G. S. Rosenkrantz (eds), *A Companion to Metaphysics*. 2nd edn (Cambridge, MA, 2009), pp. 10–18. Regardless of what might turn out to be the solution of these debates, it would not change my argument about the status of fictional narrators in film and literature.

61 Originally there is a slip here: Genette talks of Homer, rather than 'Homer' as he should.
62 Gérard Genette, *Narrative Discourse Revisited*, trans. J. E. Lewin (Ithaca, NY, 1988), pp. 85–6.
63 That she is the author does not necessarily mean she is the one who invented the stories she tells; she might have heard them from somebody. In Walton's terminology Scheherazade would be a storytelling narrator. Cf. Walton, *Mimesis as Make-Believe*, p. 368.
64 Gregory Currie, *Image and Mind: Film, Philosophy and Cognitive Science* (Cambridge, 1995), p. 265. Admittedly, an exception for paratexts such as chapter headings, table of contents, etc. should be made.
65 Seymour Chatman, *Coming to Terms: The Rhetoric of Narrative in Fiction and Film* (Ithaca, NY, 1990); Mieke Bal, *Narratology: Introduction to the Theory of Narrative*, 2nd edn (Toronto, 1999), p. 22; Shlomith Rimmon-Kenan, *Narrative Fiction: Contemporary Poetics*, 2nd edn (London, 2002), p. 91. Although the dissent usually came from linguists in arguing for speakerless sentences, it can be also found in early Chatman, and even earlier in Käte Hamburger's work published originally in 1957. See Ann Banfield, *Unspeakable Sentences: Narration and Representation in the Language of Fiction* (Boston, 1982); Seymour Chatman, *Story and Discourse: Narrative Structure in Fiction and Film* (Ithaca, NY, 1978); Käte Hamburger, *The Logic of Literature*, 2nd edn, trans. M. J. Rose (Bloomington, 1973).
66 Noël Carroll, 'Introduction' to 'Part IV: Film Narrative/Narration', in N. Carroll and J. Choi, *Philosophy of Film and Motion Pictures: An Anthology* (Malden, MA, 2006), pp. 175–84; Gregory Currie, *Narratives and Narrators: A Philosophy of Stories* (Oxford, 2010); Berys Gaut, *A Philosophy of Cinematic Art* (Cambridge, 2010); Andrew Kania, 'Against the Ubiquity of Fictional Narrators', *The Journal of Aesthetics and Art Criticism* 63.1 (2005), pp. 47–54.
67 George M. Wilson, 'Elusive Narrators in Fiction and Film', *Philosophical Studies* 135.1 (2007), pp. 73–88; Wilson, *Seeing Fictions in Film*.
68 Mario Slugan, 'An Asymmetry of Implicit Fictional Narrators in Literature and Film', *Postgraduate Journal of Aesthetics* 7.2 (2010), pp. 26–37; Mario Slugan, 'Deixis in Literary and Film Fiction: Intra-Ontological Reference and the Case of Controlling Fictional Narrators', in A. J. Bareis and L. Nordrum (eds), *How to Make Believe: The Fictional Truths of the Representational Arts* (Berlin, 2015), pp. 185–202.
69 Wilson, *Seeing Fictions in Film*, p. 121.
70 Émile Benveniste, *Problems in General Linguistics*, trans. M. E. Meek (Coral Gables, 1971), pp. 223–30.
71 Jerrold Levinson has produced an (epistemological version of the) ontological gap argument criticized successfully by Kania and Wilson. See Jerrold Levinson,

'Film Music and Narrative Agency', in D. Bordwell and N. Carroll (eds), *Post-Theory: Reconstructing Film Studies* (Madison, 1996), pp. 248–82.
72 Benveniste, *Problems in General Linguistics*, p. 227.
73 Ibid., 226–7.
74 Genette, *Narrative Discourse*, p. 214.
75 Wilson, 'Elusive Narrators in Fiction and Film'.
76 It is important to note that (7b) deals with the objections concerning propositional content. For potential objections and responses see Slugan, 'Deixis in Literary and Film Fiction'.
77 Rimmon-Kenan seems to believe that even epistolary novels have a fictional 'editor'. However, this is susceptible to the same arguments Kania makes against Levinson. We might call Rimmon-Kenan's proposal the material version of the ontological gap argument for somebody fictionally needed to compile all the letters.
78 Cf. Black, 'Genette and Film'; Chatman, *Coming to Terms*; Gunning, *D. W. Griffith*; Kozloff, *Invisible Storytellers*; Metz, *Film Language*; Verstraten, *Film Narratology*.
79 Benveniste, *General Problems of Linguistics*.
80 Francesco Casetti, *Inside the Gaze: The Fiction Film and Its Spectator*, trans. N. Andrew (Bloomington, 1998); Daniel Dayan, 'The Tutor-Code of Cinema', *Film Quarterly* 28.1 (1974), pp. 22–31; Gaudreault and Jost, 'Enunciation and Narration'; François Jost, 'The Look: From Novel to Film. An Essay in Comparative Narratology', in R. Stam and A. Raengo (eds), *A Companion to Literature and Film* (Malden, MA, 2004), pp. 71–80; Mark Nash, '*Vampyr* and the Fantastic', *Screen* 17.3 (1976), pp. 29–67; Kaja Silverman, *The Subject of Semiotics* (New York, 1983); Slavoj Žižek, *The Fright of Real Tears: Krzysztof Kieślowski between Theory and Post-Theory* (London, 2001).

It should be noted that Metz would later on explicitly deny that the great image-maker, that is, the enunciator as he would refer to it then, has any connection with the Genettian extradiegetic narrator and would go on to align himself more closely with the idea that the great image-maker should be understood as the implied author. Christian Metz, 'The Impersonal Enunciation, or the Site of Film (In the Margin of Recent Works on Enunciation in Cinema)', *New Literary History* 22.3 (1991), p. 768. This is most probably due to Cassetti's work on the filmic enunciation in which he defined the enunciator as a theoretical entity extractable from the text and in opposition to the narrator figure. Moreover, although Gaudreault, who also discussed narration in terms of enunciation, interchangeably used the great image-maker and the mega-narrator throughout his book, and in its introductory table he also identified the great image-maker with the implied author. Gaudreault, *From Plato to Lumière*, p. 7. These examples point to some uncertainty regarding the ontological status of the enunciator for its position in the works of these enunciation theorists, and particularly in Gaudreault, regularly shifts ontologically between what is fictional in the story and what theoretical models we can give for particular effects of the film. I will concentrate only on the enunciator as the narrator's analogue in film and leave the issue of the implied author aside. Suffice it to say, the above analysis of the concept of fiction allows for a clearer separation of these roles.

81 Gaudreault and Jost, 'Enunciation and Narration', pp. 47–8. Gunning's 'narrator system' is also an example of what counts as a marker of a fictional narrator.
82 Metz, 'The Impersonal Enunciation', pp. 754, 769.
83 Ibid., pp. 755–6, italics in original.
84 To be clear, when I speak of *discourse* I am speaking of Benveniste's term and not of narrative discourse.
85 Edward Branigan, 'Here Is a Picture of No Revolver!: The Negation of Images and Methods for Analyzing the Structure of Pictorial Statements', *Wide Angle* 8.3/4 (1986), pp. 8–17; David Bordwell, *Narration in the Fiction Film* (Madison, 1985).
86 Linda Hutcheon, *Narcissistic Narrative: The Metafictional Paradox* (Waterloo, 1980), p. xii.
87 Cf. Chatman, *Coming to Terms*; Gaudreault and Jost, 'Enunciation and Narration'; Gunning, *D. W. Griffith*; Robert Stam, Robert Burgoyne and Sandy Flitterman-Lewis, *New Vocabularies in Film Semiotics: Structuralism, Post-Structuralism and Beyond* (London, 1992).
88 Carroll, 'Introduction'; Currie, *Narratives and Narrators*; Gaut, *A Philosophy of Cinematic Art*; Kania, 'Against the Ubiquity of Fictional Narrators'.
89 George M. Wilson, '*Le Grand Imagier* Steps Out: The Primitive Basis of Film Narration', *Philosophical Topics* 25.1 (1997), pp. 295–318; Wilson, 'Elusive Narrators in Fiction and Film'; Wilson, *Seeing Fictions in Film*.
90 Chatman, *Coming to Terms*; Levinson, 'Film Music and Narrative Agency'.
91 Wilson, '*Le Grand Imagier* Steps Out', p. 311, italics in the original.
92 Wilson, *Seeing Fictions in Film*. This characteristic is included in order to ward off numerous criticisms put forward by Carroll, 'Introduction'.
93 Ibid.
94 Wilson, *Seeing Fictions*, p. 55.
95 I produce the argument for the mediated version of imagined seeing thesis Wilson endorses but it works for all of its versions.
96 Ibid., p. 55, italics in the original.
97 Walton, *Mimesis as Make-Believe*, p. 60.
98 Cf. ibid., note 6.23.
99 For potential responses and further analysis see Mario Slugan. 2014. 'Some Thoughts on Controlling Fictional Narrators in Fiction Film', *American Society of Aesthetics Graduate E-Journal* 6.2, pp. 1–7; and Mario Slugan, *Noël Carroll and Film: A Philosophy of Art and Popular Culture* (Bloomsbury, 2019), pp. 111–12.

Bibliography

Archives

British Film Institute
British Library
Deutsche Kinemathek
Deutsche Nationalbibliothek
Deutsches Filminstitut
Joseph Regenstein Library
Library of Congress

Selected Works Consulted

Abel, Richard, ed. 1998. *French Film Theory and Criticism: A History/Anthology, 1907–1939. Vol. 1.* Princeton: Princeton University Press.
Abel, Richard, ed. 2005. *Encyclopedia of Early Cinema.* London; New York: Routledge.
Abel, Richard. 2011. '*A Trip to the Moon* as an American Phenomenon.' In *Fantastic Voyages of the Cinematic Imagination: Georges Méliés's Trip to the Moon*, edited by Matthew Solomon, 129–42. Albany: State University of New York Press.
Albera, François and Maria Tortajada, eds. 2010. *Cinema beyond Film: Media Epistemology in the Modern Era.* Amsterdam: Amsterdam University Press.
Allen, James. 2004. *Without Sanctuary: Lynching Photography in America.* Santa Fe: Twin Palms.
Allen, Robert C. 1979. 'Contra the Chaser Theory.' *Wide Angle* 3 (1): 4–11.
Allen, Robert C. 1990. 'From Exhibition to Reception: Reflections on the Audience in Film History.' *Screen* 31 (4): 347–56.
Allen, Robert C. and Douglas Gomery. 1985. *Film History: Theory and Practice* London: McGraw-Hill.
Altenloh, Emilie. 1914. *Zur Soziologie des Kino: Die Kino-Unternehmung und die sozialen Schichten ihrer Besucher.* Jena: Diederichs.
Altman, Rick. 2004. *Silent Film Sound.* New York: Columbia University Press.
Auerbach, Jonathan. 2007. *Body Shots: Early Cinema's Incarnations.* Berkeley: California University Press.
Azlant, Edward. 1980. *The Theory, History, and Practice of Screenwriting, 1897–1920.* Madison: University of Wisconsin–Madison.

Azlant, Edward. 1997. 'Screenwriting for the Early Silent Film: Forgotten Pioneers, 1897–1911.' *Film History* 9 (3): 228–56.

Bal, Mieke. 1999. *Narratology: Introduction to the Theory of Narrative*, 2nd edn. Toronto: University of Toronto Press.

Banfield, Ann. 1982. *Unspeakable Sentences: Narration and Representation in the Language of Fiction*. Boston: Routledge & Kegan Paul.

Bazin, André. 2004. *What Is Cinema?* Edited and translated by Hugh Gray. Vol. 1. Berkeley: University of California Press.

Bazin, André. 2008. 'Every Film Is a Social Documentary.' *Film Comment* 44 (6): 40–1.

Benoit, Turquety. 2015. 'Tricks and Effects: Introduction.' *Early Popular Visual Culture* 13 (2): 103–5.

Benveniste, Émile. 1971. *Problems in General Linguistics*. Translated by Mary Elizabeth Meek. Coral Gables: University of Miami Press.

Bertolini, Pascale and Jacques Polet. 1996. 'Boniments, explications et autres bruits de scène: les accompagnements de spectacles cinématographiques muets en Belgique.' *Iris* 22: 145–60.

Biltereyst, Daniël, Richard Maltby and Philippe Meers, eds. 2011. *Cinema, Audiences and Modernity: New Perspectives on European Cinema History*. Abingdon: Routledge.

Birett, Herbert. 1994. *Lichtspiele: Der Kino in Deutschland bis 1914*. Munich: Q-Verlag.

Black, David Alan. 1986. 'Genette and Film: Narrative Level in the Fiction Cinema.' *Wide Angle* 8 (3/4): 19–26.

Blevins, Tim, Chris Nicholl and Calvin P. Otto, eds. 2006. *The Colorado Labor Wars: Cripple Creek 1903–1904, A Centennial Commemoration*. Colorado Springs: Pikes Peak Library District.

Blom, Ivo. 1999. 'Chapters from the Life of a Camera-Operator. The Recollections of Anton Nöggerath: Filming News and Non-Fiction, 1897–1908.' *Film History* 11 (3): 262–81.

Blom, Ivo and Ine van Dooren. 1996. '"Ladies and Gentlemen, Hats Off, Please!": Dutch Film Lecturing and the Case of Cor Schuring.' *Iris* 22: 81–102.

Bordwell, David. 1985. *Narration in the Fiction Film*. Madison: University of Wisconsin Press.

Booth, Wayne C. 1961. *The Rhetoric of Fiction*. Chicago. University of Chicago Press.

Bottomore, Stephen. 1984. 'Dreyfus and Documentary'. *Sight and Sound* 53 (4): 290–3.

Bottomore, Stephen. 1999. 'The Panicking Audience?: Early Cinema and the "Train Effect."' *Historical Journal of Film, Radio and Television* 19 (2): 177–216.

Bottomore, Stephen. 2007. *Filming, Faking, and Propaganda: The Origins of the War Film, 1897–1902*. Utrecht: Utrecht University.

Bottomore, Stephen. 2013. 'Eric Williams: Speaking to Pictures.' In *The Sounds of the Silents in Britain*, edited by Julie Brown and Annette Davison, 55–71. New York: Oxford University Press.

Bowser, Eileen. 1993. *The Transformation of Cinema, 1907–1915*. New York: Scribner.

Branigan, Edward R. 1986. 'Here Is a Picture of No Revolver!: The Negation of Images and Methods for Analyzing the Structure of Pictorial Statements.' *Wide Angle* 8 (3/4): 8–17.

British Film Institute. 1983. *Early Filmmakers' Catalogues*. London: World Microfilm Publications.

Buchanan, Judith. 2013. '"Now, Where Were We?" Ideal and Actual Early Cinema Lecturing Practices in Britain, Germany and the United States.' In *The Sounds of the Silents in Britain*, edited by Julie Brown and Annette Davison, 38–54. New York: Oxford University Press.

Burch, Noël. 1979. *To the Distant Observer: Form and Meaning in the Japanese Cinema*. Berkeley: University of California Press.

Burch, Noël. 1982. 'Narrative/Diegesis – Thresholds, Limits.' *Screen* 23 (2): 16–33.

Burch, Noël. 1983. 'Passion, poursuite: la linéarisation.' *Communications* 38 (1): 30–50.

Burch, Noël. 1990. *Life to Those Shadows*. Berkeley: University of California Press.

Caine, Clarence J. 1915. *How to Write Photoplays*. Philadelphia: D. McKay.

Carroll, Noël. 1983. 'From Real to Reel: Entangled in Nonfiction Film.' *Philosophic Exchange* 14 (1): 4–45.

Carroll, Noël. 1988. *Mystifying Movies: Fads & Fallacies in Contemporary Film Theory*. New York: Columbia University Press.

Carroll, Noël. 1997. 'Fiction, Non-Fiction, and the Film of Presumptive Assertion: A Conceptual Analysis.' In *Film Theory and Philosophy*, edited by Richard Allen and Murray Smith, 173–202. Oxford: Clarendon Press.

Carroll, Noël. 2006. 'Introduction' to 'Part IV: Film Narrative/Narration.' In *Philosophy of Film and Motion Pictures: An Athology*, edited by Noël Carroll and Jinhee Choi, 175–84. Malden, MA: Blackwell.

Carroll, Noël. 2008. *The Philosophy of Motion Pictures*. Malden, MA: Blackwell.

Casetti, Francesco. 1998. *Inside the Gaze: The Fiction Film and Its Spectator*. Translated by Nell Andrew. Bloomington: Indiana University Press.

Chanan, Michael. 1996. *The Dream That Kicks: The Prehistory and Early Years of Cinema in Britain*, 2nd edn. London: Routledge.

Chatman, Seymour. 1978. *Story and Discourse: Narrative Structure in Fiction and Film*. Ithaca, NY: Cornell University Press.

Chatman, Seymour. 1990. *Coming to Terms: The Rhetoric of Narrative in Fiction and Film*. Ithaca, NY: Cornell University Press.

Christie, Ian. 2011. 'First Footing on the Moon: Méliès's Debt to Verne and Wells and His Influence in Great Britain.' In *Fantastic Voyages of the Cinematic Imagination: Georges Méliès's Trip to the Moon*, edited by Matthew Solomon, 65–80. Albany: State University of New York Press.

Christie, Ian, ed. 2012. *Audiences: Defining and Researching Screen Entertainment Reception*. Amsterdam: Amsterdam University Press.

Coleridge, Samuel Taylor. 1884. *Biographia Literaria*. New York: Harper and Brothers.

Condon, Denis. 2009. 'Irish Audiences Watch Their First US Feature: *The Corbett-Fitzsimmons Fight* (1897).' In *Screening Irish-America: Representing Irish-America in Film and Television*, edited by Ruth Barton, 135–47. Dublin: Irish Academic Press.

Crangle, Richard. 2001. '"Next Slide Please": The Lantern Lecture in Britain, 1890–1910.' In *The Sounds of Early Cinema*, edited by Richard Abel and Rick Altman, 39–47. Bloomington: Indiana University Press.

Crangle, Richard, Stephen Herbert and David Robinson, eds. 2001. *Encyclopaedia of the Magic Lantern*. London: The Magic Lantern Society.

Currie, Gregory. 1990. *The Nature of Fiction*. Cambridge; New York: Cambridge University Press.

Currie, Gregory. 1995. *Image and Mind: Film, Philosophy and Cognitive Science*. Cambridge; New York: Cambridge University Press.

Currie, Gregory. 1996. 'Film, Reality, and Illusion.' In *Post-Theory: Reconstructing Film Studies*, edited by Noël Carroll and David Bordwell, 325–44. Madison: University of Wisconsin Press.

Currie, Gregory. 2010. *Narratives and Narrators: A Philosophy of Stories*. Oxford; New York: Oxford University Press.

Currie, Gregory and Anna Ichino. 2016. 'Imagination and Make-Believe.' In *The Routledge Companion to Aesthetics*, 3rd edn, edited by Berys Gaut and Dominic McIver Lopes, 320–9. New York: Routledge.

Davies, David. 2007. *Aesthetics and Literature*. London: Continuum.

Davies, David. 2013. 'Fiction.' In *The Routledge Companion to Aesthetics*, 3rd edn, edited by Berys Gaut and Dominic McIver Lopes, 330–9. New York: Routledge.

Dayan, Daniel. 1974. 'The Tutor-Code of Classical Cinema.' *Film Quarterly* 28 (1): 22–31.

Dimick, Howard T. 1915. *Photoplay Making; A Handbook Devoted to the Application of Dramatic Principles to the Writing of Plays for Picture Production*. Ridgewood, NJ: The Editor Co.

Doane, Mary Ann. 2007. 'The Indexical and the Concept of Medium Specificity.' *differences* 18 (1): 128–52.

Doložel, Lubomír. 1998. *Heterocosmica: Fiction and Possible worlds*. Baltimore: Johns Hopkins University.

Dulac, Nicolas and André Gaudreault. 2006. 'Circularity and Repetition at the Heart of the Attraction: Optical Toys and the Emergence of a New Cultural Series.' In *The Cinema of Attractions Reloaded*, edited by Wanda Strauven, 227–44. Amsterdam: Amsterdam University Press.

Dupré la Tour, Claire. 2005. 'Intertitles and Titles.' In *Encyclopedia of Early Cinema*, edited by Richard Abel, 471–6. London; New York: Routledge.

Dym, Jeffrey A. 2003. *Benshi, Japanese Silent Film Narrators, and Their Forgotten Narrative Art of Setsumei: A History of Japanese Silent Film Narration*. Lewiston, NY: Edwin Mellen Press.

Elsaesser, Thomas. 1986. 'The New Film History.' *Sight and Sound* 55 (4): 246–51.

Elsaesser, Thomas. 2004. 'The New Film History as Media Archeology.' *Cinémas: revue d'études cinématographiques/Cinémas: Journal of Film Studies* 14 (2–3): 75–117.

Esenwein, Berg J. and Arthur Leeds. 1913. *Writing the Photoplay*. Springfield, MA: The Home Correspondence School.

Ferri, Anthony J. 2007. *Willing Suspension of Disbelief: Poetic Faith in Film*. Lanham: Lexington Books.

Fielding, Raymond. 1968–9. 'Hale's Tours: Ultrarealism in the Pre-1910 Motion Picture.' *Smithsonian Journal of History* 3 (4): 101–21.

Fielding, Raymond. 1970. 'Hale's Tours: Ultrarealism in the Pre-1910 Motion Picture.' *Cinema Journal* 10 (1): 34–47.

Fielding, Raymond. 1973. 'Hale's Tours: Ultra-Realism in the Pre-1910 Motion Picture.' In *The American Cinema*, edited by Donald E. Staples. Washington: U.S. Information Agency.

Fielding, Raymond. 1983. 'Hale's Tours: Ultrarealism in the Pre-1910 Motion Picture.' In *Film Before Griffith*, edited by John Fell, 116–30. Berkeley: University of California Press.

Frank, Hannah. 2016. 'Traces of the World: Cel Animation and Photography.' *Animation* 11 (1): 23–39.

Friend, Stacie. 2008. 'Imagination, Fact and Fiction.' In *New Waves in Aesthetics*, edited by Kathleen Stock and Katherine Thomson-Jones, 150–69. Basingstoke: Palgrave Macmillan.

Friend, Stacie. 2011. 'Fictive Utterance and Imagining II.' *Aristotelian Society Supplementary Volume* 85 (1): 163–80.

Friend, Stacie. 2012. 'Fiction as a Genre.' *Proceedings of the Aristotelian Society* 112 (2): 179–209.

Garncarz, Joseph. 2005. 'Filmprogramm im Varietés: Die "Optische Berichterstattung".' In *Geschichte des dokumentarischen Films in Deutschland. Vol. 1. Kaiserreich, 1895–1918*, edited by Uli Jung and Martin Loiperdinger, 80–100. Stuttgart: Reclam.

Garncarz, Joseph. 2005. 'Nicht-fiktionale Filmformen in Varietés und Wanderkinos.' In *Geschichte des dokumentarischen Films in Deutschland. Vol. 1. Kaiserreich, 1895–1918*, edited by Uli Jung and Martin Loiperdinger, 71–4. Stuttgart: Reclam.

Garncarz, Joseph. 2005. 'Der nicht-fiktionale Film im Programm der Wanderkinos.' In *Geschichte des dokumentarischen Films in Deutschland. Vol. 1. Kaiserreich, 1895–1918*, edited by Uli Jung and Martin Loiperdinger, 108–120. Stuttgart: Reclam.

Gaudreault, André. 2009. *From Plato to Lumière: Narration and Monstration in Literature and Cinema*. Translated by Timothy Barnard. Toronto: Toronto University Press.

Gaudreault, André. 2013. 'Titles, Subtitles, and Intertitles: Factors of Autonomy, Factors of Concatenation.' *Film History* 25 (1–2): 81–94.

Gaudrault, André. 2014. 'La cinématographie-attraction chez Méliès: une conception durable.' In *Méliès, carrefour des attractions: Suivi de Correspondance de Georges*

Méliès (1904–1937), edited by André Gaudreault and Laurent Le Forestier, 27–43. Rennes: Presses universitaires de Rennes.

Gaudreault, André and François Jost. 1999. 'Enunciation and Narration.' In *A Companion to Film Theory*, edited by Toby Miller and Robert Stam, 45–63. Malden, MA: Blackwell.

Gaudreault, André and Germain Lacasse, eds. 1996. 'Le bonimenteur de vues animées/ The Moving Picture Lecturer.' *Iris* 22.

Gaudrault, André and Tom Gunning. 2009. 'Introduction: American Cinema Emerges (1890–1909).' In *American Cinema, 1890–1909: Themes and Variations*, edited by André Gaudrault, 1–21. New Brunswick, NJ: Rutgers University Press.

Gaudrault, André and Philippe Marion. 2015. *The End of Cinema?: A Medium in Crisis in the Digital Age*. Translated by Timothy Barnard. New York: Columbia University Press.

Gaut, Berys. 2010. *A Philosophy of Cinematic Art*. Cambridge: Cambridge University Press.

Gauthier, Philippe. 2009. 'The Movie Theater as an Institutional Space and Framework of Signification: Hale's Tours and Film Historiography.' *Film History* 21 (4): 326–35.

Genette, Gérard. 1980. *Narrative Discourse: An Essay in Method*. Translated by Jane E. Lewin. Ithaca, NY: Cornell University Press.

Genette, Gérard. 1988. *Narrative Discourse Revisited*. Translated by Jane E. Lewin. Ithaca, NY: Cornell University Press.

Gerow, Aaron Andrew. 2010. *Visions of Japanese Modernity: Articulations of Cinema, Nation, and Spectatorship, 1895–1925*. Berkeley: University of California Press.

Gordon, William Lewis. 1914. *How to Write Moving Picture Plays*. Cincinnati: Atlas.

Grau, Oliver. 2003. *Virtual Art: From Illusion to Immersion* Translated by Gloria Custance. Cambridge, MA: MIT Press.

Gray, Frank. 1998. 'James Williamson's "Composed Picture": *Attack on a China Mission – Bluejackets to the Rescue*.' In *Celebrating 1895: The Centenary of Cinema*, edited by John Fullerton, 203–11. Sydney: John Libbey.

Gray, Frank. 2004. '*The Kiss in the Tunnel* (1899), G. A. Smith and the Emergence of the Edited Film in England.' In *The Silent Cinema Reader*, edited by Lee Grieveson and Peter Krämer, 51–62. London; New York: Routledge.

Griffiths, Alison. 2008. *Shivers Down Your Spine: Cinema, Museums, and the Immersive View*. New York: Columbia University Press.

Gunning, Tom. 1986. 'The Cinema of Attraction: Early Film, Its Spectator and the Avant-Garde.' *Wide Angle* 8 (3/4): 63–70.

Gunning, Tom. 1989. 'An Aesthetic of Astonishment: Early Film and the (In)Credulous Spectator.' *Art and Text* 34 (1): 31–45.

Gunning, Tom. 1989. '"Primitive" Cinema: A Frame-Up? Or the Trick's on Us.' *Cinema Journal* 28 (2): 3–12.

Gunning, Tom. 1991. *D. W. Griffith and the Origins of American Narrative Film: The Early Years at Biograph*. Urbana: University of Illinois Press.

Gunning, Tom. 1993. '"Now You See It, Now You Don't": The Temporality of the Cinema of Attractions.' *Velvet Light Trap* 32: 3–12.
Gunning, Tom. 1994. 'Colorful Metaphors: The Attraction of Color in Early Silent Cinema.' *Fotogenia* 1: 249–55.
Gunning, Tom. 1994. 'The Whole Town's Gawking: Early Cinema and the Visual Experience of Modernity.' *Yale Journal of Criticism* 7 (2): 189–202.
Gunning, Tom. 1997. 'Before Documentary: Early Nonfiction Films and the "View" Aesthetic.' In *Uncharted Territory: Essays on Early Nonfiction Film*, edited by Daan Hertogs and Nico de Klerk, 9–24. Amsterdam: Stichting Nederlands Filmmuseum.
Gunning, Tom. 1998. 'Early American Film.' In *The Oxford Guide to Film Studies*, edited by John Hill and Pamela Church Gibson, 255–71. Oxford; New York: Oxford University Press.
Gunning, Tom. 1999, 'The Scene of Speaking: Two Decades of Discovering the Film Lecturer.' *Iris* 27: 67–80.
Gunning, Tom. 2007. 'Moving Away from the Index: Cinema and the Impression of Reality.' *differences* 18 (1): 29–52.
Gunning, Tom. 2009. 'The Attraction of Motion: Modern Representation and the Image of Movement.' In *Film 1900: Technology, Perception, Culture*, edited by Annemone Ligensa and Klaus Kreimeier, 165–73. Bloomington: Indiana University Press.
Gunning, Tom. 2013. 'A Trip to the Moon (1902).' In *Film Analysis: A Norton Reader*, 2nd edn, edited by Jeffrey Geiger and R. L. Rutsky, 40–56. New York: W. W. Norton.
Hamburger, Käte. 1973. *The Logic of Literature*, 2nd edn. Translated by Marilynn J. Rose. Bloomington: Indiana University Press.
Hansen, Miriam. 1991. *Babel and Babylon: Spectatorship in American Silent Film*. Cambridge, MA: Harvard University Press.
Harding, Colin and Simon Popple, eds. 1996. *In the Kingdom of Shadows: A Companion to the Early Cinema*. London: Cygnus Arts.
Harrison, Rebecca. 2018. *From Steam to Screen: Cinema, the Railways, and Modernity*. London: I.B. Tauris.
Hayward, Susan. 2018. *Cinema Studies: The Key Concepts*, 5th edn. Abingdon; New York: Routledge.
Henderson, Brian. 1983. 'Tense, Mood and Voice in Film.' *Film Quarterly* 36 (4): 4–17.
Hoagland, Herbert Case. 1912. *How to Write a Photoplay*. New York: Magazine Maker.
Holmberg, Jan. 2003. 'Ideals of Immersion in Early Cinema.' *Cinémas: Revue d'études cinématographiques/Cinémas: Journal of Film Studies* 14 (1): 129–47.
Holmes, Burton E. 1901. *The Burton Holmes Lectures. Vol. 1*. Battle Creek: The Little-Preston Company.
Huhtamo, Erkki. 2013. *Illusions in Motion: Media Archaeology of the Moving Panorama and Related Spectacles*. Cambridge, MA: MIT Press.
Hutcheon, Linda. 1980. *Narcissistic Narrative: The Metafictional Paradox*. Waterloo: Wilfrid Laurier University Press.

Jost, François. 2004. 'The Look: From Novel to Film. An Essay in Comparative Narratology.' In *A Companion to Literature and Film*, edited by Robert Stam and Alessandra Raengo, 71–80. Malden, MA: Blackwell.

Kaes, Anton, ed. 1978. *Kino-Debatte: Texte zum Verhältnis von Literatur und Film 1909–1929*. München: Deutscher Taschenbuch-Verlag; Tübingen: Niemeyer.

Kania, Andrew. 2005. 'Against the Ubiquity of Fictional Narrators.' *The Journal of Aesthetics and Art Criticism* 63 (1): 47–54.

Keil, Charlie. 2001. *Early American Cinema in Transition: Story, Style, and Filmmaking, 1907–1913*. Madison: University of Wisconsin Press.

Keil, Charlie. 2006. 'Steel Engines and Cardboard Rockets: The Status of Fiction and Nonfiction in Early Cinema.' In *F Is for Phony: Fake Documentary and Truth's Undoing*, edited by Alexandra Juhasz and Jesse Lerner, 39–49. Minneapolis: University of Minnesota Press.

Kekatos, Kirk J. 2002. 'Edward H. Amet and the Spanish-American War Film.' *Film History* 14 (3/4): 405–17.

Kember, Joe. 2000. '"It Was Not the Show, It Was the Tale That You Told": Film Lecturing on the British Fairground.' In *Visual Delights: Essays on the Popular and Projected Image in the Nineteenth Century*, edited by Simon Popple and Vanessa Toulmin, 61–70. Trowbridge: Flicks Books.

Kember, Joe. 2009. *Marketing Modernity: Victorian Popular Shows and Early Cinema*. Exeter: Exeter University Press.

Kessler, Frank. 2006. '"Fake" in Early Non-Fiction.' *KINtop* 14/15: 87–83.

Kessler, Frank. 2011. '*A Trip to the Moon* as *Féerie*.' In *Fantastic Voyages of the Cinematic Imagination: Georges Méliès's Trip to the Moon*, edited by Matthew Solomon, 115–28. Albany: State University of New York Press.

King, Norman. 1984. 'The Sound of Silents.' *Screen* 25 (3): 2–15.

Kirby, Lynne. 1997. *Parallel Tracks: The Railroad and the Silent Cinema*. Durham: Duke University Press.

Kozloff, Sarah. 1988. *Invisible Storytellers: Voice-Over Narration in American Fiction Film*. Berkeley: University of California Press.

Kracauer, Siegfried. 1960. *Theory of Film: The Redemption of Physical Reality*. New York: Oxford University Press.

Kripke, Saul. 1980. *Naming and Necessity*. Cambridge, MA: Harvard University Press.

Lacasse, Germain. 1996. 'Du bonimenteur québécois comme pratique resistante.' *Iris* 22: 53–66.

Lacasse, Germain. 2000. *Le bonimenteur de vues animées: Le cinéma muet entre tradition et modernité*. Québec: Éditions Nota bene.

Lacasse, Germain. 2012. 'The Film Lecturer.' In *A Companion to Early Cinema*, edited by André Gaudreault, Nicolas Dulac and Santiago Hidalgo, 487–97. Malden, MA: Wiley-Blackwell.

Lamarque, Peter and Stein Haugom Olsen. 1994. *Truth, Fiction, and Literature: A Philosophical Perspective*. Oxford; New York: Oxford University Press.

Levinson, Jerrold. 1996. 'Film Music and Narrative Agency.' In *Post-Theory: Reconstructing Film Studies*, edited by David Bordwell and Noël Carroll, 248–82. Madison: University of Wisconsin Press.

Levy, David. 1982. 'Re-Constituted Newsreels, Re-Enactments and the American Narrative Film.' In *Cinema 1900–1906: An Analytical Study*, edited by Roger Holman, 243–58. Brussels: FIAF.

Lewis, David. 1978. 'Truth in Fiction.' *American Philosophical Quarterly* 15 (1): 37–46.

Livingston, Paisley. 2013. 'The Imagined Seeing Thesis.' *Projections: The Journal for Movies and Mind* 7 (1): 139–46.

Loiperdinger, Martin. 2004. 'Lumière's Arrival of the Train: Cinema's Founding Myth.' *The Moving Image* 4 (1): 89–118.

Loiperdinger, Martin. 2007. '"The Audience Feels Rather at Home...": Peter Marzen's "Localisation" of Film Exhibition in Tier.' In *Networks of Entertainment: Early Film Distribution 1895–1915*, edited by Frank Kessler and Nanna Verhoeff, 123–30. Eastleigh: John Libbey.

Loiperdinger, Martin. 2014. 'Missing Believed Lost: The Film Narrator, Then and Now.' In *Performing New Media, 1890–1915*, edited by Kaveh Askari, Scott Curtis, Frank Gray, Louis Pelletier, Tami Williams and Joshua Yumibe, 87–94. New Barnet: John Libbey.

Maltby, Richard. 2011. 'New Cinema Histories.' In *Explorations in New Cinema History: Approaches and Case Studies*, edited by Richard Maltby, Daniel Biltereyst and Philippe Meers, 3–40. Chichester: Wiley-Blackwell.

Malthête, Jacques. 1996. *Méliès: Images et illusions*. Paris: Exporégie.

Mannoni, Laurent. 2000. *The Great Art of Light and Shadow: Archaeology of the Cinema*. Edited and translated by Richard Crangle. Exeter: University of Exeter Press.

Mannoni, Laurent, Donata Pesenti Campagnoni and David Robinson. 1995. *Light and Movement: Incunabula of the Motion Picture, 1420–1896 = Luce e movimento: incunaboli dell'immagine animata, 1420–1896*. Gemona: Giornate del cinema muto; Paris: Cinémathèque française-Musée du cinéma; Torino: Museo nazionale del cinema.

Matravers, Derek. 2014. *Fiction and Narrative*. Oxford: Oxford University Press.

Metz, Christian. 1974. *Film Language: A Semiotics of the Cinema*. Translated by Michael Taylor. New York: Oxford University Press.

Metz, Christian. 1982. *The Imaginary Signifier: Psychoanalysis and the Cinema*. Translated by Celia Britton. Bloomington: Indiana University Press.

Metz, Christian. 1991. 'The Impersonal Enunciation, or the Site of Film (In the Margin of Recent Works on Enunciation in Cinema).' *New Literary History* 22 (3): 747–72.

Moore, Elbert. 1915. *Elbert Moore's Text Book on Writing the Photoplay*. Chicago: E. Moore.

Moran, Richard. 1994. 'The Expression of Feeling in Imagination.' *The Philosophical Review* 103 (1): 75–106.

Muddle, E. J. 1911. *Picture Plays and How to Write Them*. London: The Picture Play Agency.

Musser, Charles. 1981. 'The Eden Musée in 1898: The Exhibitor as Creator.' *Film & History: An Interdisciplinary Journal of Film and Television Studies* 11 (4): 73–96.

Musser, Charles, et al. eds. 1984. *Motion Picture Catalogs by American Producers and Distributors, 1894–1908*. Frederick, MA: University Publications of America.

Musser, Charles. 1990. *The Emergence of Cinema: The American Screen to 1907*. New York: Scribner.

Musser, Charles. 1993. 'Passions and the Passion Play: Theatre, Film and Religion in America, 1880–1900.' *Film History* 5 (4): 419–56.

Musser, Charles. 1994. 'Rethinking Early Cinema: Cinema of Attractions and Narrativity.' *Yale Journal of Criticism* 7 (2): 203–32.

Musser, Charles. 2006. 'A Cinema of Contemplation, A Cinema of Discernment: Spectatorship, Intertextuality and Attractions in the 1890s.' In *The Cinema of Attractions Reloaded*, edited by Wanda Strauven, 159–80. Amsterdam: Amsterdam University Press.

Musser, Charles and Carol Nelson. 1991. *High-Class Moving Pictures: Lyman Howe and the Forgotten Era of Traveling Exhibition, 1880–1920*. Princeton, NY: Princeton University Press.

Nagels, Katherine. 2012. '"Those Funny Subtitles": Silent Film Intertitles in Exhibition and Discourse.' *Early Popular Visual Culture* 10 (4): 367–82.

Nash, Mark. 1976. '*Vampyr* and the Fantastic.' *Screen* 17 (3): 29–67.

Niver, Kemp R. 1971. *Biograph Bulletins, 1896–1908*. Los Angeles: Locare Research Group.

Oettermann, Stephan. 1997. *The Panorama: History of a Mass Medium*. New York: Zone Books; Cambridge, MA: MIT Press.

Paisley, Livingston. 2013. 'The Imagined Seeing Thesis'. *Projections: The Journal for Movies and Mind* 7 (1): 139–46.

Paget, Derek. 1998. *No Other Way to Tell It: Dramadoc/Docudrama on Television*. Manchester: Manchester University Press.

Pavel, Thomas. 1986. *Fictional Worlds*. Cambridge, MA: Harvard University Press.

Peirce, Charles S. 1966. *The Collected Papers of Charles Sanders Peirce, Vols 7–8*, edited by Arthur W. Burks. Cambridge, MA: Harvard University Press.

Peirce, Charles S. 1974. *The Collected Papers of Charles Sanders Peirce, Vols 5–6*, edited by Charles Hartshorne and Paul Weiss. Cambridge, MA: Harvard University Press.

Peterson, Jennifer Lynn. 2013. *Education in the School of Dreams: Travelogues and Early Nonfiction Film*. Durham: Duke University Press.

Plantinga, Carl. 2005. 'What a Documentary Is, After All.' *The Journal of Aesthetics and Art Criticism* 63 (2): 105–17.

Ponech, Trevor. 1997. 'What Is Non-Fiction Cinema?' In *Film Theory and Philosophy*, edited by Richard Allen and Murray Smith, 203–20. Oxford: Clarendon Press.

Popple, Simon and Joe Kember. 2004. *Early Cinema: From Factory Gate to Dream Factory*. London: Wallflower.

Pudovkin, Vsevolod I. 1958. *Film Technique and Film Acting*. Translated by Ivor Montagu. London: Vision Press.

Rabinovitz, Lauren. 1998. *For the Love of Pleasure: Women, Movies, and Culture in Turn-of-the-Century Chicago*. New Brunswick, NJ: Rutgers University Press.

Rabinovitz, Lauren. 2001. '"Bells and Whistles": The Sound of Meaning in Train Travel Film Rides.' In *The Sounds of Early Cinema*, edited by Richard Abel and Rick Altman, 167–80. Bloomington: Indiana University Press.

Rabinovitz, Lauren. 2004. 'More Than the Movies: A History of Somatic Visual Culture through *Hale's Tours*, Imax, and Motion Simulation Rides.' In *Memory Bytes: History, Technology and Digital Culture*, edited by Lauren Rabinovitz and Abraham Geil, 99–125. Durham: Duke University Press.

Rabinovitz, Lauren. 2006. 'From *Hale's Tours* to *Star Tours*: Virtual Voyages, Travel Rides, and the Delirium of the Hyper-Real.' In *Virtual Voyages: Cinema and Travel*, edited by Jeffrey Ruoff, 42–60. Durham: Duke University Press.

Rabinovitz, Lauren. 2012. *Electric Dreamland: Amusement Parks, Movies and American Modernity*. New York: Columbia University Press.

Rimmon-Kenan, Shlomith. 2002. *Narrative Fiction: Contemporary Poetics*, 2nd edn. London; New York: Routledge.

Robinson, David. 2005. 'Magic Lantern Shows.' In *Encyclopedia of Early Cinema*, edited by Richard Abel, 581–5. London; New York: Routledge.

Rosen, Miriam. 1987. 'Méliès, Georges.' In *World Film Directors: Volume I, 1890–1945*, edited by John Wakeman, 747–65. New York: The H. W. Wilson Company.

Ruoff, Jeffrey, ed. 2006. *Virtual Voyages: Cinema and Travel*. Durham: Duke University Press.

Russell, Bertrand. 1905. 'On Denoting', *Mind* 14 (56): 479–93.

Ryan, Marie-Laure. 2007. 'Toward a Definition of Narrative.' In *The Cambridge Companion to Narrative*, edited by David Herman, 22–36. Cambridge: Cambridge University Press.

Sánchez Salas, Daniel. 1996. 'A History of the Lecturer in Spanish Silent Cinema.' *Iris* 22: 171–82.

Sargent, Epes Winthrop. 1913. *The Technique of the Photoplay*. New York: Moving Picture World.

Schivelbusch, Wolfgang. 2014. *The Railway Journey: The Industrialization of Time and Space in the Nineteenth Century*. Berkeley: University of California Press.

Searle, John. 1975. 'The Logical Status of Fictional Discourse.' *New Literary History* 6 (2): 319–32.

Shail, Andrew. 2011. 'The Great American Kinetograph: News, Fakery and the Boer War.' In *Reading the Cinematograph: The Cinema in Short Fiction, 1896–1912*, edited by Andrew Shail, 104–28. Exeter: Exeter University Press.

Shepherd, David J. 2013. *The Bible on Silent Film: Spectacle, Story and Scripture in the Early Cinema*. Cambridge: Cambridge University Press.

Shepherd, David J. 2016. *The Silents of Jesus in the Cinema (1897–1927)*. New York: Routledge.
Silverman, Kaja. 1983. *The Subject of Semiotics*. New York: Oxford University Press.
Singer, Ben. 1995. 'Modernity, Hyperstimulus, and the Rise of Popular Sensationalism.' In *Cinema and the Invention of Modern Life*, edited by Leo Charney and Vanessa R. Schwartz, 72–99. Berkeley: University of California Press.
Singer, Ben. 2001. *Melodrama and Modernity: Early Sensational Cinema and Its Contexts*. New York: Columbia University Press.
Slugan, Mario. 2010. 'An Asymmetry of Implicit Fictional Narrators in Literature and Film.' *Postgraduate Journal of Aesthetics* 7 (2): 26–37.
Slugan, Mario. 2014. 'Some Thoughts on Controlling Fictional Narrators in Fiction Film.' *American Society of Aesthetics Graduate E-Journal* 6 (2): 1–7.
Slugan, Mario. 2015. 'Deixis in Literary and Film Fiction: Intra-Ontological Reference and the Case of Controlling Fictional Narrators.' In *How to Make Believe: The Fictional Truths of the Representational Arts*, edited by Alexander J. Bareis and Lene Nordrum, 185–202. Berlin; Boston: De Gruyter Press.
Slugan, Mario. 2017. 'Taking Bazin Literally.' *Projections: The Journal for Movies and Mind* 11 (1): 63–82.
Slugan, Mario. 2019. *Noël Carroll and Film: A Philosophy of Art and Popular Culture*. London: Bloomsbury.
Solomon, Matthew. 2010. *Disappearing Tricks: Silent Film, Houdini, and the New Magic of the Twentieth Century*. Urbana: University of Illinois Press.
Sopocy, Martin. 1998. *James Williamson: Studies and Documents of a Pioneer of the Film Narrative*. Madison, NJ: Fairleigh Dickinson University Press.
Springer, John Parris. 'The Newspaper Meets the Dime Novel: Docudrama in Early Cinema.' In *Docufictions: Essays on the Intersection of Documentary and Fictional Filmmaking*, edited by G. D. Rhodes and J. P. Springer, 27–42. Jefferson: McFarland & Co.
Springer, John Parris and Gary D. Rhodes. 2006. 'Introduction.' In *Docufictions: Essays on the Intersection of Documentary and Fictional Filmmaking*, edited by G. D. Rhodes and J. P. Springer, 1–9. Jefferson: McFarland & Co.
Staiger, Janet. 1992. *Interpreting Films: Studies in the Historical Reception of American Cinema*. Princeton, NJ: Princeton University Press.
Stam, Robert, Robert Burgoyne and Sandy Flitterman-Lewis. 1992. *New Vocabularies in Film Semiotics: Structuralism, Post-Structuralism and Beyond*. London; New York: Routledge.
Stamp, Shelley. 2000. *Movie-Struck Girls: Women and Motion Picture Culture after the Nickelodeon*. Princeton, NJ: Princeton University Press.
Stewart, Jacqueline Najuma. 2005. *Migrating to the Movies: Cinema and Black Urban Modernity*. Berkeley: University of California Press.
Stock, Kathleen. 2016. 'Imagination and Fiction.' In *The Routledge Handbook of Philosophy of Imagination*, edited by Amy Kind, 204–16. New York: Routledge.
Stoddard, John L. 1897. *John L. Stoddard's Lectures*. Vol. 1. Boston: Balch Bros.

Stoddard, Ralph P. 1911. *The Photo-Play, a Book of Valuable Information for those Who Would Enter a Field of Unlimited Endeavor*. Cleveland.
Stokes, Melvyn and Richard Maltby, eds. 1999. *American Movie Audiences: From the Turn of the Century to the Early Sound Era*. London: BFI.
Streible, Dan. 2008. *Fight Pictures: A History of Boxing and Early Cinema*. Berkeley: University of California Press.
Stromgren, Richard L. 1998. 'The Moving Picture World of W. Stephen Bush.' *Film History* 2 (1): 13–22.
Thomasson, Amie L. 2009. 'Fictional Entities.' In *A Companion to Metaphysics*, 2nd edn, edited by Jaegwon Kim, Ernest Sosa and Gary S. Rosenkrantz, 10–18. Cambridge, MA: Wiley-Blackwell.
Toulmin, Vanessa. 1996. 'The Fairground Bioscope.' In *In the Kingdom of Shadows: A Companion to the Early Cinema*, edited by Colin Harding and Simon Popple, 191–206. London: Cygnus Arts.
Toulmin, Vanessa. 2006. *Electric Edwardians: The Story of the Mitchell & Kenyon Collection*. London: BFI.
Tsivian, Yuri. 1994. *Early Cinema in Russia and its Cultural Reception*. Translated by Alan Bodger. London; New York: Routledge.
van Beusekom, Ansje. 1996. 'The Rise and Fall of the Lecturer as Entertainer in the Netherlands: Exhibition-Practices in Transition Related to Local Circumstances.' *Iris* 22: 131–44.
Verstraten, Peter. 2009. *Film Narratology*. Toronto; Buffalo: University of Toronto Press.
Waller, Gregory A. 1995. *Main Street Amusements: Movies and Commercial Entertainment in a Southern City, 1896–1930*. Washington: Smithsonian Institution Press.
Walton, Kendall L. 1990. *Mimesis as Make-Believe: On the Foundations of the Representational Arts*. Cambridge, MA: Harvard University Press.
Walton, Kendall L. 2008. *Marvelous Images: On Values and the Arts*. Oxford; New York: Oxford University Press.
Whissel, Kristen. 2002. 'Placing the Spectator on the Scene of History: The Battle Re-Enactment at the Turn of the Century, from Buffalo Bill's Wild West to the Early Cinema.' *Historical Journal of Film, Radio and Television* 22 (3): 225–43.
Whissel, Kristen. 2008. *Picturing American Modernity: Traffic, Technology, and the Silent Cinema*. Durham: Duke University Press.
Wilson, George M. 1997. '*Le Grand Imagier* Steps Out: The Primitive Basis of Film Narration.' *Philosophical Topics* 25 (1): 295–318.
Wilson, George M. 2007. 'Elusive Narrators in Fiction and Film.' *Philosophical Studies* 135 (1): 73–88.
Wilson, George M. 2011. *Seeing Fictions in Film: The Epistemology of Movies*. Oxford: Oxford University Press.
Woods, Amy. 2009. *Lynching and Spectacle: Witnessing Racial Violence in America, 1890–1940*. Chapel Hill: University of North California Press.

Wollen, Peter. 1969. *Signs and Meaning in the Cinema.* Bloomington: Indiana University Press.

Wolterstorff, Nicholas. 1980. *Works and Worlds of Art.* New York: Oxford University Press.

Yumibe, Joshua. 2012. *Moving Color: Early Film, Mass Culture, Modernism.* New Brunswick, NJ: Rutgers University Press.

Žižek, Slavoj. 2001. *The Fright of Real Tears: Krzysztof Kieślowski between Theory and Post-Theory.* London: BFI.

Index

The 4.7-Inch Naval Gun in Action at the Battle of Pretoria 133
The 5-Inch Siege Guns in Action at the Battle of Pretoria 133

actuality film 1–2, 12, 17, 22, 26, 31, 37, 47, 55, 70, 88, 99, 144, 174, 207
   and fake film 109–10, 123, 132–3
   and war film 115, 130–4
aesthetics
   analytic 3, 11, 12, 14–15, 16, 18, 21–2, 29, 56, 60, 79, 93, 96–7, 143–4, 165, 167, 174, 179, 191–2, 199, 207, 214 n.36, 243 n.60
   philosophical 2–3, 10–11, 14, 20, 210
Admiral Cigarette 206–7
advertising film 206–7
The Arrival of a Train/L'Arrivée d'un train en gare de La Ciotat 2, 11–12, 19, 22–3, 25–6, 31, 33, 37, 38, 41, 59, 79, 170–1, 173, 215 n.13
The Arrival of the Paris Express 34
The Astronomer's Dream or the Man in the Moon/La lune à un metre 1–2, 10, 11, 18, 42–3, 47, 51–3, 54, 57, 205, 208–9
attractional package 42, 44
author 9, 70, 165–6, 172–3, 176, 182, 185, 189, 192, 194, 241 n.18
   as fictional narrator 186–7, 190, 242 n.43, 244 n.63
   implied 165–6, 245–6 n.80
authorization *see* mandate

barker 137, 152–4, 156
benshi 138–40
The Big Swallow 151, 177–8, 185, 198, 202
The Birth of a Nation 7–10, 79
Blacksmith Scene 119
A Boat Leaving Harbor 74, 78
Bombardment of Matanzas 103, 116, 122–3

Boston and New York Express 51
boxing film *see* fight film
Brooklyn Bridge 82, 170

The Cabinet of Dr. Caligari/Das Cabinet des Dr. Caligari 46, 220 n.81
canned theatre 24–6, 32, 42, 44, 46, 52
Capture of Boer Battery by the British 124–6
cinema of attractions 22, 57, 71, 167, 171–2, 205, 206
cinema of narrative integration *see* transitional era
The Corbett-Fitzsimmons Fight 16–17, 101
Corbett and Fitzsimmons, Films in Counterpart of The Great Fight 101–2, 111–12, 122, 229 n.11

Deadwood Sleeper 95
Death of Macao and His Followers 131
The Defence of the Flag – Camp Meade, Pa 132
deixis 152–3, 156–8, 163, 165, 186–7, 190–7, 203, 208, 241 n.18, 242 n.29, 243 n.58
Demolishing and Building up the Star Theatre 56
diegesis 57, 161, 172, 187–90
direct recording 13, 100–2, 104–6, 108–18, 122–3, 126, 132–3, 231 n.41
direct representational content 27–8, 52–3, 57–8, 216 n.24, 216 n.25
disbelief 16, 21, 32, 33, 39–42, 52, 99, 205
documentary 1, 10, 17, 21, 23, 26–7, 31, 37, 53, 109, 118–19, 123, 125, 146, 157, 159, 161, 163, 198, 210, 217 n.32
double nature film 172

Empire State Express 36, 55
Enoch Arden 148, 155–6, 240 n.81
enunciation 136, 156, 163, 194–6

enunciator 195, 245-6 n.80
  see also great image-maker
The Execution of Mary, Queen of the Scots 206

fake film 12, 13, 97, 99, 118, 205, 206
  and deception 13, 100-5, 109-14, 123-4
  and exhibition context 127-30
  and fake news 106-9, 123
  and fiction 12, 115, 119, 123, 126, 134
  and illustration 12, 112, 128-34
  and imagination 13, 126-8, 130-4
  as mislabelling 100, 105-6, 114
  promotion of 101-6, 111-12, 118, 127, 131-4
  reception of 109-14, 115, 133-4
  as re-enactment 13, 99-101, 104-6, 111, 114-15, 120, 126, 131-4, 229 n.14
  and staging 13, 99-104, 107, 110, 113-16, 118-20, 122-4, 126, 207, 232 n.73, 233 n.88
false belief 13, 16, 32-3, 37, 41, 59, 61-2, 64, 66-70, 85-7, 93, 96, 99, 109-10, 113, 114, 123-4, 127, 142, 205, 208
Faust 148, 238 n.60
fiction *see* mandate, theory of fiction
fictional showing 11, 14, 60, 97, 163, 167, 173-4, 177-8, 181-2, 199-202, 243-4 n.44
fight film 2, 13, 16-17, 22, 101-7, 109, 111-13, 118, 120, 122, 138, 144, 145, 149, 181, 229 n.11, 229 n.14
The Four Troublesome Heads/Un homme de têtes 12, 33, 42-3, 47, 51-2

Gans-Nelson Contest, Goldfield, Nevada, September 3, 1906 106-7, 112-13, 232 n.67
genuine film *see* direct recording
Grand Hotel to Big Indian 95
grand imagier *see* great image-maker
great image-maker 165-6, 194, 199-200, 241 n.24, 245-6 n.80

Hale's Tours 11, 13, 59-61, 79-80, 82-5, 96-7, 99, 126, 134, 142, 167, 170, 205-6, 208, 226 n.74
  and hybridity 88-9, 92-3
  and imagining seeing 93-6, 228 n.112
  and narrative 170
  promotion of 87-8, 95
  reception of 85-8
The Haverstraw Tunnel 75-6, 81, 171, 174, 225 n.48
historical film 206
The Hold-Up of the Rocky Mountain Express 89-93, 94-5
Holmes, E. Burton 14, 70, 136-7, 144, 157-64, 167, 177, 187, 191, 202, 240 n.86, 242 n.43
How a French Nobleman Got a Wife through the 'New York Herald' Personal Columns 174-5

illusion 2-3, 16, 38-9, 44, 60, 205
  cognitive 2, 32, 37, 41, 61, 85-7, 93, 96, 123 (*see also* false belief)
  of depth 38-41, 49, 56, 68, 69
  diegetic 57, 62, 140, 142, 144, 148-9, 208
  and fiction 2-3, 11, 16, 63, 70, 75, 93, 208
  and imagination 12-13, 40, 49, 59, 61-2, 63, 66-9, 70-1, 85, 87, 88, 93, 99, 127, 142, 207
  and immersion 59-70, 85, 96, 99, 207-8
  in magic theatre 33, 38-41, 47, 52, 54, 56
  of movement 38-41, 49, 56, 61, 68, 223 n.9
  perceptual 32, 33, 37-41, 49, 56, 61, 99 (*see also* looming effect)
  of presence 66, 68-9, 85-7, 127
  optical 32
  stage 44-5, 47
illustrated lecture 136-9, 143, 146-7, 150-1, 157-61, 163, 191, 224 n.26
illustration 12, 13, 18, 27, 67, 72-5, 80-1, 112, 124, 128-34, 205, 207-8, 216 n.21, 233 n.88
imagined seeing 9-11, 14, 60, 207, 226 n.62
  face-to-face 17-19, 75-6, 79, 93-4, 96, 167, 208
  and fictional showing 60, 97, 174, 200-2
  and mandate 17-19, 67, 75-6, 96, 163, 167, 225 n.40
  modest 79, 93, 96, 228 n.12

immersion 11, 16, 49, 58, 85, 86, 88–9, 224 n.15, 227 n.92, 237 n.38
   as being present 49, 61, 63–4, 66, 68–9, 76, 78–9
   definition of 63–4, 66–8, 70, 208
   and imagination 16, 61, 62, 66–70, 74–6, 78, 85, 96, 99, 207, 225 n.42, 225 n.53
   and lecturer 141–3, 224 n.26
   techniques of visual 13, 58, 59, 61, 64, 96, 205–6
Impersonations by Harry Tate 121
incredulity *see* disbelief
indexicality 99, 115–18, 210
Indian Charge 132
In and Out of Picture 148–9
intertitle 137, 138, 139, 143–4, 179, 182, 183–5, 237 n.25

The Kiss in the Tunnel 92

Lava Slides in Red Rock Canyon 80
leader *see* intertitle
lecturer 14, 70, 136–9, 159, 163–4, 178–9, 183, 206, 207–8, 224 n.26
   as controlling fictional narrator 162–4
   and film text 140, 153
   and trade-press advice 149–57, 158
   see also E. Burton Holmes, John L. Stoddard
looming effect 12, 32–4, 36–7, 40, 56, 77, 99, 205
Lynching Scene 231 n.41

magic lantern 136, 140, 149, 151
magic theatre 2, 12, 24–6, 32, 33, 38–42, 44, 47, 51–2, 56, 99, 119, 205, 207
mandate 7–9, 11–12, 16–17, 24, 64, 120, 125–6, 128, 173, 196, 210, 216 n.23
   and fake film 13, 122–4, 126–7, 130, 206 234 n.121
   feedback loop 75–6, 126, 133–4
   and Hale's Tours 13, 59–60, 88, 91–3, 95–6, 167, 170
   historicizing 11, 15, 21, 29, 56, 59, 80, 82, 96, 124, 135, 163, 207, 208, 209 (*see also* temporal instability of non-fiction)
   and illusion 40, 49, 52, 63, 68, 69, 207

   and immersion 69, 78, 207
   and impersonation 121–2
   implicit 9–10, 164, 165, 186, 193–4, 203, 207
   and lecturer 137, 144, 148, 150–1, 153–7, 158–63
   and magic theatre 40–2, 119
   and narrator 14, 96, 136, 163–4, 165, 173, 175, 177–8, 179, 182–3, 185, 186–7, 193–94, 195, 197–9, 202, 242 n.43
   and non-existing object 27–8
   and non-representational work 28
   normativity of 15–16
   and phantom ride 60, 75–8, 80–1, 93, 167, 170–1
   and photograph 17–19
   and scenic 61, 73, 96
   and screenwriting manual 182–5
   and surf film 74, 78, 124, 169, 225 n.42
   and train film 19, 33–4, 36–7, 41, 48–51, 55, 56–7, 59, 61–2, 93, 99, 124, 170–1
   and travelogue 61, 70–1, 73, 75, 96
   and trick film 42–4, 47, 51–3, 56–7
   see also make-believe theory of fiction, institutional theory of fiction
metanarrative 196–8
mimesis 161
Mohammedan Inhabitants of Crete Massacring Christian Greeks/ Massacres en Crète 107
monstrator 97, 173–5, 241 n.24, 242–3 n.45
myth of the panicking audience 2, 12–13, 31, 32, 37, 38, 41, 47, 57, 59, 61, 87, 208

narrative 10, 14, 241 n.19
   and attraction 53, 57, 71, 172, 205
   cinema 9, 10, 58, 124, 136, 164, 165–6, 191, 195, 203, 206, 209, 228 n.112
   comprehension 137–40, 142–4, 146–8, 161, 178–80, 183
   definition of 167–9, 181
   discourse 172–3, 175–8, 179, 182–3, 185, 243 n.44, 246 n.84
   and fiction 24, 91–2, 99, 115, 118, 123–6, 169–70, 181–2, 188–90, 207

and Hale's Tours 96
level 187–91, 194
and narrator 14, 16, 165–7, 172–3, 175–6, 181–3, 185, 191, 194–5, 199, 203, 242–3 n.44
phantom 148, 238 n.59
and phantom ride 91–2, 169–72
present 14, 159, 161
programme 145
and train film 169–72
verbal 182–3, 186, 190, 191–4, 241 n.18
see also metanarrative
narrator 16, 167, 173, 176, 181–2, 183, 185–7, 191–2, 194, 242 n.43, 242–3 n.44, 243 n.60, 245–6 n.80
controlling 9–10, 14, 60, 96–7, 136, 157, 162–4, 166, 190–1, 193–4, 195–203, 207–8
extradiegetic 140, 166–7, 186–90, 194, 237 n.35
film 11–12, 14, 16, 58, 96–7, 136, 140, 143, 157, 159, 165–7, 172–8, 179, 185–6, 187, 191, 194–203, 205, 207–8, 237 n.36, 241 n.24, 246 n.81
and intertitles 185
intradiegetic 187–91
literary 165–7, 173, 176–7, 182–3, 185–7, 190–4, 197, 202, 207, 241 n.18
as obtruding personality 182–3, 185–6, 192
storytelling 244 n.63
system 140, 166–7, 176, 197, 246 n.81
voice-over 146, 155, 166
see also monstrator, enunciator, great image-maker
new cinema history 211 n.3
new film history 2–3, 15–16, 18–19, 21–2, 60–1, 79, 96, 140–1, 165, 174, 207, 210, 211 n.3
non-fiction 10, 13, 21, 64, 144, 189
criteria of 2, 4, 12, 16, 22–3, 25–31, 48, 53, 56, 212 n.9, 216 n.23, 217 n.31
and fake film 99–100, 119, 126
and hybridity 13, 59, 88–9, 99
and illustration 27, 216 n.23
and imagination 70–1
and immersion 64

and phantom ride 75, 80, 86
temporal instability of 1–2, 10–13, 15, 29–31, 33, 37, 41, 47, 56–7, 62–3, 80, 86, 207–9, 217 n.30
and travelogue 70–1, 75

ontological gap argument 187, 189, 193–4, 195, 200, 244–45 n.71
Othello 153, 155

panorama 13, 61, 64–70, 73, 75, 76–8, 85, 93, 96, 99, 136, 168, 224 n.26
Panoramic View of Haverstraw Tunnel, N.Y. 81
Panoramic View of Hell Gate 80
passion play 30–1, 57, 138, 144–7, 149, 154, 172
Passion Play (1897) 146
The Passion Play (1898) 30–1, 154–5, 239 n.78
Passion Play of Oberammergau 146
Personal 174–5
Phantasmagoria 136
phantom ride 2, 11, 13, 19, 22, 59–61, 75–82, 84, 86, 88–9, 92–6, 99, 142, 144, 167, 169–72, 174, 178, 202, 205–9, 225 n.53
Phantom Ride on the Canadian Pacific 80
principles of generation 8–10, 96
prop 6–10, 12, 21, 26–7, 28–9, 34, 36, 69, 71, 93, 123, 135, 144, 151–2, 155, 157, 158–9, 162–3, 165, 187, 199, 205–6, 208, 210

Quick Lunch 95

Railroad Tunnel Scene 81
re-enactment 13, 97, 99–101, 104–7, 110–11, 114–15, 120, 126, 131–34, 229 n.14
and Buffalo Bill's Wild Wild West 110, 127–30
and impersonation 125
see also fake film
Repulse of Spanish Troops at Santiago by the American Forces 131–2
The Rivals 49, 51

scenic 60–1, 71, 73, 96, 144, 168, 225 n.53
screenwriting manual 14, 164, 178–81, 182–5, 203–4, 208, 228 n.112
The Song of the Shirt 176–7
South Africa – A Train Ride by the Hex River Mountain 81
staging 13, 23, 89, 99–105, 107, 110, 113–14, 116, 207, 232 n.73
  as deception 122–4, 228 n.103
  as event 119–20
  and fiction 115, 118–23, 125, 126, 215 n.13, 233 n.88
  as narrative representation 125–6
  as representation 120–2
  see also fake film
Stoddard, John L. 146, 158–9
surf film 74, 78, 82, 88, 96, 126, 169, 206–7

theory of fiction
  institutional 12–13, 15, 22, 31–2, 37, 51, 55–6, 59–60, 61–2, 71, 82, 125, 126, 135–6, 159, 207–8, 216 n.23, 217 n.31
  intentionalist 4–5, 12, 29–31, 37, 48, 56, 60, 135, 207, 217 n.31
  make-believe 3–10, 21, 26, 37, 47–8, 56–7, 79, 94, 142, 144, 149–56, 159–63, 205, 207–8
  possible world 3–5, 243 n.60
  speech act 4–7
  textualist 12, 22–7, 37, 48, 56, 89, 91, 207, 215 n.13, 216 n.23
Tracked by Bloodhounds 107–8, 122–3
train effect 12, 32–3, 36, 38, 40, 47–8, 56–7, 99, 205, 217 n.36
  see also train film
train film 2, 11–12, 19, 22, 32–3, 47–8, 61, 64, 82, 88, 124, 126, 134, 205–8, 215 n.8
  and exhibition context 37–41
  and imagined seeing 78–9, 93, 96, 202

and narrative 169–72
and narrator 173–4
promotion of 48–51, 54–7
reception of 33–7, 40–1, 66, 68–70, 74
see also Hale's Tours, phantom ride, train effect
trick film 1–2, 12, 22–3, 33, 205–7
  and double nature film 172
  and fake film 106–7, 114
  promotion of 51–2, 54–6, 57
  reception of 41–4, 47–8
A Trip to the Moon/Le Voyage dans la Lune 22–7, 29, 31, 33, 44, 46–8, 51, 53, 57, 220 n.85
transitional era 14, 46, 70, 75, 96, 141, 144–5, 147, 149, 157, 167, 178–9, 203–4
transparency thesis 214 n.36
travelogue 2, 12, 14, 22, 60–1, 70–5, 80, 96, 99, 136, 138, 144–5, 149, 157, 163–4, 205, 215 n.11

Uncle Josh at the Moving Picture Show 151
Uncle Tom's Cabin 1, 10–11, 18, 26, 141, 205, 208–9, 237 n.38

Vanishing Lady 51
The Vanishing Lady/Escamotage d'une dame chez Robert-Houdin 41–3, 47
Third Avenue Elevated Train, New York 51

war film 13, 100–7, 110–11, 113–14, 117–19, 123–4, 126–7, 130–4, 144, 149, 233 n.88, 234 n.121
The Waterer Watered/L'Arroseur arrosé 169
water film *see* surf film
willing suspension of disbelief 2–3, 62–4, 127, 208
Wrecking an Armoured Train 131

www.ingramcontent.com/pod-product-compliance
Lightning Source LLC
Chambersburg PA
CBHW070023010526
44117CB00011B/1690